Multi-Ethnic France

Immigration is one of the most significant and persistent issues in contemporary France. It has become central to political debate with the rise, on one side, of Jean-Marie Le Pen's extreme right-wing party and, on the other, of Islamist terrorism. In *Multi-Ethnic France* Alec G. Hargreaves unmasks the prejudices and misconceptions faced by minorities of Muslim heritage and lays bare the social and political neglect behind the riots of 2005.

This new edition of *Immigration, 'Race' and Ethnicity in Contemporary France* spans politics and economics, social structures and cultural practices and has been updated to cover events which have occurred on the national and international stage since the first edition was published. These include:

- recent developments in the 'banlieues' including the riots of 2005
- the growing visibility of sub-Saharan Africans in France's evolving ethnic mix
- the reverberations in France of international developments such as 9/11, the second Intifada and the Iraq Wars
- the renewed controversy over the wearing of the Islamic headscarf
- the development of anti-discrimination policy and the debate over 'positive discrimination'.

Including a glossary and chronology, a fully updated bibliography and information on internet sites, this second edition is essential reading for all students of French politics and international relations everywhere.

Alec G. Hargreaves is the Director of the Winthrop-King Institute for Contemporary French and Francophone Studies and Ada Belle Winthrop-King Professor of French at Florida State University, Tallahassee. His publications include *Post-Colonial Cultures in France*, edited with Mark McKinney (Routledge, 1997) and *Racism, Ethnicity and Politics in Contemporary Europe*, edited with Jeremy Leaman (1995).

Multi-Ethnic France

Immigration, politics, culture and society

Second edition

Alec G. Hargreaves

Routledge
Taylor & Francis Group

NEW YORK AND LONDON

First published 1995
by Routledge
270 Madison Ave, New York, NY 10016

Simultaneously published in the UK
by Routledge
2 Park Square, Milton Park, Abingdon, Oxon OX14 4RN

Reprinted 1999

Second edition 2007

Routledge is an imprint of the Taylor & Francis Group, an informa business

© 1995, 2007 Alec G. Hargreaves

Typeset in Baskerville by
HWA Text and Data Management, Tunbridge Wells
Printed and bound in Great Britain by
Antony Rowe Ltd, Chippenham, Wiltshire

British Library Cataloguing in Publication Data
A catalogue record for this book is available from the British Library

Library of Congress Cataloging-in-Publication Data
Hargreaves, Alec G.
   Multi-ethnic France : immigration, politics, culture, and society /
   Alec G. Hargreaves. – 2nd ed.
       p. cm.
   Rev. ed. of: Immigration, 'race' and ethnicity in contemporary France,
   1995.
    Includes bibliographical references and index.
   1. France – Emigration and immigration.   2. Immigrants – France.
   3. Ethnicity – France.   4. France – Race relations.
   I. Hargreaves, Alec G. Immigration, 'race' and ethnicity in
   contemporary France. II. Title.
JV7925.H375 2007
305.800944–dc22   2006032877

ISBN10: 0–415–39782–0 (hbk)
ISBN10: 0–415–39783–9 (pbk)
ISBN10: 0–203–96279–6 (ebk)

ISBN13: 978–0–415–39782–7 (hbk)
ISBN13: 978–0–415–39783–4 (pbk)
ISBN13: 978–0–203–96279–4 (ebk)

For Margaret Hargreaves, to whom Robert and Alec owe so much

Contents

Illustrations

Acknowledgements

Earlier versions of parts of Chapter 5 were originally published as 'Half-Measures: Anti-Discrimination Policy in France', *French Politics, Culture and Society*, 18(3) (Fall 2000), 83–101, and republished in Herrick Chapman and Laura L. Frader (eds), *Race in France: Interdisciplinary Perspectives on the Politics of Difference* (New York and Oxford: Berghahn, 2004), 227–45.

Valuable comments and suggestions were made in the formative stages of the first edition of this book by Martin Schain, Claire Duchen, Peter Morris, Brian Jenkins, Philip Ogden, Beverley Abad, Patrick Weil and Gary Freeman. Several of these early advisers were kind enough to offer more detailed comments on drafts of various chapters. At Loughborough University, I benefited from the advice of Jeremy Leaman and Paul Byrne. I drafted parts of the book while holding Visiting Fellowships at the Centre for Research in Ethnic Relations at the University of Warwick and at the Institute for European Studies at Cornell University, where I am particularly grateful to Zig Layton-Henry and Susan Tarrow respectively for the warmth of their hospitality. It is also a pleasure to acknowledge the assistance given by Catherine Wihtol de Wenden, Michèle Tribalat, Véronique de Rudder, Jacques Denantes, Moncef El Bahri and Françoise Lorcerie. Patricia, Kate and Rose Hargreaves provided vital support on the home front and generously tolerated my absences while I was absorbed in the preparation of the book. Patricia's unfailing eye for detail strengthened the typescript in many ways. In preparing the second edition, I benefited greatly from the advice of Dominic Thomas and Jeremy Lane. At Florida State University, I received valuable technical support from Sophie Romeuf, Wolfgang Adolph, Matt Kemp and Hope Stewart. FSU's Winthrop-King Memorial Fund enabled me to pursue my research in France, where Patrick Simon gave me the benefit of his statistical expertise. Guests and Visiting Professors at FSU's Winthrop-King Institute for Contemporary French and Francophone Studies who shared valued insights with me include Jean Baubérot, Azouz Begag, Sophie Body-Gendrot, Sébastien Fath, Jeremy Gunn, Rémy Schwartz and Michel Wieviorka. For any errors or inadequacies which remain I am of course solely responsible.

AGH
Florida State University
August 2006

Abbreviations and acronyms

AIF	Association Islamique en France
AIS	Armée Islamique du Salut
CEM	Commission Extra-Municipale aux Étrangers
CFCM	Conseil Français du Culte Musulman
CFRES	Centre de Formation et de Recherche de l'Éducation Surveillée
CGT	Confédération Générale du Travail
CNCDH	Commission Nationale Consultative des Droits de l'Homme
CNF	Code de la Nationalité Française
CNIL	Commission Nationale de l'Informatique et des Libertés
CNLI	Commission Nationale pour le Logement des Immigrés
CNPI	Conseil National des Populations Immigrées
CODACs	Commissions d'Accès à la Citoyenneté
CORIF	Conseil de Réflexion sur l'Avenir de l'Islam en France
CRAN	Representative Council of Black Associations
CRE	Commission for Racial Equality
CRMF	Conseil Représentatif des Musulmans de France
CSA	Conseil Supérieur de l'Audiovisuel
DOM-TOM	Départements d'Outre-Mer et Territoires d'Outre-Mer
EC	European Community
FAS	Fonds d'Action Sociale pour les Travailleurs Immigrés et leurs Familles
FASILD	Fonds d'Action et de soutien pour l'intégration et la lutte contre les discriminations
FIS	Front Islamique du Salut
FN	Front National
FNMF	Fédération Nationale des Musulmans de France
FSNA	Français de souche nord-africaine
GIA	Groupe Islamique Armé
HALDE	High Authority against Discrimination and for Equality
HCI	Haut Conseil à l'Intégration
HLM	Habitation à Loyer Modéré
HVS	Habitat et Vie Sociale

IGAS	Inspection Générale des Affaires Sociales
INED	Institut National d'Études Démographiques
INSEE	Institut National de la Statistique et des Études Économiques
JALB	Jeunes Arabes de Lyon et sa Banlieue
LCO	Langues et Cultures d'Origine
LDH	Ligue des Droits de l'Homme
LICRA	Ligue Internationale Contre le Racisme et l'Antisémitisme
MGIS	Mobilité Géographique et Insertion Sociale
MN	Mouvement National
MRAP	Mouvement contre le Racisme et pour l'Amitié entre les Peuples
OMI	Office des Migrations Internationales
ONI	Office National d'Immigration
OFPRA	Office Français de Protection des Réfugiés et Apatrides
PCF	Parti Communiste Français
PS	Parti Socialiste
RONA	Rapatriés d'origine nord-africaine
RPR	Rassemblement pour la République
SONACOTRA	Société Nationale de Construction pour le Logement des Travailleurs
SONACOTRAL	Société Nationale de Construction de Logements pour les Travailleurs Algériens
UDF	Union pour la Démocratie Française
UOIF	Union des Organisations Islamiques de France
ZAC	Zone d'Aménagement Concerté
ZEP	Zone d'Éducation Prioritaire
ZUP	Zone à Urbaniser en Priorité
ZUS	Zones Urbaines Sensibles

Introduction

In November 2005, the French government declared a state of emergency in response to the nation's most serious civil disturbances since 1968. Unlike the student and worker demonstrations of 1968, which took place in city centers, factories and university campuses, the disorders of 2005 occurred in disadvantaged urban areas known as the _banlieues_, where they pitted mainly minority ethnic youths against thousands of French police. In 1995, in the first edition of this book, I wrote:

> Far from being a serious attempt at severing their links with the rest of society, the challenge to local police thrown down by young people involved in recent urban disorders is first and foremost a distress signal: by attracting the attention of the media, those concerned hope to force the authorities to redress the lack of opportunities open to ethnicized groups relegated to the banlieues.
>
> (Hargreaves 1995a: 148)

Ten years later, every word of this diagnosis remained true. Except for their scale, there was nothing substantively new in the riots of 2005. At a lower level of intensity, similar disorders had been occurring intermittently in the banlieues since the late 1970s and early 1980s, with periodic flare-ups such as those on which I commented in the mid-1990s. If the disturbances of 2005 were unprecedented in scale, this was in no small measure because, over a sustained period, governments of both left and right had failed to take effective action against the long-standing problems in which the disorders were rooted: deep-seated socio-economic inequalities exacerbated by entrenched patterns of discrimination against immigrant minorities originating in former colonies.

In the title of the first edition of this book – _Immigration, 'Race' and Ethnicity in Contemporary France_ – the reference to 'immigration' reflected the centrality of that word in French discourse in the 1980s and early 1990s. In everyday usage, 'immigration' denoted not simply the process of movement from one country to another, but everything associated with the permanent settlement of people of foreign origin within the receiving society (Tribalat 1993: 1911). The use of the word 'immigration' to encompass what in many respects were post-migratory processes was symptomatic of the difficulties experienced by the French in coming to terms – both literally and ontologically – with the settlement of immigrant minorities, especially those originating in former colonies in Africa and elsewhere. In the English-speaking world, such people are commonly referred to as 'ethnic minorities' or 'minority ethnic groups', and a large part of what in France is called 'immigration' is commonly known as 'race relations'. Terms such as 'race' and 'ethnicity' were at that time almost completely rejected in France and are still largely eschewed. Since the mid-1990s, however, significant changes have taken place in the language and thinking of French politicians, journalists and officials. Although 'immigration' is still a live issue, the spotlight has shifted increasingly to the problems of the banlieues – coded language for places of minority ethnic settlement – and genuine but still largely ineffective attempts have been made to address the problem of racial and ethnic discrimination. New buzz words such as 'diversity', 'visible minorities' and 'equal opportunities' have now made it possible to speak in a politically correct fashion (by French standards) about issues such as multiculturalism, ethnic minorities and anti-discrimination without directly using those words. While at one level the use of this coding reflects a continuing reluctance to explicitly recognize the existence of ethnic minorities, at another level it reflects a shift away from questions of immigration control towards a more direct engagement with issues relating to the permanent settlement of minority ethnic citizens. These and other changes are reflected in the title of the new edition of this book, *Multi-Ethnic France: Immigration, Politics, Culture and Society*.

The central question around which the book is structured has been at the forefront of French public life for the past quarter of a century: how effectively are recent immigrants and their descendants being incorporated into French society? This is a complex issue, embracing politics and culture as much as economic and social structures, and the attitudes of social actors are often as significant as – and sometimes at odds with – *de facto* developments on the ground. These tensions are reflected in the analytical framework of my study, which attempts to delineate and chart the interaction of three main dynamics: the attitudes and aspirations of the majority population, those of immigrants and their descendants, and the empirically observable pattern of social intercourse between majority and minority groups. Precisely because they are in a constant process of interaction, it is impossible wholly to separate any one of these strands from the others. For analytical purposes, the main focus of each chapter (except the first) falls on one or other strand, but it is important not to lose sight of the fact that they are bound together in a dialectical rather than a linear relationship. Chapter 1 presents an overview of the problematic. Chapters 2 and 3 focus on the experiences and attitudes of minority groups, spanning socio-economic, cultural and political issues, while Chapters 4 and 5 deal mainly with the majority population, focusing particularly on the political mediation of attitudes towards immigrants and their descendants.

For this new edition, the book has been comprehensively updated and expanded, reflecting the many developments which have taken place since the mid-1990s. The evidence which has accumulated in the last ten years confirms in essence what I argued in 1995. Contrary to frequent claims that recent immigrant *problems do not come from immigrants themselves but the new society they have immigrated to*

minorities cannot be successfully incorporated into French society because they are supposedly unwilling to adapt to its cultural norms, there is overwhelming evidence to show that the principal barriers come from socio-economic disadvantage and racial and ethnic discrimination by members of the majority ethnic population.

During the 1980s and 1990s, politicians and public opinion were obsessed with what was widely portrayed as a serious threat to French national identity and social cohesion arising from the settlement of minorities originating in predominantly Islamic countries, mainly former French colonies in North and West Africa. During that period, the central notion in political discourse about those minorities was the need for 'integration'. To the extent that 'integration' was not proceeding at the desired speed, this was commonly blamed on the alleged inability or unwillingness of Muslims to adjust to the cultural norms dominant in France. The evidence available up to 1994 (when I completed the typescript of the first edition of this book) showed that this was untrue: as the length of settlement grew and new generations put down roots, so they became increasingly imbued with the values dominant among their majority ethnic peers. Further confirmation has come since then, notably in the findings of large-scale sociological surveys such as those published by Tribalat (1995, 1996) and Lefèvre and Filhon (2005). Tribalat's findings – revealingly encapsulated in the title of her 1996 book, *De l'immigration à l'assimilation: enquête sur les populations d'origine étrangère en France* (From Immigration to Assimilation: A Survey of Populations of Foreign Origin in France) – were also among the first to document clearly what had long been suspected, namely that second-generation members of post-colonial minorities suffered disproportionate levels of disadvantage as a result of discrimination (Tribalat 1995: 174–82). Further evidence of discrimination accumulated rapidly during the 1990s and early years of the new century (Bataille 1997; Amadieu 2004, 2005). A simple but revealing example was cited in the preamble to the 2006 Equal Opportunities Law, drafted in response to the 2005 riots: among equally qualified job candidates, those from the most disadvantaged of the banlieues were only half as likely as other candidates to be offered an interview, while those of Maghrebi origin were five times less likely than majority ethnic candidates to be given the chance of an interview. The anger and resentment generated by grossly unequal opportunities have led to periodic explosions of violence in the banlieues. If 'integration' has proceeded more slowly than wished, this is not because of resistance against it by minorities but because politicians have been too slow in taking action against what, amidst the rubble of the 2005 riots, President Chirac called the 'poison of discrimination' (Chirac 2005).

Because it hinges on a complex mixture of behavioral, discursive and attitudinal factors, the question of how far immigrants and their descendants may be said to 'belong' to French society traverses many disciplinary boundaries. In the course of my study, I have drawn not only on my own research in the cultural and political spheres but also on the findings of specialists in many fields ranging from political science, sociology, history and economics to anthropology, social psychology and geography. While a number of studies have been published by anglophone researchers on specialist aspects of this canvas, to the best of my knowledge this book is the most comprehensive available in English on ethnic relations in contemporary France.[1] My analysis aims to serve both students and researchers in the field of French studies who have little prior knowledge of ethnic relations *per se* and anglophone scholars active in the field of ethnic relations seeking a detailed understanding of recent developments in France.

While French perceptions and policies in the field of immigration are the subject of a number of specialist studies by anglophone researchers,[2] until recently, relatively little scholarly literature has been available in English on the minority side of ethnic relations in France.[3] I hope that my own study helps to correct this imbalance. It deals essentially with the period since 1974, and more particularly since the early 1980s, when what the French termed 'immigration' – a large part of which would more commonly be known in the English-speaking world as 'race' or ethnic relations – became a major preoccupation in French public life.

Where appropriate, I have tried to relate developments in France to the theoretical frameworks within which similar experiences have been analyzed in English-speaking countries, while at the same time seeking to convey the specificity of the French experience and the particular terms in which it has been articulated by francophone scholars, politicians and ordinary members of the public. Without an understanding of the terms in which the French debate has been constructed, it is impossible fully to comprehend the way in which minority groups have fared in French society.[4]

Immigrants originating in Africa and Asia, and particularly those from Islamic countries, are at the heart of this debate. In the 1980s it became commonplace to assert that unlike earlier minority groups, who came mainly from Europe, those originating outside Europe were difficult if not impossible to incorporate into French society. Claims of this kind were advanced not only by extreme right-wing politicians such as Jean-Marie Le Pen (1984: 99–114) and apparently swallowed whole by the general public (see, for example, the Indice-Opinion poll in *Le Magazine-Hebdo*, April 1984, and the BVA poll in *Paris-Match*, 14 Dec. 1989), but were also given credence by mainstream politicians on both the left and the right (on the emergence of this consensus see Silverman 1992: 70–94). Similar ideas have also been influential among academics. Safran (1986), for example, suggested that Muslims of North African origin in France were less socio-economically adaptable and far more resistant to cultural change than were earlier waves of Jewish immigrants from eastern Europe;[5] Fitzpatrick (1993) presented a similar view. Heisler and Schmitter Heisler argued that this sort of pattern obtained not only in France but across western Europe as a whole, with 'large numbers of culturally essentially alien migrants' leading to 'the emergence of a socioeconomic and political underclass' (Heisler and Schmitter Heisler 1986: 12, 19).

Variants of this view resurfaced during the 2005 riots. Philosopher Alain Finkielkraut (2005) denied that the disturbances were a reaction to poverty or racism and claimed instead: 'The problem is that most of these youths are Blacks or Arabs, with a Muslim identity. … It is clear that this is a revolt with an ethno-religious character.' Hélène Carrère d'Encausse, permanent secretary of the Académie Française, blamed the disorders on the polygamous marital practices of Muslim immigrants from West Africa who, she said, were incapable of controlling their teenage children (*Le Monde*, 17 Nov. 2005). No evidence was adduced in support of these claims, made, it should be noted, by intellectuals with no first-hand knowledge or research experience in the banlieues. Not a single statement is on record of rioters saying the disturbances were motivated by an Islamic agenda. When Islamic organizations in France commented on the disorders, far from stoking the violence they consistently called for an end to it. A huge body of research data produced by sociologists, political scientists and other investigators (reviewed in Chapter 3) shows that the second and third generations of post-colonial minorities – from whose ranks the rioters came – have overwhelmingly acculturated to the norms dominant in France. The values and aspirations of most minority ethnic youths are similar to those of their majority ethnic peers. Their protests were prompted by frustration over the denial of equal opportunities to fulfil those aspirations. Culturally, the French model of integration has been highly successful. Its failures have been in social and economic policy, which has been woefully inadequate in the face of unemployment levels running at more than twice the British and US rates, entrenched social inequalities and widespread ethnic discrimination which has gone almost completely unchecked.

It is certainly true that recent immigrants are often reluctant to abandon the cultural codes which they internalized in their countries of origin, but there is nothing new in this. Few adults seek to annihilate the culture which they learnt during their formative years. Most seek to transmit what they inherited to their own children. Only in exceptional circumstances, however, do international migrants succeed in inculcating in their descendants a level of attachment to pre-migratory cultural codes which is in any way comparable to their own. In most cases, the necessary precondition for this has been a degree of political control amounting to colonial or quasi-colonial authority. Europeans who migrated to colonial Africa and Asia succeeded in maintaining their cultural heritage despite being numerically weak because they were politically and economically strong. To a lesser extent, the privileged status enjoyed by German settlers in Russia and neighboring lands enabled them to achieve something similar.

The experience of immigrants from former colonies in France and other parts of Europe has been directly the opposite of this. Economically weak and politically excluded, they have found the odds stacked heavily against them in the struggle to sustain their cultural inheritance across succeeding generations. As is shown in Chapters 3 and 5, after a mild flirtation with notions of cultural diversity during the late 1970s and early 1980s, the French state has returned to the well-worn and still successful tradition of acculturating as fully as possible second- and third-generation members of minority groups through the public educational system. Television and other electronic media have done the rest. The cultural norms internalized in this way are, of course, by no means purely French. The essential point, however, is that to a very large extent immigrant-born youths share through the mass media and state education in the same cultural system as their French-born peers.

This is not to say that minorities of recent immigrant origin are being successfully incorporated into the fabric of social and economic life in France. Contrary to the claims advanced by Safran, the high rates of unemployment, low levels of social mobility and poor-quality housing to which many second-generation members of minority ethnic groups find themselves condemned cannot be convincingly attributed to 'the inability of their unassimilated parents to provide role-models for cultural adaptation' (Safran 1985: 55). The principal obstacles to the incorporation of post-colonial minorities into French society lie not in cultural differences but in the radical restructuring of the labour market since the mid-1970s, greatly reducing the opportunities open to minority groups, and in the discriminatory treatment which they have suffered in the competition for jobs and scarce resources. These socio-economic developments are the subject of Chapter 2, while the factors contributing to the hierarchical ethnicization of immigrants and their descendants are examined in Chapter 4.

Wherever ethnic relations are analyzed and debated, there are fierce arguments over terminology. The conceptual framework for my own study is outlined in Chapter 1, where definitions of key terms are outlined in the context of a historical survey of immigration in France. Most of the terms adopted here will be familiar to specialists in the field of ethnic relations, and while my own usage of them will not necessarily command universal assent, it is, I hope, clearly explained and internally coherent. Several less standard expressions require a preliminary word of explanation. As used here, 'people of immigrant origin' encompasses immigrants (i.e. people born in a country other than that in which they now live) together with their children and grandchildren. 'Immigrant-born' people are to be understood as second-generation members of minority ethnic groups, i.e. people born in the receiving country to immigrant parents or who, while born abroad, were brought to the receiving country while still children. The defining feature of those whom I describe as immigrant-born lies in the fact that, in contrast with their parents, who spent their formative years in the sending country, they are socialized largely, if not exclusively, in the receiving country. This distinction is important for understanding the long-term development of ethnic relations, for patterns of socialization play a fundamental role in shaping inter-generational trends.

Many scholars distinguish between immigrants and their descendants on the one hand and the 'native' or 'indigenous' population on the other. The latter terms are best used sparingly, not least because the distinction between natives and people of immigrant origin is in practice far less clear-cut than it might appear at first sight. Basing her analysis on a span of three generations, Tribalat (1991: 43, 65–71) estimated that about a quarter of the people living in France were either immigrants themselves or had at least one immigrant parent or grandparent. If the analysis of ancestral origins were pushed back a further generation or two, the population of immigrant origin would appear larger still. Yet if a quarter or even less of a person's ancestry is foreign, of what significance is that compared to the three-quarters or more which is 'native' to France? If the succeeding generations have all been socialized in the receiving country, what does it matter if all four grandparents were foreign? In their everyday lives, many people descended from immigrants are quite ignorant of their foreign origins or attach little or no importance to them. They are apt to consider themselves – and to be regarded by others – as part of France's indigenous population, especially if they are white. By contrast, second- and even third-generation non-whites are less likely to be treated as part of the indigenous population, despite the fact that all those born in a given country, including the children or grandchildren of immigrants, are, in the literal sense of the term, natives of that territory.

Because of its contamination by socially constructed hierarchical differences of this kind, the word 'native' is generally avoided in the present study, except in a limited number of contexts where its literal meaning is appropriate. More commonly, I distinguish between majority and minority groups. The latter consist of people of immigrant origin (as defined above), while the former encompasses that part of the population which was born in France with no immediate immigrant ancestry (i.e. immigrant parents or grandparents). Because of gaps in official statistics and family memories, discussed in Chapter 1, it is not always clear whether particular individuals should be formally ascribed to one side or the other of the majority/minority divide. It should also be remembered that the relatively high level of social acceptance enjoyed by most second- or third-generation whites means that their formal minority status (as defined here) is of little significance when compared with the stigmatization experienced by many of the children and grandchildren of post-colonial migrants.

1 Overview

1.1 Introduction

The riots which rocked France in November 2005 were the most serious civil disturbances experienced by the nation in almost forty years. They took place in urban areas known as the banlieues, now a by-word for disadvantaged neighborhoods containing dense concentrations of minority ethnic populations. The disorders were blamed by some on the supposed incompatibility between mainstream French society and recently settled immigrant minorities, above all those of Muslim heritage. Similar anxieties and suspicions had manifested themselves in widespread public support for a 2004 law banning the wearing of Islamic headscarves in French state schools. Feelings of insecurity fueling support for the new law had also been at work in the 2002 presidential elections, in which extreme right-wing leader Jean-Marie Le Pen scored a shock first-round result by beating Socialist Prime Minister Lionel Jospin and finishing second only to centre-right incumbent Jacques Chirac.

These events were the latest in a long series of convulsions which during the last quarter of a century have surrounded relations between France's majority and minority ethnic populations. Yet beneath the sound and fury which have so often held the headlines, divisions between majority and minority groups are less radical than is often thought. On the minority ethnic side, second- and third-generation members of recently settled immigrant groups, including those of Muslim heritage, have acculturated overwhelmingly to the cultural norms dominant in France. Those who took to the streets in 2005 were motivated not by any desire to build an Islamic alternative to French consumer society but rather by anger at their exclusion from that society, whose secular values they largely share.

On the majority ethnic side, reactions to the riots of 2005 demonstrated that attitudes had changed considerably compared with those prevalent ten or twenty years earlier. During the 1980s and 1990s, it was commonplace to blame the failures of French 'integration' policy on the alleged unwillingness of immigrant minorities to adjust to the cultural norms dominant in France. In 2005, those who advanced such arguments were relatively isolated voices. Except for Jean-Marie Le Pen's extreme right-wing Front National and a smattering of politicians in other parties, most politicians rejected suggestions that the riots were rooted in

Islamic culture or politics. This was also true of most of the mainstream media, including right-of-centre newspapers such as *Le Figaro*, which in the past had peddled Islamophobic misrepresentations of the banlieues. While some, such as Interior Minister Nicolas Sarkozy, blamed the riots on criminality – in doing so, Sarkozy outraged many in the banlieues by describing disruptive youths there as *racaille* (scum) – there was widespread concurrence with the findings of the Renseignements Généraux (France's domestic intelligence services), according to which the disorders were a consequence of social inequality and exclusion (*Le Parisien*, 7 Dec. 2005). In other words, the disturbances in the banlieues arose not from some alien cultural force preying on France from without but from failings within the fabric of French society itself, for which the responsibility lay to a very considerable extent on the majority ethnic side. In particular, as President Chirac told his fellow-citizens: 'Nothing lasting can be built in our society without combating the poison of discrimination' (Chirac 2005). Thus while the problems laid bare by the riots were far from easy to solve, the nature of those problems was at last being recognized with greater clarity than in the past.

In the 1980s France had been to a large extent a nation in denial, with many refusing to believe that immigrant minorities originating in former colonies in Africa and elsewhere could be incorporated into French society. Symptomatic of this conceptual blockage was the refusal to use terms which might appear to give recognition or legitimacy to immigrant minorities as structural parts of French society. Terms such as 'minority', 'ethnicity', 'race relations', 'multiculturalism' and 'affirmative action', widely used in the English-speaking world, were taboo in France (Lloyd 1991; de Rudder and Goodwin 1993; Hargreaves 1997b), except among a number of academics, particularly in urban sociology and anthropology who, inspired in many cases by the Chicago School of sociology (which pioneered the study of relations between blacks and whites in the United States), were adapting the Anglo-American problematics of 'race' and more particularly 'ethnic relations' to their own field of study (Balibar and Wallerstein 1988; de Rudder 1990; Battegay 1992). A key reason for the general rejection of such terms lay in the fear of giving even verbal recognition to the settlement of people seen as enduringly different from the indigenous majority. Fearful that the use of such terms might encourage the entrenchment of ethnic differentiation within French society, social scientists such as Schnapper (1990: 88–92) argued that the notion of 'ethnic groups' was an unacceptable Americanism. Like most of France's intellectual and political elite, she preferred to speak of 'integration', a term adopted in French public policy as a means of designating the incorporation within French society of people originating outside it. As such, the notion of 'integration' has served as the functional equivalent in France of 'race' or 'ethnic relations' in Britain or the US. Whereas the concept of 'race relations' appears to imply the recognition of permanently distinct groups, 'integration' has been predicated on the assumption that social differentiation is or should be in the process of being reduced (Weil and Crowley 1994: 113–20). Thus even when the social heterogeneity resulting from immigration has been implicitly recognized, as in the discourse of integration, the terms of that recognition have presupposed its actual or future effacement.

Only in very recent years has the legitimacy of cultural difference been recognized through the adoption of the now fashionable notion of 'diversity'.

Although the 1990s brought growing recognition that recently settled immigrant minorities were in France to stay, policy-makers still refused to speak of 'ethnic minorities' and remained almost unanimous in insisting that 'multiculturalism' was fundamentally incompatible with France's 'republican' model of integration. If the notion of 'integration' betokened acceptance of immigrants and their descendants, as commonly used it also implied that they would be absorbed into French society in such a way as to make them virtually indistinct from the majority ethnic population. Yet even while pursuing steps designed to facilitate that absorption, centre-right governments introduced other measures, such as the nationality law reform of 1993 and the anti-headscarf law of 2004, which had the effect of stigmatizing immigrant minorities. Crucially, almost nothing was done to curb everyday acts of discrimination by members of the majority ethnic population against citizens of minority ethnic origin. Because of discrimination of that kind, the high levels of unemployment prevailing in France since the late 1970s impacted disproportionately on minority ethnic youths, many of whom felt permanently excluded from the labor market and the wider social opportunities to which this gave access. The seething resentment resulting from this exclusion erupted periodically in riots in the banlieues. By the late 1990s, politicians on both the right and the left had understood that if they were to stem such disturbances they would have to be seen to be taking steps to curb discrimination. Since then, policy-makers, journalists and others have begun to break through some of the verbal taboos by which they had previously been constrained. While 'ethnicity' and 'multiculturalism' still remain largely off limits, it has become increasingly common to speak of 'visible minorities' and even of *discrimination positive* (a French equivalent of 'affirmative action'). Yet even while changing their discourse in ways which previously seemed inconceivable, policy-makers have often appeared half-hearted in their initiatives, leaving minority ethnic youths deeply skeptical as to the seriousness of their intent. The growing frustration and disaffection of those youths erupted in the riots of November 2005, the scale and duration of which far exceeded those of earlier disturbances in the banlieues. The replacement of denial by schizophrenia was a classic case of too little, too late.

1.2 Naming and numbering

The policy debate of over immigration and integration has shaped not only the framework in which majority and minority ethnic populations have interacted but also the terms in which knowledge itself has been constructed. Academics often rely for much of their data on information collected by state agencies such as census authorities. In countries like Britain and the US, it is standard practice to categorize the population into groups defined by racial or ethnic origins. Census and other data collected in this way are used to pinpoint problems requiring public intervention and to monitor the effects of such initiatives. In France, the state refuses to collect nationwide information of this kind and, through its data protection laws, makes it difficult for others to do so.[1]

France does publish statistics on what are known in migration studies as population flows, i.e. the number of people entering and to a lesser extent those leaving the country over a given period of time, but only fragmentary data are available on migration stocks, i.e. people born outside France and now resident there, and still less information is compiled on their descendants. Deficiencies in records of immigrants who have died or left the country make it impossible to calculate those stocks simply on the basis of recorded inward and outward flows. The body responsible for conducting censuses, the Institut National de la Statistique et des Études Économiques (INSEE), does record the birthplace of every resident. However, until very recently little of the census data released by INSEE made any reference to place of birth, and no information at all was collected on the birthplace of people's parents. For most practical purposes, the closest one could get to official information on the ethnic origins of the population – and it was a very rough approximation indeed – was through data published on the nationality status of residents.

The 'common sense' equation which is often drawn between foreigners and immigrants is seriously flawed. Not all immigrants are foreigners; nor are all foreigners immigrants; significant numbers of people are neither foreigners nor immigrants, but are often perceived and treated as such. By focusing on nationality to the exclusion of immigration status or ethnic origins, official data have made it extremely difficult to conduct reliable analyses of the impact of immigration on French society at large. The statistical lacunae generated by the state reflect a long-standing unwillingness at the highest level officially to recognize immigrants and their descendants as structurally identifiable groups within French society.

It is true that most immigrants are foreigners. As non-citizens, foreigners stand, by definition, outside the national community and are formally identifiable on this basis. However, foreigners who fulfil certain residence requirements may apply for citizenship through a procedure known as naturalization, which grants formal admission into the community of French nationals. Others become entitled to citizenship if they marry a French national. All those who acquire French nationality disappear from the official ranks of the foreign population. Censuses do record the previous nationalities of people officially classified as *Français par acquisition*, i.e. individuals born without French nationality who have since acquired it, but published information of this kind is seldom sufficiently disaggregated to facilitate detailed socio-economic or spatial analyses. Most of the children born to immigrants automatically become French nationals on reaching adulthood or in some cases at birth without having to go through any formal application procedures. The grandchildren of immigrants are all automatically French from birth. Strictly speaking, children of foreign birth who become French nationals on reaching the age of majority are *Français par acquisition*; in practice, the majority are declared in census returns as having been born French (Tribalat 1991: 28). By the same token, they, like all the children and grandchildren of immigrants born with French nationality, have in statistical terms been lost almost without trace.

Thus in the official mind of the state, the formal integration of immigrants and their descendants has until recently gone hand in hand with their obliteration as a distinct component of French society.

During the last ten years, significant changes have been taking place in this official mindset. Beginning in the early 1990s, a number of French social scientists began to press for greater recognition of immigration and ethnicity in the collection and analysis of census and other data. Foremost among them was Michèle Tribalat, who made a breakthrough when she persuaded INSEE to collaborate with the Institut National d'Études Démographiques (INED) in what in effect was the first major state-sponsored survey of minority ethnic groups in France, though the word 'ethnicity' was played down. The research project was officially entitled 'Mobilité Géographique et Insertion Sociale' (Geographical Mobility and Social Incorporation – MGIS) and the principal publications arising from it referred to their subject matter not as ethnic minorities but as 'les immigrés et leurs enfants' (immigrants and their children) and 'les populations d'origine étrangère' (populations of foreign origin) (Tribalat 1995, 1996). Although Tribalat's approach provoked fierce resistance from more conservative researchers at INED (Le Bras 1998), the publications of both INED and INSEE gradually began to make growing use of the category of 'immigrants' – defined as people living in France who were born abroad without French nationality – where previously that of 'foreigners' had predominated. The trend was very apparent in connection with the 1999 census where, in contrast with the previous census in 1990, a significant part of the data published by INSEE focused on the distinction between immigrants and non-immigrants rather than on the criterion of nationality (INSEE 2002a, 2005).

Important methodological problems remained, however. As relatively few data published by INSEE prior to the 1999 census use the distinction between immigrants and non-immigrants, studies of changes over time still rely largely on the criterion of nationality. No less importantly, INSEE has yet to address the need for census data on the descendants of immigrants. In countries such as Britain and the United States, data on second- and third-generation members of minority ethnic groups are routinely collected through census questions either on the birthplace of respondents' parents or on their racial or ethnic affiliations. No such data are collected in France.

While many French officials remained opposed to such a practice, by 2005 the question of ethnic monitoring, i.e. data collection based on ethnic criteria, was nevertheless being taken sufficiently seriously in government circles that the newly appointed Minister for Equal Opportunities, Azouz Begag, decided to commission a survey to ascertain the extent to which ethnic monitoring would be acceptable to the public. The results of the research were no less remarkable than the fact of its commissioning. Contrary to the long-standing assertions of senior officials and politicians including President Chirac himself, according to whom ethnic monitoring would not be tolerated by the general public in France, the vast majority of those interviewed in the survey said they would accept such a practice (Simon and Clément 2006).

1.3 Immigration in French history

The refusal until recently to consider according an explicit role to ethnicity in state-sponsored data collection within metropolitan France was matched by an almost total absence of references to immigration in public monuments and other formal expressions of French national history (Noiriel 1992b). It was not until 2004 that the centre-right government of Jean-Pierre Raffarin announced the creation of a Cité Nationale de l'Histoire de l'Immigration (National Centre for Immigration History), to be inaugurated in 2007 (Raffarin 2004). Interestingly, the site chosen for the new institution had until then been occupied by the Musée National des Arts d'Afrique et d'Océanie (National Museum of African and Oceanic Arts), which had originally been built to house the Musée des colonies et de la France extérieure (Colonial and Overseas France Museum) as part of the 1931 Colonial Exhibition, widely regarded as the high water mark in public celebrations of the French colonial empire. The painful and humiliating way in which the overseas empire was liquidated, culminating in the independence of Algeria in 1962 after an eight-year military conflict in which France attempted unsuccessfully to resist the global tide of decolonization, helped to make of French colonialism another field of public amnesia (Stora 1991; Aldrich 2005). Until only a few years ago, there were few state-sponsored commemorations of the overseas empire, which many public officials felt it best to forget. The 1931 Colonial Museum was one of many public buildings renamed at the time of decolonization in such a way as to efface their colonial origins. If, in recent years, memories of the colonial period have forced themselves onto the public agenda in France, this is in part because of the settlement of immigrant minorities originating in former colonies. It is those minorities who have been at the centre of the public debates surrounding immigration during the past quarter of a century. The growing recognition that these minorities have suffered high levels of discrimination has alerted policy-makers and the public at large not only to the role of ethnicity as a significant force in French society but also to the legacy of French colonialism, a fundamental aspect of which was institutionalized racial and ethnic discrimination against non-Europeans. While seemingly absent from public policy in metropolitan France, ethnic categories were omnipresent during centuries of French colonial domination overseas (see section 5.5) and echoes of that period remain very much alive today.

Memories of the colonial period echo in contemporary France not only around immigrant minorities of African and Asian origin but also through the presence of significant numbers of former European settlers, known as *pieds-noirs*, who fled to France en masse when Algeria gained independence in 1962. In February 2005, centre-right sympathizers with the *pieds-noirs* voted through Parliament a legal requirement that high school teachers in France instruct their students on the 'positive' role of French colonialism, notably in North Africa. The anguished debate engendered by this and other strands of colonial memory – in 2001, Parliament had voted a law declaring slavery in the French colonial empire to have been 'a crime against humanity' – reached a frenzy in December 2005, with opponents

[handwritten margin note: discussion]

of the new law on history teaching suggesting that the plight of stigmatized post-colonial minorities, which had been pivotal in fomenting the previous month's riots, was similar in spirit to the treatment accorded to colonized peoples in the overseas empire (Mouvement des Indigènes de la République 2006; Moulier Boutang 2005). The reluctant but growing recognition of the role of ethnicity within French society has thus gone hand in hand with increased awareness that France is also traversed by a colonial legacy that remains highly salient almost half a century after the formal end of empire (Bowen 2006a).

The founding myths of the French state were created over many hundreds of years under the centralizing monarchical system which prevailed until the end of the eighteenth century, when they were recast by the French Revolution into the modern forms associated with the ideal of a unified nation-state. The central myths of national identity were thus in place before the rise of large-scale immigration into France during the nineteenth century. Entranced by the spell of those myths, historians in France paid little attention until recently to the contribution of immigrants to the national experience even when, by the middle of the twentieth century, sustained migratory inflows had for several generations been an integral part of French society. By contrast, in countries like the United States, immigration and nation-building were intimately intertwined. The overwhelming majority of present-day Americans are descended from immigrants who entered the US after its official establishment as an independent state at the end of the eighteenth century. Immigration is in this sense an integral part of American national identity, and it is recognized as such in American historiography (Noiriel 1988; Green 1991).

It was not until the 1980s that the preoccupation with immigration in contemporary France brought an upsurge of interest in historical studies of this phenomenon over a much longer period (Citron 1987; Noiriel 1988; Lequin 1988; Ogden and White 1989). Such studies were long overdue, for it is an important matter of historical fact that during the greater part of the last two centuries France has received more immigrants than any other country in Europe (Dignan 1981). Indeed, for much of the twentieth century, after the US imposed tight quotas in the 1920s, France was the most important country of immigration in the industrialized world. By 1930, foreigners accounted for a larger share of the population in France than they did in the US (Noiriel 1988: 21).

As formally defined by INSEE and other agencies of the French state, immigrants are people who, irrespective of their current citizenship status, were born abroad without the nationality of the country in which they now live. Thus defined, the number of immigrants in France rose to a little over four million for the first time in the census of 1982 and neared five million early in the new century.[2] At the time of the 1991 census, 31 per cent had acquired French nationality; the proportion stood at 40 per cent a decade later. In addition, Tribalat estimated in 1991 that about five million people (the great majority of whom were French nationals) were the children of immigrants, and that a similar number had at least one immigrant grandparent. Thus in all, about fourteen million people living in France – a quarter of the national population of nearly fifty-seven million in 1990

– were either immigrants or the children or grandchildren of immigrants (Tribalat 1991: 43, 65–71).

In explaining migratory flows, a distinction is usually drawn between 'push' and 'pull' factors. Industrialization, combined with the country's relatively low rates of natural population growth compared with most of her neighbors, were the principal 'pull' factors inclining France to accept and in some cases actively recruit inflows of foreigners. Heavy population losses suffered during the First World War and to a lesser extent during the Second World War gave an additional impetus to pro-immigration policies. Those who migrated to France felt 'pushed' from their home countries by a variety of factors. Most commonly, these were of an economic nature. When they compared their present circumstances with those they hoped to find elsewhere, migrants motivated by economic considerations calculated that, by moving to another country, they would have a higher chance of improved living standards. In some cases, political pressures weighed more heavily than purely economic concerns. State persecution of individuals or groups, pursued sometimes to the point of genocide, induced many of those targeted in this way to seek refuge elsewhere. Ever since the revolution of 1789, France has cultivated an international reputation as a country committed to the defense of human rights, making it a natural destination for would-be refugees (Noiriel 1991).

Three further general points should be made concerning the pattern of migratory flows. First, it would be a mistake to view those flows as a mechanical outcome of impersonal forces. While substantial numbers of people have sometimes been forcibly transported from one country to another (as slaves or convicts, for example), most international migrants have themselves made the decision to move. Often, of course, the choice has been made in circumstances in which they would have preferred not to find themselves (such as poverty or persecution), but in each case the decision to migrate has nevertheless depended on an act of personal volition, without which 'push' and 'pull' factors would have been no more than analytical abstractions. One place does not push or pull against or towards another. Places have the power to attract or repel only to the extent that they are perceived positively or negatively within the personal projects constructed by individual human beings (Begag 1989).

Second, the relative weight of push and pull factors may be perceived differently in the sending and receiving states. If unemployment or inter-ethnic tensions rise in a receiving country, voters and politicians may seek to halt or even reverse migratory flows. If, at the same time, the situation worsens or simply remains stable within a sending country where people already consider their lot to be intolerable, they may seek to enter the other country in spite of the barriers placed in their way. Contradictions of this kind have become increasingly visible since the mid-1970s, when most west European states declared a formal halt to inward labor migration. As living standards and political conditions have stagnated or worsened in many African and Asian countries since then, would-be migrants have turned increasingly to illegal modes of entry into European labor markets.

Third, the choice of a particular destination on the part of an individual migrant is always conditioned by a complex set of calculations in which immediate opportunities and constraints are weighed against the chances of securing long-term objectives. Thus countries with less than ideal conditions but relatively low barriers may pull in more migrants than states which are perceived as highly attractive but to which access is tightly policed. Geographical proximity, transport systems and social networks based on friends or relatives who have already migrated may also play a role.

During a large part of the nineteenth and twentieth centuries, French perceptions of the need for immigrants, and more particularly immigrant workers, dovetailed more or less closely with the calculations made by would-be or actual migrants in nearby countries. There have, however, been important exceptions to this pattern. An economic downturn in the late nineteenth century was marked by growing antagonism towards foreign workers in some sections of French society, particularly those who feared for their jobs. Anti-Italian sentiments became especially strong in southern France, where a number of violent attacks took place. The most serious of these occurred in 1893 at Aigues-Mortes, where at least eight Italians were killed and dozens more injured. During the slump of the 1930s, the French authorities organized the forcible repatriation of trainloads of Poles (Ponty 1988: 309–18).

Until the First World War, France exercised only weak immigration controls, effectively leaving most population movements to the free play of market forces. Even after official controls were instituted,[3] these were often circumvented with the more or less open connivance of the state. For example, the majority of immigrant workers who entered the French labor market during the economic boom of the 1960s did so illegally, but the state was happy to 'regularize' their situation *ex post facto* by issuing residence and work permits to foreigners who, by taking up jobs, were helping to ease labor shortages. Even today, when the state appears to be more earnest in its opposition to illegal immigrants, many find jobs (usually of a precarious and poorly paid nature) because their employers calculate that their own interests are well served by the recruitment of undocumented workers. In this way, employers bypass and yet at the same time benefit from the regulatory intervention of the state, for the fear of deportation prevents undocumented workers from complaining about poor wages or working conditions.

During the nineteenth century, labor shortages in France's expanding industrial sector induced considerable internal migration from rural to urban areas. However, these internal population flows proved insufficient to meet the demand for labor, and foreign workers came in increasing numbers. Census data on the foreign population were first collected in 1851. Figure 1.1 shows the number of foreigners, expressed as a percentage of the total population, at every census conducted since then. It shows a steady rise in the foreign population from 1 per cent of the national total in 1851 to almost 3 per cent in the 1880s, when economic circumstances entered a more difficult phase. The figure remained fairly stable until after the First World War, then quickly doubled to 6 per cent by the time of the 1931 census. The economic slump of the 1930s saw a sizeable fall in the foreign population, though it remained at a higher level than that seen prior to the First World War. The strong growth rates achieved during what the French

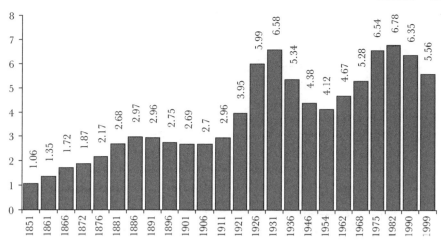

Figure 1.1 Foreigners as percentage of the total population of France, 1851–1999

Source: INSEE 1992a: tables R2, R3; 2005: table 1.6).

call *les trente glorieuses*, i.e. the thirty years immediately following the Second World War, brought the figure back up to above 6 per cent, where it has remained since the mid-1970s despite the much weaker economic growth and higher rates of unemployment which have prevailed since then.[4]

Until the post-war period, non-Europeans accounted for only a tiny fraction of France's foreign population. Beginning in the 1950s, their numbers grew rapidly. By the time of the 1982 census, Europeans represented less than half of the foreign population although, as a proportion of the immigrant population (including naturalized immigrants as well as immigrants who remained foreign nationals), Europeans remained in the majority until as recently as the 1990 census (Figures 1.2 and 1.3). Up to and including the 1968 census, the majority of the foreign population in France came from directly neighboring countries. Prior to the 1920s, Belgium and Italy alone accounted for over half of all foreign residents. Belgians, attracted by job opportunities in the coal, steel and textile industries just over the border in north-east France, outnumbered Italians until the beginning of the twentieth century. Italians, who were traditionally concentrated in unskilled jobs in south-eastern France, then took over as the single largest national group, which they remained until being overtaken by the Spaniards when their numbers peaked in 1968. Spanish immigrants were particularly numerous in south-western France, where many worked as agricultural laborers (Dreyfus and Milza 1987; *Cahier de l'Observatoire de l'intégration* 1994).

Between the wars, a large Polish community had also developed. Most Polish immigrants took jobs on the land or in the mines. They quickly became the largest expatriate community originating in a country without a shared border with France, and second only in size to that of the Italians. By 1931, they accounted for half of all foreign workers in the mining industry. The slump hit this sector particularly hard, forcing tens of thousands of Poles to return home. Up to 100,000 more

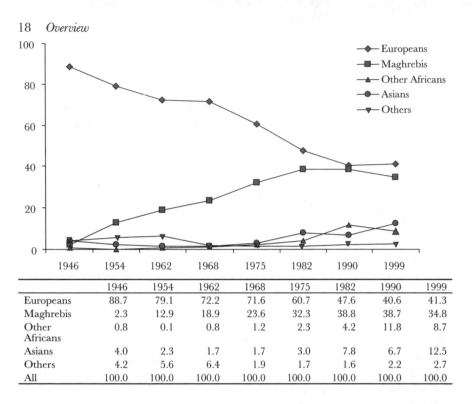

	1946	1954	1962	1968	1975	1982	1990	1999
Europeans	88.7	79.1	72.2	71.6	60.7	47.6	40.6	41.3
Maghrebis	2.3	12.9	18.9	23.6	32.3	38.8	38.7	34.8
Other Africans	0.8	0.1	0.8	1.2	2.3	4.2	11.8	8.7
Asians	4.0	2.3	1.7	1.7	3.0	7.8	6.7	12.5
Others	4.2	5.6	6.4	1.9	1.7	1.6	2.2	2.7
All	100.0	100.0	100.0	100.0	100.0	100.0	100.0	100.0

Figure 1.2 Main nationality groups as percentage of France's foreign population, 1946–99

Sources: INSEE 1992a: table R6; 2002a: table P6B.
Note
As defined by INSEE, Asians include Turks.

followed them immediately after the Second World War. When the Iron Curtain sealed Poland's borders shortly afterwards, the remaining community in France stagnated and then declined rapidly in importance (Ponty 1988).

While economic motives were to the fore among the four main national communities which dominated migratory flows to France until the middle of the twentieth century, political factors also played a significant role in two of them. Throughout the nineteenth century, political exiles from Italy had found a refuge in France, and their numbers were swollen following Mussolini's accession to power in 1922. Political refugees began leaving Spain almost as soon as the Civil War began in 1936. When it ended three years later with the defeat of the Republicans, almost half a million Spaniards crossed into France; though many later returned home, at least half of them stayed.

A number of smaller immigrant communities were formed mainly as a result of political persecution. Armenians, for example, regrouped in France during the 1920s after fleeing a campaign of genocide instigated by Turkey. At about the same time, more than 100,000 Russians hostile to the Bolshevik Revolution settled in France, mainly in the Paris area. Before the First World War, about 40,000 Jews had fled to France from the Russian Empire, where they were threatened

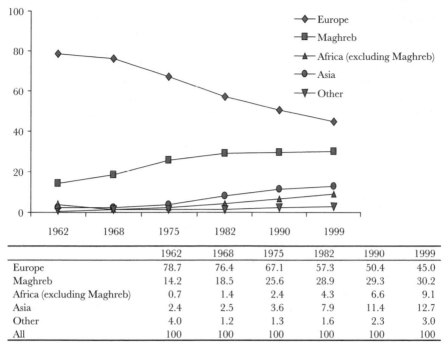

	1962	1968	1975	1982	1990	1999
Europe	78.7	76.4	67.1	57.3	50.4	45.0
Maghreb	14.2	18.5	25.6	28.9	29.3	30.2
Africa (excluding Maghreb)	0.7	1.4	2.4	4.3	6.6	9.1
Asia	2.4	2.5	3.6	7.9	11.4	12.7
Other	4.0	1.2	1.3	1.6	2.3	3.0
All	100	100	100	100	100	100

Figure 1.3 Main regions of origin as percentage of France's immigrant population, 1962–99

Source: INSEE 2005: table 1.8.1.
Note
As defined by INSEE, Asia includes Turkey.

by widespread pogroms. With the rise of fascism during the 1930s, well over 100,000 Jews from Germany and eastern Europe sought refuge in France. During the Second World War foreigners – particularly those who had come to France because of political persecution – were to play a vigorous role in the Resistance, thereby contributing to the liberation from Nazi occupation (Courtois 1989).

After the war, plans drawn up by the French government foresaw a need for substantial numbers of immigrants to assist in reconstruction work and to compensate for the country's weak demographic growth. In the debate over the orientation of immigration policy, there were two main camps: economists such as Jean Monnet, who were mainly concerned to remedy immediate labor shortages, and demographers such as Alfred Sauvy and Georges Mauco, who favored permanent immigration by families to compensate for France's low population growth. There was also considerable debate over whether or not to impose ethnic quotas similar to those operated by the United States until 1965. While there was widespread agreement that Africans and Asians were less desirable than Europeans, those whose main concern was the labor market were less anxious to formalize an ethnic hierarchy than were those who saw immigration as vital for France's demographic future. A compromise eventually emerged when the foundations of France's post-war immigration policy were laid in a government ordinance issued on 2 November 1945 (Weil 1991: 53–62).

One of the most important aspects of the regulations laid out in this ordinance was the separation of residence and work permits. Although it was expected that most immigrants would in the first instance be foreign workers, the right to live in France was not made conditional on being in employment. Thus while labor recruitment quickly outpaced demographic considerations as the dominant concern shaping immigration policy (Tapinos 1975), the regulatory framework readily permitted family settlement, and would later make it difficult for the state to subordinate residence rights to narrowly economic criteria.

No ethnic quotas were laid down in the 1945 ordinance, but in implementing these formal regulations, successive governments sought as far as possible to encourage European rather than African or Asian immigrants. Thus the Office National d'Immigration (ONI),[5] a state-run agency established under the 1945 ordinance with the task of regulating migratory inflows, immediately opened recruiting offices in Italy while leaving other countries untouched. The pattern of inflows which subsequently developed was, however, very different from what had been expected. Italians and other Europeans were less attracted to France than had been hoped. The fastest growing groups originated in the Maghreb, i.e. the western part of North Africa, consisting of Algeria, Morocco and Tunisia. Their share of the foreign population leapt from just 2 per cent in 1946 to 39 per cent in 1982. From the mid-1970s onwards, other non-Europeans – principally South-East Asians, Turks and Africans from south of the Sahara (mainly former French colonies in West and Central Africa) – also grew rapidly in number, further eroding the share of Europeans among the immigrant population. This shift is in part a reflection of the fact that differences in living standards between different parts of western Europe have generally lessened during the post-war period, particularly since the creation of the European Economic Community in 1957, and this has reduced the incentives for intra-European migration. At the same time, the gap in living standards between Europe and formerly colonized regions in Africa and elsewhere has grown, making migration towards the rich North an increasingly attractive prospect to those in the impoverished South.

After the Second World War, France's overseas empire, which until then was second in size only to that of Britain, was gradually decolonized. Independence was granted to French Indochina in 1954 and to French West and Central Africa in 1960. The last major step in this process came with the independence of Algeria in 1962. Until then, Algeria had been officially regarded as an integral part of French territory and all its inhabitants – including those of non-European descent – had the formal status of French nationals. Neighboring Morocco and Tunisia were also under French rule until 1956, but as these states had the juridical status of protectorates (implying a milder type of colonial domination than that obtaining in Algeria), their citizens were not officially classed as French. The formal equality enjoyed by Algerians under a new statute applied to their country in 1947 gave them complete freedom of movement in and out of metropolitan France, i.e. France as commonly understood, as distinct from overseas territories under French sovereignty, and they retained this right for several years after independence. They were by the same token exempt from the regulatory powers of the ONI. From a mere 22,000 in 1946, their numbers grew to 805,000 in 1982, making Algerians the largest national group among the foreign population in France.

If international migrants are defined without regard for current or past nationality as people living in a country other than that in which they were born, one of the largest groups of international migrants in France consists of people of European descent who left the Maghreb at the time of independence. French citizens from birth and generally indistinguishable in their somatic (i.e. bodily) appearance from the majority of the French population, these 'white' settlers from former colonies are never referred to as immigrants in official or popular discourse, but are instead known as *rapatriés* (repatriated citizens) or, more colloquially, as *pieds-noirs*. France still retains a few overseas possessions, known as the DOM-TOM (Départements d'Outre-Mer et Territoires d'Outre-Mer, i.e. overseas departments and territories). The most important of these possessions are the four Départements d'Outre-Mer: Guadeloupe, Martinique and French Guyana (in the Caribbean) and Réunion (in the Indian Ocean). As French citizens, their inhabitants are exempt from French immigration controls and do not feature in official statistics on the foreign population. However, as they are mainly of African or Asian descent and easily recognizable by virtue of their somatic features as originating outside France, at a popular level they are often treated as 'immigrants' in a way that the *rapatriés* are not.

At the time of the 1999 census, 357,000 people born in the DOM-TOM were living in metropolitan France. If, excluding the *rapatriés*, residents of France who were born elsewhere are classified by their country of origin, irrespective of their nationality status, those originating in the DOM-TOM at present constitute the sixth largest immigrant group in metropolitan France (Figure 1.4). If population groups in France are classified by foreign nationality alone, the DOM-TOM

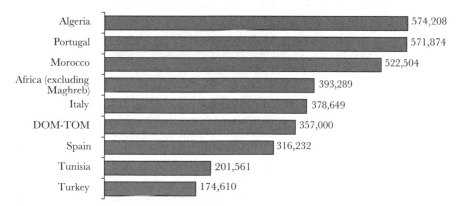

Figure 1.4 Main countries of origin of international migrants (excluding rapatriés) and French citizens born in territories currently of DOM-TOM status living in metropolitan France in 1999

Source: INSEE 2002b; 2005: tables 11, 12.

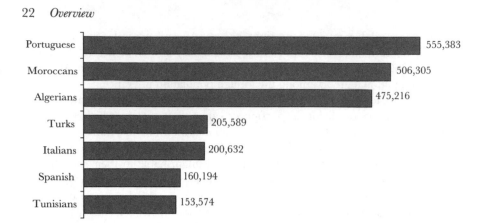

Portuguese	555,383
Moroccans	506,305
Algerians	475,216
Turks	205,589
Italians	200,632
Spanish	160,194
Tunisians	153,574

Figure 1.5 Main nationalities among France's foreign population, 1999

Source: INSEE 2002a: table P6B.

group disappears from the picture, and the rank order of the others is modified as a consequence of different rates of naturalization (Figure 1.5).

The Iberian peninsula has provided the only major exception to the post-war decline of Europeans among France's foreign population. The number of Spaniards in France grew from 302,000 in 1946 to a peak of 607,000 in 1968, falling back to 216,000 in 1990. The rise of the Portuguese community was the most rapid of all. During the 1960s, under the dictatorship of Antonio de Oliviera Salazar, Portugal became engaged in a series of wars designed to prevent its African colonies from becoming independent. Rather than fight, hundreds of thousands of young Portuguese men fled the country, and most of them headed for France, where the authorities unofficially waived normal entry regulations (Weil 1991: 68). Unlike the Spanish, they had no previous tradition of mass migration to France. Between the 1962 and 1968 censuses, the number of Portuguese expatriates in France rose from a mere 50,000 to 296,000. By the time of the following census, in 1975, the figure stood at 758,000, the largest for any national group in France.

While the size of the Portuguese population subsequently remained fairly stable, the number of non-Europeans continued to rise. Maghrebis, who were the first non-Europeans to make their presence felt on a significant scale, have since 1982 represented around 30 per cent of the total immigrant population, making them by far the largest non-European minority in France. During the last thirty years rapid rates of growth have been recorded among other Africans (up from 2.4 per cent of the immigrant population in 1975 to 9.1 per cent in 1999) and Asians (up from 3.6 to 12.7 per cent during the same period). Non-Europeans have thus been by far the most dynamic components in recent migratory inflows.

Before the Second World War, when most of these countries were under colonial rule, relatively few of their inhabitants migrated to France. During the First World War over half a million 'native' troops were enlisted in the French armed forces and more than 200,000 'colonial workers', mainly from the Maghreb and Indochina, were brought over to ease civilian labor shortages in France, but as there was a deliberate policy of repatriation as soon as the conflict ended only about 6,000 remained by 1920 (*Hommes et migrations* 1991b). Small numbers of Algerians had begun migrating to France before the First World War, and these flows resumed during the inter-war period. Unlike European migrants, many of whom settled permanently in France with their families, the overwhelming majority of Maghrebis came to France alone, worked there for a few years and then returned to their families in their country of origin. Often, they were replaced by a relative or sometimes a neighbor from the same village, in what became known as the 'rotation' system. In all, it is estimated that as many as 500,000 Algerians may have migrated temporarily to France during the inter-war period, though the number present at any one time was very much smaller than this (Gillette and Sayad 1984; MacMaster 1997).

During the Second World War, hundreds of thousands of 'native' troops were mobilized in support of the liberation of France. Most were repatriated to the colonies after the war and their role was largely forgotten by the general public in France until the release of Rachid Bouchareb's movie *Indigènes* (Natives) in 2006 drew attention to the sacrifices of troops from French North Africa. Immediately after the war the French government had encouraged family immigration from Italy and other European countries (Weil 1991: 63). Family reunification was also rapidly facilitated for the Portuguese migrants who arrived during the 1960s and early 1970s (Rogers 1986: 45; Amar and Milza 1990: 263). A very different attitude was taken towards immigrants from Africa and Asia. In 1956, faced with growing numbers of Algerian migrant workers living in extremely poor housing, the government set up a state-run agency to provide them with hostel accommodation; while the initiative was in some respects clearly beneficial, it was hoped that, as the accommodation was unsuitable for families, this would discourage the wives and children of Algerians from coming to join them in France (Weil 1991: 60). After independence, the authorities in Algeria and other ex-colonies concurred with their counterparts in France in seeking to discourage permanent family settlement, partly because it reduced the flow of remittances sent home by expatriate workers (Weil 1991: 70–1). However, they were to prove increasingly unsuccessful in this.

The trend towards family settlement is clearly visible in Table 1.1. Within the French population, there is a roughly equal balance between the sexes, with the longer life expectancy of women reflected in the slight numerical superiority of females over males. Among foreign nationals, men usually outnumber women. This is because most (but not all) immigrant workers have initially been men; spouses and children have usually joined them at a later stage while some have remained in the country of origin. The current imbalance in favor of females among the Polish community reflects the unusual age pyramid of this group, more than half of whom are aged 65 or over; the longer life expectancy of women consequently weighs particularly heavily here. The general imbalance in favor of men is far less pronounced among Europeans than among Maghrebis. Throughout the post-war period, family settlement has been the norm among Italians and Spaniards. While the few Portuguese in France during the early post-war period were mainly men,

Table 1.1 Females as percentage of selected nationalities in France, 1946–99

	1946	1954	1962	1968	1975	1982	1990	1999
French	53.1	52.6	51.9	51.8	51.8	51.8	51.8	51.7
Italians	45.2	42.7	42.7	44.0	43.7	43.0	42.8	43.2
Polish	48.5	47.9	47.8	50.2	54.0	58.5	61.3	61.8
Portuguese	24.8	27.0	30.0	35.5	46.2	46.0	46.8	46.7
Spanish	39.7	42.1	44.1	46.8	47.3	47.3	48.0	49.8
Algerians	2.3	6.5	16.0	26.7	32.0	38.3	41.3	42.8
Moroccans	1.7	9.3	16.2	21.8	26.7	38.9	43.8	45.5
Tunisians	8.5	24.6	31.5	33.3	30.9	38.2	41.1	41.3

Source: INSEE 1986: table 8; 1992a: table 10; 2002a: table N3.

as soon as mass migration began in the mid-1960s families quickly followed and within a decade a gender balance similar to that of other European groups was achieved.

Family reunification was much slower among Maghrebis. Although Algerians far outnumbered the Portuguese during the early post-war decades, it was not until the mid-1960s that a trend towards family settlement began to gather pace among Algerian immigrants. Even today, half a century after the rise of mass Algerian migration, Algerians have still not achieved quite the gender balance attained by the Portuguese in little less than a decade. During the last thirty years, family settlement has nevertheless become the norm among Maghrebis, with a female-to-male ratio close to that of Europeans. A similar pattern is also apparent among other non-Europeans. According to the 1999 census, 46.4 per cent of nationals from former French colonies south of the Sahara were female; among Turks the figure was 47.2 per cent and among South-East Asians 50.1 per cent (INSEE 2002a: table P6).

1.4 Immigration after the 'end' of immigration

In 1974, France officially halted inward migration. This was one of the most important early policy decisions taken under the center-right presidency of Valéry Giscard d'Estaing, who was head of state from 1974 to 1981. The halt – formally termed a 'suspension' – of immigration was not all that it seemed. It has in one sense become a classic example of what the French call *le provisoire qui dure* (a lasting temporary measure), for thirty years later the 'suspension' (a seemingly interim arrangement) still has not been lifted. At another level, however, the moratorium was never as sweeping as it appeared. From the start, there were several important gaps in the seemingly blanket interdiction on inward migration; other blindspots later became apparent.

The decision to suspend immigration came in the aftermath of the Middle East War of 1973, when a sharp rise in oil prices sparked widespread fears over the prospects for economic growth throughout western Europe. France, like other labor-importing countries, decided to close her borders to fresh inflows of immigrant workers because of fears of rising unemployment. As a member of the European Community, however, she was not allowed to impede the entry of EC nationals. Nor did the ban on labor migration apply to asylum-seekers, who were covered by entirely different legal and procedural arrangements. Certain categories of professional and highly skilled personnel were also exempt, and there were provisions for making other exceptions if the need arose in particular sectors of the economy.

If these exceptions did not appear to cut across the principle of a ban on 'immigration', this was in part because of unstated but nonetheless powerful stereotypes attached to that term in everyday discourse. Because of the dominance of the labor market in shaping the basic thrust of migratory flows, *immigrés* (immigrants) had come to be regarded as synonymous with *travailleurs immigrés* (immigrant workers), who were in turn equated with unskilled workers rather than professionally qualified personnel (Sayad 1979). As the victims of political persecution, asylum-seekers and refugees stood outside this economic matrix, and were consequently not associated with popular notions of immigrants. Because most unskilled foreign workers were non-Europeans, immigrants as a whole had come to be seen essentially as people of color, whereas European and other Western residents were more commonly referred to as *étrangers* (foreigners). The degree to which the 1974 ban on immigration was perceived to have taken effect would therefore depend on the extent to which people of non-European origin became less visible to the general public. In the event, exactly the opposite was to happen. Far from tapering off, the presence of non-European immigrants and their descendants became ever more visible in virtually every sphere of French society.

This increased visibility has been partly a consequence of growing numbers, despite the formal ban on immigration. One of the main reasons for this lies in a complex web of domestic and international law which has prevented the state from subordinating the rights of foreigners to the crude dictates of the labor market (Hollifield 1992). A crucial instance was the failure of the government's attempts to impose a ban on family reunifications. Such a ban was announced as part of the 1974 freeze on immigration, but it soon proved unworkable and in 1978 the Conseil d'État, France's highest administrative court, declared it to be unlawful. While procedural obstacles have continued to hamper dependants wishing to join family heads in France, the principle of their right to do so overrides the ban on new labor migrants, and family reunifications have been the single most important element in documented migratory inflows during the last three decades.

This has helped to bring about a major structural change in the population originating outside Europe. Whereas men of working age had been dominant until the early 1970s, families subsequently became the norm. Before family reunification, many immigrant workers had been housed in hostels and other forms of accommodation which kept them apart from the majority of French nationals. The arrival of families led to a much deeper penetration into the mainstream housing market. At the same time, the children of immigrants were enrolled as a matter of course in French schools. In this way, immigrant groups which had seldom been encountered outside the workplace became visible on a daily basis in a growing number of neighborhoods. Their increased visibility would not, of course, have been so marked had it not been for one other crucial point: far more than earlier generations of immigrants, those originating in Africa and Asia were instantly recognizable because of their skin color and other somatic features.

By 1977, the government had reached the view not only that the temporary suspension of immigration announced three years earlier should become permanent, but also that the existing immigrant population should, if possible, be reduced. This task was entrusted to Lionel Stoléru, Minister of State for Immigrant Workers from 1977 to 1981, who focused his efforts on inducing non-EC, essentially Maghrebi, immigrants to return home. Financial incentives designed to encourage voluntary repatriation under a system known as *l'aide au retour* (repatriation assistance) launched in 1977 met with little success. Most of those who took up the offer were Spanish or Portuguese immigrants who had probably decided to return home in any case, partly because the political climate there had recently improved with the end of the Franco and Salazar dictatorships; very few Maghrebis, at whom the program was primarily aimed, took advantage of it.

In collaboration with the Interior Minister, Christian Bonnet, Stoléru therefore devised a scheme under which immigrant workers and their families could be forcibly repatriated if they were deemed to be surplus to current labor requirements. Such a system would require a radical overhaul of the regulations governing work and residence permits, but legislative proposals brought forward in 1979–80 to facilitate mass expulsions of this kind failed to command the necessary parliamentary majority. The Interior Ministry used discretionary powers to expel as many individual foreigners as possible, but the numbers involved – on average, about 5,000 a year between 1978 and 1981, most of them young Maghrebis – were far smaller than the hundreds of thousands explicitly targeted in Stoléru's mass repatriation plans (Weil 1991: 107–38).

With hindsight, it seems clear that these strong-arm tactics were counter-productive. Precisely because they feared losing access to the French labor market if they returned home – as Maghrebis had traditionally done under the rotation system – many decided to remain in France, and to bring in their families, thereby increasing the population of non-European origin. That population was further swollen in two other main ways: by a rise in the number of asylum-seekers and by inflows of illegal immigrants.

Under the Constitution adopted in 1946, France committed herself to granting asylum, i.e. formal refugee status including full residence rights, to anyone persecuted for acting to uphold liberty. The grounds for entitlement to refugee status were widened by France's signature of the 1951 Geneva Convention (subsequently updated by the New York Protocol of 1967), which applies to people fleeing their country out of a well founded fear of persecution because of their race, religion, nationality, membership of a particular social group or political opinions. The operation of the convention in France is managed by the Office Français de Protection des Réfugiés et Apatrides (OFPRA). Until the late 1970s, all but a tiny fraction of those granted refugee status by OFPRA were Europeans, most of whom had fled the Soviet bloc. This began to change after the Vietnam war, between the Communist North and a US-backed régime in the South. When the war ended with a Communist victory in 1975, it was followed by an exodus of asylum-seekers who became known as 'boat people' because of the small craft in which many of them fled. Vietnamese exiles were soon joined by Cambodians fleeing the authoritarian régime of Pol Pot and Laotians who feared for their safety because they had assisted the US during the Vietnam war. Most went to the US, but about 100,000 – divided more or less evenly between Vietnamese, Cambodians and Laotians – entered France, which until 1954 had ruled Indochina as part of its colonial empire; several thousand Chinese nationals, who had a long history of commercial activity in the region, came with them. Most were granted refugee status.

Because they were clearly perceived as victims of political intolerance and because Vietnamese nationals in particular were held to have valuable entrepreneurial skills (many fled their country following the blanket nationalization of the private sector in 1978), asylum-seekers from South-East Asia aroused relatively little hostility in France. During the 1980s, however, when asylum-seekers from other regions, notably Africa, grew in number, a less welcoming attitude developed. During this period, requests for asylum grew sharply across the whole of western Europe, and there were widespread suspicions that many applicants were really economic migrants attempting to circumvent the ban on labor migration imposed in the mid-1970s. In France, the number of applicants rose from fewer than 20,000 in 1981 to 61,000 in 1989; at the same time, the rate of rejection grew from 22 to 72 per cent (OFPRA 1994), a clear indication that the authorities were increasingly inclined to view claims of political persecution as a cover for economic motives.

Many of those to whom asylum was refused remained in the country illegally, partly because the often lengthy procedures involved in asylum cases were such that, by the time a decision was reached, applicants had in practice become settled in France. By 1990, about 100,000 rejected aslyum-seekers were estimated to be living illegally in France. That year, the government sought to reduce cases of this kind by speeding up decision-making procedures, reducing the average length from three years to six months. This, combined with the high rate of rejections, appears to have acted as a disincentive to new asylum-seekers, for the number of applications each year fell steadily from a peak of 61,000 in 1989 to 17,000 in 1996, but they began to rise again the following year, reaching 52,000 in 2003. In 2005, the total number of OFPRA-recognized refugees living in France stood at 119,000 (excluding children). Almost 53,000 of them were from Asia, 33,000 from Europe and 29,000 from Africa (OFPRA 2006: 64).

For many years prior to the 1974 suspension of labor migration, most foreign workers had technically broken the law by taking up employment without the required residence and work permits. Because of labor shortages, the government had willingly acquiesced in this, issuing the necessary documents *a posteriori* under a procedure known as 'regularization'. When the 1974 suspension was announced, many thousands of undocumented workers found themselves trapped without papers; others later joined them, often in the belief that the freeze was only a temporary measure. When the left came to power in 1981, it declared an amnesty for illegal immigrants, provided they had entered France before 1 January and provided they had proof of employment. In all, 132,000 illegal immigrants were regularized in this way during the winter of 1981–2 (Marie 1988). The number of undocumented immigrants is estimated to have grown subsequently at the rate of about 30,000 a year, making a total of perhaps 300,000 by the early 1990s (*L'Expansion*, 19 March 1992). Current government estimates put the total at between 200,000 and 400,000 (*Le Monde*, 29 Nov. 2005).

While the numbers and origins of undocumented residents cannot, by definition, be known with certainty, it is likely that most come from outside Europe. This was certainly the case of those regularized in 1981–2, some 61 per cent of whom were Africans, with Maghrebis alone accounting for 46 per cent (Marie 1988). When a partial amnesty for rejected asylum-seekers was declared in 1991, 49,000 came out of clandestinity in the hope of securing residence permits; a similar number are thought to have remained in hiding. Africans and Asians accounted for 90 per cent of the 12,000 whose applications were successful (Lebon 1993: 104).

Besides undocumented additions to France's immigrant population, well over 100,000 foreigners take up residence each year under recognized procedures. In 1992, resident permits were issued to 116,558 newly entering foreigners (Lebon 1993: 85–7). In 2003, the number was 172,096, among whom 52 per cent were Africans, 28 per cent were Europeans (mainly from EU countries) and 13 per cent were Asians (HCI 2004: 22; INSEE 2005: table 2.1.1). Excluding entrants from the EU, only 6,500 came to take up jobs while 9,790 were granted refugee status; almost all the others – over 100,000 in all – were granted residence permits for family reasons. Until recently, most family entrants came under a procedure formally known as *regroupement familial* (family reunification), reuniting family members with foreigners, mainly immigrant workers, living in France. Since the late 1990s there has been a rapid rise in the number of spouses and other family members of foreign nationality granted the right to join French citizens living in France. Many of the sponsoring citizens are naturalized immigrants or descendants of immigrants holding French citizenship. By 2004, the majority of residence permits issued for family reasons went to family members of French citizens, many of whom were sponsoring spouses from their country of origin or that of their parents (Van Eeckhout 2006).

Despite regular inflows of this kind, there has been no change in the proportion of immigrants among the general population, which has remained stable at 7.4 per cent at every census from 1975 through to 1999 while the proportion of foreigners has fallen from a high of 6.8 per cent in 1982 to 5.6 per cent in 1999. The single most important factor contributing to this statistical dip in the foreign population has been the acquisition of French nationality by a steady flow of foreign residents.

Each year over 100,000 foreigners become French (Table 1.2). About half are immigrants who do so by naturalization, a process which requires a formal request for citizenship after five years of residence in France. Most of the others

Table 1.2 Acquisitions of French nationality by foreigners

	1996	2000	2003
By naturalization	50,730	68,750	67,326
By reintegration	7,368	8,728	9,776
By marriage to French spouse	19,127	26,056	30,921
Automatically at age of majority	–	8,570	4,710
By declaration prior to age of majority	–	35,883	29,419
By 'expression of choice'	29,845	–	–
Other	2,753	2,038	2,488
Total	109,823	150,025	144,640

Source: INSEE 2005: table 1.3.1.

Note
Data do not include children born French of foreign parents.

Table 1.3 Foreigners acquiring French nationality by countries of origin (per cent)

	1995	2000	2003
Europe	25.0	16.5	14.5
EU	20.0	10.6	8.9
Spain	2.0	0.8	0.6
Italy	2.1	1.1	0.7
Portugal	14.8	7.9	6.9
Africa	53.5	59.6	63.9
Maghreb	43.7	48.4	49.1
Other African countries	9.8	11.3	14.8
Asia	17.7	19.8	16.6
Turkey	5.7	8.6	7.5
South-East Asia*	6.7	5.1	3.1
Other	3.8	4.1	5.0
Total	100.0	100.0	100.0

Source: INSEE 2005: table 1.3.3.

Notes
* ex-French Indochina.
Data do not include children born French of foreign parents.

are divided roughly evenly between foreigners acquiring French citizenship through marriage to a French spouse and children born in France to foreign parents who automatically become French on reaching the age of majority if they have not already exercised their right to French citizenship. More than half of the foreigners acquiring French citizenship are of African origin; Asians are the next largest regional category, followed by Europeans (Table 1.3).

Prior to 1993, automaticity was the norm for the children of immigrants, i.e. they became French on reaching the age of majority without any action being required on their part. In the early 1990s, around 24,000 young men and women – most of whose parents were of non-European origin – were estimated to be acquiring French nationality in this way each year under Article 44 of the French Nationality Code (CNF). In addition, more than 17,000 children born each year to foreign parents, mainly Algerians and Africans from former French colonies south of the Sahara, were French from birth under Article 23 of the CNF, which conferred French nationality automatically on any one born in France having at least one parent who was also born on French territory. Because Algeria and certain other former colonies, principally in West and Central Africa, were deemed to be part of French territory prior to independence, the children of immigrants originating in those countries were not formally classified among the ranks of foreigners acquiring French nationality, for they were by law French from birth.

In response to claims that French nationality laws were giving citizenship too easily to young people of immigrant origin, the automaticity of Article 44 was abolished by the center-right government elected in 1993. This meant that, during the mid-1990s, children of immigrants acquired French citizenship only if they formally requested it by performing what was called *une manifestation de volonté* (expression of choice). On returning to power in 1997, the left restored automaticity and made it possible for young people of immigrant origin to take French citizenship before reaching the age of majority by making a formal declaration to that effect. Table 1.2 shows that these legal changes made very little difference to the number of second-generation foreigners acquiring French citizenship. In the absence of automaticity, the numbers doing so in 1996 by 'expression of choice' (29,845) were similar to the estimated 24,000 who automatically became French each year prior to the 1993 reform. When the left restored automaticity and opened up the option of acquiring French citizenship by declaration prior to the age of majority, most of the young people concerned exercised that option: 29,419 did so in 2003 while 4,710 acquired citizenship by automaticity.

While the 1993 reform amended Article 23 so that it no longer applied to children born since then to Africans from former French colonies south of the Sahara, it remained valid for the vast majority of children born to Algerian immigrants and for anyone born in metropolitan France or territories still administered by France overseas (i.e. the DOM-TOM), provided at least one of their parents was also born there.

It follows from all this that statistics on nationality provide no more than a very rough guide to the number of immigrants living in France, and they offer an even poorer index of the minority ethnic population, i.e. immigrants together with their descendants. At the time of the 1999 census, some 5.9 million people living in metropolitan France (i.e. France including Corsica, but excluding the DOM-TOM) were born elsewhere (Figure 1.6). Of these, 1.6 million – mainly *rapatriés* and people originating in the DOM-TOM – were French nationals from birth. If we define immigrants as people living in France who were born abroad as foreign nationals, 4.3 million residents of this kind were recorded in the 1999 census. More than a third of these – some 1.6 million – had acquired French nationality. At the same time, there were at least half a million second-generation foreigners in France who, having been born there, were not immigrants; most were likely to become French on or before the age of majority.[6] As the core of Article 23 of the CNF was not affected by the 1993 reform, the third generation, i.e. children born in France of parents who were themselves born there to immigrants, will all be French from birth.

A similar pattern has been at work throughout the twentieth century. More than nine million people living in France today are either the children or grandchildren of immigrants (Tribalat 2004b). As the vast majority were born in France and have French nationality, all but around half a million of them – immigrant-born children who have not yet acquired French citizenship – appear simply as 'French' in Figure 1.6. As noted earlier, the absorption of people of foreign origin into the national community has left relatively few monuments in the collective memory of France. The seeming invisibility of past generations of immigrants and of those who are today descended from them is often regarded as proof of the success with which they have been incorporated into French society. Immigrants who have settled in France during the post-war period, and more particularly those who have come to the fore during the last thirty years, are often felt to threaten this tradition. It is widely claimed that non-Europeans are much harder to 'integrate' than Europeans. Far from disappearing without trace, they have actually increased in visibility at a time when successive governments have been claiming that immigration has been halted. While there is a marked reluctance to speak of them as ethnic minorities – as if the very use of the term might somehow make a reality of the specter which has come to haunt French public debate – there is a widespread fear that immigration has been leading to the formation of permanently distinct minorities within French society.

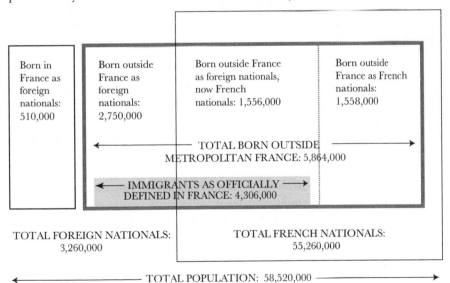

Figure 1.6 Population of metropolitan France in 1999 by place of birth and nationality

Source: Derived from INSEE 2005: tables 1.1, 1.6.

1.5 Ethnicity and integration

Ethnicity and a range of associated concepts play a central role in migration studies in the English-speaking world. They are often mistrusted in France (de Rudder and Goodwin 1993), and it should be said that certain aspects of British and American usage may justify some of these misgivings. The French preference for a discourse of integration has been regarded with equal mistrust in Britain, again often for understandable reasons. It would be a mistake to side uncritically with either camp. No less importantly, it would be foolish to disregard potentially valuable insights derived from one or other approach. Understanding of this kind is possible only if terms are defined and applied with care. Unfortunately, both the discourse of integration and that of ethnicity have been characterized by enormous diversity and not a little confusion.

There is fairly general agreement that the core of ethnicity lies in a sense of group belonging. Theorists and practitioners of ethnic studies disagree, however, over the types of groups involved and the criteria by which belonging is established.[7] Even when – as is the case in the present study – the field of ethnic relations is confined to phenomena associated with international migration, there are many variations in the approaches adopted. A first difficulty concerns the relationship between subjectively felt identities and groups delineated on the basis of empirically observed criteria. Are ethnic groups the subjective creations of social actors, or should they be defined through empirical procedures devised by outside investigators? Bearing in mind that a group of people stigmatized by others may not *ipso facto* share a sense of community, if scholars accept that ethnic groups are the creations of social actors what should be the relative importance accorded to exclusionary as compared with self-inclusionary practices? The specific criteria by which ethnic groups may be subjectively or objectively delineated are very diverse. Three main strands may be usefully distinguished: biological, politico-territorial and cultural. Few if any conceptions of ethnicity rest on just one of these components. Most involve a complex hierarchy of elements.

In the United States, the most common notion of ethnicity has been based on the relatively objective criterion of national origins. A person may be said to belong to a particular ethnic group to the extent that he or she comes from or is descended from someone originating in a particular country. While territorial origins are the prime element in this view of ethnicity, a biological dimension is also involved via the question of ancestry. Biological ancestry is fundamental to another form of inter-group analysis pioneered in the US, that of 'race relations'. Here somatic features, notably skin color, serve to delineate different groups, above all 'blacks' and 'whites'. In recent years the fairly neat distinction between these two approaches has become blurred (Yinger 1985: 153; Lee 1993: 86), partly because it has been recognized that both involve more subjective constructions than may at first meet the eye. For a person whose ancestors come from a variety of countries, there is a large element of subjectivity involved in identifying with one ethnic group rather than with another. Similarly, the seemingly objective fact of somatic difference becomes significant only when human beings make it so in their social dealings. Bearing in mind that the majority of blacks in the US have at least one white among their ancestors, it is impossible to draw a purely biological line between blacks and whites. 'Blacks' were constructed as such by 'whites' as part of a process of social domination and exclusion.

In British academic and political discourse, which has drawn on and adapted American models, ethnic minorities are conventionally defined as groups subjected to discriminatory behavior by members of the majority population. Because carefully controlled tests have shown that people who are somatically different from the 'white' majority suffer from particularly severe discrimination, until recently they alone were officially recognized as ethnic minorities by bodies such as the Commission for Racial Equality (CRE). As the CRE's name implies, its main purpose is to fight against 'racial' discrimination. The quotation marks are necessary because there is now broad agreement among scholars that the idea of biologically distinct races of human beings has no scientific foundation. 'Racial' categories are not, as the expression may unfortunately be taken to imply, objective facts but products of racialization, i.e. patterns of meaning in which 'social relations between people have been structured by the signification of human biological characteristics in such a way as to define and construct differentiated social collectivities' (Miles 1989: 75). The socially constructed nature of 'racial' differences is regrettably obscured by the British and American habit of talking about 'race relations', a phrase which misleadingly suggests that objectively distinguishable 'races' exist and interrelate.[8] Somatic differences between individuals do of course exist, but the relationships at the heart of 'race relations' are between social actors who view each other through the lenses of invented – and often pernicious – notions of racialized group boundaries.

For scholars working within the race relations paradigm, racial and ethnic minorities are one and the same thing (Jones 1993) and are generically defined by skin color: ethnic minorities are that part of the national population which is not classified as 'white'. In the UK, the only significant exceptions to this are the Irish, who, while classified as 'white', are recognized by the CRE as a group suffering significant levels of discrimination. Within the CRE's classification system, minority groups are subdivided by regions of origin, all of which lie outside the UK. This reflects the fact that the stigmatization of 'non-white' somatic features is a consequence of their association with distant territorial origins: dark skins have served to mark ethnic groups treated by members of the majority population as not belonging fully or legitimately to the national society in which they live. These biological and territorial factors are often implicitly linked in turn with cultural assumptions: people originating outside Britain have often been felt not to 'fit in' because of linguistic, religious or other cultural traditions associated with foreign countries.

A differently structured combination of biological, territorial and cultural criteria characterizes the notion of 'ethnic Germans'. This is the standard English translation of *Volksdeutsche*, and *deutsche Volkszugehörigen*, terms denoting individuals who are formally recognized as belonging to the German people. The legal foundation of this concept is a 1913 law basing German citizenship on *jus sanguinis*, i.e. biological descent rather than territorial residence. The law was designed to enable people of German origin living outside Germany, particularly in eastern Europe and what is now the former Soviet Union, to retain German citizenship rights. While the initial driving force behind this system was German self-inclusion, it has at the same time carried important exclusionary implications. Because of their different biological and territorial origins, most immigrants of non-German descent who settle in Germany remain permanently outside the national community, and the same applies to their children and grandchildren.

It would be oversimplistic to see this system as an expression of crude biological racism. Brubaker (1992) has argued that it is ethnocultural rather than ethnoracial in intent, if not in effect. As parents generally attempt to rear their children in the cultural traditions which they themselves have inherited, the transmission of nationality through filiation is the juridical corollary of this cultural transaction. Significantly, when the rights of ethnic Germans in the Soviet bloc were strengthened by additional laws adopted in Germany after the Second World War, evidence of German culture was officially recognized as an acceptable alternative to proof of biological descent for those wishing to exercise these rights.

Rather than focusing on biological or territorial origins, a directly cultural view of ethnicity takes as its starting point participation in a shared system of meaning and values. Thus defined, ethnic minorities are characterized by linguistic, religious or moral codes different from those of the dominant population. The Spanish-speaking population in the US, Hindus in Britain and Muslims in France are examples of groups liable to be categorized in this way. The cultural view of ethnicity involves no biological component. In common with the other approaches already considered, however, it includes a politico-territorial dimension. Minority and majority groups appear as such only when they are positioned within politically structured spaces. Hispanics are not a minority group in Mexico; nor are Hindus in India nor Muslims in Algeria. They appear so only within the confines of a territory which is under the sovereignty of a state dominated by cultural norms of a different order.

Whether the emphasis falls on biological, territorial or cultural criteria, the cardinal feature of ethnic minorities is that they are in some way marked as originating outside the national society within which they now live. The central question to which this gives rise is how far minorities of this kind genuinely stand apart from the majority population. Do the members of minority ethnic groups belong wholly or primarily to their countries of origin, to the national societies in which they live, to separate collectivities in the margins of both, or to wider transnational entities? While the terminology of 'ethnic minorities' is seldom used in France, fundamentally similar questions lie at the heart of the French debate over 'integration'. When academics and politicians talk of a crisis of integration (Wieviorka 1990), they mean there is a danger that people of immigrant origin are being inadequately incorporated into French society.

Unlike their German neighbors, the French have a long tradition of mixing *jus sanguinis*, giving citizenship through filiation, and *jus soli*, through which birth within the national territory brings entitlement to citizenship. An important underlying assumption has always been that both methods of bestowing citizenship were built on a strong foundation of cultural cohesion. While immigrants from other countries could be naturalized only if they furnished proof of cultural assimilation, it was assumed that their children, socialized from birth in France, would be sufficiently French in outlook to justify the automatic acquisition of citizenship on reaching adulthood. These and many other related assumptions have been called into question in recent years.

Until quite recently, the overwhelming majority of immigrants came from countries which share with France a tradition of Catholicism. Today, large numbers come from countries where the dominant faith is Islam, a religion which until their arrival had virtually no significant history within France.[9] Most Muslim immigrants come from North and West Africa and are visually recognizable as originating outside the country. Because their children display similar somatic features, it is widely (though not always correctly) assumed that they, too, are Muslims. Controversies such as the Islamic headscarf affair, which began in 1989 when three Muslim girls refused to remove their headscarves during school classes, have been symptomatic of widespread anxieties over the compatibility of Islamic culture with French norms. Doubts over the commitment of young people of immigrant origin to the dominant values of French society found their most powerful symbolic expression in the reform of French nationality laws enacted in 1993 so as to require immigrant-born youths to request French nationality instead of receiving it automatically.

The immigrant populations which have been settling in France in recent decades have been doing so in a context of high unemployment, fitful growth and major economic restructuring. The opportunities for effective socio-economic incorporation have therefore been far less plentiful than during earlier periods. It is indeed arguable that the roots of present fears concerning ineffective integration lie far more in socio-economic circumstances than in cultural differences between post-colonial migrants and their European predecessors. As Noiriel (1988: 247–94) has pointed out, bouts of xenophobia similar to that currently directed against non-European immigrants marked the economic downturns of the 1880s and the 1930s, when Italians and Poles were castigated as 'unassimilable', which in the language of the day was equivalent to saying they were impossible to integrate.

Charges of this kind were less a reflection of the cultural differences characterizing immigrants than of an unwillingness among the French themselves to incorporate relative newcomers at a time of economic difficulty. In this respect, the problematic of integration runs closer than it might sometimes appear to that of race relations, for both are concerned (albeit from different perspectives) with patterns of social differentiation marked by discriminatory behavior against people of foreign origin. In France, as in Britain, the somatic features of people of color frequently arouse exclusionary attitudes. Immigrants of African and Asian descent originating in the DOM-TOM often suffer from discrimination of this kind, despite the fact that they are French by nationality and to a large extent by cultural affiliation. Paradoxically, exclusionary reflexes among the French themselves have been tending to create in all but name racially constructed ethnic minorities of precisely the kind that cut across the much vaunted project of integration.

It is doubtful, however, whether it makes sense to import wholesale into France the discourse of race relations. While discriminatory behavior triggered by somatic features may be described in broad terms as racist, there are no 'races' in France (any more than there are in Britain) among whom 'relations' can be said to exist. Even if they are triggered by skin color, many acts of discrimination rest on cultural prejudices against people of foreign origin rather than on theories of biological racism. More fundamentally, the rhetoric of 'racial' or cultural discrimination may be little more than a cloak for the more hard-nosed objective of imposing unfair handicaps on easily targeted groups in the competition for scarce resources such as jobs and housing. To categorize all this as 'race relations' is unhelpful from an analytical point of view, for it carries the risk of reifying epiphenomena instead of looking beyond these to the root causes of social differentiation.

The discourse of integration has its own drawbacks. The most important of these has been a tendency among those who speak of integration to assume that the effacement of differentiation through ever fuller incorporation into the national community is not simply a useful model for analytical purposes but also a self-evidently desirable goal. As Beaud and Noiriel (1991) have pointed out, integration has often been implicitly and uncritically equated with assimilation, i.e. the wholesale elimination of differences through the generalization of pre-existing national norms. A classic exposition of the analytical model of assimilation with particular reference to the US is that of Gordon (1964). In France, the normative equation of integration with assimilation has been championed explicitly by officials such as Barreau (1992). In a milder form, similar presuppositions have structured many governmental and academic analyses in France. In this respect, the discourse of integration has tended to function as part of the project of nationalization (Miles 1993: 175–6, 207–11; Lorcerie 1994a).

In contrast with normative approaches of this kind, functionalist views of integration focus on the social, economic or political participation of people of minority origin without assuming that the end product of this process is, or should necessarily be, their assimilation into pre-existing French norms. Stretched between these normative and functionalist poles, 'integration' has been used in very diverse and often ill-defined ways (Bonnafous 1992; Bastenier and Dassetto 1993). When schematic definitions have been attempted, they have varied from one analyst to another. Lapeyronnie (1993) distinguishes between integration, defined as identification with national cultural norms, and participation, defined as involvement in the processes of socio-economic production and exchange. Dubet (1989) prefers a threefold distinction between socio-economic integration, cultural assimilation and national identification, the latter being associated with political participation. The state-appointed Haut Conseil à l'Intégration (High Council for Integration, HCI) appears to propose a functionalist definition of integration based on the notion of participation in French society (HCI 1991: 18–19), but its reports have implicitly favored a normative approach by claiming to measure the 'progress' of integration by reference to indicators such as crime rates, educational qualifications and mixed marriages (HCI 1991: 38–48).

In view of these difficulties, I will refrain in the present study as far as possible from using the word 'integration'. However, because of its ubiquity until very recently in popular, academic and political discourse in France, the term cannot be avoided altogether. It will be used only when citing statements or arguments advanced by those who use the term in France. When its meaning is clear in the original source, I will explicate it accordingly. As many users leave the word undefined, explication is not always possible, and in such cases the reader is left to infer from the context what may be meant.

The word 'assimilation' will also be avoided, except when referring to the use made of this term by others. In general, I find it more useful to speak of acculturation, meaning the acquisition of pre-existing cultural norms dominant in a particular society. Assimilation tends to imply not only acculturation but also the complete abandonment of minority cultural norms. As will be shown in Chapter 3, this is a rather simplistic way of conceiving of the cultural intercourse generated by international migration. Acculturation does not necessarily imply the obliteration of cultural differences, for it is perfectly possible for people to be simultaneously competent in more than one culture.

One of the most important and least scrutinized aspects of the paradigm of integration lies in the assumption that the framework of social incorporation is, or should be, coterminous with the boundaries of the nation-state. Such an assumption was never wholly valid, and the increasingly global scale on which labor, capital, goods and services circulate is rendering it ever more obsolescent. International migration is itself one of the most tangible expressions of this process. Yet there is an important sense in which immigrants (or rather, certain groups of immigrants), more than others, remain constrained by the power of the nation-state. Since the 1950s, obstacles to intra-European migration have been steadily removed by a growing number of states, at any rate where their own nationals are concerned. To facilitate freedom of movement within the European Union, member states have been increasingly driven to harmonize their entry policies *vis-à-vis* third-country (i.e. non-EU) nationals by creating a common policy on external frontiers. Once inside the EU, however, immigrants from non-member states remain almost entirely subject to the regulatory framework of the particular country to which they have been admitted. Their residence and work permits do not extend beyond the boundaries of that country, and even within it their rights are restricted in ways that do not apply to EU nationals. The horizon of opportunities open to non-EU nationals is in this respect bounded by the state on whose territory they reside. For this reason, it makes sense to analyze their experiences within such a framework.

The fundamental issue with which the present study is concerned is the extent to which recent immigrants and their descendants, when compared with the rest of the population, are characterized by a process of 'differential incorporation' (Rex 1986b: xii) within French society. Incorporation is both a subjective and an objective process. Individuals are incorporated objectively within a society to the extent that they are *de facto* participants in the full range of activities and relationships which characterize the national collectivity. Subjective incorporation depends both on self-perceptions and the perceptions of others. While immigrants and their descendants may feel a personal identification with the national community or at least characteristic parts of it, members of the majority population may adopt exclusionary attitudes. There is a constant cross-over between subjective and objective processes. How people interact depends in part on their perceptions and aspirations; the manner in which an individual is treated by others affects in turn the way he or she feels and thinks.

For analytical purposes, three main axes of social experience may be distinguished: the economic (concerned with the production and consumption of material resources), the cultural (centered on the construction and communication of meaning and value) and the political (focusing on the acquisition and use of power). Few, if any, experiences are ever mono-dimensional. In practical terms, power cannot be wielded without using cultural instruments, most obviously language. Control over economic resources gives a very real kind of power, even if it is not expressed through the channels of formal politics and public policy-making (elections, state intervention, etc.). Cultural production is impossible without access to certain economic resources, and cultural products may in turn take the form of commodities bought and sold in the marketplace. It is clear that if we wish to measure the breadth and depth of social incorporation, all three axes must be considered, including the ways in which they reinforce or cross-cut each other.

The main emphasis of Chapters 2 and 3 is on the experiences and attitudes of minority groups. Chapters 4 and 5 focus on the majority population. In Chapter 2, we shall consider the extent to which people of immigrant origin occupy a distinctive position in France's socio-economic structure. Chapter 3 asks how far minority and majority groups are separated by different systems of meaning and value. Chapter 4 considers how and why the citizenship rights of immigrants and their descendants have been redefined in recent years. As the key to incorporation into formal politics, citizenship is of major symbolic importance. French politics and public policy have also had enormous practical consequences for the population of immigrant origin. These are examined in Chapter 5.

Should we describe people of immigrant origin as ethnic minorities? To the extent that they originate in territories outside France, there is an objective sense in which they could be classified in this way. The nub of the issue, however, is how far they now belong to the society in which they live. Within the race relations paradigm, their stigmatization by members of the majority population would suffice to label them as ethnic minorities. It would, however, be a mistake for social scientists to model their own concepts on the prejudices of particular social actors. At least as important as the attitude of the majority population is the extent to which immigrants and their descendants feel committed to French society, as well as their *de facto* participation in its structures. To avoid ambiguity, I think it wise to make these important conceptual differences explicit in the present analysis. Accordingly, a tripartite distinction will be made between what I propose to call *ethnic groups, ethnicized groups* and *ethnocultural groups*.

In the present context, membership of a minority ethnic group is defined by the objective fact of common origins in a territory outside the state in which the group now resides, and within which (an)other group(s) occupy/ies a dominant position. Those foreign origins may be direct (in the case of immigrants) or indirect (in the case of their descendants). Whether this territorial and biological legacy is of real social significance depends to a large extent on how it is perceived by different social actors. A minority ethnicized group is one whose members are considered by members of the majority population to be in a significant sense separate from the national community;[10] racialized minority groups (categorized by somatic features such a skin color) are a subtype of ethnicized minorities. An ethnocultural group is one whose members feel united by a shared system of meaning and value associated with common origins.

None of these three types of group is necessarily united by formal organizational structures, though ethnocultural groups are generally more inclined than the others to organize themselves in such a way. Some sociologists of ethnic relations, notably Rex (1986a), prefer to speak of unorganized groups as quasi-groups, but this seems unnecessary provided the use of the word 'group' is carefully defined, as above. The formal organization of minority ethnocultural groups, through associational and community structures, is discussed in Chapter 3.

The boundary lines between ethnic, ethnicized and ethnocultural groups are seldom if ever neatly isomorphic (cf. Mason 1990, 1991). Majority ethnic members of the French population are inclined to talk about anyone with the physical appearance of a Maghrebi as an 'Arab', though many Maghrebis in fact come from Berber- (rather than Arab-) speaking areas. In this respect, 'Arabs' as an ethnicized group are very different from 'Arabs' as defined by shared territorial or cultural origins. Many of the children of Arab immigrants identify only weakly or intermittently with the cultural heritage of their parents; as such, while they are generally perceived by the public at large as part of the ethnicized Arab population, they belong only marginally to the ethnocultural Arab community.

As will be shown in Chapters 3 and 4, if the French are often anxious over what is seen as the threat of ethnocultural minorities, it is in part because they mistake the phantoms created by their own ethnicization of minority ethnic groups for the much more diffuse modes of ethnicity which characterize many people of immigrant origin. Before examining these attitudinal indicators, however, I shall begin by considering in the next chapter some basic data on the position of recent immigrants and their descendants within the socio-economic structure of France.

2 Socio-economic structures

2.1 Introduction

Economic production sets the material framework within which social structures
and individual life opportunities are shaped. Together with child-rearing, which
continues to impact differentially on men and women, the business of earning a
living takes up more of the average adult's waking life than any other activity. At
the same time, it provides the resources which are indispensable to virtually every
other part of life. The single most important resource to which it gives access is
housing, the location and quality of which provide the context for numerous other
social experiences. If people of immigrant origin are atypical in their employment
and residential patterns, compared with the rest of the population, they are by the
same token marked as significantly different in some of the most basic aspects of
social incorporation.

People suffering from acute disadvantage in the labor market are referred
to by certain commentators as an 'underclass', and localities containing dense
concentrations of those affected in this way are sometimes labeled as 'ghettos'.
Both terms are customarily linked with notions of ethnic alterity: ghettos and
the underclass associated with them are equated primarily with concentrations of
disadvantaged minority ethnicized groups.[1] In the United States, where both terms
are more widely used than in Britain or continental Europe, they were forged into
an explicit collocation by Wilson (1987, 1989), whose work has focused on mainly
black inner-city areas of acute disadvantage in major American conurbations.
Earlier American usage of these terms was adapted to the context of British
'race relations' by sociologists such as Rex and Tomlinson (1979; cf Rex 1988),
and have featured more recently in discussions of continental Europe, including
France (see, for example, Lapeyronnie 1993).

However, European social scientists generally prefer not to use these terms,
for two main reasons. First, everyday usage has become heavily politicized, with
strong connotations of moral opprobrium: in political debate, membership of the
ghetto and its underclass is frequently attributed to dysfunctional behavior such
as high crime rates and low standards of personal morality. Wilson and others
have done their best to dispel such myths, grounding their analysis in empirical
investigations of social disadvantage. Even at this second level, however, the

applicability of such an approach to Europe is generally doubted, mainly because few if any European cities contain ethnicized concentrations of the density found in the US (Wacquant 1992). In France, traces of both approaches became fused in censorious references to the ghetto as an Anglo-Saxon (i.e. British and American) model which must not be allowed to develop in French cities.[2] Viewed from this perspective, the ghetto is the antithesis of successful integration: a spatially distinct enclave inhabited by people who deviate from the moral and material norms of the majority population.

Because they are so ideologically tainted, terms such as 'ghetto' and 'underclass' are probably best avoided in scholarly analyses. The questions which they raise are nevertheless highly pertinent to an understanding of the social incorporation of immigrants and their descendants. How far do minority ethnic groups in France occupy distinct positions in the labor and housing markets? This is the guiding theme of the present chapter. While it is important and relatively simple to formulate this question, it is far more difficult to produce an empirically reliable answer. The most important reason for this lies in the general absence of official data on a large part of the population of immigrant origin. Until very recently, census, labor force and other surveys in France usually distinguished only between French nationals and foreigners; because most people born to immigrant parents become French on or before reaching adulthood, it has generally been impossible to identify them and their children in surveys of this kind. If minority ethnic groups can be said to occupy particular positions in the class structure, this implies a considerable degree of stability. Longitudinal data, i.e. information documenting trends over time, are therefore potentially very significant, and the most convincing evidence of this kind would be inter-generational. The blindspots in most official statistics have made it difficult to establish a reliable picture of the employment patterns and spatial distribution of second- and third-generation members of minority ethnic groups, but a number of studies conducted during the last fifteen years have begun to shed light on these important questions.

2.2 Employment

Before the labor recruitment freeze imposed in the mid-1970s, immigrants throughout western Europe were characterized by high rates of economic activity and low rates of unemployment. Unlike the indigenous populations, a large proportion of which consisted of young and retired people outside the labor market, foreigners were far more likely to be in paid employment, and they were heavily concentrated in badly paid, low-skilled jobs. It was therefore possible to argue with some justification that, together with indigenous workers at the lower end of the socio-economic hierarchy, they were objectively part of the working class, even if this was not acknowledged subjectively by all of the individuals concerned (Castles and Kosack 1973). Since then, there have been major demographic and economic changes. At the time of the 1946 census, some 60 per cent of all foreigners in France were part of the formal labor force (i.e. were economically active in the sense of holding a job or seeking one), compared with

51 per cent of French nationals. By the end of the 1960s, family settlement was already sufficiently advanced to have reduced the share of the foreign population that was economically active to 48 per cent, compared with 41 per cent among French nationals. By 1990, only 45 per cent of France's foreign population was economically active, a figure almost identical to that of the national population as a whole (INSEE 1992a: 19). At the same time, unemployment had risen sharply, particularly among non-nationals. Among French nationals, the unemployment rate (defined in the census as the share of the economically active population out of work, whether receiving unemployment benefit or not) stood at 10 per cent in 1990, compared to 20 per cent among the foreign population (INSEE 1992a: tables 13 and 19). By 1999, the unemployment rate had risen to 12 per cent among French nationals and 24 per cent among foreigners. While the jobless rate among Europeans remained similar to that of French nationals (around 12 per cent), non-Europeans suffered particularly sharp rises. More than one in three Maghrebis, sub-Saharan Africans and Turks were out of work in 1999. Among these groups, the unemployment rate was roughly three times as high as among Europeans (Table 2.1).

Historically, the female participation rate in the formal labor market has always been lower than that of men, but since the late 1960s it has risen steadily. In 1999, some 49 per cent of non-immigrant women aged 15 or more were economically active, compared with 61.7 per cent of non-immigrant men. Among immigrants,

Table 2.1 Unemployment rates by nationality and sex, 1990 and 1999 (%)

	All		Male		Female	
	1990	*1999*	*1990*	*1999*	*1990*	*1999*
French	10.4	12.1	7.5	10.1	14.1	14.3
Foreign	19.5	24.1	16.3	22.0	26.8	27.5
EC/EU	11.3	11.6	8.6	10.6	16.0	13.0
Spanish	12.5	13.8	10.3	12.8	16.3	15.3
Italians	12.2	13.9	9.3	11.5	20.9	19.4
Portuguese	10.2	11.1	7.4	10.7	14.5	11.8
Algerians	27.5	35.9	23.1	32.5	42.3	42.8
Moroccans	25.4	34.2	20.7	30.1	42.5	43.9
Tunisians	25.7	35.6	22.0	32.6	41.7	44.3
Other Africans*	27.6	35.0	21.5	30.5	45.2	42.3
S-E Asians†	26.8	29.3	19.5	23.1	38.6	38.5
Turks	28.9	34.7	23.0	28.3	47.9	51.4

Sources: INSEE 1992a: tables 13, 19; 2002a: tables A1, A4.

Note
* ex-French sub-Saharan Africa; † ex-French Indochina.

the labor participation rate was 42.9 per cent for women and 64 per cent for men. Participation in the formal labor market remains low among women from the Maghreb and Turkey, a pattern which appears in part to reflect the cultural norms prevailing in Islamic countries, where female employment outside the home is often discouraged.[3] Women from these countries seeking work in France experience extremely high unemployment levels (Table 2.1), making them doubly disadvantaged where socio-economic incorporation is concerned. At the beginning of the 1990s, unemployment rates were roughly twice as high among women as among men (immigrant and non-immigrant alike). In the course of the decade the gender gap narrowed, mainly because of a faster rise in unemployment among men.

It is a mark of how economic conditions have changed in the industrialized world that today, when some analysts of social stratification attempt to locate minority ethnic groups within the parameters of an underclass, they appeal to very different criteria from those invoked by Castles and Kosack in their 1973 study of immigrant workers. Instead of hyper-concentration in low status jobs, wholesale disconnection from the labor market is advanced by Wilson, Lapeyronnie and others as a cardinal feature of the 'underclass'. During the years of post-war economic expansion, immigrant workers served as what, in Marxist terminology, is known as a reserve labor army. The international division of labor had created in ex-colonial and other territories large pools of unemployed or underemployed people. By drawing on this reserve workforce, capital was able to remedy labor shortages in industrialized countries without increasing wage costs unduly, for the status of most of those recruited in this way was too insecure to permit them seriously to challenge employers over pay or working conditions. The high unemployment rates now suffered by foreign workers and their concentration in insecure, low-grade jobs suggests that they have become a reserve labor army which is based within France, rather than outside its borders (Talha 1989: 165–237; Marie 1992: 27–8). Moreover, there is growing evidence, discussed below, that second-generation members of post-colonial minorities tend to occupy a structural position which is similar to that of their parents.

Cross (1995), who rejects the 'underclass' as a useful analytical concept, has instead proposed a three-pronged approach for assessing the extent to which minority groups are differentially incorporated into society as a consequence of their position within the labor market. Using Cross's grid in a slightly modified form (his own definitions are somewhat narrower than those employed here), we may speak of *segmentation* as the concentration of certain groups of workers within particular sectors of the economy and at certain levels of the occupational hierarchy. *Marginalization* is the condition of workers who hold particularly insecure jobs. Those who are unemployed, particularly over long periods, may be described as the victims of *exclusion*. On all three counts, post-colonial minorities are generally less well placed than the rest of France's population, including European immigrants.

Segmentation

We may usefully begin by considering the overall distribution of foreign workers within the French economy; concentrations of particular ethnic groups will be highlighted later in this chapter. The foreign labor force has traditionally been overrepresented in the industrial sector. In 1975, two-thirds of foreign workers held industrial jobs, including more than a quarter in the construction industry (Table 2.2). By contrast, well over half of French nationals were employed in the service sector. Many of these had left industrial jobs during the post-war boom, taking more attractive opportunities in the tertiary, i.e. service, sector. Less desirable jobs vacated in the industrial sector were filled by immigrant workers. Since the mid-1970s, widescale restructuring has brought an overall decline in manufacturing industry, and an ever stronger tertiarization of the economy as whole. In 1990, almost two-thirds of French nationals were employed in the service sector, as was half of the foreign labor force. By the end of the decade, the proportion of foreigners employed in the service sector had risen to 60.7 per cent, more than twice the proportion which had prevailed in 1975; during the same period, the share of the foreign labor force working in industry (including construction) had dropped from 68.6 to 36.1 per cent.

There are marked differences in the employment patterns of men and women (Tables 2.3 and 2.4). Men, particularly non-nationals, have traditionally been to the fore in industrial jobs, whereas women have always been heavily concentrated in the service sector. Foreign men have been especially overrepresented in the construction industry, where very few women are present. But the structural changes undergone by the French economy in the course of the final quarter of the twentieth century were such that by 1999, most male foreign workers were in the service sector, with only 43.7 per in industry, compared with 72 per cent in 1975. Among the female labor force, in 1999 some 85.1 of foreign workers were in the service sector, almost exactly the same proportion as among French women. Despite similarities in overall sectoral trends among French and foreign members of the labor force, there are major differences in the types of jobs held (Tables 2.5 and 2.6). In 2002, the proportion of female immigrants employed in the 'personal service' sector, usually implying low-status domestic work, and in manual labor, generally poorly paid, was more than twice as high as among non-immigrant women, while the proportion of female immigrants who were junior managers or professionals was half that of non-immigrant women (Zimmermann 2005). Male immigrants were similarly underrepresented in managerial and professional positions and overrepresented in manual jobs.

After halting labor migration in 1974, the administration presided over by Giscard d'Estaing had hoped to curb unemployment among French nationals by encouraging foreign workers to return home; forcible repatriations were also planned, though it proved impossible to effect them. An important assumption underlying this strategy was that French nationals would be willing to fill the jobs vacated by departing foreigners. Government ministers were irritated when a report which they had commissioned called this assumption into question. Taking

Table 2.2 Sectoral distribution of French and foreign labor force by percentage, male and female combined, 1975–99

	1975		1982		1990		1999	
	French	*Foreign*	*French*	*Foreign*	*French*	*Foreign*	*French*	*Foreign*
Agriculture	10.3	5.7	8.2	4.4	5.8	3.4	4.2	3.2
Industry*	28.8	38.7	26.0	33.7	22.5	26.2	18.4	21.4
Construction	7.8	26.9	8.2	22.3	6.6	20.6	5.3	14.7
Services	53.1	28.7	57.6	39.6	65.1	49.8	72.1	60.7
Total	100.0	100.0	100.0	100.0	100.0	100.0	100.0	100.0

Sources: INSEE 1992a: table R10; 2005: tables A9, A12.

Note
* excluding construction.

Table 2.3 Sectoral distribution of French and foreign male labor force by percentage, 1975–99

	1975		1982		1990		1999	
	French	*Foreign*	*French*	*Foreign*	*French*	*Foreign*	*French*	*Foreign*
Agriculture	11.6	6.3	8.9	4.9	6.7	3.8	5.3	4.0
Industry*	31.8	39.5	30.3	35.3	27.6	28.4	23.8	21.5
Construction	11.6	32.5	12.6	28.5	10.5	28.0	8.8	22.2
Services	45.0	21.7	48.2	31.3	55.2	39.8	62.1	52.3
Total	100.0	100.0	100.0	100.0	100.0	100.0	100.0	100.0

Sources: INSEE 1992a: table R10; 2005: tables A9, A12.

Note
* excluding construction.

Table 2.4 Sectoral distribution of French and foreign female labor force by percentage, 1975–99

	1975		1982		1990		1999	
	French	*Foreign*	*French*	*Foreign*	*French*	*Foreign*	*French*	*Foreign*
Agriculture	8.4	3.0	7.1	2.6	4.7	2.0	2.8	1.9
Industry*	23.6	35.2	19.4	27.5	15.9	20.6	11.8	11.9
Construction	1.4	1.6	1.5	1.2	1.4	1.3	1.1	1.1
Services	66.6	60.2	72.0	68.7	78.0	76.1	84.3	85.1
Total	100.0	100.0	100.0	100.0	100.0	100.0	100.0	100.0

Sources: INSEE 1992a: table R10; 2005: tables A9, A12.

Note
* excluding construction.

Table 2.5 Occupational groups as percentage of employed labor force, 2002

	Male and female combined			Male		Female	
	Total labor force	Non-immigrants	Immigrants	Non-immigrants	Immigrants	Non-immigrants	Immigrants
Farmers	2.7	2.8	0.7	3.5	0.7	2.0	0.7
Artisans, tradespeople, company heads	5.9	5.8	8.2	7.4	10.7	3.8	4.6
Senior managers and professionals	14.7	15.0	10.4	17.6	11.8	12.1	8.2
Junior managers and professionals	21.5	22.3	12.4	21.6	12.9	23.1	11.8
Non-manual workers	29.3	29.4	27.8	13.2	11.5	48.6	52.2
personal service staff	6.2	5.6	12.3	1.2	3.0	10.9	26.1
Manual workers	25.9	24.7	40.5	36.7	52.4	10.4	22.5
skilled	16.9	16.4	23.4	26.9	35.0	3.9	5.8
unskilled	9.0	8.3	17.1	9.8	17.4	6.5	16.7
Total	100.0	100.0	100.0	100.0	100.0	100.0	100.0

Source: INSEE 2005: table 4.5.1.

Table 2.6 Occupational groups as percentage of employed immigrant labor force by country of origin, 2002

	Spain	Italy	Portugal	Other Europe	Algeria	Morocco	Tunisia	Other Africa	Turkey
Farmers	3	2	1	2	0	0	0	0	1
Artisans, tradespeople, company heads	8	9	8	9	7	8	10	4	17
Senior managers and professionals	9	12	2	24	7	9	9	9	2
Junior managers and professionals	15	16	9	20	15	10	8	11	5
Non-manual workers	33	27	30	24	30	22	24	38	11
personal service staff	15	10	21	8	8	8	8	15	4
Manual workers	32	34	50	21	41	51	49	38	64
skilled	20	24	32	13	25	24	28	18	33
unskilled	12	10	18	8	16	27	21	20	30
Total	100	100	100	100	100	100	100	100	100

Source: INSEE 2005: table 4.5.3.

the construction and automobile industries as examples, Le Pors (1977) reported that, as the posts occupied by foreigners were mainly of the kind that the French themselves had been keen to quit, it was unlikely they would now return to such jobs, even at a time of rising unemployment. In both absolute and proportional terms, these industries were at that time the two largest employers of foreign labor in France. In different ways, they exemplified the fact that immigrant workers, concentrated in certain segments of the labor market, were a structural rather than a temporary feature of the national economy.

The building trade was characterized during the post-war period by increasingly poor rates of pay, compared with those offered in other sectors, and carried particularly unattractive working conditions – high accident rates, poor hygiene, low job security, etc. French nationals who found job opportunities elsewhere were increasingly inclined to leave the industry, leaving immigrants to fill the gaps. A similar trend was visible in the car industry, where automation had lowered the general level of skills required of the workforce, for whom repetitive assembly line tasks were the norm; shiftwork and the anti-social hours which this implied were a further disincentive. While robotization led to wide-scale redundancies among immigrant car workers from the late 1970s onwards, this brought few job opportunities for French nationals. According to labor force surveys, between 1973 and 1982, the number of foreigners employed in the car industry dropped by 151,000; because many of these jobs disappeared altogether, it was estimated that no more than 10,000 French nationals found employment as a result (Hessel 1988, vol. 2: 43).

There was heavy labor-shedding in the building industry, too, and foreign workers bore the brunt of this. Non-nationals accounted for three-quarters of all the construction jobs lost between 1975 and 1982 (Marie 1992: 27). While this helped to protect French workers from the worst of the recession, as overall employment levels in this sector declined the laying off of large numbers of foreign workers created relatively few new jobs for French nationals.

Public cleaning services in large cities such as Paris offer a rare example of the systematic substitution of French for foreign workers. In 1976, the Paris City Council stopped recruiting foreigners to sweep the streets. Because permanent employment by central and local arms of the state is reserved by law for French nationals, the council was able to effect this shift without breaking other statutes forbidding racial discrimination. Until 1976, most street-sweepers had had the formal status of temporary auxiliaries, which had enabled the council to hire foreigners. By 1985, 1,500 of them had left their jobs, while 2,000 French nationals had been taken on. This reduced the proportion of foreigners among the city's street-sweepers to 32 per cent in 1985, compared with 72 per cent in 1975. Even here, however, major improvements in pay and working conditions made the process a less than direct substitution of nationals for non-nationals, for the jobs taken up by the former were substantially upgraded in comparison with those vacated by the latter (Merckling 1987: 81).

Marginalization

The concentration of foreign workers in unattractive segments and at low levels of the economic hierarchy is compounded by their vulnerability to job insecurity. This insecurity, which in one sense marginalizes them, is nevertheless structurally important. Capitalist economies are increasingly characterized by what are known as split or dual labor markets (Berger and Piore 1980). The primary market offers relatively stable, skilled and well-paid jobs, whereas in the secondary market employment is more likely to be insecure, poorly paid and unskilled. It is no accident that foreign workers are heavily overrepresented in the construction industry, for this, more than any other, is characterized by high levels of job insecurity (Beaugé 1990). Textile manufacture, which has also relied heavily on immigrant workers, is another industry vulnerable to sharp fluctuations in the demand for labor (Berrier 1985). The shift from industrial to service sector jobs has brought few benefits in this respect. The fact that permanent employment by the state has been reserved for French nationals (recently widened to include EU nationals) has excluded foreigners from the most secure part of the tertiary sector; non-nationals are concentrated in services such as domestic work and catering (in hotels, cafés, restaurants, etc.), where employment is often poorly paid and subject to seasonal and other fluctuations (Verhaeren 1990: 128–30; Maurin 1991: 48–9).

Since the late 1970s, economic restructuring forced by the quickening pace of globalization has been marked in France, as in many western countries, by the decline of manufacturing industry, the growth of the service sector, higher levels of female economic activity and increased casualization, i.e. the introduction of weaker employment contracts than those previously enjoyed by employees. The effect of these closely intertwined trends has been to favor the development of the secondary labor market. Some of this has been achieved by substituting part-time and/or temporary contracts for full-time, permanent jobs; increased subcontracting by large firms has pushed in the same direction (Abou Sada 1990). Legally sanctioned forms of casualization have been accompanied by the development of the informal or underground economy, which circumvents legislation designed to protect the labor force. By not declaring part or all of their activities to the authorities, employers escape tax and social security payments as well as regulations on health and safety, minimum wage levels, maximum working hours and security of employment. By the same token, those employed in this way work in extremely insecure conditions. Undocumented immigrants are only a small part of the total underground economy, but their fear of expulsion if reported to the authorities makes them one of the most vulnerable groups within it (HCI 1993b: 100).

The jobs initially taken by immigrant workers have generally been in the secondary labor market (Piore 1979; Courault 1990). The fixed-term contracts prescribed in the official procedures laid down in 1945 by the Office National d'Immigration (ONI) for the recruitment of foreign workers were designed to ensure flexibility. Seasonal workers – tens of thousands of whom are still granted temporary work permits each year, mainly in the agricultural sector – represent a continuing and acute form of institutionalized impermanence. The ONI never succeeded in fully controlling the recruitment process. Algerians were always exempt from it, and during the 1960s most other foreign workers obtained residence and work permits only after they had taken up jobs, reversing the order of the formally prescribed procedures. The dividing line between the formal and informal parts of the secondary market was thus relatively weak: undocumented foreign workers who, in breach of the law, obtained temporary contracts of employment found it easy to regularize their situation.

As their period of settlement lengthened, immigrants generally acquired longer term residence and work permits, together with more stable employment, while nevertheless remaining subject to more frequent changes of jobs than French nationals (Maurin 1991: 42). After the labor migration freeze imposed in 1974, the more difficult economic climate which was then developing probably slowed the pace at which settled labor migrants were able to move from the secondary to the primary labor market (Tribalat 1991: 196). Following the second oil crisis of 1979, economic restructuring brought huge job losses in sectors with heavy concentrations of foreign workers, among whom unemployment rates rose steeply, forcing a renewed willingness to accept insecure work rather than none at all (Courault 1990). At the same time, the state's refusal to accept new foreign workers sharpened the divide between the formal and informal parts of the secondary market. Despite rising unemployment, many employers welcomed illegal immigrants, whose weak bargaining position they were keen to exploit (HCI 1993c).

An analysis by Marie (1988) of those who benefited from the amnesty declared by the incoming Socialist administration in 1981–2 provides a telling picture of the role of undocumented foreign workers within the French economy. Most were non-Europeans, reflecting the dominance of Africans and Asians in recent migratory flows. The great majority held jobs in sectors dominated by small firms. Two-thirds worked for businesses employing less than ten people. Construction, catering, domestic service and the clothing industry together accounted for more than half of all those regularized. As Marie (1992: 31) later observed, this sectoral profile matches up very closely with the most dynamic features of the role currently played by foreign workers in the formal labor market. A follow-up survey conducted two years after the amnesty found that more than 80 per cent of the total now held regular jobs, usually in the same sector where they had previously been working illegally. This was clear evidence that, as undocumented workers, they had been meeting a structural need within the French economy. Their working conditions after regularization changed very little. Low pay, long and anti-social working hours and insecure contracts of employment were the hallmarks of this system, enabling employers to respond to shifts in demand with maximum flexibility (Marie 1988: 554–74). An analysis of police reports concerning employers accused of circumventing the laws regulating hired labor in 1989–90 found that the pattern had changed very little: two-thirds of the reported cases concerned the building, catering and retail distribution sectors (Marie 1992: 32).

While most of those regularized in 1980–1 were young men, a fifth were women. Again, this replicated almost exactly the gender balance among salaried foreign workers in the formal labor market (Marie 1992: 30). Three-quarters of the regularized women were unmarried. The largest single group among them – almost a third of the total – was composed of Portuguese nationals. They accounted for the bulk of undocumented domestic staff, who together represented half of the female contingent in the regularization operation. About a fifth of undocumented women were employed as cleaners or clothing workers. Even after regularization, two-thirds of women were being paid less than the official minimum wage, as were a quarter of regularized men.

Among undocumented workers as a whole, a tendency towards ethnic segmentation was clearly visible, with Turks, Moroccans and Tunisians together accounting for almost two-thirds of those regularized in the building industry; sub-Saharan Africans represented 41 per cent of other industrial workers, and the Portuguese alone accounted for an identical share of regularized domestic staff. In many, though not all respects this, too, parallels the sectoral and occupational distribution of national groups within the formal economy (Tables 2.7–2.9). Ethnic concentrations were still more marked among the 20 per cent of regularized workers employed by foreign nationals. Some 75 per cent of those working for

Table 2.7 Sectoral percentage distribution of employed labor force by nationality, male and female combined, 1990 and 1999

	Agriculture		Industry excluding construction		Construction industry		Services		Total
	1990	*1999*	*1990*	*1999*	*1990*	*1999*	*1990*	*1999*	
French	5.8	4.2	22.5	18.4	6.6	5.3	65.1	72.1	100
Foreign	3.3	3.3	26.3	18.1	20.6	14.7	49.8	63.9	100
EC/EU	3.3	3.2	24.3	18.1	24.7	18.4	47.7	60.3	100
Spanish	6.1	4.3	24.4	9.4	19.4	13.4	50.1	62.9	100
Italians	2.2	1.5	28.4	23.3	27.1	17.0	42.3	58.2	100
Portuguese	2.6	3.1	24.0	17.3	29.9	25.1	43.5	54.5	100
Algerians	0.6	0.9	26.9	17.8	21.9	12.6	50.6	68.7	100
Moroccans	10.6	9.7	29.6	20.0	18.9	12.7	40.9	57.6	100
Tunisians	3.3	3.5	21.8	15.5	24.6	16.9	50.3	64.1	100
Other Africans*	0.3	0.5	23.6	11.4	6.9	5.0	69.2	83.1	100
S-E Asians†	1.1	1.6	42.7	32.0	3.4	2.3	52.8	64.1	100
Turks	4.3	3.8	43.7	31.2	28.5	27.2	23.5	37.8	100

Sources: INSEE 1992a: table 18; 2002a: table A12.

Note
* ex-French sub-Saharan Africa; † ex-French Indochina.

Table 2.8 Sectoral percentage distribution of employed male labor force by nationality, 1999

	Agriculture	Industry excluding construction	Construction industry	Services	Total
French	5.3	23.8	8.9	62.0	100
Foreign	4.0	21.6	22.2	52.2	100
EU	3.9	22.0	30.1	44.0	100
Spanish	5.7	25.4	22.1	46.8	100
Italians	1.7	26.6	22.9	48.8	100
Portuguese	3.9	20.4	41.8	33.9	100
Algerians	1.1	21.9	17.5	59.5	100
Moroccans	11.8	24.1	16.7	47.4	100
Tunisians	4.2	17.3	21.4	57.1	100
Other Africans*	0.6	14.8	7.8	76.8	100
S-E Asians†	1.6	33.3	3.3	61.8	100
Turks	3.9	30.7	33.4	32.0	100

Source: INSEE 2002a: tables A9, A12.

Note
* ex-French sub-Saharan Africa; † ex-French Indochina.

Table 2.9 Sectoral percentage distribution of employed female labor force by nationality, 1999

	Agriculture	Industry excluding construction	Construction industry	Services	Total
French	2.8	11.9	1.0	84.3	100
Foreign	1.9	11.9	1.1	85.1	100
EU	2.3	12.6	1.2	83.9	100
Spanish	2.4	11.0	1.3	85.3	100
Italians	1.0	14.9	1.7	82.4	100
Portuguese	2.1	12.9	1.4	83.6	100
Algerians	0.4	8.0	0.8	90.8	100
Moroccans	3.4	8.4	0.9	87.3	100
Tunisians	1.0	9.4	1.3	88.3	100
Other Africans*	0.3	4.6	0.3	94.8	100
S-E Asians†	1.6	29.6	0.4	68.4	100
Turks	3.9	33.0	3.2	59.9	100

Source: INSEE 2002a: tables A9, A12.

Note
* ex-French sub-Saharan Africa; † ex-French Indochina.

Algerians were themselves of Algerian nationality; among Turks the equivalent figure was 80 per cent, and among Tunisians and Moroccans it exceeded 90 per cent (Marie 1988).

Exclusion

It is a cruel irony that immigrants, who in popular discourse used to be synonymous with immigrant workers, now suffer from exceptionally high levels of unemployment. Until the late 1970s, while marginalized and segmented, they were nevertheless more fully integrated into the world of work – in the simple sense of holding jobs of one kind or another – than French nationals themselves. Today, while far more settled in France than was the case thirty years ago, many foreigners face a much higher risk of social exclusion as a consequence of unemployment.

There is a sharp distinction here between Europeans and others. While documented unemployment levels among EU nationals are very similar to those of the French, Africans and Asians are almost three times as likely to be out of work (Table 2.1). The steep rise in unemployment among non-Europeans has been partly a consequence of their concentration in unskilled jobs within sectors which have shed particularly large numbers of workers. The shake-out was particularly vigorous in the late 1970s and early 1980s. In the industrial sector as a whole (including construction), foreigners represented two-fifths of the jobs lost between 1979 and 1982, though they accounted for only about a tenth of the total industrial labor force (Anstett 1992: 113).

In 1982, foreigners constituted about a sixth of the building industry's labor force, but they had suffered seven out of every ten job losses over the previous ten years (Anstett 1992: 114). At the time of the 1975 census, vehicle production was the second largest industrial employer of foreign labor. With robotization, the industry suffered heavy job losses in the early 1980s, and most of the manual workers replaced in this way were non-nationals. By 1990, the foreign workforce had been reduced by more than half, while French nationals in this sector were down by only a sixth.

Contrasts of this kind cannot always be accounted for by differences in the level of skills offered by French and foreign workers. In the electrical industry, for example, unskilled non-nationals suffered job losses during the 1980s at a rate five times higher than French workers in the same category (Maurin 1991: 44). While its effects are difficult to quantify with precision, discrimination by employers appears to have disadvantaged certain groups of foreign workers, particularly non-Europeans, within the formal labor market. At the same time, the generally poor level of qualifications found among Africans in particular is in itself a serious handicap when competing for jobs in expanding sectors demanding higher levels of skills than were required in some declining industries.

Tribalat (1991: 195–237) has suggested that differential unemployment rates during the 1980s reflected the relatively recent nature of migratory flows from certain countries. The available data provide only limited evidence in support of this. While Africans and Asians who arrived in France during the 1980s, mainly within the framework of family reunification procedures, suffered even higher unemployment levels than their longer established compatriots, this was not true of newly arriving Europeans, among whom the jobless rate was very similar to that of French nationals (HCI 1993b: 37). Recent entrants may be handicapped by poor language skills, but there is no reason to believe that non-Europeans are worse affected by this than Europeans. As most of those from Africa and Asia come from former colonies where French is still widely used, they should if anything have an advantage in this respect. Lack of qualifications and discrimination on the part of employers are more likely explanations.

As the educational systems in many formerly colonized regions are far less developed than those in European states, African immigrants in particular appear to be disadvantaged in this regard. Labor force surveys in the early 1990s indicated that 75 per cent of Maghrebis had no formal qualifications at all, compared with only 35 per cent of French workers. Yet even when controlled comparisons were made with French nationals of identical age and skills, Maghrebis were almost twice as likely to be out of work, strongly suggesting that they were the victims of discriminatory practices. Similarly, as only 45 per cent of South-East Asians lacked qualifications, compared with 82 per cent of Portuguese workers, it is likely that the much higher levels of unemployment suffered by the former were due in part to discrimination against them (Maurin 1991: 39–41).

The cumulative effect of all this has been to push a growing proportion of non-Europeans into long-term unemployment. A labor force survey conducted in 1992 found that 40 per cent of unemployed foreigners had been out of work for over a year, compared with 32 per cent of French nationals. While long-term joblessness affected 25 per cent of unemployed Portuguese nationals, among out-of-work Maghrebis the rate was 44 per cent and among other Africans it stood at 48 per cent (INSEE 1994: 85).

Youth unemployment

Notwithstanding the fact that a disturbingly high proportion of non-Europeans are jobless, if long-term or permanent unemployment is fundamental to membership of an 'underclass', it is clear that only a minority of foreigners fall within it. If an underclass can be said to exist, it is rather among the younger age segments of post-colonial minorities, most of whom are French. Because the census authorities and other government agencies do not collect ethnically based data, there is a paucity of statistical information on second- and third-generation members of minority ethnic groups. Recent studies have, however, produced strongly concordant indicators suggesting that unemployment rates among young men and women of non-European origin are extremely high. Census data show that in chronically disadvantaged urban areas known as Zones Urbaines Sensibles (ZUS), where minority ethnic groups are overrepresented, the jobless rate among the 15–19 age group in 1990 was 26.4 per cent for males and 36.3 per cent for females (Table 2.10).

Table 2.10 Youth unemployment rates by type of locality, 1990 and 1999 (%)

	France		Urban areas containing ZUS		Zones Urbaines Sensibles (ZUS)	
	1990	1999	1990	1999	1990	1999
Male unemployment rate						
Age 15–19	16.3	24.1	19.1	29.7	26.4	44.0
Age 20–24	14.8	22.5	16.7	25.2	23.5	37.2
Female unemployment rate						
Age 15–19	28.6	35.1	29.1	36.4	36.3	50.7
Age 20–24	25.3	28.4	24.1	27.4	33.0	39.5

Source: INSEE data in HCI 2003: 38.

As the census data do not distinguish between ethnic groups, it is probable that they conceal even higher unemployment rates among minority ethnic youths, who are hampered in the labor market by widespread discrimination. This was confirmed by the path-breaking 'Mobilité Géographique et Insertion Sociale' (Geographical Mobility and Social Incorporation – MGIS) survey led by Tribalat in the early 1990s, which found that the unemployment rate among second-generation ethnic Algerians aged 20–29 was 40 per cent for women and 42 per cent for men (Tribalat 1995: 175). In the course of the 1990s, youth unemployment in the ZUS rocketed, reaching 44 per cent for men and 50.7 per cent for women (all ethnic groups combined) in 1999. Extrapolating from Tribalat's findings at the beginning of the decade, it is reasonable to suppose that jobless rates among minority ethnic youths at the end of the 1990s were even higher. The disproportionate impact of unemployment on post-colonial minorities was confirmed in another large-scale survey conducted by INED in conjunction with INSEE, the 'Enquête Famille' (Family Survey – EF), based on data collected in 1999, where Meurs *et al.* (2005) found that second-generation non-Europeans had higher jobless rates and more insecure forms of employment than young people of French origin with the same level of qualifications. Like the authors of other studies before them (Céreq 2004), Meurs *et al.* concluded that discrimination had played a key role in reducing the employment opportunities of second-generation members of minority ethnic groups. For well over a decade, youth unemployment among visible minorities had been so high that many young people of Maghrebi, sub-Saharan African and Caribbean origin had come to despair of ever finding regular employment. That despair, combined with resentment over discrimination, was a major factor in the riots which swept through the banlieues in November 2005 (Clémentine *et al.* 2006; Mucchielli 2006; Moulier Boutang 2005).

Although not as widespread as in 2005, similar disturbances pitting minority ethnic youths against the police, seen as representatives of a discriminatory and repressive social order, had been erupting periodically in disadvantaged urban areas since the late 1970s. Extensive media coverage of these events in the early 1980s was revived by a new upsurge of rioting in the Lyonnais banlieue of Vaulx-en-Velin in 1990 and continued intermittently in response to similar events in many cities throughout the 1990s (Begag and Delorme 1994: 107–21; Hargreaves 1996).

The disturbances in Vaulx-en-Velin in 1990 coincided with the first significant attempt to measure youth unemployment among the minority ethnic population. This too had been the work of Tribalat. It focused on immigrant-headed households, which, at the time of the 1990 census, contained 1,030,000 people in the 15–24 age bracket, two-thirds of whom were born in France. The contrasts which emerged between Europeans and non-Europeans in this younger age group were similar but not identical to those characterizing first-generation members of different immigrant groups. Calculated on the basis of the 1990 census data, the nationwide unemployment rate among 22-year-old men, including those in non-immigrant households, was 19 per cent. Among men of that age in immigrant-headed households, the rates were 12 per cent in homes headed by an immigrant from Portugal, 23 per cent where the head was from Spain, 39 per cent where the head was from Morocco and 51 per cent where the head was from Algeria (Tribalat 1993: 1940–1). Tribalat did not give any comparable 1990 data for women, but in a more limited household survey conducted in the 1980s she had found a substantially similar pattern among both sexes. The unemployment rate among 21 year olds still living with French mothers was 12 per cent for men and 18 per cent for women; among the sons and daughters of Portuguese women the figures were 7 and 18 per cent respectively, compared with 39 and 49 per cent among those born to Algerian mothers (Tribalat 1991: 165).

Exact comparisons with young people from households headed by South-East Asians and sub-Saharan Africans were difficult because a larger proportion of them were still in full-time education, but their unemployment rates were certainly lower than those of young Maghrebis. The stronger rates of participation in higher education among the children of South-East Asians served to reproduce the superior qualifications found among this group, compared with other immigrants, and this was clearly beneficial in the employment market. Research on the educational attainment of the children of immigrants has consistently shown that the socio-professional status and educational qualifications of parents (which tend to be interlinked) are by far the most important variables, as they are for youngsters among the French population at large. Foreign children generally fare less well at school than French nationals. Certain groups, such as young Maghrebis, do particularly badly. With poorly educated manual workers accounting for a large proportion of Maghrebi immigrant parents, these same groups are characterized by high levels of socio-economic disadvantage. When children from similar socio-economic backgrounds are compared, the educational differences between national groups are almost insignificant; if anything, foreign children tend to do slightly better than their French peers (Aissou 1987; Boulot and Boyzon-Fradet 1988; Conseil Économique et Social 1994: 58–79).

Compared with the school population as a whole, young Maghrebis leave full-time education much earlier, and with much poorer qualifications. Yet this alone does not suffice to explain their chronic rates of unemployment. The children of Portuguese immigrants also tend to finish their education early, but their unemployment rate is well below the national average. Young people of Portuguese origin benefit from family and other networks in finding jobs, particularly in the building industry, and it is clear that they suffer far less discrimination than young Maghrebis.

The rise in unemployment seen in most west Europeans countries since the beginning of the 1980s hit young people particularly hard, forcing governments to devise a variety of schemes designed to alleviate the problem. In France, the first such initiative was the creation in 1982 of Missions locales pour l'insertion professionnelle et sociale des jeunes, local advice centers targeting young people (essentially in the 16–25 age group) experiencing serious difficulties in finding work. Since then, state-aided youth employment, work experience and training schemes have also been introduced. In 1992, the labor inspectorate produced a report on the experiences of young people of immigrant origin in the employment market based on information collected through these local advice centers (IGAS 1992). The official ban on ethnic monitoring made it impossible to produce exact figures (for reasons already explained, nationality is an inadequate indicator), but local officials estimated that youngsters from immigrant families, who probably made up less than 15 per cent of the 16–25 age group as a whole (Tribalat 1993: 1930) accounted for between 30 and 60 per cent of their clients (IGAS 1992: 17). As the Missions locales are designed to assist young people facing particularly acute employment problems, there was strong evidence here that the descendants of immigrants were encountering exceptionally severe difficulties.

It is true that immigrant-born youngsters are over-represented in relatively poor households with unskilled family heads, and that this pattern tends to reproduce itself in an inter-generational way regardless of ethnic origins. The inspectorate found, however, that in addition to the handicap of poor qualifications, which they shared with many unemployed youths from non-immigrant families, youngsters of immigrant origin were subject to widespread discrimination. Every local advice center reported that this was the case. Bearing in mind that discrimination has been prohibited by law since 1972, the frequency with which employers engaged in such practices even when dealing with official agencies of the state was very striking. The full force of these practices can best be conveyed by quoting from the report:

> All the Missions locales and local employment offices included in the survey emphasized the growing importance of discrimination in job offers, based on the origins, the name or simply the address of candidates, particularly if this is an area where disturbances have occurred.
>
> The unwillingness to take on certain people is not always spelled out explicitly. The employer may indicate reservations or refusals of certain candidates by saying nothing at all or simply rejecting them without explanation; in some

cases, employers explain their refusals by saying they already have too many foreigners on the payroll or blame refusals on the reaction of other members of staff or customers, when the job involves dealing with the public. Often, though, particularly when contacting local employment offices, employers are straight to the point, signaling their refusal with remarks such as 'no colored people', 'no Arabs', 'no Maghrebis'.

The Missions locales included in the survey estimated that one in three and in some cases one in two job offers were discriminatory.

(IGAS 1992: 49–50)

As one of the co-authors of the report noted, those worst hit by practices of this kind were young people from Maghrebi and sub-Saharan African families, as well as those originating in the DOM-TOM (Lemoine 1992: 175). Although many of the former and all of the latter were French nationals, this was clearly unimportant in the eyes of those discriminating against them. These post-colonial minorities were being negatively ethnicized by majority ethnic gate-keepers because of their origins.

Throughout the 1990s, evidence of discrimination and high levels of unemployment suffered by minority ethnic youths accumulated at an accelerating pace (de Rudder *et al.* 1994; Bataille 1997) but politicians were slow to react. They generally played down the issue of discrimination, denying that a significant problem existed. Instead of tackling discrimination, the center-right government which held office from 1993 to 1997 invested a huge amount of energy in the symbolic politics of the nationality law reform, which cast doubt over the 'Frenchness' of post-colonial minorities and implicitly lent legitimacy to those who discriminated against them. Only when the left returned to power in 1997 was anti-discrimination policy accorded for the first time a significant position on the government's agenda but even then effective action was slow (Hargreaves 2000). It was not until 2005, five years after an EU Directive requiring each member-state to set up an independent anti-racism authority similar to Britain's Commission for Racial Equality, that President Chirac inaugurated the Haute Autorité de Lutte Contre les Discriminations et pour l'Egalité (High Authority against Discrimination and for Equality – HALDE). In the mean time, conditions in the banlieues had deteriorated steadily, with official unemployment rates among young men in the ZUS (all ethnic groups combined) leaping from 26.4 per cent in 1990 to 44 per cent in 1999 (Table 2.10). Because of discrimination – research conducted in 2004 on job applications from candidates of different ethnic origins with identical experience and qualifications found that a candidate of Maghrebi origin was five times less likely than a candidate of French origin to be called for interview (Amadieu 2004) – it is probable that unemployment rates among minority ethnic youths were higher still. Small wonder that in 2005 the banlieues were burning.

Ethnic business

The term 'ethnic business' is widely used to denote economic activities by people of minority ethnic groups who are self-employed, and who in many cases also employ others.[4] In France and other countries, the last twenty years have brought a marked rise in small businesses of this kind. In the present context, these businesses raise two questions which are particularly pertinent: how far have they served to alleviate the difficulties experienced in the labor market by minority ethnic groups, and how far have they strengthened or diluted the segmentation of these groups?

The statistical data available in France usually distinguish three main categories among the self-employed: artisans (i.e. skilled manual workers), people in the retail, wholesale or catering trades (generically referred to hereafter as tradespeople) and the owners of businesses employing ten or more people. All but 7 per cent of self-employed foreigners fit into the first two categories (Echardour and Maurin 1993: 510). As foreign entrepreneurs employing more than a handful of people are few in number, there is relatively little scope for the development of full-blown 'enclave economies', i.e. concentrations of particular minority groups within businesses owned, managed and staffed entirely on a mono-ethnic basis (Portes 1981).

In comparison with their share of the general population, foreigners have traditionally been underrepresented among the self-employed, partly because of restrictive regulations which were not lifted until 1984. Not surprisingly, those wishing to set up in business have been characterized by above average naturalization rates, as a consequence of which statistics based on nationality significantly underestimate the number of self-employed immigrants. Since the mid-1970s, however, there has been a steady rise in the number of self-employed foreigners. This began even before the restrictions on them were lifted.

From only 2 per cent of all artisans in 1975, foreign nationals rose to 4 per cent in 1982 and 6 per cent in 1990, a figure only fractionally less than their share of the total labor force (Auvolat and Benattig 1988: 39; INSEE 1992a: table 17). It is no accident that this rise took place at a time of radical economic restructuring and weaker job security. Many large companies were increasing the share of their activities subcontracted out to small businesses sometimes consisting of one 'self-employed' individual who, because of that status, was formally exempt from the security of employment traditionally enjoyed by salaried employees. In the mid-1980s, a survey by Auvolat and Benattig (1988) found that half of all recently registered artisans, both French and foreign, had previously been out of work. Among foreign artisans, southern European (particularly Portuguese) and Maghrebi nationals were dominant. Most set up in sectors where they had previously worked as employees. More than two-thirds of foreign artisans, compared with only two-fifths of French artisans, were in the building industry, where there had been heavy job losses, particularly among immigrant workers, since the late 1970s. Significantly, two-thirds of the self-employed foreigners in the construction sector surveyed by Auvolat and Benattig were subcontractors, compared with less than a third of French nationals. Thus many self-employed foreigners appeared to owe their status to a combination of labor-shedding and subcontracting practices devised by larger French firms to gain flexibility in the hiring and firing of their workforce (Garson and Mouhoud 1989). In these circumstances, it is only in a relatively weak sense that the majority of foreign artisans might be included under the umbrella of 'ethnic business'. While certainly overrepresented in certain segments of the labor market, they remain to a very large extent dependent upon, and dominated by, contracts in the mainstream economy.

A clear pattern of ethnic segmentation is also visible among tradespeople of immigrant origin. In 1990, foreigners represented 5 per cent of all tradespeople in France, compared with 3 per cent in 1982 (Echardour and Maurin 1993: 510). In the mid-1980s, Ma Mung and Guillon (1986: 108) found that in the Paris conurbation, more than 60 per cent of foreign-owned small businesses were accounted for by grocery stores and catering establishments such as cafés and restaurants. French tradespeople were far more widely spread. The businesses in which foreigners were most strongly represented were either in decline among French tradespeople (this was true of both grocery stores and catering in general) or offered 'exotic' produce unavailable in French establishments (the cuisine proposed by foreign-owned restaurants being the best example). Certain nationalities were also heavily overrepresented, with Maghrebis accounting for 61 per cent of all foreign tradespeople, against only 39 per cent of the foreign population at large. This was partly because, under the terms of the Evian agreement granting independence to Algeria in 1962, Algerians had been exempted from the controls on self-employment by foreigners. It should also be said that because of exceptionally high naturalization rates among South-East Asians, their business activities – which are particularly strong in the catering sector – are always grossly underestimated in analyses based on nationality.

A survey by Ma Mung (1992) based on ethnic origins (as judged by family names) rather than nationality confirmed the dynamism of tradespeople of immigrant origin and the predominance among them of Maghrebis and Asians, with a marked segmentation in particular niches. More than one in five of all the shops and catering establishments in the Paris conurbation which changed hands in the first half of 1989 were bought by Maghrebis (15 per cent of the total) or Asians (5.6 per cent); as measured by nationality, these groups account respectively for just 2.5 and less than 1 per cent of the general population. While gradually extending into a wider range of businesses, both groups remained heavily concentrated in food shops and catering, with Maghrebis to the fore in general grocery stores and Asians strongly represented in the restaurant trade.

The extent to which a particular pattern of economic activity may be described as 'ethnic business' depends on the ethnic complexion of four main variables: the capital with which businesses are acquired, the staff who run them, the services or products sold, and the customers for whom they cater. The more these variables correspond to the same ethnic group, the more the businesses in question function as a distinct economic circuit outside the dominant patterns of the national economy. While businesses run by people of immigrant origin in France are frequently dependent for their capital on minority ethnic networks and some target clienteles which are primarily of a similar ethnic complexion, most depend for the lion's share of their custom on the majority population. According to Ma Mung and Guillon (1986: 128), the two most typical types of foreign-run small businesses are Maghrebi-owned grocery stores selling a 'normal' (i.e. unexotic) range of products in mainly French districts and Asian restaurants serving Oriental dishes to French customers.

It should be remembered that both the retail food and catering sectors have been in decline among French tradespeople, who have proved increasingly unwilling to work the long and anti-social hours which are necessary to make a success of such businesses. Businesses of this kind certainly attest to the dynamism found among groups of immigrant origin, and it is also true that small, user-friendly grocery stores in mainly French districts play a valuable public relations role on behalf of minority ethnic groups, but they also tend to reinforce the pattern of ethnic segmentation noted earlier in connection with salaried workers without necessarily bringing real independence or even higher living standards to the self-employed.

2.3 Housing

Housing and employment are linked in two main ways. At a regional level, the practicalities of daily travel are such that most people live fairly close to their place of work. More locally, housing opportunities are heavily conditioned by income levels, which in turn depend primarily on employment. France's immigrant population is heavily concentrated in urban areas (Figure 2.1), reflecting the

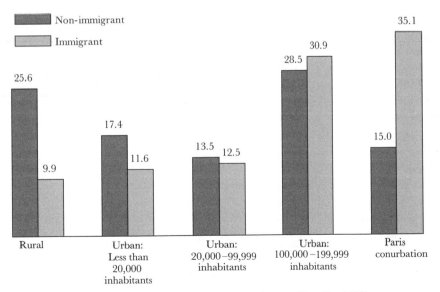

Figure 2.1 Population distribution by percentage and type of locality, 1999

Source: INSEE 2005: table 5.3.1.

historical predominance of industrial employment among non-nationals. Only 10 per cent of immigrants live in rural areas, compared with 26 per cent of non-immigrants. Immigrants are more concentrated than the general population in large cities, with Greater Paris, France's largest conurbation, accounting for 37.5 per cent of the immigrant population, compared with only half that proportion of the general population.

The Paris conurbation makes up the bulk of the population in Île-de-France, one of the twenty-two administrative regions into which metropolitan France is divided. Each region contains on average four or five départements, which are roughly equivalent to British or American counties. As can be seen from Table 2.11, 57.5 per cent of the immigrant population, compared with 36 per cent of the population as a whole, is concentrated in just three of these regions: Île-de-France (centered on the City of Paris, which, uniquely, also has the status of a

Table 2.11 Regional distribution of immigrant population, 1999

	Total population (thousands)	Share of total immigrant population (%)	Immigrant share of regional population (%)
Île-de-France	10,947	37.5	14.7
Rhône-Alpes	5,664	11.0	8.4
Provence–Alpes–Côte d'Azur	4,505	10.0	9.5
Languedoc-Roussillon	2,296	4.8	8.9
Nord–Pas-de-Calais	3,994	4.0	4.3
Midi–Pyrénées	2,552	4.0	6.8
Lorraine	2,309	3.9	7.4
Aquitaine	2,908	3.7	5.4
Alsace	1,732	3.4	8.5
Centre	2,440	2.8	5.0
Picardie	1,857	1.9	4.4
Bourgogne	1,609	1.9	5.1
Haute-Normandie	1,780	1.5	3.6
Champagne-Ardenne	1,341	1.5	4.9
Franche-Comté	1,117	1.5	5.9
Pays de la Loire	3,221	1.4	1.9
Auvergne	1,308	1.3	4.3
Bretagne	2,908	1.1	1.6
Poitou-Charentes	1,638	0.9	2.4
Basse-Normandie	1,423	0.7	2.0
Limousin	711	0.6	3.7
Corse	260	0.6	10.0
Total	58,520	100.0	

Source: INSEE 2002a: table L1.

département), Rhône-Alpes (where the largest city is Lyon) and Provence–Alpes–
Côte d'Azur (of which Marseilles is the administrative center). Île-de-France is by
far the most important region in both absolute and proportional terms. It contains
well over a third of France's total immigrant population, and the immigrant
share of the regional population is far greater here than in any other part of
France. Other important concentrations include those in the old northern and
eastern industrial regions of Nord–Pas-de-Calais, Alsace and Lorraine. The least
industrialized parts of France lie in the west of the country, where foreigners are
in general far less numerous.

As they are concentrated in relatively low-level jobs and exposed to high levels
of unemployment, most foreign workers have below average incomes (INSEE
1994: 91). Africans and Asians generally have larger families than French and EU
nationals, which further depresses their per capita income levels. Their purchasing
power in the housing market is therefore tightly constrained. Discrimination by
gatekeepers such as landlords and estate agents has imposed additional limits.
People of immigrant origin have consequently tended to become concentrated
in certain localities and types of housing. The informal mutual support networks
associated with 'chain' migration have also contributed to this process. When first
seeking work or accommodation, many immigrants head for localities where family
members or people originating in the same village or region have already settled,
thus creating a recruitment chain by word-of-mouth (Sayad 1975). In some cases,
these informal recruitment chains are strengthened by a desire for mutual support
and protection in the face of racist behavior. There have also been cases of what
the Americans call 'white flight', i.e. large-scale departures to other localities by
members of the majority population who, fearing an influx of visible minorities,
precipitate a self-fulfilling prophecy (Battegay 1992).

During the early post-war period, when France faced an acute housing shortage,
some immigrant workers were provided with hostel-style accommodation by their
employers, but most had to fend for themselves. Many lived in cheap lodging
houses in dilapidated inner-city districts, which in some cases were run by
marchands de sommeil (sleep merchants), racketeers who rented out beds on a shift
basis. Others – particularly those who were joined by their families – moved into
bidonvilles (shantytowns) set up on spare ground, often in outlying districts. Most
of the makeshift buildings in these shantytowns lacked the basic facilities, such as
mains electricity, running water and sewers, that the majority of the population
took for granted. By the mid-1960s, 75,000 people were officially classed as living
in bidonvilles, though the true figure was probably at least three times as high
(Lallaoui 1993: 44–5). As four-fifths of the officially acknowledged total were
foreigners – among whom half were Maghrebis and a quarter Portuguese – the
bidonvilles exemplified the way in which unbridled market forces tended to create
dense, ghetto-like concentrations of economically weak ethnic groups.

Some of the public policy initiatives designed to remedy excesses of this kind
have also proved segregationist in their effects. The first such initiative came in
1956, with the creation of the Société Nationale de Construction de Logements
pour les Travailleurs Algériens (SONACOTRAL), a state agency set up to

provide hostel accommodation for Algerian immigrant workers. In 1963, the organization was renamed Société Nationale de Construction de Logements pour les Travailleurs (SONACOTRA), when its remit was extended to include foreign workers of all nationalities. The hostels built by SONACOTRA certainly offered better basic facilities than many tenants had been able to find in the private sector, but as the accommodation was intended solely for foreign workers, it effectively separated them from the mass of the population (Ginesy-Galano 1984). From the mid-1970s onwards, this type of housing was called increasingly into question, partly as a consequence of growing disquiet over the regimented living conditions characterizing many hostels, and because of their unsuitability for family occupation at a time when family settlement had largely displaced the rotation of 'lone' immigrant workers. Even so, almost 100,000 foreigners – virtually all men, and 85 per cent Africans – still lived in hostel accommodation at the time of the 1990 census (INSEE 1992a: 81).

Recognizing the shift towards family settlement and committed since the early 1970s to the eradication of bidonvilles, the state ceased investing in the construction of new hostels in 1975 and at the same time began directing substantial sums of money into public housing for immigrant families. A key mechanism for this lay in the adaptation of a payroll tax initially created in 1953 to help ease the overall housing shortage in France. All companies with more than ten employees were required to invest 1 per cent of their total payroll in housing programs. Beginning in 1975, companies were instructed to earmark one-fifth of their contributions to the housing of immigrant workers, and most of the funds created in this way were invested in family-style accommodation in Habitations à Loyer Modéré (HLMs), the French equivalent of British council housing and American housing projects. Although these funds were sometimes misused and the overall level of the payroll tax was later reduced, as was the share earmarked for immigrants, the net effect was to substantially increase the presence of immigrant families within the public housing sector. Many of these families had previously lived in bidonvilles; others had been forced out of run-down inner-city areas when these were transformed by property developers into up-market units beyond the purchasing power of low-income families.

In 1975, only 15 per cent of households headed by a foreign national lived in HLMs. By 1982, the figure had climbed to 24 per cent, and in 1990 it stood at 28 per cent, compared with only 14 per cent of households headed by a French national. In the 1999 census, the majority of households headed by non-immigrants and immigrants from EU countries were owner-occupiers. The owner-occupation rate was very much lower among immigrants from the Maghreb, sub-Saharan Africa and Turkey, while those from South-East Asia were approaching the level of the general population. These differentials reflect the lower income levels generally found among non-Europeans, especially Africans, who find it much harder to raise the level of funds required to become home-purchasers. A similar contrast is visible in the rented sector, where private accommodation is usually more costly than social housing. French and European tenants are more numerous in the private than in the public rented sector, whereas Africans and Asians are heavily concentrated in HLMs. Almost half of the households headed by immigrants from Algeria, Morocco and Turkey live in HLMs, compared with only about 16 per cent of those headed by EU immigrants and across the population in general (Table 2.12).

The majority of HLMs constructed after the war took the form of large-scale high-rise developments in suburban districts, many of which were designated as Zones à Urbaniser en Priorité (ZUPs). Although ZUPs were officially superseded in 1967 by Zones d'Aménagement Concerté (ZACs), the term has remained in common usage as a label for large estates consisting mainly of social housing. While HLMs were built primarily to accommodate tenants of limited means, significant numbers of lower middle-class French families lived there during the early post-war period. By the late 1970s many of these had moved out, becoming owner-occupiers in the private sector. French tenants who remained in HLMs often felt trapped in an urban environment where social facilities had seldom been good and were often visibly deteriorating. The growing presence of immigrant families was sometimes regarded by French tenants as a mark – if not indeed the cause – of the deteriorating conditions in HLM estates. Instead of being spread evenly across those estates, foreign tenants were generally allocated to less popular, more run-down properties, rather than to new units financed by the payroll tax (Boumaza *et al.* 1989; Weil 1991: 254–6; Blanc 1992; de Rudder 1992).

Since the late 1970s, a variety of government policies have been devised to assist urban areas experiencing acute social difficulties. At the time of the 1990 census, more than 500 districts containing a total of almost three million inhabitants were receiving special assistance in programs jointly run by city councils, regional

Table 2.12 Housing tenure patterns by percentage and origin of head of household, 1999

	Owner-occupiers	Tenants	HLM tenants	Free housing	Total
All households	54.7	40.7	16.0	4.6	100
Immigrant	41.9	53.8	27.9	4.3	100
EU	57.6	37.0	15.7	5.4	100
Spanish	59.5	35.9	17.3	4.6	100
Italian	68.4	26.7	12.5	4.9	100
Portuguese	47.6	46.3	22.2	6.1	100
Algerian	23.8	74.0	49.1	2.2	100
Moroccan	22.6	74.2	46.1	3.2	100
Tunisian	29.8	67.5	37.5	2.7	100
Other African*	16.7	80.5	46.2	2.8	100
S-E Asian†	41.2	56.2	34.2	2.6	100
Turkish	24.1	74.1	46.1	1.8	100

Source: INSEE 2002a: table LG1.

Note
* ex-French sub-Saharan Africa; † ex-French Indochina.

authorities and the central state. As recorded by the census, unemployment across France as a whole was 11 per cent. Within jointly aided districts the figure was 20 per cent, and almost a third of the jobless in these neighborhoods had been out of work for at least two years. A study by Castellan *et al.* (1992) showed that non-Europeans were overrepresented in these localities. While non-nationals made up only 6 per cent of the general population, they accounted for 18 per cent of the inhabitants of jointly aided districts. Non-EU nationals represented 63 per cent of the foreign population as a whole, but their share of the foreign population within jointly aided districts was 81 per cent.

Most of these districts were located in the suburbs of large cities. Neighborhoods of this kind are commonly referred to as banlieues, a term which until the 1980s denoted suburban districts in general, but which has now become synonymous with areas of acute social disadvantage containing dense concentrations of minority ethnic groups (Hargreaves 1996). In the English-speaking world, suburbs generally connote relatively pleasant living conditions, in contrast with those obtaining in inner-city areas, where the densest concentrations both of poverty and of minority ethnic groups are to be found. There are relatively few districts of this kind close to the center of French cities. In Paris, the best-known examples are La Goutte d'Or, just to the north of the Gare du Nord (Toubon and Kessamah 1990; Vuddamalay *et al.* 1991) and Belleville, to the east of the Place de la République (Simon 1992). Even here, redevelopment programs have been pushing many low-income families out into suburban areas offering cheaper public sector accommodation.

Though differently located, the French banlieues, as currently connoted, are the sociological equivalent of British and American inner-city areas. Typically, these districts are dominated by high-rise HLM estates catering for the poorest sections of society. The northern and western suburbs of Paris contain many such estates in districts such as La Courneuve, Nanterre and Sartrouville. Similar districts in the eastern suburbs of Lyon include Vaulx-en-Velin and Vénissieux. In Marseille, the main concentrations of this kind are known as *les quartiers du Nord* (the northern districts). Often, these neighborhoods are hemmed in by communications arteries which, paradoxically, separate them from other parts of the city. Seven out of ten are close to railway lines, but only four out of ten are served by a station. A third are bounded on at least one side by an *autoroute* (i.e. motorway or freeway); more than four-fifths are boxed in by other major roads (Castellan *et al.* 1992).

The peripheral location of most jointly aided districts, their poor facilities and physical separation from other parts of the city, combined with high unemployment levels and dense concentrations of mediocre or poor-quality housing have turned these areas into a byword for social exclusion (Dubet and Lapeyronnie 1992). As noted earlier, youths of non-European origin suffer exceptionally high unemployment rates. They have often been to the fore in street disorders in the banlieues provoked by what they see as aggressive policing. Little reported incidents of this kind occurred in districts such as Nanterre and Vaulx-en-Velin during the 1970s. Greater publicity was given to similar incidents on the Minguettes housing estate in Vénissieux in the early 1980s, and a veritable torrent of media coverage was unleashed during the early 1990s when serious disorders occurred in localities such as Vaulx-en-Velin, Sartrouville and the Val-Fourré estate in Mantes-la-Jolie, fifty miles to the west of Paris (Begag and Delorme 1994: 107–21). Most of these disturbances were characterized by a very similar pattern: typically, an unarmed youth of immigrant origin involved or suspected of involvement in petty crime (most commonly, the theft of a motor vehicle) was injured or killed by a police officer, and this was followed by an outbreak of street violence by other youths (Hargreaves 1996). The riots of November 2005 fitted the same mold. They began with the death by electrocution of two minority ethnic youths who had sought refuge in an electrical substation rather than submit to a police identity check. Although the deaths were accidental, they were blamed by other youths in the banlieues on aggressive policing and triggered the most serious civil disturbances seen in France in almost forty years.

In media coverage of these events, frequent comparisons have been made with American inner-city areas marked by heavy concentrations of poverty, crime and minority ethnicized groups, mainly blacks (Girard 2006). In drawing this connection, French journalists and politicians have often referred to the most disadvantaged of French banlieues as 'ghettos'. As Wacquant (1992) has shown, however, the parallel is far from exact. The sheer scale of racialized ghettos in major American cities has no direct equivalent in France. The black ghetto of Chicago's South Side contains between 400,000 and 700,000 inhabitants; there are similar concentrations in the South Central and Compton districts of Los Angeles, and almost a million people live in the black ghettos of New York City's Harlem, Brownsville and South Bronx districts. In French cities, the largest comparable concentrations come nowhere near this. Val-Fourré, France's biggest single ZUP, has around 30,000 inhabitants. Even at its height (several tower blocks have now been demolished), the population of the Minguettes estate in Vénissieux was 35,000. America's black ghettos are sufficiently large to contain a complex division of labor, which in the past enabled some of these districts to function almost as closed micro-societies (with the departure of many middle-class blacks this is less true today). Despite deficiencies in public transport, most inhabitants of French ZUPs who have jobs work outside the estates where they live; although people from other districts tend not to enter disadvantaged areas, there are regular flows in the other direction.

In the US, it is not uncommon for large neighborhoods to be almost entirely mono-ethnic, i.e. inhabited almost exclusively by members of a single ethnicized group, particularly blacks. In France, areas containing relatively large concentrations of residents of foreign origin are almost always multi-ethnic, i.e. it is common to find people of many different national origins within the same neighborhood; while a few groups often dominate, it is extremely rare for a single group to make up virtually the whole of the minority population. In Val-Fourré, for example, where non-nationals account for around half of the total population, the largest single group is composed of Moroccans, who represent two-fifths of the foreign contingent and just under a fifth of all residents (Poiret and Guégan 1992: 172). Similarly, in the département (county) of Seine-Saint-Denis, in the northeastern banlieues of Paris, which contains France's poorest urban areas and largest concentrations of visible minorities, many different ethnic groups are present, including Maghrebis, Africans from south of the Sahara and DOM-TOMiens (mainly of Caribbean origin) as well as majority ethnic French. Although living conditions in many HLM estates compare unfavorably with other parts of France, they generally benefit from better welfare provision than disadvantaged areas of American cities. Violent crime is also far less prevalent in the French banlieues. Fire-arms are far less widely available than in the US and homicide rates are well below those found in American ghettos. Even the riots of November 2005, which had their epicenter in Seine-Saint-Denis, were far less destructive than the disturbances seen in many American cities during the late 1960s and in the South Central district of Los Angeles in 1992.

2.4 Group profiles

Residential concentrations of particular ethnic groups are conditioned not only by employment patterns and other factors already mentioned, but also by social networks and culturally specific opportunities or constraints. Taken together, these factors have produced considerable diversity in the pattern of settlement characterizing different groups.

Europeans

Though now much smaller in number than in the past, Italians dominated migratory inflows into France during a large part of the twentieth century. Recent calculations by Borrel and Simon (2005: 435) using a statistical methodology not previously applied to French census data indicate that there are more second-generation ethnic Italians than there are second-generation members of any other immigrant group in France. Almost all are French nationals and many are now quite elderly. There is still a strong Italian presence in old industrial regions such as Nord–Pas-de-Calais and Lorraine, together with south-eastern regions, which are geographically close to Italy, and the Greater Paris area. The Spanish are mainly concentrated in southern France, as well in the central part of the Paris conurbation. The southern concentrations reflect the proximity of the border with Spain, across which there is a long tradition of agricultural laborers coming to work on French farms. The Spanish population of southern cities such as Bordeaux and Toulouse was also swollen by the arrival of political exiles after the Fascist victory in the Spanish Civil War. In the Paris area, Spaniards are found particularly in well-to-do central *arrondissements* (districts) such as the seventh, eighth and sixteenth, and up-market suburbs such as Neuilly-sur-Seine and Saint-Mandé. This is seldom because they are themselves well off, but because many Spaniards – particularly women – are employed as domestic staff by wealthy families, who require them to live in (Taboada-Leonetti 1987).

The Portuguese are the largest national contingent among the foreign population as a whole, though they are outnumbered by Algerians among the immigrant population. Female labor participation rates are particularly high, with strong concentrations in the domestic service sector. Non-European women are far less frequently employed in French homes. The Portuguese are more scattered than many other groups, partly because Portuguese men are overrepresented in the building industry, where employment tends to be quite widely spread and often requires considerable mobility. More than 40 per cent of Portuguese men in employment hold construction industry jobs, a far higher share than is found among any other national group. This is one of the reasons why, despite their large absolute numbers, they are less immediately visible than other, particularly non-European, groups. Similarly, the subordinate position of Spanish and Portuguese domestic staff in households providing free accommodation prevents them from displaying visible markers of their presence within wealthy areas. Foreign tenants in poorer districts may feel less inhibited, and for tradespeople serving minority groups or hoping to attract French customers in search of exotic cuisine a prominent display of ethnic markers is often judged to be good for business (de Rudder and Guillon 1987). For these and other reasons, including most obviously skin color, even relatively dense concentrations of Europeans tend to be less visible than those of other groups (Taboada-Leonetti 1989; White 1989).

Maghrebis

Algerians constitute France's oldest and largest immigrant group of colonial origin (Gillette and Sayad 1984; MacMaster 1997). They remain heavily concentrated in regions where significant numbers of them were first hired as manual laborers: in the suburbs of major conurbations, notably Paris (particularly northern districts), Lyon and Marseilles, and in the old industrial regions of the north and east. Within those regions, they are especially overrepresented in districts which have experienced severe economic decline and loss of population (Desplanques and Tabard 1991: 56, 61). As they have tended to remain in these districts and are underrepresented in areas of strong technology-led job creation, they are particularly vulnerable to unemployment and urban decay. About half of the Maghrebi labor force, as of the Portuguese, consists of manual workers, but the Portuguese are far less concentrated in densely working-class districts (Desplanques and Tabard 1991: 59). Maghrebis are especially concentrated in suburban HLM estates (the banlieues). In 1990, they made up 39 per cent of the nationwide foreign population but accounted for 56 per cent of foreigners residing in chronically disadvantaged urban areas receiving special government support while EU nationals represented 36 per cent of all foreign residents but only 19 per cent of foreigners in those acutely disadvantaged districts (Champion *et al.* 1993: 27).

The 1999 census puts the Algerian population at 475,000. As with other national groups, this leaves out of account naturalized immigrants and people of immigrant descent who automatically acquire French nationality. Where Algerians are concerned, there is a further complication arising from the process of decolonization. During the war of independence, Algerian auxiliary troops known as *harkis* were used by the French in their struggle against the nationalist guerrillas.

With the advent of independence in 1962, many *harkis* were killed by nationalist forces, but tens of thousands escaped to France, together with other Algerian Muslims who had sided with the French. Today, they and their descendants are more than 500,000 strong. All are and always have been French nationals, yet they are regarded as outsiders by many members of the native population, and have experienced extreme marginalization in both the housing and employment markets. When they first arrived in France, many *harkis* were housed in old army camps and similar forms of makeshift accommodation in isolated locations. Gradually, most were rehoused in less remote areas near the Mediterranean littoral, together with northern towns such as Roubaix and Amiens. They often remain in dense micro-concentrations, however, and suffer acute unemployment levels (Roux 1991; Hamoumou 1993). In the summer of 1991, when unemployment among the 18–25 age group in *harki* families was reported to be running at 80 per cent (*Le Monde*, 30 June 1991), youngsters in southern towns such as Narbonne staged violent street demonstrations similar to those which had recently occurred in more northerly cities characterized by acute social disadvantage.

Although Moroccans now exceed Algerian nationals in number, their migratory history is more recent. Many found manual jobs in the car industry during the 1960s, and this helps to explain their concentration in the western part of Île-de-France, stretching from the western suburbs of Paris along the Seine valley to Mantes-la-Jolie. Others worked in the now defunct coal mines and other declining industries of the north, where significant numbers of Moroccans still live. Moroccans are more widely distributed across rural parts of the south-west, and account for more than half the foreign population in Corsica; in both cases, agricultural employment – which occupies a larger share of the total Moroccan labor force than of any other national group – is to the fore.

The Tunisian population in France is only about a third of the size of each of the other Maghrebi groups. The settlement of Tunisians is also more recent than that of Algerians and Moroccans. There are few Tunisians in the old industrial regions of the north and east. They are more concentrated than other Maghrebis in the central parts of major conurbations such as Paris and Lyon (Rimani 1988).

Africans from south of the Sahara

Africans from south of the Sahara provide a prime example of how, among certain groups, immigration has rapidly accelerated since the formal 'end' of non-EC migration to France. A year after the freeze on migration was announced, the 1975 census recorded only 82,000 nationals of African countries, excluding those of the Maghreb. By 1982, the total had almost doubled to 158,000, and by 1990 it had climbed to 240,000, reaching 282,000 in 1999. The vast majority come from former French colonies in West and Central Africa, together with the ex-Belgian colony of Zaire and the former British Indian Ocean colony of Mauritus, in both of which French is widely spoken. Within the formal economy, non-Maghrebi Africans are more highly concentrated in the service sector than any other group, including French nationals: almost all employed women and three out of four men hold service sector jobs. These are generally low-grade jobs, particularly in sectors such as cleaning and street-vending. Like most other groups of recent immigrant origin, sub-Saharan Africans are heavily overrepresented in the Île-de-France region, especially the département of Seine-Saint-Denis (Barou 1992b; INSEE 1992a: table 35).

The true size of these groups is generally acknowledged to be considerably larger than the official figures suggest, partly because polygamous families – of which there are significant numbers among the population of West African origin compared with very few among Maghrebis – experience major difficulties in securing appropriate documentation. The precise number of polygamous African families in France is not known. In the early 1990s, the most reliable estimates put the number of polygamous households in the Île-de-France region at between 3,000 and 15,000 (Poiret and Guégan 1992). As each household involved a minimum of two wives, each of whom was likely to have several children, the total number of people concerned was by no means insignificant, even on the lower estimate. Tribalat (1996: 78, 122) estimated that in France as a whole there were around 8,000 polygamous households containing a total of about 90,000 people (adults and children combined), representing in all about a third of the population originating in Africa south of the Sahara.

For polygamous families, the quest for suitable housing is often extremely arduous. These difficulties were highlighted by the prominence of African families in demonstrations by homeless migrants during the early 1990s. The most widely publicized of these involved dozens of Malian families evicted from their run-down Paris homes in 1992 to make way for property developers. They were offered makeshift accommodation by the local authorities only after camping for six months in parkland near the château de Vincennes (Sindonino 1993). Shortly afterwards, Africans from south of the Sahara were prominent among victims of the Pasqua laws of 1993, which pushed tens of thousands of foreigners into the status of illegal residents (*sans-papiers*), provoking a fresh round of demonstrations.

The shortage of affordable accommodation large enough to decently house polygamous families, combined with the reluctance of both public- and private-sector gatekeepers to respond to their needs, has forced those concerned to rely heavily on their own social networks. When polygamous families succeed in finding suitable accommodation, they not uncommonly pass the word to others, who may well seek to move into the same area. In this way, dense micro-concentrations sometimes develop. During the 1980s, for example, special promotional deals on properties built in new towns on the edge of the Paris conurbation unexpectedly enabled a small number of African families to move into localities such as Evry and Marne-la-Vallée. In a period of four years, several blocks in the district of Emerainville, in Marne-la-Vallée, were sold almost entirely to foreign purchasers, most of whom were polygamous Africans. With low incomes, these families were at one and the same time massively indebted and seriously overcrowded. Each African household contained on average eight people (compared with three among their French neighbors), and their per capita income was estimated to be 40 francs per day, against 200 francs per person in French households and an official poverty line of 50 francs per day (Poiret and Guégan 1992: 234–58).

South-East Asians

Small numbers of Asians have been present in France throughout the twentieth century, but large-scale settlement on their part, like that of sub-Saharan Africans, dates essentially from the mid-1970s. Most are from South-East Asia and more specifically the former colonies of Vietnam, Cambodia and Laos, which were grouped together in French Indochina until independence in 1954. Their numbers grew rapidly in the late 1970s and 1980s, when many fled from Indochina following the 1975 communist victory in the Vietnam war. Compared with migrants of African origin, they were generally better educated and had higher levels of certified skills. Although of non-European origin, they generally encountered less suspicion or hostility than Africans, partly because, in a world polarized between communist and capitalist blocs, they were seen as victims of communist authoritarianism rather than as post-colonial minorities.

With exceptionally high rates of naturalization – by the time of the 1999 census more than two-thirds of immigrants from Indochina had taken French citizenship – the size of their presence is grossly underestimated if measured solely by nationality. In 1999, France had 50,000 residents of Vietnamese, Cambodian or Laotian nationality but almost 160,000 immigrants originating in those countries. The statistical picture is further complicated by the fact that most of those who fled Indochina in the mid-1970s were of Chinese origin, though they were of Vietnamese, Cambodian or Laotian nationality (Yok-Soon 1991: 121). Mainly tradespeople, particularly restaurateurs and shopkeepers, they were joined by Chinese traders from Taiwan and Hong Kong who entered France as self-employed entrepreneurs; often, the capital necessary for this was raised through a global network of family and social contacts which has made Chinese traders a uniquely mobile group (Ma Mung and Guillon 1986; *Migrations société* 1992).

An older established and little noticed concentration of Chinese settlers, mainly from what since 1949 has been the People's Republic, was already present in the Arts et Métiers neighborhood of Paris's third arrondissement. Ethnic Chinese entering after the end of the Vietnam war regrouped near the Porte de Choisy, on the southern edge of the thirteenth arrondissement of Paris, and to a lesser extent in Belleville. Today the Porte de Choisy offers a rare example of an almost mono-ethnic micro-district. The majority of businesses in a small area known as the Choisy Triangle are now ethnic Chinese, and in a few apartment blocks there are similar residential concentrations (Guillon and Taboada-Leonetti 1986). Compared with France's total immigrant population, the number of Chinese living in the Choisy Triangle is of course very small, and the area remains untypical of the districts inhabited by the majority of the foreign population.

There are strong concentrations of South-East Asians in the Greater Paris area, with the rest fairly widely scattered across other urban areas. With higher levels of educational attainment than most migrants from other formerly colonized regions and more ready access to capital, South-East Asians have generally found it easier to set up their own businesses. They are very active in the textile and clothing industries and in services such as catering and retail shops. These businesses make extensive use of a low-wage and sometimes undocumented labor force; not uncommonly, they also rely on unpaid work by family members. Because so much of the work is done within family businesses or, in the case of the garment industry, as outwork (Brunel 1992: 205), the higher rates of female economic activity found among South-East Asians, compared with those of Turkish and Maghrebi women, do not necessarily imply a wider network of social contacts.

Turks

Until the 1970s there were very few Turks in France. In the 1968 census, they totaled less than 8,000. By the time of the next census in 1975, the number had leapt to 50,000 and it almost quadrupled in the course of the next fourteen years, reaching 197,000 in 1990. Turks have relatively low levels of employment in the service sector. Alone among non-Europeans, a majority of Turkish men are employed in industrial jobs. Women of Turkish nationality have higher rates of industrial employment than those of any other significant national group in France. Turks of both sexes have a strong presence in the textile and clothing industries, which often rely on labor-intensive small businesses characterized by low rates of pay and a significant element of undocumented employment (Morokvasic *et al.* 1986; Morokvasic 1990). Turks are mainly concentrated in Île-de-France, Rhône-Alpes, Alsace and Lorraine, the last two of which are close to the border with Germany, where by far the largest part of the Turkish diaspora is found (*Migrations société* 1992). On many statistical indicators, they are the most closed-in upon of themselves of immigrant minorities in France (see section 3.7).

DOM-TOMiens

The DOM-TOM, French overseas départements and territories where most of the inhabitants are of non-European origin – their ancestors were generally brought there as slaves – are characterized by lower living standards and higher levels of unemployment than those prevailing in metropolitan France. As French citizens, DOM-TOMiens have unfettered access to metropolitan France, where many have sought work. Most of the 357,000 DOM-TOMiens now resident in France come from three of the overseas départements: the Caribbean islands of Guadeloupe and Martinique and the Indian Ocean island of Réunion. About a quarter of the entire population born in Martinique and Guadeloupe now lives in metropolitan France. The labor force participation rates of DOM-TOMiens tend to exceed those of foreign immigrants, and are particularly high among women, a significant proportion of whom came as economic migrants in their own right rather than as dependants of male breadwinners.

Most DOM-TOMiens live in the Île-de-France region, often in areas containing dense concentrations of foreign immigrants from formerly colonized regions, whom they also resemble by their low levels of owner-occupation and high rates of HLM tenancy. They are strongly concentrated in two départements: the City of Paris, particularly the working-class northern and eastern arrondissements, which include La Goutte d'Or and Belleville, and the contiguous département of Seine-Saint-Denis. This predilection for the Paris region, where the central administrative organs of the state are located, is partly explained by the exceptionally high concentrations of DOM-TOMiens in public-sector employment, to which they have access as French nationals. Foreign immigrants are largely excluded from state employment. Despite this important difference, there is an underlying similarity in the low level of the jobs acceded to by most foreigners and DOM-TOMiens. Less well qualified than women native to metropolitan France, those originating in the DOM-TOM are overrepresented in low-grade hospital and other health service jobs, while men are concentrated in the lower ranks of the postal service, school ancillary work and other parts of the public sector. Unemployment among immigrants from the DOM-TOM is only a little higher than the national average, but among their children, as among those born to foreign immigrants, it is much higher. While poor qualifications offer a partial explanation, labor inspectorate reports indicate that discrimination by employers also weighs heavily in the high jobless rates among young people descended from DOM-TOMiens, most of whom are black (Marie 1993: 10–11; IGAS 1992).

2.5 Conclusion

The experiences of people originating in the DOM-TOM are one among many elements indicating that, despite its conventional centrality in official thinking, formal nationality status is of less significance than other factors in shaping the incorporation of immigrants and their descendants into French society. The social capital that immigrants bring with them, particularly in the form of certified skills, together with discriminatory treatment by members of the native population, are of much greater importance in the employment and housing markets. The discrimination suffered by certain groups shows that despite their *de facto* presence within French society, at an attitudinal level people of immigrant origin – especially those originating in former colonies – may still be regarded as outsiders. In practical terms, their occupational segmentation and uneven spatial distribution may also make it difficult for some groups – particularly Africans and Asians – to establish more than superficial social contacts with the indigenous population. Because of their lower rates of participation in the formal labor force, women tend to be particularly constrained in this respect. Yet in their cultural practices and aspirations, post-colonial minorities, like other minorities of immigrant origin before them, are strongly inclined to embrace French values, seeking inclusion rather than exclusion. It is to a consideration of the cultural and political dimensions of their experience that we now turn.

3 Minority ethnic identification and mobilization

3.1 Introduction

Most labor migrants initially expected to be only temporary residents in France. Under the 'rotation' system of labor recruitment, which initially prevailed in colonized or formerly colonized regions, dependants generally remained in the country of origin, where they were supported by remittances sent home by workers in France. Even when they were joined by their families in France, many immigrant workers saw this as a temporary arrangement, at the end of which they would return to their country of origin, having saved enough to buy a more comfortable home than they could previously afford or perhaps set up a small business. Like the native population in France, they saw the migratory process as an essentially, if not indeed exclusively, economic phenomenon. In reality, it carried important cultural implications from the outset, and these have become steadily more apparent with the passage of time, especially with the development of permanent family settlement. Participation in the labor market demands at least a minimal level of acculturation, i.e. the acquisition of cultural codes prevalent in the receiving country. At the same time, immigrants carried into France a large and very different store of cultural baggage accumulated in their countries of origin. With the increasing visibility of differences of this kind, a significant part of French public opinion became persuaded that immigration – particularly from Islamic countries – represented a fundamental threat to the cultural cohesion of the nation.

The main purpose of this chapter is to assess the extent to which recent immigrants and their descendants are culturally distinct from the majority population in France. All minority groups have in some degree acculturated, but this is not necessarily incompatible with the retention of pre-migratory cultural practices and/or the development of new syntheses drawing on a variety of sources. Some analysts regard acculturation as part of a process of 'modernization', but this term is in my view best avoided partly because it often implies, even if only at an unconscious level, a positive value judgement in favor of acculturation and a negative view of its presumed opposite, 'traditionalism'.[1] No less importantly, it misleadingly implies that extremely complex processes can be understood in terms of a simple polarization between binary opposites, with a one-way street connecting the two. Immigrants and their descendants are not confined to tramlines carrying them ineluctably through acculturation to complete assimilation, with the only significant variable being the pace at which they adopt the norms of the receiving society while simultaneously abandoning those of the sending society. As we shall see, the cultural options open to minority groups are far wider than this.

Cultures, nations and states

The word 'culture' is used in many different ways, so it is important to spell out its meaning in the present context. In its most basic sense, culture may be understood as the human production of meaning and value. Beyond this generic sense we may speak of particular cultures as group codes of meaning and value. Ethnocultural groups, as defined in Chapter 1, are characterized by shared codes associated with common origins. Individual members of ethnocultural groups do not always agree in every particular, but can at least disagree in mutually intelligible ways, for they share and communicate with each in the same cultural codes. The most fundamental of cultural codes is language. The ability or inability to speak French, Portuguese, Arabic or Turkish gives access to or excludes a person from a wealth of communicative acts. Other fundamental cultural codes govern cosmological beliefs, personal morality and a sense of territorial belonging.

Just as it is impossible wholly to disentangle culture and economics, so there are significant overlaps between culture and politics. While some cultural practices are a purely private matter or, if publicly visible, are not subject to state regulation, others are formally codified in law. Some of these touch on extremely intimate parts of personal life, such as sexuality and family relationships. Others concern potent symbols of national identity, such as language and, in certain cases, religion. Yet only very rarely do the boundaries of cultural practices match up exactly with those of political geography. Although English, French and other tongues are often referred to as 'national' languages, and are indeed enshrined in law as the official languages of certain states, the spatial distribution of English- and French-speakers is by no means isomophoric with the boundaries of those countries. Nor do the boundaries of linguistic groups necessarily coincide with those of religious or other cultural groups.

Basques in Spain and France, Berbers in the Maghreb and Kurds in Turkey and neighboring countries are examples of the many linguistic minorities scattered within or across state boundaries. Some important cultural traditions, including religions such as Christianity, Buddhism and Islam, are more or less global in their reach. The myth of a culturally distinct and homogeneous nation-state has nevertheless been central to the political history of modern Europe. With decolonization it has been taken up by many African and Asian states. The many wars which punctuated European history up to 1945, and which after the end of the Cold War were renewed in eastern Europe, like those in post-independence Africa and Asia, have often been marked by a disjunction between political and cultural boundaries.

Wholly distinct and autonomous national cultures have never existed. In at least two major respects, however, modern states have pushed towards the nationalization of cultures. Often at the cost of hugely destructive wars, they have pursued this project externally by attempting to establish international boundaries consonant with the spatial distribution of certain cultural groups. Within its own frontiers, the state has exercised enormous – though never exclusive – power over the means of cultural reproduction.

Today, three main forces predominate in the transmission of cultural systems. The earliest influence in the life of every individual is the family. Next comes the formal system of education through which the child passes in preparation for adulthood. Concurrently with this and throughout the rest of his or her life, the mass media disseminate images and information which have a powerful influence on the individual's view of the world. While it is difficult for the state to exercise direct control over day-to-day family life,[2] it exerts a strong and sometimes decisive influence over education and the media.

In the modern world, the state controls most, and in some cases all, of the formal educational process. Not surprisingly, the knowledge dispensed by state educational systems tends to take the nation as its 'natural' frame of reference. The national language occupies pride of place, while history and geography lessons familiarize the child with landmarks and events of national significance.

State control over the media has generally been less complete, though in authoritarian countries it is often very extensive. Before the rise of electronic media such as radio and television, communication processes were dominated by print media and to a lesser extent by the cinema. Economies of scale and the central role of formal education in creating a readership literate in a common language favored the rise of a national press even when this remained in private, rather than state ownership; at the same time, technological limitations made it difficult to distribute newspapers much beyond the national territory within an acceptable time frame. The electronic media have in many ways cut through these constraints. Radio dispensed with the need for a literate audience, though language barriers still imposed significant limits on the medium. Moving pictures, first developed via the pre-electronic technology of the cinema, traverse linguistic and other boundaries far more easily. While the cinema is relatively cumbersome and limited in its audience penetration, television has brought instantaneous audio-visual communication into the home, and with the rise of satellite technology audiences are increasingly global in scale. When television broadcasting was limited to a handful of terrestrially based frequencies in each country, it was in principle relatively easy for the state to regulate the system. In practice, the high production costs associated with television often made it necessary to purchase programs abroad. The advent of domestic video recorders together with cable and satellite broadcasting further weakened state control over the medium.

Immigration and culture

The children of immigrants, like those born to the native population, are initially exposed primarily to family influences. Linguistic, moral and other codes inherited from the country of origin naturally dominate during these early years. The mutual support systems associated with chain migration provide a wider network of social contacts drawing on cultural practices shared by immigrants originating in the same village or region. These are often supplemented by formally constituted associations pursuing welfare, cultural and sometimes political objectives.

Until 1981, these efforts were hampered in France by legal restrictions on foreigners' rights of association. After these restrictions were removed by the incoming Socialist-led administration, the number of associations mushroomed (*La Tribune Fonda* 1991). Even so, the sending and receiving states continued to exert a significant influence over voluntary associations. The limited resources available on a self-help basis obliged many associations to seek public subsidies (cf. Schmitter Heisler 1986: 82–6). Some sending states attempted to control practically all the organizational activities of their nationals and harass emigrants who set up independent associations (Miller 1981: 38–40), but they were seldom successful in this. In a study of Marseilles, Cesari (1993) found that subsidies awarded by the French state, either centrally or through the city council, were of crucial importance in shaping the activities of local associations run by people of immigrant origin. Until recently, public funding of this kind was channeled mainly through the Fonds d'Action Sociale pour les Travailleurs Immigrés et leurs Familles (Social Action Fund for Immigrant Workers and their Families – FAS). The prime purpose assigned to the FAS, controlled by the Ministry for Social Affairs, was to support the state project of integrating immigrants and their descendants into French society. It assisted voluntary associations run by members of minority ethnic groups whose activities were conducive to integration, but not if they were driven by separatist ambitions.[3]

Within the formal educational system, the cultural codes of migrants are overwhelmingly marginalized in favor of those prevalent among the majority population.[4] In France all children, regardless of their nationality, are required by law to attend school from the age of 6 to 16. Generous state provision of nursery schools means that the majority of children enter the educational system three or even four years before the age of 6; most remain in it well beyond the minimum school-leaving age. Immigrants are not entirely powerless in the face of the state educational system. Under French law, they are free to set up schools of their own. In practice, most immigrants have neither the economic resources nor the organizational skills necessary for such an undertaking. In the 1990s, among foreign children of primary school age only 3 per cent were educated outside the state sector; at the secondary school level the figure was 7 per cent (Conseil Économique et Social 1994: 45). It is often wrongly thought that the 1905 law on *laïcité* removed all state support from religious organizations. In fact, the Republic has continued to fund the upkeep of most existing religious buildings and it provides generous funding for thousands of private religious schools, most of them Catholic. Muslims, now the largest religious minority in France, have so far received no funding of this kind. In the whole of France, there is only one Muslim high school, which opened in Lille in 2003 after twice being refused a permit by the educational authorities. It depends entirely on private funding.

Private school fees are normally affordable only to relatively affluent parents. For most immigrant-born children, the schooling provided free of charge by France's state educational system is the only practical option. Small elites within minority ethnocultural groups often try to counterbalance this pattern by organizing extra-curricular classes, and sending states sometimes provide trained personnel and other assistance, but the resources at their disposal are no match for those poured into the mainstream educational system.

Low levels of literacy among many immigrants, particularly those from formerly colonized regions, have placed severe limitations on their use of print media, though there is a long history of newspaper and magazine production by cultural elites of foreign origin in France (Presse et mémoire 1990). The electronic media are more easily accessible to large audiences. Radio broadcasts from home countries can often be picked up quite easily on receivers in France. During the 1970s, a brisk trade in imported audio cassettes developed, enabling immigrants to hand-pick programs to suit their own listening tastes (Lehembre 1984). Since 1981, when the newly elected Socialist-led administration liberalized the air-waves, dozens of local radio stations run by and for minority ethnocultural groups have been licensed (Barbulesco 1985). While these have often helped to build a sense of community among such groups, the state has nevertheless exercised considerable control over them. Rather than risk fostering cultural separatism, the state-appointed agencies responsible for granting licences have generally favored multi-ethnic rather than single-ethnic stations (HCI 1992b: 131). Many of them depend on public subsidies, channeled mainly through the FAS, which insists that those benefiting from its support subscribe to the objective of integration (Moreau-Desportes 1990).

Television, by far the most powerful mass medium, has in its dominant forms been the least responsive to minority interests (UNESCO 1986). Until the mid-1980s, France had only three terrestrial channels, all of them state-owned. Although the number of channels had doubled by the mid-1990s, commercial pressures dictated programming aimed at maximizing mass audiences, rather than catering for minority groups (Hargreaves 1992b). A small amount of specialist programming on terrestrially based state channels was funded by the FAS (Humblot 1989; Hargreaves 1993b), but for a fuller diet minority ethnocultural groups were obliged to turn to other forms of television.

Domestic video recorders became widely available in France during the 1980s. Significantly, they quickly became one of the few consumer durables in which foreign-headed households were better equipped than those headed by French nationals (*Le Monde*, 11 June 1991). With substantial video cassette production centers in both Asia and the Arab world and easily accessible retail outlets in French cities, many people of immigrant origin were for the first time able to construct home viewing schedules reflecting their ethnocultural roots. It should not be assumed, however, that facilities of this kind were used in a mono-ethnic fashion. While the children of Asian immigrants, for example, enjoyed imported martial arts films (a genre which was also popular among a significant number of French youngsters), they were avid viewers of American movies, and also enjoyed both French and American rock music videos. The viewing habits of their French peers often involved a similar transnational amalgam (Raulin 1990). While Maghrebi immigrants sometimes watched Islamic cassettes, their children generally had more secular tastes (Chaabaoui 1989). Kastoryano (1986: 99) reported a similar split between the viewing habits of first- and second-generation members of the Turkish population in France.

Since the 1990s, cable and satellite television have greatly widened the viewing choices available in suitably equipped homes. The broadcasting licensing authority, the Conseil Supérieur de l'Audiovisuel (CSA), was initially reluctant to allow television stations based in the home states of immigrants access to the French cable network – which would effectively remove editorial control from French hands – despite the technical feasibility of this. The Moroccan channel 2MI was first made available to cable subscribers in the northern town of Roubaix in 1989. The service was later extended to Mantes-la-Jolie and other towns with substantial concentrations of Maghrebis, but it was discontinued in 1993. It was far less easy for the French authorities to control satellite broadcasting by foreign states. During the early 1990s, TV channels based in countries ranging from Morocco and Tunisia to Turkey and Poland became available to viewers in France equipped with suitable satellite dishes.

In 1995, a survey conducted for the European satellite company Eutelsat indicated that 21 per cent of Arabic-speaking households in France had invested in satellite receivers, compared with 4 per cent of the general population (*Le Monde*, 29–30 Oct. 1995). A year later, the number of Arabic-speaking households with satellite dishes was believed to have doubled (*Le Monde*, 29 Nov. 1996). By the end of the decade, satellite TV had become a standard fixture in the homes of most Maghrebi immigrants. Research conducted in such homes showed that there were significant generational differences in the viewing patterns of Maghrebis. While immigrants were using the new technology to watch 'home' country channels, their children were generally more interested in the opportunities for accessing more American-based programs (Hargreaves and Mahdjoub 1997). At the same time, the internet had begun to make available electronic resources which in the twenty-first century are now multiplying exponentially the sources of information and entertainment available to all ethnic groups in France and across the globe (*Hommes et migrations* 2002).

French anxieties over cultural imports, particularly in the audio-visual sector, were a major factor in the 1993 GATT negotiations on world trade. Only when her negotiating partners agreed to exempt cultural goods from free trade measures did France finally clear the way for the conclusion of a world-wide deal. Under this agreement, France continues to imposed tight quotas on foreign programs broadcast on prime time terrestrially based television. The main target of these protectionist measures lies not, of course, in any of the African and Asian countries in which most immigrants originate, but in the United States, which has long occupied a globally dominant position in the field of popular culture. A long series of similar protectionist measures has failed to prevent the partial Americanization of many aspects of French culture during the post-war period.

To speak of 'French culture' as if it were a wholly autonomous national entity is indeed, and always has been, seriously misleading. Like the culture of every other nationally defined space, it is composed in part of elements which extend and in some cases originate beyond the country's frontiers. Before the current influx of Americana, France and her European neighbors exchanged many cultural influences. For example, her Judeo-Christian heritage has its origins in the Middle East. While it is permissible to speak of French culture as a set of norms which are dominant in France, it is important to remember that not all of them are exclusive to France; nor are they shared to an identical extent by every French national. While the French language is now common to practically the whole of the indigenous population, there is still considerable diversity over matters such as religious belief and personal morality.

This is not always fully appreciated by the French themselves. Like the natives of other states, they have been encouraged to think of themselves as a more coherent and self-contained cultural community than they really are. Research conducted among members of minority ethnocultural groups has often found a similar appearance of national consciousness dominating over cultural diversity. Le Huu Khoa, for example, reports that, when given *carte blanche* to define their identity, Vietnamese respondents in France always spoke first and foremost of themselves as Vietnamese and in some cases as French, or a mixture of the two; though many were Buddhists or Catholics, none spontaneously defined themselves by their religious affiliation (Le Huu Khoa 1985: 173–82). Kastoryano found a more ambiguous overwriting of religious by national identity among Turkish immigrants and their descendants. When she asked the children of immigrants to state their religion, most replied: 'I'm a Turk' (Kastoryano 1986: 89), perpetuating an equation between religious affiliation and national belonging commonly found among their parents. In Turkey, the state has formally distanced itself from the religious sphere more than is the case in virtually any other predominantly Islamic country. While the state tells its citizens that they are first and foremost Turks, Islamic beliefs remain strong, particularly in the rural areas where many immigrants originate. The potential gap between the two strands is elided by using 'Turkish' as a synonym for 'Muslim'.

Culture and identity

The limits of state propaganda machines are vividly illustrated by Kastoryano's findings. Despite (or perhaps because of) their relatively limited education, the Turks interviewed by Kastoryano inflect the official view of national identity with a more religious slant than the state might wish. Their replies also illustrate some of the enormous complexities which often lie behind the seemingly simple concept of 'identity'. Following Hall (1992), we may usefully distinguish between three main approaches to this concept. The first, inherited from the Enlightenment, views identity as a relatively fixed and autonomous form of selfhood, an inner personality largely immune to outside influences. A second approach, symbolic interactionism, developed during the early decades of the twentieth century, putting the emphasis on social influences in the construction of more malleable personal identities. Most recently, theorists of post-modernism have argued for an unanchored, constantly open and self-generating form of identity. As these contrasting approaches suggest, one of the main difficulties attaching to the term 'identity' is the fact that in everyday usage it is often understood to denote something fixed, whereas social psychologists and other researchers have produced abundant evidence to show that few if any human beings may be said to have an entirely stable, unchanging identity.

If we define identity as the pattern of meaning and value by which a person structures his or her life, it is clear that this involves a dynamic process rather than an immutable condition. Individuals construct meaning and value with the aid of cultural codes shared by particular groups. Personal identity is in this sense inseparable from – though not necessarily reducible to – socio-cultural identity. It is not uncommon for a person to switch between codes. By the same token, he or she moves between a variety of socio-cultural identities.

Socio-cultural ties based on collective origins distinct from those of other groups are the foundation of ethnic identities. The cultural codes associated with ethnic identities have been described by Geertz as 'primordial attachments' (1963: 109). There are at least three senses in which this description might appear apt. First, the cultural codes on which ethnic identities are built tend to be of a fundamental nature, setting a general framework of meaning within which particular acts are constructed. This applies to language, for example, as well as to religious beliefs. Secondly, cultural codes of this kind are usually, though not always, learnt at an early age, and in this sense enjoy ontological primacy. Thirdly, they are by the same token associated with deep-seated affective ties which may make them difficult to dislodge or replace. New codes may be learnt in later life, however, and in certain circumstances may supersede those acquired at an early age. Moreover, code-switching is not necessarily an essentially affective affair. Individuals or groups may invoke ethnic identities in a calculated fashion, sometimes with the aim of achieving objectives which owe relatively little to the original codes inherited by ethnocultural groups. This is sometimes referred to as an instrumentalist (as against a primordial) form of ethnicity. Drawing on rational choice theory, Banton (1983) and Hechter *et al.* (1982) have argued that ethnic allegiances owe more to this kind of calculation than to primordial sentiments.

The behavior of all human beings is marked by a mixture of rational and affective features. The rational dimension is most easily visible in the economic sphere, where employers and employees make calculated judgements about the most effective ways of maximizing their material gains. When they first migrate, foreign workers often expect to pursue an economic project without this affecting their cultural identity. In reality, it is impossible to keep the two wholly separate, just as it is impossible to separate politics from culture. As already noted, the state plays a major role in cultural reproduction. At the same time, certain kinds of cultural competence are indispensable to effective economic participation. Most immigrant workers are obliged to acquire at least minimal competence in the language of the receiving country if they are to function effectively in the employment and housing markets. They may take a purely instrumental view of foreign language acquisition, thereby retaining a primordial attachment to their native tongue, but in this and other respects their cultural repertoire widens significantly as the length of their stay extends.

However, the most important challenge to minority ethnocultural groups concerns the second and third generations (Liebkind 1989). The majority of immigrants arrive in the receiving country as adults, with their primordial cultural attachments already formed in the country of origin. By contrast, the formative years of their children are spent in the land to which the older generation has moved. These youngsters are often encouraged by their parents to work hard at school, for education is seen as a passport to better jobs than those held by most immigrant workers. At the same time, many parents are initially anxious to ensure that the cultural codes inherited from the country of origin are sustained by the younger generation. Their children are therefore expected to profit instrumentally from school while remaining affectively distanced from the cultural norms dominant in the receiving country. In most cases, it proves impossible wholly to reconcile these contradictory demands. As they pass through the educational system and mix with children from the majority population, immigrant-born youngsters tend to internalize the cultural codes of the dominant population not simply as means to an end but as desirable objects in their own right.

During the colonial period, European minorities were able to sustain their ethnocultural identity by virtue of their privileged position in overseas territories. Today's post-colonial immigrants occupy a diametrically opposite position: they are disempowered minorities, without citizenship in most cases and with very little leverage over the formal education system. As Banton (1983: 154) has observed, in the industrialized world only a handful of cases can be cited of minority ethnocultural groups which have succeeded in remaining almost wholly separate from the majority populations over more than three generations. The best known examples are the Amish communities in the US, which have managed to exist as almost entirely self-contained entities, controlling entry and exit, information flows, employment for adults and the education of children. This has been possible only because of their spatial isolation in rural communities. There are very few examples of a comparable degree of ethnocultural separation being sustained in cities, where the physical proximity of densely packed and diverse population groups make inter-group contacts almost inevitable.

As noted in Chapter 2, immigrants and their families are heavily concentrated in urban areas, and they are particularly overrepresented in France's largest conurbations, notably Paris. Mono-ethnic districts are virtually non-existent, except for a few micro-localities. Some groups, such as the *harkis*, were initially housed in isolated areas, but their children have all been educated in state schools and their parents are in any case fiercely pro-French, having fought against Algerian independence. Kastoryano's fieldwork on Turkish immigrants reveals an interesting contrast between those who settled in the Paris conurbation and those she interviewed in Terrasson, a small provincial town in south-west France. Though smaller in absolute numbers than their compatriots in Paris, the Turks in Terrasson were more densely concentrated, and this made it easier to establish social networks beneficial for the reinforcement of their distinct cultural codes. Yet even here, separation from the indigenous population was by no means absolute. Almost all the men worked in nearby French factories, while their children all attended local state schools. The erosion of their ethnocultural identity was less marked than among Turks dispersed across the Paris conurbation, but it was nonetheless under way (Kastoryano 1986; cf. Tripier 1990: 211–66).

Measuring ethnicity

Measuring the strength of ethnocultural groups is no easy task. It should be remembered that these are not the same as ethnic groups, whose members are defined for the purposes of the present study simply on the basis of shared territorial origins. Despite the inadequacies of official statistics, we saw in Chapter 2 that data on nationality do enable us to conduct at least partial socio-economic analyses of minority ethnic groups in France. No directly comparable data are available on ethnocultural groups. There are no census questions, for example, on language usage or religious beliefs. With a few recent exceptions, we therefore have to rely on much smaller surveys conducted by a variety of researchers. The representativeness of sampling procedures is often open to question, and there are huge variations in the methodologies used by different researchers, making accurate comparisons based on their data difficult if not impossible.

The central role of subjective processes in the constitution of cultural groups raises even more fundamental difficulties. Unlike employment and housing patterns, which are in principle open to direct empirical observation, ethnocultural belonging revolves around intellectual and attitudinal processes which cannot be directly apprehended by an outside observer. Traces of those processes are visible in behavioral patterns, but their interpretation is by no means a simple or mechanical task. It is, of course, possible to ask people about their values and beliefs (many of the surveys drawn on later in this chapter do so), but this always involves complex methodological problems, and there is no guarantee that potential interviewees will be willing to respond to questions in such personally sensitive areas or, if they do, that their replies will be wholly truthful.

In assessing the strength of ethnocultural groups, it is useful to distinguish between cultural *competence*, cultural *performance*, ethnic *identification* and ethnic *mobilization*. Cultural competence, the capacity to use a particular cultural code, is intertwined but not identical with cultural performance, i.e. the actual use of such codes. Ethnic identification, the affective association of an individual with an enthnocultural group, may lead to involvement in ethnic mobilization, i.e. the collective organization of such a group, but this is not automatic.

In many cases, cultural competence is acquired unreflectingly through cultural performance. Perhaps the best example of this is the acquisition of a person's native language. That language is often known as the mother tongue because it is learnt by deciphering and copying utterances heard during the child's earliest years, when parental influences are at their strongest. While parents often correct errors in particular utterances made by their children, they seldom if ever give formal grammar lessons. Yet at an unconscious level, the child masters an enormously complex set of rules governing the formulation of intelligible utterances in the language concerned. In this way, linguistic competence is derived from linguistic performance. When second or third languages are learnt later in life, often at school, the pattern is usually very different. Although there are considerable variations in language instruction methods, it is not uncommon for teachers to begin by explaining general rules, which are then illustrated and practised through particular utterances. In this way, linguistic performance is preconditioned by linguistic competence.

It is important to note that neither linguistic competence in particular nor cultural competence in general is a zero-sum game. Just as individuals may acquire new languages without this in any way reducing their competence in their native tongue, so they may grasp other types of cultural code without losing those already mastered. Elements drawn from diverse cultures frequently coexist within a person. While conflicts may sometimes arise, this is by no means always the case. Frequently, cultural diversity provides a stimulus for the creation of new syntheses.

At the same time, an individual may be competent in a particular code and make active use of it without identifying with the ethnocultural group with which it is most closely associated. For instance, immigrants often learn to use the dominant language of the society in which they live while nevertheless regarding it as a code which remains fundamentally foreign to them. Even if the native tongue falls into disuse, at an affective level it is likely to retain a strong hold on the mind of the immigrant, for whom it remains a more natural vehicle of expression or communication. Similar observations apply to non-linguistic codes. Spiritual values, for example, may be understood and, in some cases, religious practices may be performed without the person concerned necessarily believing in the doctrines on which they are based. Children are often encouraged to join in the religious practices of their parents, and may feel pressurized to conform outwardly with them as long as they remain in the family home even if their inner thoughts are at variance with these traditions. Cultural performance cannot therefore be equated with ethnic identification.

As a general rule, ethnic mobilization is a more reliable sign of ethnic identification (Olzak 1983). While individuals may sometimes feel pressurized into joining or supporting 'voluntary' organizations, on the whole these are run by activists who are strongly committed to particular goals. It is nevertheless important to distinguish between mobilization *for* ethnicity and mobilization *through* ethnicity. Some associations – those promoting language teaching or religious observance, for example – draw on the bonds of ethnic affiliation to further cultural objectives. Others may be organized by and for members of ethnicized or ethnocultural groups, but not necessarily with the aim of strengthening ethnic identity. Membership of certain anti-racist organizations, for example, may be ethnically based, but the objective may be equality of treatment alongside the indigenous population rather than the promotion of distinctive cultural codes.

3.2 Language

Competence in French

Although most immigrants were poorly educated and learnt little if any French at school, they generally acquire at least a minimal level of competence in the language, particularly if their working environment requires this. Few employers offer linguistic training. Adult literacy classes are organized by a number of voluntary agencies, but the availability of courses is patchy; women, particularly from Islamic countries, have often found it difficult to attend, partly because their menfolk are reluctant to endorse female activity outside the domestic sphere.

A household survey conduced jointly by INSEE and INED in 1992 found a close correlation between the length of settlement of immigrants and the degree of proficiency which they had acquired in the French language (Table 3.1). Only a minority had had any formal education in French, with those from former colonies in a slightly stronger position in this regard. The proportion of Algerian men who said they had had some schooling in French was twice as large as that reported by Portuguese men, and with a longer average period of settlement Algerian men still speaking little or no French were far less numerous than their Portuguese counterparts.

The lower rates of linguistic competence generally reported by women migrants are primarily a reflection of their later arrival in France, but there are some significant differences between different national groups. In spite of having the same average length of settlement as Portuguese women and slightly greater exposure to French while at school, Algerian women were much weaker in the language. Some 57 per cent said they could speak little or no French, compared with only 35 per

Table 3.1 French language competence among immigrants by nationality, sex and date of arrival in France, 1992

	Average date of arrival in France	Schooling included some French (%)	Difficulty in understanding French TV news (%)	Speak little or no French (%)
Portuguese, male	1970	17	14	38
Portuguese, female	1972	20	20	35
Algerian, male	1964	35	10	16
Algerian, female	1972	25	46	57
Moroccans and Tunisians, male	1972	35	26	40
Moroccans and Tunisians, female	1979	29	51	65
Turks, male	1977	10	65	83
Turks, female	1979	0	85	100

Source: INSEE 1994: 61.

cent of Portuguese women, who, uniquely, reported higher levels of proficiency than men of the same nationality. It is likely that this reflects employment patterns. As many Portuguese women are employed as domestic staff by French nationals, they work in a basically French-speaking environment, whereas men employed in the construction industry – as are many Portuguese – are more liable to work in ethnically segmented teams. Participation rates in the formal labor market are much lower among Algerian women than among those of Portuguese nationality, and very few work within a French residential environment. Their greater isolation at home is reflected in lower levels of competence in French. Still greater linguistic difficulties are reported by Turkish women, who suffer from all three handicaps: a comparatively short period of residence in France, no schooling whatever in French and very low levels of employment outside the home.

Few of their children experience comparable difficulties. Those who arrive in France after reaching school age are often handicapped initially, but special support classes are provided to help reduce the linguistic gap as quickly as possible. Among those born in France, the initial trauma of stepping from a home dominated by the mother tongue into the French-speaking environment of school is soon overcome. So complete is the mastery of French acquired by most immigrant-born children that it generally supplants the mother tongue as their primary language. Frequently, their command of the mother tongue becomes stunted, failing to progress beyond the level reached at the beginning of their schooling. Very commonly, the younger generation uses French within the family home. At first, parents may continue speaking to their children in their native language, while receiving replies in French. Later, many parents find themselves forced to switch to French. In some cases, parents deliberately use French because they believe that proficiency in this language will give their children better opportunities in the French labor market. Le Huu Khoa (1985: 210), for example, reports this to have been common among Vietnamese families.

A large-scale survey conducted by INED and INSEE in 1999 confirmed that among all immigrant groups, as the number of generations present in France increases so too does the loss of the first generation's mother tongue. This applies as much to Arabic and Turkish as it does to Spanish and Italian. A rare exception is Portuguese, which appears to be resisting this erosion better than most other languages, partly because of more frequent visits to the 'home' country, to which many Portuguese migrants still expect to return (Héran *et al.* 2005).

Mother tongue teaching

In the mid-1970s, the French government agreed to allow sending states to provide, at their own expense, tuition in 'Langues et Cultures d'Origine' (Homeland Languages and Cultures – LCO) for the children of immigrants within French primary schools. By the early 1980s, agreements had been signed with eight states, but despite considerable investment in specialist teaching only a minority of immigrant-born children have been covered by these programs (*Revue de linguistique et de didactique des langues* 1990). In 1998, less than a fifth of children eligible for lessons in immigrant languages were receiving them and the numbers were falling. In 2002–3, only 70,000 schoolchildren were enrolled, compared with 140,000 twenty years earlier. The number of teachers supporting the program had also been halved (Petek 2004: 49). In the school year 1988–9, the proportion of foreign children receiving language instruction paid for by the sending state was as follows: Algerians 14 per cent, Moroccans 15 per cent, Tunisians 15 per cent, Spaniards 23 per cent, Italians 137 (sic) per cent, Portuguese 31 per cent, Turks 35 per cent, Yugoslavians 20 per cent (Ministère de l'Éducation Nationale 1989: table 4). Other sending states, such as those in sub-Saharan Africa and South-East Asia, funded no classes of this kind. The fact that the number of primary school children learning Italian was larger than all those of Italian nationality combined reflects the fact that some French parents were using the system as a way of obtaining early foreign language tuition for their own children. Other languages spoken by minority ethnic groups exert no comparable attraction. Even among nationals of the countries concerned, there are often misgivings about attending these classes, for in many cases this means missing other parts of the curriculum. Affective ties with the country of origin are not uncommonly outweighed by the low status attached to 'immigrant' languages in the eyes of the majority population and a concern to maximize skills directly applicable within France.

The LCO program is paid for entirely by the governments of countries from which migrants come. The French state provides no funding for it. An important consequence of this is that the languages in the LCO program are often other than the mother tongues of the children to whom they are taught. This is because the governments concerned are prepared to fund only their official national languages, whereas many migrants and their children speak regional dialects or completely different languages. Thus many children of North African origin learn Berber from their parents, rather than the official language of their home country, Arabic (Chaker 1988). For them, the LCO program is in effect an encounter with a foreign language rather than support for their mother tongue. And as the program provides only a few hours of tuition each week, often for only a year or two, the competence acquired by pupils is very limited.

Mother tongue teaching is even more marginalized at the secondary school level. Although major languages spoken in a number of sending countries are in principle available on demand, very few immigrant-born youngsters opt to study them. Like their French peers, the overwhelming majority choose English as their first foreign language. This is partly because of the negative images associated with languages spoken by immigrants of low socio-economic status, in sharp contrast with the images of glamour and commercial utility associated with English. In 1984–5, Portuguese was being studied by no more than 15 per cent of Portuguese secondary schoolchildren; only 7 per cent of Maghrebis were learning Arabic (Boulot and Boyzon-Fradet 1987: 179), and the proportion has since declined. Only fragmentary information is available on language classes organized by voluntary associations, but their efforts are unlikely to significantly alter the overall picture of very limited formal education in the mother tongue of most immigrant-born children (Bazin and Vermes 1990).

Language surveys conducted jointly by INSEE and INED indicate that all the main immigrant groups are fighting a losing battle on the home front. A survey conducted in 1992 (Héran 1993) asked approximately 2,000 parents living in France who were brought up speaking a language other than French which language they usually spoke when addressing their children. As dozens of different native languages – including some spoken by regional, rather than immigrant minorities – were included in this aggregate total, sample sizes for individual languages were often small. The results should therefore be treated as indicative rather than as definitive measures of language performance. Certain overall trends nevertheless emerge very clearly.

Though it is not their native tongue, the overwhelming majority of interviewees say they usually speak in French to their children (Table 3.2). The main variations between different groups of immigrants are accounted for by differences in the length of settlement. Berber parents, for example, who use French with their children more frequently than Arabic-speakers, have on average lived in France for a longer period. A similar point applies to Italian- and Spanish-speaking parents, compared with Portuguese-speakers. The very small use of French reported by Turkish interviewees reflects their recent arrival in France. Sub-Saharan Africans are also relatively recent arrivals, but it is likely that they were more exposed to the French language than Turks before emigrating, hence their greater propensity to use French with their children. Right across the board, the practice of conversing within the family in French increases steadily with the length of settlement, irrespective of the parents' native tongue or indeed of their sex. Given an equal period of residence in France, women, who are sometimes portrayed as more conservative guardians of tradition than men, in fact have a slightly higher propensity to use French when talking to their children.

Table 3.2 Language usage by parents resident in France brought up speaking a language other than French, 1992

Language of parents	Proportion usually speaking French to their children (%)
Creole (DOMs and Mauritius)	90
Italian	90
Spanish	80
Portuguese	55
Arabic	50
Berber	70
Turkish	5
Vietnamese	55
Miscellaneous sub-Saharan	75

Source: INSEE-INED 1992 Education Survey in Héran 1993: 2.

It would be wrong to jump to the conclusion that the habit of speaking mainly in French can be directly equated, as Héran (1993: 2) rather misleadingly puts it, with the 'rate of loss' of the parental language. In a survey conducted by the Education Ministry almost simultaneously with the INED–INSEE survey, the proportion of foreign parents who said they regularly spoke to their children in a language other than French was as follows: 99 per cent of Turks, 91 per cent of both Spaniards and Portuguese, 88 per cent of Moroccans, 87 per cent of South-East Asians, 83 per cent of Algerians and 82 per cent of Tunisians (Conseil Économique et Social 1994: 77). These findings are not necessarily at odds with those of the survey previously quoted. It is perfectly possible for parents to speak 'usually' in French while nevertheless also speaking 'regularly' in their native tongue, though their children may well reply in French. Even if, at the level of day-to-day performance, French clearly dominates, linguistic competence is not a zero-sum game: while acquiring competence in French and perhaps other languages, the children of immigrants are likely to retain at least a passive understanding of their mother tongue even if their active command of it is largely lost. Precisely because it is the language of their parents, many young people continue to identify affectively with their mother tongue even when they lack competence in it altogether, a posture summed up in a remark made by a young interviewee of Algerian origin questioned in a survey by Dabène and Billiez (1987: 66): 'Arabic is my language but I can't speak it'.

This affective relationship is clearly different and less intense, however, from that felt by immigrants who are wholly at one with their native tongue. In purely practical terms, moreover, few second-generation members of minority groups are in a position to pass on their mother tongue to their own children, though many express an idealistic desire to do so. In most cases they have so internalized the French language that it comes as naturally to them as their native tongue to their parents. Functionally, it has in fact replaced their native language, for it serves not only instrumental purposes at school or at work but also as the principal vehicle of self-expression, whether in personal relationships (such as within the family) or for creative purposes such as literary production.

Variants and inflections

For many immigrants from former colonies, French is still perceived, even if only at an unconscious level, as a language of external domination. Traces of such anxieties are sometimes found among their children, despite their formal mastery of French, and this perhaps helps to explain a frequent tendency to inflect the language in directions which decenter it. By injecting liberal doses of slang and expressions imported from other tongues, they reappropriate the language so as to make it perceptibly their own. A form of slang much favored by young people of immigrant origin is *verlan* (backslang), which reinvents words by reversing the order of their syllables (Bachmann and Basier 1984; Mela 1988). A now famous example of this is the neologism *Beur*, which was initially adopted as a self-designation by young Parisians of Maghrebi origin during the 1970s. *Beur* is a partial contraction and reversal of *Arabe*, a word which in French usage often carries pejorative connotations inherited from the colonial period. Anyone of Maghrebi appearance is liable to be referred to by a French observer as an Arab, despite the fact that many of those concerned are from Berber families. Aware that when they were called Arabs this frequently connoted an inferior status, young Maghrebis began calling themselves Beurs. As the term was completely new, its meaning was molded by its creators instead of being tainted by negative accretions from the past.

The word entered public usage in 1981, when Radio Beur became one of the first local radio stations to be licensed in Paris. Within a few years, heavy usage of the term by the mass media made it part of the vocabulary of the general public throughout France. Precisely because of this, those to whom the term 'Beur' was applied became increasingly reluctant to accept it, for they no longer controlled its meaning, which in media usage became increasingly intertwined with negatively connoted images of the banlieues, echoing earlier stereotypes associated with *Arabes* (Durmelat 1998). This has not dampened the enthusiasm of young Maghrebis for the principle of backslang. Provided terms reappropriated by outsiders are renewed by the in-group (*Rebeu*, for example, is sometimes used as a reversal of *Beur*), a sense of community can be sustained by linguistic inflections of this kind.

One of the great attractions of verlan is that it enables language users to position themselves outside the standard categories of social identification. Those who called themselves Beurs circumvented the simplistic choice with which outsiders tended to confront them, insisting that they be labeled as *either* French *or* Arab (Barbara 1986: 135). Open identification with France is a particularly sensitive matter for the descendants of Algerians, since their parents generally supported the nationalist movement during the struggle for independence. Although the younger generation owes more of its cultural repertoire to France than to Algeria, there is a tendency to emphasize sub- or supra-national elements within the French cultural space, thereby avoiding directly national forms of identification (Hargreaves 1992a, 1993a). For example, forms of slang unique to a particular region or town are often cultivated, while at the other end of the scale there is a strong interest in international youth culture, especially when marked by American and/or black influences.

Mixtures of this kind frequently mark the literary production of young Maghrebis, scores of whom have published mainly autobiographical novels since the early 1980s (Hargreaves 1997a). The emphasis on local roots is exemplified in the title of Azouz Begag's *Le Gone du Chaâba* (1986; translated as *Shantytown Kid* 2007). While the author's Arab ancestry is signaled in *Chaâba*, the Arabic name of the shantytown where Begag was brought up in the city of Lyon, *gone* (kid) is part of the local slang indigenous to the town. Only those who really belong to a locality can fully master its slang. Begag was born in Lyon, and by calling himself a *gone*, he signals the depth of his roots in France's second city. While this implicitly cuts across those who argue that people of immigrant origin can never be part of the French national community, the emphasis on local slang enables the author to establish his French credentials without directly identifying himself with a specifically national representation of French culture.

The title of Soraya Nini's autobiographical novel, *Ils disent que je suis une Beurette…* (They Call Me a Beurette… 1993), reflects the wariness now felt by many young Maghrebis in relation to the term Beur and its feminine variant, Beurette, which is sometimes used by French journalists. There is also a deep reluctance among many young women to accept the gender roles traditionally assumed in Maghrebi families (an issue explored in greater detail later in this chapter). When talking with her Maghrebi girlfriends, Nini's fictional alter ego, Samia, mixes linguistic codes so as to escape the repressive surveillance of her family. The girls' secret language blends together verlan, southern French slang and English, producing cocktails of the following kind:

> – La mother a técontra au KGB que tu treren tous sel srios présa eighteen o'clock! (La mother a raconté au KGB que tu rentres tous les soirs après dix-huit heures.) (Nini 1993: 112)
> – Mother told the KGB [a nickname for Samia's elder brother] that you don't get home until after six o'clock each evening.

While the English expressions which pepper this and other pieces of writing by young Maghrebi authors may sometimes draw on school lessons, they are more commonly inspired by the mass media, which are deeply impregnated with material originating in the US despite the efforts of the French state to hold back the tide. The title of another autobiographical narrative, Ferrudja's Kessas's *Beur's Story* (1990), is directly inspired by two American movies, *West Side Story* and *Love Story*, both of which feature romances between an American boy and an immigrant-born girl. When the Maghrebi-born Smaïn, who in the 1990s became one of the most popular entertainers in France, staged his first major show he called it 'A Star is Beur', a playful allusion to the Judy Garland movie *A Star is Born*. In his autobiography, Smaïn recalls that his childhood was saturated with American influences transmitted nightly on French television. His first role model was the American humorist Jerry Lewis, the first record he bought was a George Gershwin album (which he could not resist because of its photograph of New York at night), and he dreamt constantly of waking up to find himself in Hollywood-sur-Seine (Smaïn 1990).

American popular culture is no more monolothic than the cultural practices of the many countries into which it has penetrated. While Smaïn fell under the spell of white entertainment establishment figures, many other young Maghrebis in France, particularly those who have become political activists, have been more influenced by black Americans. Some of the most important tensions which lie just below the surface of American popular culture are exemplified in the field of rock music. Although rock and roll first came to international prominence through white American performers, the musical forms on which they drew were largely the creation of black Americans. Today, many variants of rock music – including some of its most politicized forms – are dominated by black rather than white performers. It is significant that the earliest stirrings of political mobilization among younger members of France's post-colonial minorities were organized at the beginning of the 1980s under the title Rock Against Police. The name was directly inspired by the Rock Against Racism concerts organized a few years earlier in Britain by young Afro-Caribbeans, who in turn looked for their own role models to black Americans. Thus in France, the English label 'Rock Against Police' was a way of attracting young supporters through the excitement associated with rock music while at the same time pointing to the political example provided by minority groups in Britain and North America, where mobilization against racism was more advanced (*Questions clefs* 1982: 52–63).

A similar dynamic has been at work in the French rap music scene. Originally created in the 1980s by African Americans in the US, rap was taken up in France by multi-ethnic bands which in the 1990s made it the most popular musical form among young people as a whole, including those of majority ethnic origin. As in the US, the rap scene in France embraces many different variants both musically and politically, from the softer, more lyrical MC Solaar to the more provocative and subversive NTM (Cachin 1996). Among the most successful bands is the Marseilles-based IAM, whose members are of Italian, Malian, Algerian and Spanish origin. According to the band members their name – pronounced 'I am', as in English – is an acronym derived from an invented English expression, 'Imperial Asiatic Men'. In a musical mold borrowed from African American rappers, their songs combine a fierce attachment to their native city with the celebration of a myth of pharaohism centered on Egypt. While IAM's music certainly includes borrowings from the ancestral cultures of band members, their personal roots do not directly connect up with the cultural spaces – Asia, the Middle East and above all what Paul Gilroy (1993) has called the Black Atlantic – privileged in their music. This fusion of the local and the global, in which the national state is seen as an oppressive or irrelevant construction, is encapsulated in the title of their 1991 album, '… de la planète Mars' (from/about the planet Mars), where Mars is both a contraction of a specific locality, the city of Marseilles, and a cultural amalgam that is planetary in scale (Cannon 1997).

The use of English by people of minority ethnic origin is a complex and politically ambivalent phenomenon. Some, such as Smaïn, equate it with an ethic of personal socio-economic advancement, while for others it is an emblem of collective mobilization by oppressed minorities. No less important is the cultural ambivalence of English usage, which allows young people of immigrant origin to position themselves both within and beyond the cultural norms dominant in France. English is now such a standard part of international youth culture that its adoption places the descendants of immigrants on a par with their French peers without their ostensibly submitting to a specifically French norm, which would be deeply troubling to many of their parents.

3.3 Gender roles and family relationships

Personal values

Family relationships are of importance not only in the transmission of cultural values from one generation to the next but also as a key locus in which individuals establish their personal status within the framework of collectively structured signifying practices. The cultural structuring of gender roles is a crucial part of this process. Historically, men have tended to ascribe to themselves a dominant role in most, though not all, socio-cultural systems. In recent decades, legislation has been adopted in many industrialized countries aimed at establishing at least formal equality between men and women, though in practice many inequalities persist. Most immigrants of African and Asian origin come from countries where even formal equality does not exist: power is vested primarily in the father, whose authority extends over most decision-making areas and who generally serves as the bread-winner while the mother attends primarily to domestic tasks.

There are exceptions to this general pattern. In parts of West Africa, for example, matrilineal kinship systems place mothers at the center of family units (Barou 1992a: 48). When the ancestors of Afro-Caribbeans – some of whom are descended from families of this type – were forcibly transported across the Atlantic as slaves, they suffered major socio-cultural dislocation and were often prevented from forming stable family units. Today, a relatively high proportion of Afro-Caribbean households consist of single-parent families, which are almost always headed by women. In the US, a similar pattern applies to black Americans. It is replicated in turn by immigrants from the Caribbean who have settled in European countries such as Britain, France and the Netherlands. The 1990 census found that a quarter of the families in metropolitan France originating in the French West Indies were headed by a single parent, almost invariably female; this proportion is roughly twice the national average (Marie 1993: 12). The high profile of Afro-Caribbean women as bread-winners is reflected in the exceptional levels of female emigration and labor force participation found among the population originating in the DOM-TOM, noted in Chapter 2.

In many regions outside the industrialized world, fertility is a highly prized female attribute. Women achieve status and respect by bearing children, and this favors fertility rates which are high when compared with those prevalent among the indigenous population in industrialized countries such as France. These fertility rates are initially replicated by women migrants, but the gap almost always closes as the length of settlement increases. Among Algerians in France, for example, the fertility rate fell from 8.5 children per woman of child-bearing age in the early 1960s to 4.2 in the early 1980s. At the same time, a narrower gap between French nationals and women migrants from southern Europe virtually disappeared. In the early 1960s, it was not uncommon for women of southern European origin to have three or four children each. By the early 1980s, their fertility rates were very similar to the French average of about 1.8 children per woman of child-bearing age (Desplanques 1985: 39).

The rising living standards and improved health care associated with industrialization are generally accompanied by what is known as the demographic transition: a fall in mortality rates accompanied (sometimes a little later) by a reduction in birth rates. The net effect has been smaller families, with each member enjoying greater life expectancy than in pre-industrial societies. Some African and Asian countries have yet to make this demographic transition but among women migrants originating in these states there is a steady decline in fertility rates as their length of settlement increases. Between 1981 and 1990, when the average number of children per French woman of child-bearing age remained more or less stagnant (slipping from 1.8 to 1.7), there were sharp falls among women of African and Asian origin. The average number of children fell from 4.2 to 3.2 among Algerian women, from 5.2 to 3.5 among Moroccans, and from 5.3 to 3.7 among those of Turkish nationality. Although the fall – from 5.1 to 4.8 – was less marked among nationals of sub-Saharan African states, whose arrival in France is particularly recent, there is nevertheless already a widening gap between them and women remaining in the countries of origin, where on average each woman has more than six children (INSEE 1992b).

The long-term trend towards families similar in size to the French norm is undoubtedly sustained among the descendants of immigrants, though as most are French nationals by the time they reach child-bearing age it is difficult to document this with precision. A significant indicator is a rise in the average age at which immigrant-born women marry, compared with their mothers. An analysis by Tribalat of INSEE survey data collected in 1982 found that while 70 per cent of Algerian migrant women had been married before the age of 20, this was true of only 15 per cent of their daughters. A similar trend was apparent among Moroccans and Tunisians. The relatively low age at which the daughters of Turkish women were marrying was attributed to the fact that, compared with Maghrebis, Turks had tended to migrate at a later age. Because of this, many had daughters of marriageable age who had been socialized in rural parts of Turkey, where early marriages were still the norm. Young women of Maghrebi origin, who had spent longer in France, were thought to be delaying marriage partly because they were in some cases unwilling to accept Muslim spouses proposed by their parents (Tribalat 1991: 151–8).

The desire to exercise personal control in the fields of sexuality and matrimony is indicative of important attitudinal changes among young people of immigrant origin compared with their parents. Second- and third-generation members of minority ethnic groups tend to model themselves on their French peers, most of whom regard sexual relations and marriage as matters in which personal decision-making should be paramount. By contrast, in many parts of Africa and Asia extra-marital sexual relations are strictly taboo and matrimony is seen as a matter to be arranged between families. When families migrate, the choice of marriage partners becomes of crucial importance for the inter-generational reproduction of ethnocultural differentiation. The higher the rate of endogamy, i.e. marriage within an ethnocultural group, the better are the chances of sustaining its distinctive cultural values. Exogamy, i.e. marriage outside the group, often reflects a desire for personal independence and signals the erosion of the group's traditions.

In much of Africa and Asia it has been customary for parents to arrange marriages for their children. Those who migrate often expect to retain this prerogative and to use it in such a way as to ensure that succeeding generations remain faithful to the cultural heritage of their ancestors. Immigrants seeking to arrange marriages in this way, usually through extended family and social networks, are engaged in a very important form of ethnic mobilization. As children brought up in France are inclined to expect the same personal freedoms as their French peers, they sometimes find themselves on collision course with their parents. In a survey by the Centre de Formation et de Recherche de l'Éducation Surveillée (CFRES) conducted among 500 teenagers in the late 1970s, 68 per cent of Maghrebi interviewees, compared with only 29 per cent of the Iberian (i.e. Portuguese and Spanish) sample and 27 per cent of their French peers, said their parents were opposed in principle to marriages between people of different nationalities. Asked to give their own opinion, only 9 per cent of Maghrebi boys and 15 per cent of Maghrebi girls took the same view. The figures among Iberian youths were 4 and 13 per cent; among French interviewees they were 8 and 7 per cent (Zaleska 1982: 186–8). Whatever their origins, most interviewees said that neither nationality nor religion mattered where their own preferences for a marriage partner were concerned; the important thing would be personal attraction (Taboada-Leonetti 1982: 224). A survey by Muxel of three similarly defined groups of teenagers in the mid-1980s found almost universal agreement for the proposition that cohabitation outside marriage was acceptable (Muxel 1988: 932) – a view with which very few Muslim parents would be likely to agree.

There are also deep inter-generational differences over gender roles. Some 85 per cent of the young Maghrebis questioned in the CFRES survey said their fathers felt women should stay at home and look after the family while men went out to work; 68 per cent said their mothers agreed. The equivalent figures were 67 and 60 per cent among Iberian interviewees compared with 33 and 24 per cent among the French. When asked to state their own views, the younger generation favored a more equal distribution of roles among men and women, though boys were less committed to this than girls. Only 10 per cent of Maghrebi girls, compared with 38 per cent of boys, agreed with the traditional distribution of gender roles. The figures were almost identical among young Iberians, while among French girls and boys they were 3 and 20 per cent respectively. Muxel's survey found a very similar inter-ethnic convergence on the question of gender roles among young people from native French, immigrant Catholic and immigrant Muslim backgrounds (Muxel 1988: 932).

Parental expectations tend to constrain daughters more than sons, for the dominant role traditionally enjoyed by men makes exogamous marriages contracted by male descendants appear less threatening than those of females. In Islamic countries, non-Muslim women who marry Muslim men are expected and sometimes legally required to accept that their children will be brought up as Muslims; because of the dominant role traditionally attributed to men, marriages between Muslim women and non-Muslim men are strongly discouraged and may not be legally recognized at all. In France, daughters of Muslim immigrants marrying a non-Muslim run a much higher risk of being shunned by their families than do sons who take non-Muslim spouses (Streiff-Fenart 1993).

It is difficult to know how many marriages are contracted between partners from different ethnocultural groups. The nationality of spouses is often a relevant indicator, but the data compiled in France do not include marriages contracted in the home countries of immigrants. Moreover, as the descendants of immigrants are generally French nationals by the time they reach adulthood, it is impossible to make even approximate estimates of inter-generational trends based on the nationality of spouses. A study conducted on the basis of nationality showed that marriages between foreigners and French nationals generally increase with the length of settlement and that foreign men enter more frequently than women into unions of this kind (Munoz-Perez and Tribalat 1984). While this gender balance no doubt corresponds in part to the statistical dominance of men in adult migratory inflows, it may also reflect the heavier pressures brought to bear on women by members of groups anxious to sustain a separate ethnocultural identity through endogamous unions (Abelkrim-Chikh 1991).

The first large-scale study to produce data on unions between partners of different ethnocultural groups, the MGIS survey led by Tribalat, found that endogamy was generally more common among minorities originating in predominantly Muslim countries than among those originating in Europe (Tribalat 1996: 101–3) but the gap should not be exaggerated. Two-thirds of second-generation Portuguese males reported relationships with majority ethnic partners, as did half of second-generation Algerian men. Among second-generation women, mixed unions were reported by 43 per of those of Portuguese origin and 32 per cent of those of Algerian origin (Tribalat 1995: 70, 89). A more recent large-scale study, the Family Survey (EF) based on data collected in 1999, found that the highest rates of endogamy were among immigrants from Turkey, South-East Asia and Portugal; the rates among Algerians and Tunisians were significantly lower, close to those of Italians and Spaniards (Filhon and Varro 2005: 488–9).

Studies of mixed marriages, i.e. those between spouses of different ethnic origins, show that it is difficult, if not impossible, to insulate the family home from the wider political struggles between the different cultural traditions in which the partners have their roots. As a general rule, these marriages are marked by a cultural imbalance against the minority group. Thus immigrants in mixed unions are less likely than those married to a partner of the same ethnic origin to use their mother tongue when speaking to their children (Héran 1993: 3). The names given to the children of mixed unions are highly symbolic indicators of identity. When parents choose names, they implicitly indicate how they want their children to be perceived in relation to their diverse ethnocultural origins. Those perceptions depend in part on popular preconceptions attaching to different ethnicized groups. Varro and Lesbet (1986) report that as Franco-American couples generally consider their two countries of origin to enjoy roughly equal public esteem, they tend to favor names which are common to both. More commonly, immigrants fear that the nominalization of foreign origins may expose their children to discriminatory treatment. For this reason, French names are often preferred.

The historical legacy of colonization invests the deliberations of some couples with particular sensitivity. Algerian immigrants who experienced the war of independence are generally reluctant to accept French names for their children or grandchildren, though they know that Arab names render social acceptance more difficult in France. In most mixed unions, the desire not to handicap children with stigmatized names eventually wins out over the wish to display a sense of historical pride. In a study of the names given to 600 children of mixed Franco-Maghrebi (mainly Franco-Algerian) parentage, Streiff-Fenart found that 58 per cent had identifiably French names, compared with only 18 per cent that could be classified as Arab. This overall imbalance was compounded by gendered inequalities. Among couples where the Maghrebi partner was male French names still predominated, with 44 per cent of the total, but the proportion of Arab names rose to 29 per cent. By contrast, where the female partner was Maghrebi 73 per cent of names were French and only 6 per cent Arab (Streiff-Fenart 1993: 235).

Almost a quarter of the names given to the children of Franco-Maghrebi couples were found to be 'neutral', i.e. they could be identified with both cultural traditions or neither. Popular examples straddling the cultural divide included Nadia for girls and Hedi/Eddie (the Americanized diminutive for Edouard) for boys. Names such as Joris, Tahnee, Vadim and Nolwen were drawn from cultural spaces such as Scandinavia, which were free from the rivalry and/or stigmatization marking Franco-Maghrebi relations. These names are important symbols of the capacity for renewal and invention often seen in the cultural practices of ordinary individuals faced with the contrasting traditions of majority and minority groups. As Streiff-Fenart (1989) and others (Muller 1987; Déjeux 1989; Barbara 1993) have shown, similar compromises and creative syntheses in matters ranging from language and dress to schoolwork and leisure permeate the daily lives of families based on mixed unions.

Legal clashes

Syntheses of this kind are possible because both partners in mixed unions share a personal bond which enables them to look beyond the cultural boundaries of the groups in which they originate. In other circumstances, cultural differences sometimes lead to serious conflicts. Some of the most basic aspects of personal relationships are codified in laws governing kinship systems, which vary from one state to another. Practices which are perfectly lawful in an immigrant's home country may render him or her liable to prosecution in France (HCI 1992b). Family law in France is based on the premise of monogamy. In recent years, immigration from countries where polygamy is widely practised has opened up a legal minefield.

Although polygamous practices existed before Islam, they were formally codified in the Koran, which permitted husbands to take up to four wives provided they were all treated equally. In many parts of the Islamic world, including the

Maghreb, polygamy has now fallen into disuse, and some predominantly Islamic countries, such as Tunisia, have made it unlawful. Most of the polygamous families in France are Muslims originating in the Soninké, Bambara and Toucouleur peoples of Mali and Senegal, in former French West Africa, where the practice is both widespread and lawful. While French nationals are not allowed to be married to more than one person at a time, under French law foreigners resident in France are in principle governed in family matters by the laws of their own country. Until recently, citizens of Mali, Senegal and other states where polygamy is lawful were therefore allowed to bring more than one wife to France, together with their children, provided the marriages were contracted in the country of origin (Rude-Antoine 1991).

Since 1993, however, the laws governing family reunification have restricted admissions to only one spouse and set of directly dependent children per resident foreign citizen (Costa-Lascoux 1994a: 29–31). Moreover, even before then, immigrants wishing to be joined by their families were required to prove that they had sufficient income and adequate housing to meet the needs of their dependants. As few polygamous Africans had the material resources to satisfy these requirements, their wives often circumvented the regulations by entering France simply as visitors rather than within the framework of the formal procedures governing family reunification. When foreign visitors exceed a stay of three months, they become illegal immigrants liable to deportation. However, prior to the reform of French nationality laws in 1993, the threat of deportation was removed in the case of women originating in ex-colonies such as those in sub-Saharan Africa if they bore children while in France, for such children automatically held French nationality from birth. By the same token, neither they nor their parents could be deported from France, even if the mother's status remained that of an illegal immigrant (Rude-Antoine 1991; Poiret and Guégan 1992: 92–102). The Pasqua laws of 1993 were designed to make deportations easier. In practice, they generated so many heart-rending family break-ups and/or deportations that public support for the laws was undermined and a large part of the reforms was repealed by the Socialist-led administration which took office in 1997.

The legal maze surrounding residence rights has been compounded by the regulations concerning social security and family allowances. While allowing foreign men to live with more than one wife, the French state has always restricted social security cover to only one of the spouses, unless the others took up employment in their own right, which has generally proved possible only in a minority of cases. By contrast, family allowances are paid in respect of all children resident in France, regardless of the nationality or immigration status of their parents. The legal and regulatory framework in France has thus offered positive incentives to child-bearing within polygamous marriages: children have served as a guarantee against deportation and as their numbers have increased so, too, has the income derived from family allowances. Poiret (1992: 29, 33, 40) has argued that this situation has perverted the cultural code underpinning polygamy in the countries of origin. There, the number of wives taken by a man and the children born from these unions serve to mark his wealth and social status. In France, multiple marriages retain their value as status symbols, but as most immigrants have very low incomes the economic base on which polygamy is built in West Africa is generally lacking; in many cases, instead of symbolizing wealth children serve to compensate for poverty.

In the highly charged atmosphere surrounding the public debate over immigration, polygamous families have attracted the ire of French politicians. In a speech in 1991, for example, Jacques Chirac, Mayor of Paris, former Prime Minister and future President of the Republic, attacked alleged financial abuses by polygamous immigrant families and voiced his sympathy with those who disliked the 'noise and smell' associated with such families (*Le Monde*, 21 June 1991). At the height of the 2005 riots, Hélène Carrère d'Encausse, permanent secretary of the Académie Française, blamed the disturbances on polygamous immigrants from West Africa who, she said, were unable to control their teenage children (*Le Monde*, 17 Nov. 2005). Employment Minister Gérard Larcher made similar claims, though neither he nor Carrère d'Encausse offered any evidence to substantiate them. As Poiret and Guégan (1992: 8) observe, polygamous families have become one of the most emotive symbols incarnating French fears over immigration. Most polygamous men are poorly educated, unskilled Muslims with low incomes and large families who in some cases are housed in dense micro-concentrations. As such, they exemplify French fears of immigrants as culturally alien people 'taking over' parts of the country and abusing its laws.

While it would be foolish not to recognize the cultural clashes associated with multiple marriages and the very real material difficulties to which they give rise, it is likely that the living conditions experienced by polygamous families in France will in the long run serve to discourage this kind of kinship system. These conditions are almost invariably more stressful than those obtaining in Africa, where it is customary for each wife to have a separate home. In France, African immigrants have great difficulty in finding even one affordable home adequate for their needs, and it is rarely large enough to provide a separate room for each spouse. The daily stress of the overcrowding which results from this is frequently compounded by personal rivalries. Although it is often difficult for African women to organize independently of their husbands, the main associations which they have established in France have placed the reform or abolition of polygamy high on their agenda (Barou 1992b: 53–5; Poiret and Guégan 1992: 84–90). While their settlement is still at a relatively early stage, there is little, if any, evidence to suggest that second-generation Africans whose childhood has been spent in overcrowded and sometimes quarrelsome homes will be keen to perpetuate the polygamous practices of their parents. As French nationals, they will in any case be legally bound to monogamy.

Many parents nevertheless expect their children to retain at least some of the cultural codes inherited from the country of origin. One the most tangible marks of parental expectations is circumcision, a physical act of cultural initiation performed on children at an age when they are generally too young to control or in some cases even understand its significance. Male circumcision is practised throughout the Islamic world, as well as by Jews, and is perfectly lawful in France.

Female circumcision is less widespread, being confined principally to sub-Saharan Africa, and although the main countries where it is practised are predominantly Islamic, it is not part of the Islamic religion *per se*. Until the mid-1970s, when families from Mali and Senegal first began to emigrate in significant numbers, female circumcision was unheard of in France. According to Piet (1992: 190–2), the majority of adult women emigrating from these countries were circumcised during their childhood. With the growth of family settlement in France, many West Africans have arranged for their daughters to be circumcised there. Following the death of a 3-year-old girl on whom the operation was performed in 1982, court cases have been successfully brought against a number of parents charged with aiding in the mutilation of their daughters, and in 1991 a Malian woman hired by parents to circumcise girls was given a five-year prison sentence.

Perceptions of female circumcision vary widely, depending on the cultural context within which it is viewed. The equation of this practice with mutilation in French jurisprudence imputes to parents a malicious motive entirely at odds with their own view of the matter, for in their eyes the operation is designed to best prepare girls for adulthood. In their country of origin, uncircumcised girls would be severely handicapped in the matrimonial market. Some analysts argue that the customs on which this market is built are rooted in a project of male domination over female sexuality (M'Barga 1992: 170). Others point out that the practice is largely organized and carried out by women, and note that the associations of immigrant women campaigning against polygamy have been more reserved where female circumcision is concerned (Bourdin 1992: 182–5; Barou 1992b: 62–3). Against this, it is sometimes argued that women have been conditioned into serving as the agents of their own imprisonment within male-dominated cultures.

The extent to which individuals are free to construct their own values independently of the cultural codes which they inherit depends on a host of social and psychological variables. It is not always easy to know whether particular acts have been freely chosen, passively reproduced or grudgingly performed under psychological or even physical coercion. Girls brought up in France by Muslim parents are generally given very little personal freedom once they reach adolescence. Parents feel that their own status in the eyes of other Muslims depends on keeping their daughters insulated from any risk of pre-marital sex and on finding for them suitable husbands who share the Islamic faith. Young women placed in such a situation have very restricted opportunities for finding partners of their own choice, with little chance of their parents being prepared to accept a non-Muslim son-in-law. There have been press reports of girls running away from home to avoid arranged marriages (*Ouest-France*, 28 Nov. 1985; *Le Monde*, 11 Aug. 1988), and frequent claims that young women of Maghrebi origin have a higher suicide rate than their French-born peers (*Le Monde*, 17 March 1989; *L'Express*, 3 Nov. 1989), though there appear to be no wholly reliable statistics to confirm this. Runaways are often helped by support organizations run by women of immigrant origin who have first-hand experience of their problems (*Hommes et migrations* 1991a). In the face of high unemployment levels, unless they have access to networks of this kind capable of providing material support, many young people have little alternative but to remain in the family home, with marriage to an approved partner the only possible way out. In these circumstances, consent to a proposed partner may sometimes be perceived as the least undesirable available option rather than as a positive preference.

The distinction between acceptance of this kind and genuinely forced marriages is not always easy to draw. This has made it difficult for French courts to prevent or reverse marriages in which unproven doubts over the question of consent have been raised. A case in which court intervention succeeded involved a Moroccan girl brought up near Nancy, in north-eastern France, under the guardianship of an uncle after her parents were killed in a road accident. Shortly after her sixteenth birthday, she was taken to Morocco and married against her will to the uncle's son. Unusually, the girl was able to secure documentary proof of what had happened, so that when the newly weds returned to France she was able to obtain a court order quashing the marriage (*Le Monde*, 27 Oct. 1989). There is no way of knowing how many marriages are based more on coercion than consent, and in the absence of firm evidence it would be wrong to overgeneralize. There can be little doubt, however, that serious tensions exist in many Muslim families as a consequence of the acculturation of the younger generation. To address some of the problems arising from this, in 2006 the legal age of marriage for women in France was raised to 18, the same as for men; until then the marriage age for women (unlike men) had been 15.

In recent years there have been widely publicized cases of minority ethnic women being severely abused by young men of similar ethnic origins. A particularly horrific case was the death of 17-year-old Sohane Benziane, who was burnt alive on 4 October 2002 in the banlieue of Vitry-sur-Seine after refusing to submit to the sexual demands of her 19-year-old killer. The same year, Samira Bellil published an equally horrific first-hand account of gang rapes known as *tournantes* perpetrated by young men in the banlieues (Bellil and Stoquart 2002). It was against this background that, in 2003, young women activists from the banlieues organized a Marche des femmes des quartiers pour l'égalité et contre le ghetto (Urban Women's March for Equality and Against Ghettoes) and set up a pressure group called 'Ni putes ni soumises' (Neither sluts nor slaves) to campaign for the rights of women at risk of these and other forms of abuse (Amara and Zappi 2003). Media representations of these events suggesting that they were unique to certain ethnic groups appear to have been misleading, for documented cases of similar forms of abuse occurred more widely but were accorded less publicity (Mucchielli 2005). Nevertheless, the cases highlighted by Bellil and Amara in which young men, mainly of Maghrebi and Afro-Caribbean origin, abused women of similar origins, suggested that amid the worsening socio-economic conditions afflicting the banlieues, some were tempted to vent their frustrations on 'weaker' targets within those localities rather than confronting the wider social, economic and political forces in which the disadvantages of the banlieues were rooted.

3.4 Islam

Most immigrants of European origin, together with those originating in the Caribbean, come from countries with a long tradition of Christian, mainly Catholic, belief. About half of the immigrants from south of the Sahara are also estimated to be Christians. However, the vast majority of immigrants originating outside Europe come from predominantly Islamic countries. Smaller numbers adhere to a variety of other religions ranging from Judaism and Buddhism to Taoism and Confucianism (*Migrants-Formation* 1990; *Hommes et migrations* 1993). Research into the development of these faiths within France is very unevenly spread, and it is not possible in the space of this chapter fully to encompass them all. Instead, I shall focus on Islam, which merits particular attention for three main reasons.

One of these is numerical: while precise figures cannot be established with certainty, it is clear that Muslims now far outnumber adherents to other minority faiths in France, placing them second only to Catholics and well ahead of long-standing religious minorities such as Protestants and Jews. Second, unlike other religious minorities, Muslims have in recent years been involved in a number of major disputes concerning their rights within France. Third, these clashes have taken place at a time when Islam has become a much more potent force in international politics than any of the other faiths associated with recent migratory inflows. All these elements, which have become frequent reference points in domestic politics, have combined to induce fears among the majority population that Islam represents a serious threat to social stability in France.

These fears – reflected in a 1992 opinion poll in which two out of three interviewees said they were frightened by the development of Islam in France (SOFRES 1993: 233) – are in my view largely unfounded. The analysis which follows will show that, in at least three respects, the challenge posed by Islam to the existing structures of French society has been greatly exaggerated. In the first place, there is ample evidence to show that religious belief and observance are far weaker among the descendants of immigrants than among first-generation Muslims in France. Secondly, the organizational structures of the Islamic population are seldom aimed at disturbing the established social order and most of them are in any case too weak to present a significant threat even if their leaders were so inclined. Finally, we shall see that even the most widely publicized confrontations over the status of Islam have never mobilized more than a tiny minority of Muslims in France.

Religious beliefs and practices

As there is no census question on religious beliefs, the number of Muslims in France is not known with certainty. In the 1980s, the most commonly cited estimates were around three million; today they are between four and six million. Typically, estimates have been arrived at by totaling up the foreign residents who are nationals of predominantly Islamic countries, and then adding the estimated number of French nationals descended from them (a figure of at least a million is commonly used) together with the half million or so *harkis* and their descendants and 30,000 or more native French converts to Islam (Kepel 1987: 12–13; Leveau 1988: 108–10; Nielsen 1992: 10–11; Boyer 1998). Using a variant of this methodology based on data not previously made available by the French census authorities, Tribalat (2004b) has estimated that the total number of people in France 'liable to be Muslim' by virtue of their country of origin as immigrants, or by filiation as the descendants of immigrants from predominantly Muslim countries, is about 3.7 million. If an estimate is included for French converts, the total is around four million. Maghrebis account for about four-fifths of the total, with sub-Saharan Africans and Turks making up most of the rest. This sort of calculation is open to many criticisms (Kepel 1987: 13–16; Étienne 1989: 51–3, 89–100; Tribalat 2004a: 21–5). While it is safe to assume that the overwhelming majority of immigrants from mainly Muslim countries are of the Islamic faith, there are certainly exceptions to this. Far more questionable is the assumption that all their descendants share their faith. In numerous surveys, between a fifth and a third of young people from Muslim backgrounds regularly say they are not Islamic believers, and many of the others profess only a weak allegiance to the religion of their parents (Hargreaves and Stenhouse 1991).

The inter-generational erosion of Islam can be illustrated by examining data from surveys conducted in 1988–9 among the population of Algerian origin in the northern town of Roubaix (Table 3.3). The data cover over 1,000 interviewees, of whom the majority were *harkis* and their descendants, while the remainder were economic migrants or their descendants questioned in exit polls conducted during the presidential elections of 1988. The *harkis* and their descendants are all French nationals, and as the remainder of those questioned were interviewed after

Table 3.3 Islamic beliefs and practices among French residents of Algerian origin in Roubaix, 1988–9

	Age <26	Age 26–30	Age 31–40	Age 41–50	Age >50
Harkis and their descendants					
Prayers and Ramadan	4	8	12	61	90
Ramadan only	44	20	27	11	10
Neither, but considers self Muslim	26	47	38	28	0
Other	26	25	23	0	0
Other French nationals of Algerian origin					
Prayers and Ramadan	3	10	13	75	–
Ramadan only	42	10	25	0	–
Neither, but considers self Muslim	33	60	25	25	–
Other	22	20	37	0	–

Source: Souida 1990: 62.

participating in French elections, they too necessarily held French citizenship. This makes the sample in some ways untypical of the population of Algerian origin as a whole, for while most of the children of economic migrants automatically acquire French citizenship, the majority of their parents remain Algerian nationals. The absence of any data on 'Other [i.e. non-*harki*] French nationals of Algerian origin' over the age of 51 reflects the fact no person in that category voted, or any rate none was interviewed, in the polling stations where the exit polls were conducted. However, it is not unreasonable to suppose that, like their *harki* counterparts, Algerian economic migrants of that age are all Muslim believers. Among all the other age groups, there are close parallels between the *harki* population and the rest of the sample, and the overall trend is unmistakably towards a much weaker attachment to Islam among the younger generations.

Perhaps the most striking feature is the number of responses corresponding to the category which the survey designers diplomatically labeled 'Other'. As implicitly defined in the context of the alternatives, 'Other' means that the respondent does not consider himself or herself to be a Muslim. While there were no responses of this kind among interviewees over the age of 40, about a quarter of younger respondents replied in this way. A large majority of older respondents said they prayed regularly and fasted during Ramadan. Very few of those aged below 41 prayed. While almost half of those below the age of 25 said they observed Ramadan, it is likely that a large proportion of them were still living in the parental home, where there may have been no practical alternative to following the dietary customs of their parents. Ramadan was observed by far fewer of those aged between 26 and 40, many of whom were likely to have set up their own homes.

Despite their low rates of religious observance, the majority of younger interviewees nevertheless described themselves as Muslims. Other surveys, such as that of Gonzales-Quijano (1988), have shown that young people brought up by Muslim immigrants know very little about Islamic doctrines and often take a negative view of the dietary, sexual and other restrictions associated with it, yet most continue to say they are Muslims. In its most extreme form, the coexistence of affective identification with doctrinal detachment is summed up in a remark uttered by more than one young 'Muslim': 'I am a Muslim atheist' (Bourgeba-Dichy 1990: 634; *L'Express*, 17 Feb. 1994; cf. *Panoramiques* 1991: 109). This residual identification with Islam even among young people who consider themselves to be atheists reflects the fact that Islam is inextricably intertwined with their family roots. For many people brought up by Muslim immigrants, it would be impossible to break altogether with Islam without causing profound distress to their parents. Islam is in this sense a primordial attachment the denial of which is almost literally unthinkable. Yet this is not the same as saying that it is a primary source of values in the life projects of young Muslims. While young activists sometimes evoke their Islamic heritage as part of an anti-racist strategy, the promotion of religious doctrines or institutions seldom features among their objectives. As we shall see later in this chapter, they have been far more concerned to address social, political and economic injustices.

Organizational structures

The doctrinal ignorance of many youngsters brought up in Muslim families is a consequence of the very weak organizational infrastructure which has long characterized the Islamic population in France. Poorly educated and confined to low-income jobs, the vast majority of Muslim immigrants have lacked both the financial resources and organizational skills necessary for the effective reproduction of their Islamic heritage. In the mid-1970s, there were fewer than fifty places of Islamic worship in France. By the mid-1980s there were well over 1,000 (Kepel 1987: 229). This exponential growth has sometimes been taken as a sign of awesome power. In fact, it is first and foremost a reflection of the organizational weakness of Islam. Despite the fact that Muslims were to the fore in migratory inflows during much of the post-war period, they had very little organizational infrastructure until the mid-1970s, when a vigorous but late catching up process began. After a period of rapid growth during the 1980s, it has shown signs of leveling off (CNCDH 1993: 309).

While these organizational developments provide the basis for an enduring Islamic presence in France, they remain limited in their resource base and outreach. Very few of the places of Islamic worship established during the last thirty years are purpose-built mosques complete with minarets; most are simply a room set aside for prayers in an apartment block or hostel for immigrant workers. The main beneficiaries of these initiatives have been immigrants who were initiated into Islam before leaving their countries of origin. Their descendants have remained to a large extent beyond the reach of organized religion, despite growing attempts to draw them into its orbit. Raised in France by parents who, by virtue of their illiteracy, have been unable to offer any formal instruction or even direct access to the Koran, most of the children of Muslim immigrants have little more than a rudimentary knowledge of Islamic values and practices. In a survey of people attending mosques in Marseilles in the late 1980s, Cesari (1989: 64) found that no more than 15 per cent were aged below 36, despite the fact that this age group accounted in theory for roughly half of the three million believers then attributed to Islam across the country as a whole.

Despite the formal separation of church and state in France, Catholics continue to enjoy a privileged status. Public holidays are still built to a large extent around the Christian calendar, as is the timetable of state schools, which traditionally leave Wednesday afternoons free in order to permit the children of Catholics to attend catechism classes. Moreover, the state directly funds church-run schools in exchange for a commitment to cover the national syllabus laid down by the Ministry of Education alongside their confessional teachings. In the 1990s across France as a whole, 13 per cent of primary school children and 20 per cent of secondary school children were educated in state-funded private schools, 95 per cent of which were Catholic (Conseil Économique et Social 1994: 45). Today, while thousands of Catholic schools and hundreds of Jewish schools are funded by the Republic, there is not a single state-funded Islamic school in the whole of metropolitan France, though Muslims in France greatly outnumber

Jews. Islam has been similarly disadvantaged where the media are concerned. Until 1991, when its allocation was doubled to thirty minutes, Islam was given only a fifteen-minute slot in the sequence of religious programs broadcast on Sunday mornings by one of the state television channels; despite the fact that they were outnumbered by Muslims, Jews had an equal length of time, while Protestants had a longer slot, second only to that enjoyed by Catholics. While local radio stations run by and for Catholics, Protestants and Jews have been licensed in several cities, the authorities have been reluctant to allocate frequencies to stations which are specifically Islamic in character. Practically the only station of this kind, Radio-Orient in Paris, was hand-picked for its religious 'moderation', i.e. opposition to so-called Islamic 'fundamentalism' (*Le Point*, 6 March 1989; *Le Monde*, 13 Oct. 1994).

It is as normal for Muslims to wish to practise their religion with suitable organizational support as it is for Catholics or Jews. There is no incompatibility between the diversity of their beliefs and the fact that they all pay taxes to the same state and, if they are French citizens, vote in the same elections. Just as there is no reason to suppose that practising Catholics or Jews are *ipso facto* plotting with Rome or Jerusalem to overthrow the established social order in France, so it is unreasonable to impute a similar motive to Muslims who have links with outside countries. Because their own resources and skills are limited, many Muslim associations in France have depended on help from their home countries or oil-rich Islamic states such as Saudi Arabia, which have funded the construction of mosques and provided trained personnel. It was not until the early 1990s that the first training facilities for imams (Islamic prayer leaders) were established in France; until then, most associations had no practical alternative to relying on foreign-trained imams (*Migrations société* 1994).

After the first phase of the Islamic headscarf affair in 1989, discussed below, a clear policy commitment, shared by both left and right, emerged in favor of coopting organizations representing the Muslim population of France into a constructive dialog with the state. A key objective was to reduce foreign influences over Islamic organizations in France and weaken the potential for Islamic fundamentalism by fostering organizational structures which were compatible with the French code of *laïcité*. The French state had long recognized similar organizations as representatives of Catholics, Protestants and Jews (CNCDH 1992: 193–6). Organizations of this kind enjoy tax and other advantages, while serving as consultative channels between religious communities and the state and as authorized intermediaries in such matters as the admission of spiritual counsellors to hospitals, prisons and other public establishments as well as in the regulation of certain commercial activities (the preparation of ritually slaughtered meat, for example).[5]

The first government initiative aimed at establishing comparable channels of communication with Muslims was taken in 1990 by Socialist Interior Minister Pierre Joxe, who invited leading members of Islamic organizations to form a Conseil de Réflexion sur l'Avenir de l'Islam en France (Deliberative Council on the Future of Islam in France – CORIF). The CORIF was entrusted with the task of advising Joxe on how relations between the state and the Muslim population might best be organized. The hope was that a unified representative organization acceptable to the state, similar to those already recognized for other religious faiths, would emerge from these discussions. Dissensions between rival groups of Muslims prevented this outcome. Repeated initiatives by successive Interior Ministers in governments of both the left and the right in pursuit of the same goal also failed until 2003, when Nicolas Sarkozy succeeded in persuading France's main federations of Muslims to hold elections to a unified body called the Conseil Français du Culte Musulman (French Council for Islamic Worship – CFCM). Most of the General Assembly seats were divided between four main federations: the Union des Organisations Islamiques de France (UOIF), generally regarded as the most radically inclined of them, and three other federations dominated respectively by Muslims of Moroccan, Algerian and Turkish origin (*Le Monde*, 15 April 2003). Since then, the CFCM's operations have been marked by ongoing dissensions and rivalries, greatly limiting its ability to establish a common position on matters of mutual concern.

Islamism and terrorism

In their internal affairs, most states with predominantly Muslim populations blend principles based on Islamic law with more pragmatic elements, and they take the view that Muslims living as minorities in other countries should respect the laws prevailing there. A few states and a number of non-governmental Islamic organizations – the most notorious of which is Al-Qaida, responsible for the 9/11 attacks in the US – take a more fundamentalist line, arguing that Islamic law must be followed in every particular and imposed, if necessary by force, as widely as possible. The Iranian Revolution, which brought the Ayatollah Khomeiny to power in 1979, marked the onset of a more assertive Islamic dimension in international politics than had previously been apparent during the post-war period. It coincided with a sudden rise in the visibility of Muslims in France, who until the beginning of the 1980s had been seen merely as cogs in the chain of economic production ('immigrant workers') rather than as a settled communities with distinct cultural identities ('ethnic minorities') (Hames 1989).

Although these two developments were not directly linked, they became fused in the minds of many politicians and ordinary members of the public, who were inclined to draw a blanket equation between 'Muslims' and 'fundamentalists'. The confusion between Islam and extremism became all the easier when, in the 1980s, 'Islamism' (which could be readily misread for 'Islam') gained widespread currency as a synonym for 'fundamentalism'. Étienne (1987: 287), who conducted extensive fieldwork among Muslims in southern France, estimated that less than 1 per cent could be reasonably described as 'fundamentalists'. In 2004, the French intelligence services reported that Islamists controlled only a small minority of Islamic places of worship (*Le Figaro*, 8 Dec. 2004). The intelligence services blamed the 2005 riots on 'social exclusion' and found that Islamic organizations, whether moderate or militant, had played no role in the violence (*Le Parisien*, 7 Dec. 2005). Far from encouraging the disturbances, in statements made during the riots Islamic organizations consistently called for an end to the disorders.

Most Muslims have no desire to challenge France's existing legal order. From time to time, France has served as a place of asylum and/or terrorist activity for Muslims bent on political change in other countries. The Ayatollah Khomeiny lived in exile in France until his return to Iran in 1979. In 1986, pro-Iranian terrorists seeking to influence events in the Middle East staged a series of bomb attacks in Paris. They were aided by a handful of Maghrebis living in the Paris area but had no mass base among the immigrant population at large. During the 1990s, when the Front Islamique du Salut (FIS) was banned by the Algerian government, a bitter armed struggle waged in Algeria between the security forces and Islamist guerrilla groups such as the Groupe Islamique Armé (GIA). In 1995 the GIA attempted to put pressure on Paris, which was backing the Algerian government, by recruiting second-generation Algerians in France to conduct a bombing campaign there. Bombs planted by young recruits from the banlieues of Lyon killed ten and injured 130. The bombing campaign ended when the prime suspect in the attacks, 22-year-old Khaled Kelkal, was killed in a shoot-out with the police. Kelkal's apparent responsibility in the bombings, like the conviction in 2006 of Zacarias Moussaoui, a French citizen of Moroccan descent, for his part in preparations for the attacks of 11 September 2001 in the United States, was deeply disturbing. Yet it would be wrong to infer from these cases that the methods or objectives of such terrorists enjoy anything other than the most marginal levels of support among Muslims in France. The overwhelming majority of Algerians in France remained aloof from or positively hostile towards the FIS, whose political project had little if any relevance to their own daily concerns. According to a survey carried out in the autumn of 1994, only one in ten Muslims in France had a good opinion of the FIS and would like to see it in power in Algeria, while seven out of ten were hostile (*Le Monde*, 13 Oct. 1994). Similarly, Muslims questioned in an opinion survey conducted in France in the wake of the attacks of 9/11 were virtually unanimous in condemning such acts as contrary to Islamic values (IFOP survey in *Le Monde*, 5 Oct. 2001).

Shortly after the death of Khaled Kelkal in 1995, an interview was published in which, three years earlier, he had recounted to a German sociologist his childhood and adolescence in the Lyonnais banlieue of Vaulx-en-Velin. Describing the disturbances which had erupted on the streets of Vaulx-en-Velin in 1990, pitting minority ethnic youths against French police, Kelkal said:

> All those guys without jobs were trying to say: 'Stop! Think about us! You think everything's fine downtown, but take a look at what's happening in the *banlieues*: take a look at the poverty and the drugs.' … Why don't they give young people jobs so they can get on with their lives? People don't seem to understand anything until there are riots.
>
> (Kelkal 1995)

These words, spoken about events which took place fifteen years before the riots of 2005, are in the light of those later disturbances a sad reflection on the years of political neglect which helped to fuel the deep-seated frustration and despair in which the 2005 disorders were rooted. Kelkal's background typifies the difficult circumstances in which many second-generation Maghrebis grew up. The son of an immigrant worker who lost his job when Kelkal was in his late teens, his schooling was interrupted when he was arrested and imprisoned for theft. After serving his term, Kelkal was unable to find stable employment. Throughout his childhood and adolescence, he felt excluded and marginalized. It was in prison that he turned to Islam, guided by a Muslim cell-mate who helped him learn to read and write in Arabic. What Kelkal valued in Islam was above all a sense of community that had hitherto been denied to him. He now felt part of a universal Islamic brotherhood united by mutual respect and shared religious faith.

When interviewed in 1992, Kelkal had said that, having found inner peace in Islam, he felt there was no role for violence of the kind that had shaken the streets of Vaulx-en-Velin two years earlier. He died three years later with a revolver in his hand in a shoot-out with police who had found evidence of his involvement in the murderous 1995 bombing campaign, for which the GIA claimed responsibility. As Kelkal did not live to testify in court, the details of his apparent shift from Muslim pacifist to Islamist terrorist are unclear. A very clear pattern emerges, however, from the trials of other young Maghrebis involved in terrorist groups associated both with the 1995 bombings in France and with Islamist attacks carried out the previous year in Morocco. In both cases, young men from immigrant families disaffected by a seemingly endless cycle of disadvantage and discrimination in France were recruited by Algerian or Moroccan Islamists engaged in armed struggles against Maghrebi régimes judged to be the enemies of the true Islamic faith (Belaïd *et al.* 1996).

This was in many ways a strange partnership. The GIA handlers sent to France to organize the 1995 bombings had little interest in the problems of the banlieues. Their mission was to aid the Islamist insurgents in Algeria by bombing the French government into cutting off support for the Algerian military. The young men whom they recruited in the banlieues of Paris, Lyon and other cities had little first-hand knowledge of life in Algeria, and it was hard to see how a change of régime there could improve the lot of the Maghrebi diaspora in Europe. By throwing in their lot with insurgents seeking to build an Islamist régime on the other side of the Mediterranean, second-generation Maghrebis in the mold of Kelkal effectively signaled that they had abandoned any hope of finding a place for themselves within French society.

A similar dynamic appears to have been at work among a gang of heavily armed Maghrebis and young French converts to Islam who died in a shoot-out with the police in the northern town of Roubaix in the spring of 1996 after carrying out a series of violent robberies. Although propaganda issued by the FIS and its armed offshoot, the Armée Islamique du Salut (AIS), was found in the homes of the dead men, they did not appear to have been acting on the orders of those or other outside groups such as the GIA. Commenting on the Roubaix shoot-out, Interior Minister Jean-Louis Debré stated:

> The product of a radicalization of marginalized sections of society, a kind of revolt that was bound to express itself one way or another, violent acts of this kind are now clothed in the most assertive challenge to authority currently available in the 'ideological market': that of radical Islamism. … This conversion gives an international identity to people who are disconnected from both their roots and the host society. Hence the trend towards panislamism among this new generation of radicals: admirers of those fighting in Afghanistan, Bosnia or Chechnia, they are developing their own counter-culture, which is increasingly disconnected from the Algerian experience, on which they previously drew.
>   What comes through in this Islamic revival is less the religious dimension than its capacity for offering a framework for social protest.
>
>   (Debré 1996)

Despite this diagnosis, the accuracy of which has been confirmed by researchers such as Roy (2004: 143–6), the social marginalization to which Debré traced the violence of these young men went largely unaddressed, fueling the frustration to which, a decade later, the rioters of 2005 gave vent.

While similar in their causes, terrorist acts committed in the name of Islam are fundamentally different in their objectives and have involved much smaller numbers of young people of Muslim heritage than the kinds of street protests which reached their apogee in 2005. Like the rioters of 2005, most young people of Muslim heritage are far more intent on gaining social acceptance and equity within France than with pursuing a transnational Islamist agenda (Roy 2004: 143–6). Muslims in Europe are certainly an important battleground in the global agenda of radical Islamists (Kepel 2004). While those who fall under the spell of such movements can wreak terrible damage and destruction through acts of terrorism, the scale of that damage should not be misread as a sign of wider representativeness.

The headscarf affair

In the debate over Islam in France, no single issue has generated greater acrimony than the Islamic headscarf affair, which began in 1989 and then re-erupted in 1994 and again in 2003, culminating in a 2004 law banning the garment from French state schools. The long-running saga began when three Muslim girls were suspended from their state school in Creil, fifty kilometers (thirty miles) to the north of Paris, in October 1989 because their insistence on wearing headscarves was judged by the headmaster, Ernest Chenière, to be in contravention of French laws on *laïcité* (secularism), a term denoting the formal separation of the state from religious institutions. The teenage girls – two of whom were of Moroccan origin, the other being Tunisian – were wearing the headscarves in line with their understanding of

Islamic teachings on female dress. Chenière's decision was brought to the attention of the national media when an anti-racist organization, SOS-Racisme, appealed against it to the Minister of Education, Lionel Jospin, claiming that Chenière was breaking the law by victimizing the girls because of their religion. Another anti-racist organization, the Mouvement contre le racisme et pour l'amitié entre les peuples (MRAP), had already lodged a similar complaint with the education authorities in Creil. Over the next few months, the affair developed into a major political controversy, attracting saturation coverage in the media (ADRI 1990; Perotti and Thépaut 1990; Perotti and Toulat 1990; Siblot 1992).

When Jospin overturned Chenière's suspension order, his decision was likened by a group of leading intellectuals – among them Régis Debray and Alain Finkielkraut – to Munich (*Le Nouvel Observateur*, 2 Nov. 1989), a byword for the feckless appeasement of threatening foreign forces. At the Munich peace conference of 1938, Britain and France had given in to the expansionist demands of Nazi Germany; by implication, the Islamic bridgehead established by the three girls in Creil now represented a comparable threat to the future well-being of France. By December 1989, the controversy had enabled Jean-Marie Le Pen's anti-immigrant Front National (FN) to win a sweeping by-election victory in Dreux, fifty kilometers (thirty miles) to the west of Paris, forcing the Socialist government to rush through a series of institutional initiatives aimed at reassuring the public that immigrants and their descendants could be successfully 'integrated' into French society (see section 5.3).

In assessing the significance of the headscarf affair, it is important to correct two serious misconceptions about it. First, the confrontation in Chenière's school did not arise – as is often mistakenly thought (see, for instance, Fitzpatrick 1993: 121–2) – from a Muslim refusal to obey French law. Nor was it a rallying point uniting France's Muslim population against *laïcité*. As the following analysis will show, both these claims run counter to the empirical evidence.

Far from being caused by a challenge to French law, the Islamic headscarf affair was triggered by a particular interpretation of the law on the part of Headmaster Chenière which was found by the courts to be untenable. After overturning Chenière's decision, Jospin referred the matter to the Conseil d'État, France's highest administrative court, which ruled that the wearing of headscarves at school did not *per se* infringe the laws on *laïcité* (*Le Monde*, 29 Nov. 1989). By the same token, the Conseil d'État upheld the spirit of SOS-Racisme's complaint that it was Chenière (not his Muslim pupils) who had contravened the law, by discriminating against the girls on the grounds of their religion.

The core principles of *laïcité* were codified in the law of 1905 on the separation of churches and the state. At the heart of the 1905 law lies the protection of freedom of conscience. At the time, the Republic's law-makers were principally concerned to protect individuals from what they regarded as undue religious pressures from the Catholic Church, though the law was written in generic terms and as such applied to all religious denominations. In pursuit of their goal the 1905 law-makers prohibited the state and any of its representatives from giving any form of public support to particular religious beliefs. While the Republic continued to fund the maintenance of religious buildings, a key effect of the law was that the Catholic Church, by far the largest religious denomination in France, lost the right to teach its beliefs in the public educational system. At the same time, individuals were guaranteed the right to express any religious beliefs they might have provided these did not disturb *l'ordre public* (public order); among other things, this meant that they were not allowed to proselytize in public spaces, including public educational institutions, though (provided they were not agents of the state) they were allowed to express their opinions in such places.

It followed from this that when the law was applied, in state schools throughout France it was common practice to allow Catholics to wear crucifixes; similarly, Jewish boys were permitted to wear yarmulkas. Neither the expression of religious opinions nor the wearing of religious insignia was prohibited. What the law prohibited on the premises of state schools was *proselytism*, i.e. attempts to persuade others to accept particular religious or political opinions. Chenière and others claimed that the wearing of an Islamic headscarf constituted an act of proselytism, whereas the wearing of a crucifix or yarmulka did not. Acknowledging that religious insignia or items of dress might in certain circumstances be used for acts of proselytism – and hence put their wearers in breach of the law – the Conseil d'État ruled that it was only usage of that kind (not particular garments or insignia *per se*) that contravened the law. Subsequent jurisprudence arising from disputes in other schools similar to that in Creil confirmed that religious garments or insignia could not be banned as such, although schools had the right and indeed the duty to prevent their being used by teachers or pupils for the purpose of proselytizing.

In the autumn of 1994 François Bayrou, Education Minister in the center-right government appointed the previous year under the premiership of Edouard Balladur, nevertheless attempted to institute a tougher line by issuing a circular to headteachers asking them to ban 'ostentatious' signs of religious belief, which he equated with acts of proselytism or discrimination (*Le Monde*, 21 Sept. 1994). In a press interview, he made it clear that he intended the ban to apply to headscarves but not to yarmulkas or crucifixes, which he classified as unostentatious (*Le Point*, 10 Sept. 1994). Asked to rule on the matter, the Conseil d'État declared that there was no legal basis for declaring the wearing of the Islamic headscarf to be ostentatious or unlawful *per se* (*Le Monde*, 12 July 1995). By the same token, Bayrou's circular was rendered a dead letter.

Eight years later, opponents of the headscarf returned to the charge at the invitation of President Chirac, who was already on record as favoring a ban (*Le Monde*, 22 March 1995). In July 2003 Chirac set up a commission headed by a senior civil servant and long-time friend, Bernard Stasi, to review the workings of the 1905 law on *laïcité*. It was an open secret, widely trailed in the media for months, that what Chirac wanted was a recommendation from the commission in favor of new legislation banning the headscarf in state schools. While Chirac's objective in setting up the commission was well known, it was less clear why he chose to act against the headscarf at this particular time. As the number of girls wearing headscarves in state schools had never been large and was at it lowest for many years in 2003, it was difficult to see any particular urgency to legislate against them. Chirac's decision to proceed in this way appears to have been driven by a set of wider, loosely connected issues fueling fears of ethnic conflicts in which radical forms of Islam were seen as increasingly threatening forces. These included a sharp rise in recorded cases of anti-semitism in France – widely blamed on Arab minorities – since the beginning of the second Intifada in 2000 (CNCDH 2004: 31–69), a similar reported rise in ethnically marked forms of incivility and violence in schools in disadvantaged multi-ethnic neighborhoods (Brenner 2002) and a number of highly publicized attacks on minority ethnic women who in some cases were apparently targeted by young men of Muslim heritage for failing to wear Islamic headscarves (Amara and Zappi 2003), all of which helped to generate renewed public debate over the dangers of *communautarisme* (ethnic factionalism). Just as, in 1986, Chirac had championed a reform of French nationality laws as a means of apparently 'doing something' to address public concerns over immigration (see Chapter 4), so in 2003 he appears to have decided to act against the Islamic headscarf as a means of showing his determination to 'do something' against ethnic intolerance and conflict, especially where this was perceived to be generated by Muslims (Bowen 2006b). In both cases, while the targets against which he struck were full of political symbolism, they were in practical terms of doubtful value as solutions to the problems they were supposed to address.

When the Stasi Commission reported in December 2003, it included among its dozens of recommendations a proposal to ban from state schools the wearing of religious insignia deemed to be *ostensibles*[6] (Comité de Réflexion sur l'Application du Principe de Laïcité dans la République 2004). Ignoring the commission's other recommendations, Chirac immediately announced that legislation would be rushed through Parliament to ban the wearing of such insignia. The new law was promulgated in March 2004.

In announcing the new law, Chirac defined *signes ostensibles* (conspicuous signs) as 'those which lead to the wearer being immediately perceived and recognized by his or her religious affiliation'. The insignia to be banned included 'the Islamic veil, under whatever name,[7] the yarmulka, and manifestly over-sized crosses'. On the other hand, 'discreet insignia such as a cross, the star of David or the hand of Fatma' would be allowed (Chirac 2003). Chirac did not explain how the difference between a 'manifestly over-sized' cross and a 'discreet' crucifix would be measured. Nor did he give a direct justification for banning insignia branded as 'ostensibles' other than to claim that the wearing of them was against 'customs which have been reasonably and spontaneously respected over a long period in our society'. Chirac could not, of course, claim that wearing such insignia was unlawful for had that been the case there would be no need (as he saw it) for a new law. His claim that wearing insignia now described as 'ostensibles' ran counter to some long-established custom was untrue. The Jewish yarmulka – which was among the items now branded as 'ostensibles' and therefore unacceptable – had been worn, unchallenged, for decades in French state schools. In reality, the banning of the yarmulka was accidental collateral damage occasioned in the attack on the real target, the Islamic headscarf.

In seeking to hit that target without infringing constitutional and other legal constraints, the Stasi Commission had performed some elaborate verbal acrobatics. As a law explicitly banning only the Islamic headscarf would be unmistakably discriminatory, a more generally-worded proscription was needed. Members of the commission explained after the publication of their report that a general term such as 'visible' had been found not to fit the bill since a law banning all 'visible' religious insignia would run counter to the European Convention on Human Rights (Long and Weil 2004). Legislating more narrowly against insignia deemed to be 'ostentatoires' would also be unworkable since the Conseil d'État had already determined that the Islamic headscarf was not inherently 'ostentatoire'. At the last minute, a commission member proposed 'ostensible' as a way out of the dilemma and this word was duly adopted in the final report (Coroller 2004).

In neither the Stasi Commission's report, Chirac's speech, nor the preamble to the draft law presented to Parliament was any precise explanation given as to how the wearing of 'signes ostensibles' (conspicuous insignia) infringed the principle of *laïcité*. In other public statements, commission members most commonly claimed that the headscarf had to be banned from state schools because the wearing of it ran counter to the need to protect freedom of conscience, as guaranteed in Article 1 of the 1905 law (Long and Weil 2004). Banning religious insignia seems at face value a strange way of ensuring freedom of conscience. Commission members gave two reasons why, in their view, allowing the Islamic headscarf to be worn was incompatible with the protection of freedom of conscience: Muslim girls were being forced to wear the headscarf and the wearing of it constituted an unacceptable form of pressure on other girls to do the same. In presenting the legislation to Parliament, similar claims were made by Education Minister Luc Ferry (Assemblée Nationale, 20 Jan. 2004).

While citing anecdotal evidence of girls being forced to wear the headscarf against their will, neither the commission nor Chirac nor any member of the government adduced any quantitative data to support the notion that a significant proportion, let alone a majority, of girls dressing in this way were being coerced to do so. As for the notion that those who wore the headscarf were by the same token pressuring other students, this had already been dismissed as unfounded by the Conseil d'État. None of this mattered from a legal point of view since, by selecting the term 'ostensible' instead of 'ostentatoire' and making the wearing of garments thus qualified unlawful, the commission had conjured up a verbal way forward for legislation, for which neither convincing evidence nor a logical rationale was required.[8]

Just as it is possible that some girls are pressured into wearing the Islamic headscarf, so it is possible that other students are pressured by their parents to wear 'discreet' Christian crosses. There is plenty of evidence to suggest that many girls wearing headscarves have been doing so of their own volition (Gaspard and Khosrokhavar 1995; Keaton 2006); the same is no doubt true of many girls wearing crosses. The commission took the trouble to hear evidence in public from only two young women actually wearing headscarves, and one of its members stated openly that there was no point hearing from more of them since nothing they might have said would have changed the commission's thinking (Weil 2005: 70). In calling for a ban on the headscarf, commission members were apparently of the view that the need to protect unquantified numbers of girls from being forced to wear the garment entirely outweighed the rights of those wishing to wear it by choice. A law designed to protect young people from being forced to behave against their own will might more fairly have been directed against those pressurizing them rather than against the victims of such coercion. Similarly, had the law been intended to protect all victims of coercion it would logically have prohibited the forced wearing of any religious insignia, whether 'discreet' or 'ostensible'. The illogical relationship between the wording of the ban, with its pivotal focus on 'signes ostensibles', and the justifications given for it arose from the fact that the pressure to legislate was being driven by a single-minded determination to ban the headscarf which overrode all other considerations of evidence, logic or fairness.

Without even waiting for the Stasi Commission to report, Chirac declared in December 2003: 'In my view, for the French as they are, the wearing of the veil[9] is something aggressive which they find hard to accept' (*Le Monde*, 7 Dec. 2004) The wearing of a headscarf or a veil may be motivated by a variety of reasons such as religious piety, a sense of decorum or, perhaps, aggression towards others. It is extremely doubtful that most, let alone all, women wearing the headscarf in France are motivated by aggressive intentions. Yet for Chirac, what mattered was a mono-dimensional 'French' perception of the headscarf, as determined by him, not the diverse meanings attached to the garment by those wearing it. It was on the basis of that one-sided perception that he pushed through the anti-headscarf law.

Far from challenging the code of *laïcité*, as was often claimed, until the law was deliberately changed to place them outside it, girls wearing the headscarf had been behaving entirely lawfully. Equally misconceived is the impression, often given by the media (Tévanian 2005), that the headscarf affair was a rallying point uniting France's Muslim population against *laïcité*. Nothing could be further from the truth. This was not simply because, until 2004, the wearing of an Islamic headscarf was entirely compatible with French law. More generally, numerous surveys have shown that the overwhelming majority of Muslims in France support the principle of *laïcité* and believe their religion is entirely compatible with the laws of the Republic (see, for example, SOFRES survey in *Le Nouvel Observateur*, 15 Jan. 1998; IPSOS 2003a; Brouard and Tiberj 2005). No less significantly, the number of girls wearing the headscarf has always been small, and all the available evidence suggests that they are supported by only a minority of the Muslim population as a whole.

An IFOP opinion poll conducted among a sample of 516 Muslim interviewees at the height of the original affair found that only 30 per cent were in favor of allowing Islamic headscarves to be worn in state schools, compared with 45 per cent who opposed it (*Le Monde*, 30 Nov. 1989). In a similar survey five years later, the proportion of Muslims in favor of tolerating the headscarf at school had fallen to 22 per cent, while those against remained steady at 44 per cent; 31 per cent said they were indifferent, while 2 per cent made no reply (IFOP poll in *Le Monde*, 13 Oct. 1994). In a 2003 survey of 300 young women of Muslim heritage born in France, those in favor of an anti-headscarf law outnumbered those opposed (IFOP poll in *Elle*, 8 Dec. 2003). Although poll samples of this size can serve as only a rough guide to Muslim opinion in France, their broad findings are corroborated by a larger survey of adults of Maghrebi, sub-Saharan African and Turkish origin conducted in 2005, among whom a clear majority again supported the headscarf ban (Brouard and Tiberj 2005).

More generally, throughout the affair there was very limited Islamic mobilization in favor of the headscarf. In 1989, the organizations which first took up the case of the three girls in Creil – SOS-Racisme and the MRAP – were not Islamic associations at all. SOS-Racisme is a multi-ethnic youth organization which from its creation in 1984 until 1992 was presided over by Harlem Désir, whose mother (a native of Alsace) and Afro-Caribbean father (from the overseas département of Martinique) were both French Catholics. Like the older established MRAP, SOS-Racisme has always included anti-Semitism among the forms of racism targeted by its campaigns. These anti-racist movements were neither 'fundamentalist' nor even 'pro-Islamic', but simply opposed to unlawful discrimination against minorities, regardless of their creed or color.

After SOS-Racisme and the MRAP had taken the initiative, several Islamic organizations began mobilizing locally in favor of the Creil girls. Throughout the initial phase of the affair in 1989, the only attempt at a national demonstration by Muslims was a march through Paris on 22 October. It was organized by the Voix de l'Islam, a tiny pro-Iranian group, and the mainly Turkish Association Islamique en France (AIF). In all, out of the three million believers commonly attributed to Islam in France at that time, only 500 or 600 joined the march (*Le Monde*, 24 Oct. 1989; *Le Point*, 30 Oct. 1989).

This was a far cry from the 100,000 demonstrators who turned out in Paris at the end of the first nationwide March Against Racism, organized by young Maghrebis in 1983 (Bouamama 1994). Most of those who joined the headscarf demonstration were Turks. There was no significant involvement by Maghrebis, who accounted for the vast majority of Muslims in France, including the three girls in Creil. The most powerful organization representing mainly Maghrebi Muslims, the Algerian-dominated Grande Mosquée de Paris, refused to associate itself with the demonstration, while supporting the right of Muslim girls to wear headscarves if they wished (*Le Monde*, 21 and 24 Oct. 1989). This was hardly a subversive act. Exactly the same position was taken by both the Archbishop of Paris and the Chief Rabbi of Paris, who no doubt sensed that it would be morally and legally impossible to ban headscarves without also prohibiting crucifixes and yarmulkas. France-Plus, the foremost national organization of young Maghrebis, favored a complete ban on all religious insignia in state schools, including the headscarf (*Le Point*, 30 Oct. 1989). Vigorous opposition to the headscarf was also voiced by Djida Tazdaït, president of a leading provincial youth association, Jeunes Arabes de Lyon et sa Banlieue (JALB), and one of two women of Algerian origin elected as Members of the European Parliament earlier in 1989 (*L'Express*, 3 Nov. 1989).

When the anti-headscarf law was promulgated in March 2004, there was intense media speculation about the possibility of major demonstrations by Islamic organizations and campaigns of civil disobedience when the law took effect in the autumn of that year. In late August, a few days before the beginning of the new school year, an Islamist group in Iraq kidnapped two French journalists, demanding that in exchange for their release the French government must rescind the new law. As a mark of their solidarity with the French nation, all the major Islamic organizations in France reacted by immediately condemning the kidnappings and put an end to any talk of inciting Muslim girls to behave in defiance of the law (*Le Monde*, 31 Aug. 2004). When schools reopened in September there were only minor demonstrations and only around 600 girls attempted to defy the law, of whom all but about 200 gave in and removed their headscarves; 143 left to study in private schools, by distance learning or in other countries, while forty-seven were expelled from public education (*Le Monde*, 15 March and 11 Sept. 2005). By the autumn of 2005, only three girls were still defying the law (*Le Monde*, 30 Sept. 2005).

While the headscarf affair might appear at first sight to have favored the emergence of a form of ethnic politics in France (Feldblum 1993), on closer analysis one cannot but be struck by the minimal level of the political mobilization which it sparked among minority ethnocultural groups. Far from being a trial of strength pitting minority groups against the majority population, the controversy over the headscarf was first and foremost a Franco-French affair, i.e. a struggle between two different camps within the native population. It was they who generated most of the political heat and media coverage. Both camps, it should be noted, wanted to limit the influence of Islam; they differed less in their aim than in the means felt to be appropriate to that end (Beriss 1990; cf. Bowen 2006b). Chenière represented those who were determined to impose draconian controls on Islam; Jospin spoke for those who favored a less confrontational approach, arguing that if girls wearing headscarves were to be excluded from France's secular education system, this would be a certain recipe for pushing them back into an exclusively Islamic milieu (*Le Nouvel Observateur*, 26 Oct. 1989). This Franco-French battle was undoubtedly marked by the politicization of ethnocultural differences in the debate over ethnicized notions of Islam. However, those differences were of far greater significance in the minds of rival French actors than in motivating minority groups.

At the height of the original affair in 1989, Socialist Prime Minister Michel Rocard pointed out that while three girls in Creil and a handful elsewhere had aroused a storm of controversy because they insisted on wearing headscarves, some 350,000 other girls from Muslim families were attending state schools daily without raising any such problem (*Le Monde*, 21 Nov. 1989). The IFOP poll conducted at the same time confirmed that Muslims in France had understood and internalized the spirit of *laïcité*. Aware that religious convictions must not intrude unduly into the state educational system, a majority among those interviewed felt the headscarf should be kept out of school – a stricter interpretation of laïcité than was required by the letter of the law, as ruled on by the Conseil d'État.

The number of girls wearing headscarves in state schools has never been more than a very small proportion of those of Muslim heritage. Chenière, who was elected as a Member of Parliament in 1993, wearing the colors of the center-right Rassemblement pour la République (RPR), claimed in the autumn of that year that 700 girls were involved, while the Education Ministry put the figure at only a few dozen (*Le Monde*, 11 Nov. 1993). Pressure from Chenière and other right-wing MPs nevertheless led Bayrou to issue his ministerial circular in September 1994 aimed at excluding the headscarf from school. Early in October, Bayrou put the total number of schoolgirls wearing headscarves across the country as a whole at 1,143 (*Le Monde*, 12 Oct. 1994). Later, he stated that 2,000 girls had been wearing headscarves just before he issued his circular in September, and claimed that as a result of his action the figure had fallen to only 400 by December 1994. At the same time, uncorroborated estimates leaked to the press by the Interior Ministry put the total as high as 10,000 or even 15,000 (*Le Point*, 24 Nov. 1994; *Le Monde*, 26 Nov. and 20 Dec. 1994). Even if the highest of the Interior Ministry's figures were accurate, this would amount to at the most one in eight Muslim schoolgirls of secondary school age; on the highest estimate put forward by the Education Ministry, which was probably better informed than the Interior Ministry, it was less than one in sixty.[10] In the summer of 2003, shortly before Chirac set up the Stasi Commission to prepare the way for legislation against the headscarf, fewer than 200 girls were wearing the garment in state schools, according to the Ministry of Education (*Le Monde*, 17 June 2003). The necessity for a new law to deal with a 'problem' of that magnitude – in fact, perfectly lawful behavior – was far from self-evident.

Just as Chenière had stirred up the original confrontation in Creil by taking action of doubtful legal validity in 1989, so Bayrou's 1994 circular, subsequently invalidated by the Conseil d'État, led to a rash of confrontations in schools where girls refused to remove their headscarves. Similarly, there was an increase in the small number of girls wearing the headscarf when Chirac pushed through the 2004 law banning the garment from state schools. In 1994, as in the original affair, small groups of militant Muslims seized on the opportunity to demonstrate in support of those excluded from school because of the headscarf. Somewhat incongruously, they were joined in 1994 by French Trotskyists seeking to make their own political capital out of what they described as the discriminatory treatment being meted out to young Muslims (*Le Monde*, 6 Oct. 1994). Only very rarely did support groups form inside schools affected by these disputes. When twenty-four girls were threatened with exclusion from their high school in Mantes-la-Jolie, about 300 classmates demonstrated in sympathy with them. Significantly, they marched behind a banner bearing the republican motto 'Liberty, Equality, Fraternity' (*Le Monde*, 11 Oct. 1994). Similarly, while a number of militant Islamic groups attempted to make political capital out of the 2004 anti-headscarf law, Muslim girls demonstrating against the law made a point of dressing in the red-white-and-blue colors of the Republic; some wore the Phrygian bonnet of Marianne, the traditional personification of the Republic, while the 'Marseillaise' played from loudspeakers (*Le Monde*, 17 Jan. 2004). This kind of opposition to what they saw as the victimization of a religious minority hardly constituted an assault on the core values of French society.

It is clear that most Muslim immigrants and their descendants have adapted to the framework of law governing religious practices in France (Cesari 1998). Opinion surveys suggest that, compared with Muslims in other west European countries such as Britain, Germany and Spain, those in France identify particularly strongly with the society in which they have settled (Pew Research Center 2006). This is not the same as saying that a mechanical process of acculturation has led to the abandoning of their religious faith. Still less does it mean that they have been entirely assimilated into a pre-existing set of cultural norms. Rather, in the field of religion, as in other cultural spheres, immigrants and their descendants are forging new syntheses combining elements drawn from their pre-migratory heritage with a commitment to the overarching norms governing social intercourse in France.

3.5 Territorial belonging

'Home is where the heart is': like all folk-wisdom, this adage contains an important element of truth, while inevitably oversimplifying many complex realities. Importantly in the present context, it hints at a tension between primordial affects and instrumentalist calculations, for the maxim is implicitly framed by the unspoken assumption that while a person's 'real' home depends on emotional ties, his or her place of residence may be governed by other necessities. Still more fundamentally, it suggests that 'home' may not be a place at all, but a state of mind and/or set of relationships (Morley 2000). These tensions are exemplified in the complex processes of identification which characterize immigrants and their descendants. Most people retain deep emotional bonds with both the family into which they are born and the place where they are brought up. Immigrants who leave the land of their birth in the hope of securing better economic opportunities elsewhere usually expect to return, even if only when they retire, to the place of their primordial attachments. However, this apparently simple polarity between a place of affective origins and a place of instrumentally defined interests breaks down when immigrants begin to raise children.

While living in France, immigrant parents continue to speak of their country or village of origin as 'home', and encourage their children to think in the same terms. Yet the 'home country' of immigrants is not in any directly equivalent sense the 'home country' of children who are born and raised in France.[11] Their earliest affective ties are, of course, forged with the family. Through this, they are encouraged to identify with a distant place of which (in contrast with their parents) they may have little or no first-hand experience (Hargreaves 1995b). The topographical fact of the matter is that the family home is in France, and like all children, the descendants of immigrants feel deep affective ties not only with their family but also with the place where their earliest years are spent. As they move into adolescence and adulthood, the choices faced by the children of immigrants are therefore weighted very differently from the apparently simple polar opposites facing their parents.

Their affective ties with their parents' country of origin are real but seldom as strong as those which bind them to France. Often, their feelings of allegiance to the 'home country' have relatively little to sustain them beyond a sense of loyalty to their parents. As we have seen earlier in this chapter, in crucial cultural spheres such as language and religion, most of the descendants of immigrants lack the competence and/or the commitment necessary to function effectively within the 'home country'. During family holidays there, they are not uncommonly treated as outsiders by the local population. When they reach working age and are theoretically free to settle wherever they wish, very few seek to make a career in the country from which their parents originate. Not surprisingly, most of the immigrant-born youngsters deported to their 'home country' during the presidency of Giscard d'Estaing subsequently sought to re-enter France (Lefort and Néry 1985).

To the extent that their ties with France outweigh those with the 'home country', the descendants of immigrants also complicate the seemingly simple position of their parents. If their own children wish to remain in France, the equation initially drawn by immigrants between the land of their birth and that of the family breaks down. By the same token, the balance of affective and instrumental calculations becomes more complicated than it first appeared.

This mental shift within the older generation is reflected in a number of indicators. Monetary transfers to their home country are one such sign. Immigrant workers without families in France usually send money regularly to the home country, often to support not only members of their immediate family but also a wider village community or network of kinspeople. When family settlement develops, monetary transfers may still continue, particularly if immigrants are planning to retire to a new home in their country of origin built with the aid of their savings. Monetary flows are difficult to calculate with precision, partly because many different methods of transfer may be used, ranging from salary deductions by employers to cash in hand or payments in kind. It is nevertheless clear that while variations in political and economic circumstances are sometimes significant, the dominant trend is for monetary transfers to decline as family settlement lengthens (Garson and Tapinos 1981; Salgues 1988). Thus sub-Saharan Africans, whose settlement was relatively recent, were making substantial transfers in the 1990s (Barou 1992a: 32–3), while remittances by Algerians were very much lower after a longer period of settlement.

A second indicator of the deepening roots of immigrants within the receiving society is the lack of success of government schemes aimed at inducing them to leave. Between 1977 and 1981, when immigrant workers were under strong pressure to leave, fewer than 100,000 people (including dependants) benefited from the first scheme of this kind. By 1992, the total had risen to about 215,000 (Lebon 1993: 109). Although dependants account for the majority of this figure, it should be noted that immigrant workers unaccompanied by family members heavily outnumber those returning as part of a family unit. Between 1984 and 1992, for example, only about a third of the foreign workers repatriated with government aid were accompanied by dependants. Immigrant parents know that most of their children would find it very difficult to resettle in the 'home country'; hence the relatively small numbers of family units 'returning' there.

For young people born and brought up in France, resettlement in the 'home country' would not in fact be a 'return' at all, but an act of emigration tearing them away from their deepest roots. Because few among these younger generations are inclined to leave the country where they were raised – in Tribalat's MGIS survey only one in five second-generation Portuguese and one in ten second-generation Algerians said they had considered going to live in their parents' country of origin (Tribalat 1996: 139–40) – most immigrants wishing to remain close to their children find themselves facing the prospect of remaining permanently in France even after their retirement. The myth of return is thus pushed to its ultimate point and beyond: only after death, with a burial place in the land of their birth, will many immigrants finally accomplish the return journey of which they have dreamt since their initial departure (Chaïb 1994).

Despite being more or less permanently resident in France, immigrants are often reluctant to take French nationality. In some cases there are important practical reasons for this. Many states refuse to recognize dual nationality, forcing immigrants to renounce their citizenship rights in their country of origin if they take the nationality of the country in which they have settled. For citizens of countries such as Turkey, this means forfeiting inheritance and other rights. Affective ties with the country of origin also weigh against a change of nationality, for the symbolic status of such a step fits ill with the myth of return. Ideological factors may also play a part, for no territory can be entirely separated from the political complexion of the state which exercises sovereignty over it. In the eyes of many Algerians, for example, the ideological legacy associated with the founding myths of Algerian statehood render the taking of French nationality almost literally unthinkable (Sayad 1987).

As a general rule, the rate of naturalization among immigrants increases with the length of settlement, but there are marked differences between different national groups (Table 3.4). Among Europeans, the correlation between naturalization rates and length of settlement is fairly constant. Mass migration from Poland ceased several decades ago. Most immigrants from that country are now aged 60 or over, and more than two-thirds have acquired French nationality. At the opposite end of the scale, only a fifth of Portuguese immigrants, whose age profile is much younger, have acquired French nationality. Compared with Moroccans and Tunisians, Algerians have been slower to take French nationality, no doubt because of the bloodier conditions in which Algeria gained independence compared with the neighboring Maghrebi states.

The ideological legacy of colonization appears to weigh less heavily on immigrants from former French sub-Saharan Africa, less than 6 per cent of whom are aged over 60; already, more than a third have taken French nationality. Immigrants from former French Indochina have exceptionally high naturalization rates. In part, this reflects the fact that a large proportion of them are refugees who feel no allegiance to the state as presently constituted in their country of origin, making a return even more mythical than it is for many economic migrants.

Until the 1993 reform of the French nationality code, most children born in France to immigrant parents automatically became French nationals on reaching

Table 3.4 Proportion of immigrants having acquired French nationality by selected national origins, 1999

Current or previous nationality	% of immigrants now French nationals	% of immigrants aged >60
European	39.9	36.5
Spanish	54.5	51.8
Italian	55.3	59.6
Portuguese	20.3	14.6
Polish	69.4	58.6
Algerian	27.2	23.6
Moroccan	25.6	11.4
Tunisian	40.1	23.2
Other African	35.4	5.6
Ex-French Indochina	68.5	15.4
Turkish	15.2	7.6

Source: INSEE 2002a: tables N2, P2, P2B.

the age of majority. In principle, they were free to decline French citizenship, but very few actually did so (Catani and Palidda 1989). The position of children born to Algerian immigrants was rather different, and remained largely untouched by the 1993 reform. Those born before Algerian independence in 1962 held French nationality until then, but lost it that year unless they or their parents specifically requested to keep it. They can, if they wish, resume French citizenship, and some have exercised this right. Somewhat paradoxically, children born to Algerian immigrants since independence are automatically French from birth. At the same time, however, they are considered by the Algerian state to be Algerian nationals. This is because the nationalists who successfully fought to obtain Algerian independence refused to acknowledge the legitimacy of French sovereignty during the colonial period. As Algerian nationality law is based on *jus sanguinis*, Algerian nationals automatically pass on citizenship to their descendants, regardless of where these are born. Children born to Algerian immigrants in France since 1962 are therefore *de facto* bi-nationals from birth, for both the French and Algerian authorities regard them as citizens of their respective states (Costa-Lascoux 1983).

Because of the bitter legacy of the war of independence (Stora 1991), the nationality status of these youngsters became a matter of acute sensitivity on all sides. Almost three million Frenchmen fought in the Algerian war, leaving deep scars of suspicion and resentment towards those of Algerian origin who now live in France. The automatic acquisition of French citizenship by children whose parents supported the nationalist cause was considered by a significant part of the majority population to be unacceptable. According to the official Algerian version of events, a million Algerians died during the war (a lower but still fearsome figure is given by most historians). Their sacrifice made the tenure of French citizenship by modern-day Algerians an equally unacceptable proposition in the eyes of those with first-hand memories of the war.

The conflicting claims of France and Algeria concerning the descendants of immigrants were nowhere more sensitive than in the matter of military service, which is often regarded as the most potent symbol of national allegiance. When they began to reach their late teens at the end of the 1970s, young men born to Algerian immigrant parents after 1962 found that, as nationals of two states, they were called upon to do military service in both France and Algeria. Failure to fulfil this duty rendered them liable to imprisonment, as some discovered to their cost when they visited Algeria after ignoring or never receiving their call-up papers. In 1983, France and Algeria signed an agreement under which military service performed in one country enabled the young men concerned (though still not formally recognized by Algeria as bi-nationals) to be dispensed from being drafted by the other (Babadji 1992). According to a French Defence Ministry report issued in 1990, at the most three in ten Franco-Algerian bi-nationals were reporting for duty in Algeria; the rest chose to serve in France (Biville 1990; Faivre 1990: 33).[12]

Bearing in mind the symbolic significance of military service in the eyes of immigrant parents, and the psychological pressure often brought to bear on their children as a consequence of this, the high proportion of Franco-Algerian bi-nationals opting for France was quite striking. It should not be assumed, however, that military service had the same symbolic status in the eyes of the younger generation. For many, it was simply a legal obligation, like paying taxes or carrying an identity card; for practical purposes, it was necessary to comply in order to enjoy the benefits of citizenship, but that is not the same as saying that draftees automatically felt patriotic. The high proportion opting for France may simply have been a reflection of the greater practical difficulties associated with Algeria, where military service was longer, material conditions poorer and the prevailing cultural codes less familiar.

Opponents of *jus soli* often argued that it allowed the descendants of immigrants to enjoy the benefits of citizenship without feeling a true allegiance to the French state. Fears of an 'enemy within' reached a paroxysm during the Gulf War of 1991, when France joined the mainly western coalition against Iraq's occupation of Kuwait. Even allowing for the fact that a sizeable proportion of Maghrebi immigrants are Berbers, France has by far the largest Arab population of any country in western Europe. During the early stages of the war, the French media engaged in near-hysterical speculation over the possibility of immigrants and their descendants serving as a Fifth Column in support of Saddam Hussein (Hargreaves and Stenhouse 1992; Rachedi 1994). On the day the allied coalition forces launched their air attack against the Iraqis, *Le Monde* (17 Jan. 1991), France's most respected newspaper, reported that 'four out of five Beurs are thought to be admirers to a greater or lesser extent of Saddam Hussein'. In an opinion poll conducted a fortnight into the war, 70 per cent of French interviewees said they thought it likely there would be serious incidents involving the country's Muslim population (SOFRES 1992: 138). It was widely feared that there might be fighting between France's Arab and Jewish populations. In the event, no such disorders occurred, and when public opinion polls were conducted among the Muslim population they found that only one in five (exactly the opposite of the ratio claimed by *Le Monde*) backed Saddam Hussein; two out of three said they were opposed to his policies (SOFRES poll in *L'Express*, 8 Feb. 1991; cf. IFOP poll in *Le Figaro*, 29 Jan. 1991).

No less remarkably, in a poll conducted among young Maghrebis almost three years later, two-thirds said that if France came under military attack, they would be willing to defend the country (SOFRES poll in *Le Nouvel Observateur*, 2 Dec. 1993). Only one in five – a proportion similar to that opting for the draft in Algeria and expressing support for Saddam Hussein – said they would refuse to defend France. As the poll did not include a parallel sample of young people of French descent, no direct comparison can be made, but it is by no means impossible that a significant number of them, too, would have reservations about military engagement.

Nation-states can no longer claim to exercise a monopoly of rights over the territorial identification of their citizens. That monopoly was never complete, and it is being steadily eroded by powerful transnational forces, of which international migration is but one example. At the same time, local particularisms are reasserting themselves in new ways. These sub- and transnational currents are vividly combined in the gang cultures which have blossomed among youths of immigrant origin in the banlieues of many French cities. Modern urban spaces have long been marked by gang-style assertions of local territorial control by young men (women are less commonly involved) experiencing difficulty in establishing a secure place in the socio-economic hierarchy. A newer element in France is the prominence of young men from immigrant families displaying highly visible markers of ethnic differentiation. Most come from ethnicized groups suffering high levels of discrimination and socio-economic exclusion: above all, Maghrebis, sub-Saharan Africans and DOM-TOMiens.

Gangs are not necessarily criminally oriented. While some commit violent acts, many infringe no laws more serious than those prohibiting excessive noise or the unauthorized painting of public buildings. Fire-arms, the scourge of American gang life, are comparatively rare in the French banlieues. Excluded from socio-economic incorporation by high levels of unemployment, gang members seek self-esteem and solidarity by reappropriating anonymous urban spaces at a neighborhood level. Their assertion of territorial control over parts of the banlieues may seem at first sight to confirm French fears of ghettoization. Yet such an interpretation is in many ways misguided. Gangs of this kind seldom recruit from a single ethnic group and they never mobilize more than a small minority of the population in a given area (Dubet 1987; Jazouli 1992: 139–50).

During the disorders which broke out in several French cities in 1990–1, police were occasionally given instructions to limit their presence and/or turn a blind eye to certain offences in order to reduce tension. This led to talk of 'no-go' areas beyond the control of the state emerging in certain banlieues, but the authorities were quick to reassert themselves, ensuring that no districts were closed to them

(*Le Monde*, 30 May, 18 June 1991). The dominant forms of territorial appropriation practised by most gangs are more symbolic in nature. They function visually (by marking territory with a type of graffiti known as 'tagging'), verbally (using particular forms of slang to establish linguistic in-groups) and musically (through loud performances of rap and other imported idioms) (Kokoreff 1991).

The lingua franca of all these groups is French. While their cultural codes also draw substantially on elements originating outside metropolitan France, in most cases these are only marginally related to the ancestral cultures of the regions in which gang-members' parents have their origins. Maghrebi gang-members, for example, speak little if any Arabic, know virtually nothing of Islam, and if they refer to their parents' religion at all they do so almost solely as a provocation, knowing that it causes consternation among the majority population (Roy 1991, 1994: 65). The transnational cultural codes on which these gangs draw most heavily originate in the Black Atlantic (Gilroy 1993), a cultural archipelago stretching from sub-Saharan Africa through the Caribbean and into the black ghettos of the United States; the Maghreb (where France's largest post-colonial minorities have their ancestral roots) offers certain parallels but is not directly part of this space.

In the 1980s, the most influential model for youth gangs of immigrant origin in France was the Zulu Nation, founded in New York in 1975 by the black American activist Africa Bambatta. Referring to themselves generically as Zulus, gangs in the banlieues chose American-English names such as Black Dragon, Criminal Action Force and Fight Boys (*Le Nouvel Observateur*, 9 Oct. 1990). They dressed in the stylized fashion of young black Americans, incorporated liberal doses of American English into their linguistic codes, and adapted the rhythms of rap into newly inflected forms of French. While physically confined to small localities within particular banlieues, in their signifying practices they were part of a global post-colonial culture. As Kokoreff (1991: 36) put it: 'The Zulus [in France] live in a world situated somewhere between Manhattan, Dakar and Saint-Denis [a northern Paris banlieue]'. There is here a certain kind of ethnicity. Gang-members share linguistic and other codes and identify with particular territories, both concrete and mythical. Gang cultures do not, however, represent a continuation of the cultural traditions imported by immigrants. They owe far more to the youth cultures of France and the Black Atlantic, with which they interface through the mass media (Roy 1993).

While only a minority of immigrant-born youths are gang members, there is among them a much wider identification with the transnational nexus at the heart of gang cultures. This does not necessarily imply hostility towards French cultural norms. Many youths of French descent have also assimilated elements of both black Atlantic and white American culture through the US-dominated mass media. Although not of French origin, these are now *de facto* parts of the culture of France. In identifying with them, young people of immigrant origin leave far behind the cultural heritage of their parents while not ostensibly melting into a specifically French cultural mold. These cultural cross-currents traverse the many rock bands formed by young musicians of immigrant origin (Moreira 1987). They are perhaps best summed up in the rendering of 'Douce

France' (Sweet France) recorded by Carte de Séjour, one of the top bands formed by immigrant-born Maghrebis in the 1980s. The song, with its chorus 'Sweet France, my dear childhood home', was first made famous by the archetypal French crooner Charles Trenet. As re-recorded by Carte de Séjour in 1986, the words are sung with intermittent Arab tonalities over an American-inspired disco beat picked out in a combination of African and western instruments. There are many deliberate ironies in this, but also a deep underlying seriousness, for in the hearts of countless immigrant-born youths, France is indeed home, in the fullest sense of the word. This attachment was confirmed on a large scale by their reaction to the 1993 law requiring them to request French nationality instead of receiving it automatically. As noted in section 1.4, the vast majority of those affected by the law promptly requested French citizenship and after automaticity was retored in 1997 most opted to take citizenship early rather than waiting until the age of majority (Table 1.3).

3.6 Political mobilization

Because people of immigrant origin identify strongly with cultural codes which are not coterminous with French national boundaries, they are often mistrusted by members of the majority population, who suspect them of harboring projects of ethnic separatism. Pushed to their ultimate extreme, such projects might theoretically threaten the political integrity of the French state. Yet if we define political mobilization as collective actions designed to influence the constituent elements and decision-making machinery of the state, there is little evidence to suggest that minority ethnic groups are mobilizing in a separatist direction.

In an analysis of minority ethnic groups in Britain, Miles and Phizacklea (1977) usefully distinguish between three main modes of political mobilization: class unity, black unity and ethnic organization. Class unity brings together people of majority and minority origin in pursuit of common socio-economic interests. As understood at that time in Britain, 'black' unity signified the organizational coalescence of diverse minority ethnic groups (including Asians as well as Afro-Caribbeans) in pursuit of goals defined by their shared minority status. In the present context, it might better be termed minority ethnic unity. Ethnic organization, by contrast, is characterized by separate forms of mobilization on the part of each minority group. Applying this typology to France, we shall see that no single form of mobilization dominates.

Ethnic organization

As noted earlier in this chapter, there are many thousands of associations run by people of immigrant origin in France. The majority serve particular ethnocultural groups, rather than minority ethnic people as a whole. However, this is obviously not the same as saying that they are engaged in political separatism. Most exist to serve either the welfare needs or the cultural interests of particular groups. French nationals who give voluntary help to medical research charities or local drama societies or who are active in their local church are engaged in activities which are separate from and wholly compatible with any political activities which they might wish to pursue within the normal framework of the law. The same applies to immigrants and their descendants who set up advice centers, language classes or places of worship catering for members of particular ethnocultural groups.

Even supposing that a separatist project existed, few minority groups control an autonomous resource base sufficient to sustain it. As noted in Chapter 2, there are few if any cases of self-contained economic enclaves. Most minority groups are dependent on native employers and/or markets. Were it not for their ready access to the benefits of the welfare state, minority groups suffering from high rates of unemployment might perhaps have developed more extensive mutual support networks than those which actually exist. Yet even Schmitter Heisler (1986: 82), who has argued that groups of recent immigrant origin are unusually resistant to the processes of acculturation and assimilation, acknowledges that their inclusion in the system of material support afforded by the welfare state has to a large extent stunted the growth of autonomous financial institutions.

First-generation members of minority ethnic groups – particularly those who have come to France as political refugees – sometimes work for radical political change in their countries of origin. Expatriates from countries such as Portugal and Morocco have been allowed by their home country to elect Members of Parliament to represent them in the national legislature. Sending states pursuing such a policy have seen it as a means of retaining the loyalty of their citizens (Miller 1981: 30–82). Such activities have little direct bearing on French political life. As foreigners, most immigrants are excluded from electoral or governmental participation within France. Consultative mechanisms have been established by a number of local councils. In the 1980s, half a dozen towns allowed foreign residents to elect 'associate councillors', but the turn-out was often low, probably because those elected in this way had no voting rights within the city council (Centre des Cultures Méditerranéennes 1989: 167–227). The Maastricht Treaty, signed in 1992, gave citizens of European Union member states the right to vote in local and European (but not national) elections, but as the majority of foreign residents in France are from non-EU states, they remain wholly excluded from the electoral process.

This has suited sending states wishing to retain the active identification of their citizens. However, those states have found it virtually impossible to sustain a comparable grip on the descendants of immigrants. Until the early 1990s, for example, Algeria urged second-generation members of the expatriate population in France not to use the political rights which were theirs under the terms of French nationality laws, but this approach proved wholly ineffectual. By the second half of the 1980s, growing numbers of young Franco-Algerian bi-nationals were registering as voters and standing as candidates in French local elections. Realizing that they were acting completely independently of its own concerns, the Algerian government belatedly backtracked on its advice and encouraged the descendants of immigrants to exercise their rights as French citizens under the aegis of a newly created youth organization run by its long-established front organization in France, the Amicale des Algériens en Europe. The initiative failed almost completely, and the Amicale soon became a shadow of its former self (Hargreaves 1990).

France-Plus, the most powerful organization centered on second-generation Maghrebis, was founded in 1985. Unlike its arch-rival, SOS-Racisme, which seeks minority ethnic unity (see below), France-Plus was based on the principle of ethnic organization. Its primary purpose was to mobilize young Maghrebis as an electoral force, based on the citizenship rights enjoyed by the descendants of immigrants. France-Plus's potential power lay in the demographic importance of Maghrebis, who, if taken together, constitute the largest single minority ethnic group in France. In the run-up to the 1989 municipal elections, France-Plus fixed its sights on persuading the main parties to include Maghrebis in winnable positions on their lists of candidates. It proved quite successful in this, helping to secure the inclusion of about 1,000 Maghrebi candidates, several hundred of whom won seats on town councils (Hargreaves 1991: 362–4).

Research into candidate selection procedures suggests, however, that many of those put forward by France-Plus had little experience of grass-roots activism among the Maghrebi population (Geisser 1992; Poinsot 1993). Unlike the majority of Maghrebis, whose sympathies are heavily to the left, the candidates who won council seats were fairly evenly spread across the party lists of the left and right. There appear to have been no negotiations over the policy platforms of different parties: Maghrebis accepted as candidates simply fell in line with predefined manifestos (Bouamama 1989). France-Plus never pursued a distinctive ethnocultural agenda, such as the promotion of Islam. The organization's watchword was in fact 'integration' (*Être Français aujourd'hui et demain* 1988, vol. 1: 467–8), principally by the provision of better opportunities for Maghrebis who, as an ethnicized group, suffer severe discrimination and disadvantage. In socio-economic terms, those elected with the support of France-Plus were generally of higher status than the mass of Maghrebis. Their election as town councillors gave them additional status without necessarily bringing any tangible benefits to Maghrebis at large. In line with its own class interests as part of the upwardly mobile segment of Maghrebis, this small elite appeared to be moving steadily away from its supposed ethnic base (Cesari 1992). The urban disorders seen during the 1990s were widely interpreted as expressions of frustration by the most disadvantaged sections of that base, who felt that those in authority had abandoned them to chronic unemployment and poor housing (Begag 1991; Hargreaves 1996). Following financial irregularities including improper use of funds for the benefit of France-Plus leaders, the organization went bankrupt and was wound up in 1997 (*Le Monde*, 29 April 1997).

Until the mid-1990s, France-Plus had been by far the most prominent organization in France acting on behalf of a particular ethnic group. Since then, organizations based on ethnic groups other than Maghrebis, especially those of African and Caribbean descent, have come to the fore. The first to have a high-profile impact was the Collectif Égalité, a pressure group established in 1998 to press for more equitable representation of people of color in the French media. It scored a major coup by persuading the Conseil Supérieur de l'Audiovisuel (CSA), the regulatory body for radio and television broadcasting in France, to conduct a study of visible minorities on French television (see section 5.5). Although Collectif Égalité was in theory open to all minority ethnic groups, in practice its leadership was exclusively of African and Caribbean descent and it spoke most commonly of the need to improve the representation of *Noirs* (Blacks), which is not a label that Maghrebis identify with. In late November 2005, with the nationwide riots of that month still prominent in public debate, the 'Black' label was adopted with unprecedented clarity when the Conseil Représentatif des Associations Noires (Representative Council of Black Associations – CRAN), a federation of associations dedicated to the advancement of blacks in France, held its widely publicized inaugural meeting (*Le Monde*, 26 Nov. 2005). Denounced in some quarters as evidence of a dangerous current of *communautarisme*, the CRAN was supported by majority ethnic commentators such as sociologist Michel Wieviorka, who pointed out that, far from demanding special rights, the organization was campaigning for fair treatment of minorities who had long suffered from discrimination (*Libération*, 29 April 2006).

Yet it cannot be denied that recent years have seen an upsurge of activity by minority ethnic groups which, while understandably seeking to right past wrongs, has sometimes spilled over into narrow factionalism and in some cases racism. Ethnic Armenians, who in 2001 successfully campaigned to have France officially recognize the massacres of 1915 as 'genocide', and blacks, who the same year succeeded in having Parliament pass a law recognizing slavery as a 'crime against humanity', have been understandably concerned to have past evils recognized. But some members of minority ethnic groups have been tempted to engage in more dubious practices. The most sensitive of these have revolved around Jews (Wieviorka 2005). After the second Intifada began in the autumn of 2000, there was an upsurge of recorded anti-Semitic incidents, which for the first time since current data-keeping began exceeded recorded acts of racism against Maghrebis. Monthly figures for the Greater Paris (Île-de-France) region showed particularly sharp increases in anti-Semitic attacks at moments of acute crisis in the Middle East, such as the start of the second Intifada, the launching of Israel's Operation Defensive Shield against Palestinians suspected of terrorism and the US-led invasion of Iraq in 2003 (CNCDH 2004: 31–69). Anti-Semitic attacks took place in many places including high schools, synagogues and Jewish cemeteries. Simultaneously, there was a marked increase in the desecration of Muslim cemeteries. The upsurge in anti-Semitic attacks was frequently attributed to young Maghrebis who saw similarities between their marginalization in the banlieues and the fate of Palestinians under Israeli occupation. A government-commissioned report suggested, however, that Maghrebis may not have been predominant among the perpetrators of these acts, which were rooted rather in a French version of what the American anthropologist Oscar Lewis called the culture of poverty:

> The 'new' form of anti-Semitism thus appears to be more varied than is supposed by those who regard it as a peculiarly Maghrebi phenomenon

arising naturally from events in the Middle East. ... [Y]oung people of other ethnic origins (Africans, West Indians and even Franco-French) may, via a form of identity construction derived from the culture of poverty, come to identify with the Palestinian cause and even convert to Islam and engage in anti-Semitic attacks.

(Rufin 2004: 17)

Symptomatic of these tensions was the fact that when SOS-Racisme and an older anti-racism movement, the Ligue Internationale Contre le Racisme et l'Antisémitisme (LICRA), organized a demonstration in Paris against anti-Semitism in May 2004, two other long-established anti-racism movements, the Mouvement contre le Racisme et pour l'Amitié entre les Peuples (MRAP) and the Ligue des Droits de l'Homme (LDH), refused to participate on the grounds that singling out anti-Semitism from other forms of racism divided the anti-racist movement and favored *communautarisme* (Zappi 2004). Similarly, demonstrations in Paris and other French cities organized six months later by the MRAP and the LDH under the slogan 'Contre tous les racismes' (Against all forms of racism) were boycotted by SOS-Racisme and the LICRA, who claimed that some of the Islamic groups participating in the demonstration were anti-Semitic (Zappi 2004).

Commenting on these and related developments, *Le Monde* journalist Philippe Bernard wrote:

> This constant harping on yesterday's victims, combined with the instrumentalisation of the Israeli–Palestinian conflict, feeds a seemingly unstoppable chain: while a Jewish religious official compares the violent acts committed against synagogues in 2002 with *Kristallnacht* in Nazi Germany, certain anti-racist leaders cite colonial wounds and anti-Maghrebi racism to explain if not excuse aggressive acts by Beurs against Jews. Schoolchildren of African origin have been disrupting lessons about the extermination of the Jews in order to draw attention to the silence surrounding slavery. The situation became irredeemably confused when the humorist Dieudonné blamed the slave trade on the Jews and then claimed that he was being attacked for having criticized Israeli policies.
>
> (Bernard 2004)

The claims and counterclaims advanced in relation to the past are symptomatic of deep divisions among minority ethnic groups today. Many blacks clearly feel that they have been unfairly overshadowed by other ethnic groups, especially Maghrebis. Some among both the black and Maghrebi minorities are tempted to scapegoat Jews for the ills which afflict them. Racism of this kind is by no means predominant among minority ethnic activists but it casts an ugly element into the complex web of minority ethnic movements.

Minority ethnic unity

Attempts to unite all residents of immigrant origin in concerted political action are hampered not only by the lack of voting rights among non-citizens but also by deep differences between and indeed within different minority groups. These sometimes divide blacks against Maghrebis and/or against Jews. There is also a recurrent division between Europeans and non-Europeans. Why should Spanish or Italian immigrants share the concerns of Turks or other Muslims who feel moved to demonstrate over matters such as the headscarf affair? In its organizational structures, the Muslim population as a whole has itself been characterized by deep national and ideological divisions (Kepel 1987; Étienne 1989; Nielsen 1992: 18–19; Roy 1994: 57). Nationally defined ethnic groups such as the Turks or Vietnamese are also split by major ideological rifts (Gokalp 1992; Le Huu Khoa 1985).

The strongest bases on which to make common cause have proved to be anti-racism and mobilization against forced deportations. However, by no means all groups of immigrant origin feel equally threatened by racism or deportation. There is a wealth of evidence to show that Europeans now suffer comparatively little racism and those who are citizens of EU states face virtually no threat of deportation. The main victims are visible minorities, above all Maghrebis. Afro-Caribbeans and sub-Saharan Africans also suffer to a significant degree, whereas South-East Asians are less affected (see section 4.1 for further details). Since the beginning of the 1980s, young people of immigrant origin have led a series of anti-racist initiatives. The earliest of these was Rock Against Police, a series of concerts organized in 1980–1 (*Questions clefs* 1982). A nationwide March Against Racism in 1983 was followed by several similar demonstrations over the next few years (Jazouli 1986: 113–99). In the autumn of 1984, SOS-Racisme was launched. It quickly gained widespread media coverage by enrolling well-known figures from the world of entertainment in support of its anti-racist message (Désir 1985; Malik 1990). While young people of French descent have given support to some of these initiatives, particularly SOS-Racisme, relatively few of European immigrant origin have done so. Only a handful of young Asians joined the 1983 march and a similar one held the following year (Le Huu Khoa 1987: 78–81). Even young Afro-Caribbeans, who unquestionably suffer serious discrimination, have sometimes hesitated to join in, for as French nationals they are reluctant to publicly associate themselves with what are seen as 'immigrant' initiatives (*Le Monde*, 11 Dec. 1991).

Theoretically broad anti-racist fronts have therefore mobilized in practice rather more narrow ethnic constituencies. Like Rock Against Police, the 1983 march was dominated by young Maghrebis. Though officially called the Marche pour l'égalité et contre le racisme (March Against Racism and for Equality), it was retitled by the media the Marche des Beurs (March of the Beurs). In the follow-up march, Convergence 84, conscious efforts were made to involve Asian, Portuguese and sub-Saharan African youths alongside Maghrebis (Rodrigues *et al.* 1985), but the demonstration was plagued by internal dissension and the overall turn-out was less than half that achieved by the 1983 march (Bouamama 1994).

SOS-Racisme has always emphasized its multi-ethnic membership, but it was hampered from the outset by deep suspicions on the part of Maghrebis, who felt it had unfairly taken the limelight off them and disliked its willingness to cooperate with Jewish anti-racists (Hargreaves 1991). All but one of its presidents have been of sub-Saharan African or Caribbean origin, the exception being Malek Boutih, a second-generation Algerian who led the organization between 1999 and 2003. By then, following the collapse of France-Plus, no organization centered specifically on Maghrebis had a national presence comparable to that of the multi-ethnic SOS-Racisme.

Two other types of multi-ethnic organizations have attained a significant degree of national attention. The first arose in connection with the *sans-papiers* movement, which emerged in the mid-1990s. The *sans-papiers* (i.e. undocumented migrants threatened with deportation because of their illegal status) were supported by many different organizations. Those in which the *sans-papiers* themselves were most directly involved coalesced in a number of collectives. While sub-Saharan Africans were initially to the fore, many other ethnic groups were also involved in these collectives, but their impact was often weakened by loose organizational ties (Simeant 1998; Rawlings 2004; Freedman 2004: 71–87).

More recently, a movement called Les Indigènes de la République (Natives, i.e. non-European subjects, of the Republic) was set up in January 2005 to advance the interests of post-colonial minorities, whose condition it compared with that of colonized 'natives' in France's former colonial empire (*Le Monde*, 17 March 2005; Nous sommes les Indigènes de la République, 19 January 2005). The movement is certainly multi-ethnic, involving Maghrebis alongside activists of African and Caribbean descent, but it is less universalist in outlook than SOS-Racisme, for its concerns are tightly focused on post-colonial minorities and some of its members appear more intent on exacerbating inter-ethnic conflicts than on healing past wounds. Tensions around attitudes towards 'whites' and other internal conflicts quickly led to splits in the movement, which appears very unlikely to seriously rival SOS-Racisme in terms of national profile and cross-party support.

Class unity

Opinion surveys and exit polls conducted among people of immigrant origin traditionally show very high levels of political support for the left, particularly the French Socialist Party (PS) (see, for example, the exit poll data in Leveau and Wihtol de Wenden 1991: 4–9, and the SOFRES polls in *L'Express*, 30 March 1990, and *Le Nouvel Observateur*, 13 May 1993). As minority ethnic groups are heavily concentrated at the lower end of the socio-economic hierarchy, these findings are not especially surprising, for most French voters of a similar socio-economic standing also favor the left. There are two notable exceptions to this pattern. The first concerns the *harkis*, who are much more conservative than economic migrants in their political loyalties; the children of both groups, however, display similar leftist sympathies, which suggests that their underlying class position outweighs the peculiar political heritage of the older generation (Souida 1990: 63). Asians are the other main exception. Among those expressing an opinion in the 1990 SOFRES survey, sympathies were evenly divided between the left and the right. Again, this is consistent with the higher levels of self-employment and entrepreneurship among people of Asian origin compared with the majority of immigrants.

Against the backdrop of the accelerating crisis in the banlieues and the perceived failure of the left to deliver improvements with sufficient speed, it was widely claimed that in the 2002 elections there had been a significant shift among minority ethnic voters towards the center-right (Gabizon 2002). While there may have been a small movement in that direction, a CSA exit poll conducted during the first round of the presidential elections found that 69 per cent of voters of Maghrebi and Turkish origin had voted for the left, compared with 42 per pent of voters as a whole (CSA 2002b). Similarly, in a survey of French citizens of voting age of Maghrebi, sub-Saharan African and Turkish origin conducted in 2005, three-quarters said they felt close to the left compared with only half of a representative sample of the French electorate as a whole (Brouard and Tiberj 2005).

The triumph of class interests over ethnic origins appears to be confirmed by the poor showing of candidates campaigning on minority ethnic tickets. Very few have succeeded in mobilizing even the financial resources necessary to stand as candidates. In the 1986 regional elections, for example, which were fought under a list system in each département, a slate of minority ethnic candidates was fielded in just one département, Val-de-Marne, where it took less than 0.5 per cent of the vote. In those elections, all the main parties had included for the first time a few candidates of Maghrebi origin on their lists. However, they were tiny in number and none was placed in a winnable position under the system of proportional representation used in those elections.

For young people of immigrant origin hoping to escape from the low socio-economic status to which most of their parents were confined, education is of pivotal importance. In the autumn of 1986 and again in 1990, nationwide demonstrations by high school and university students were marked by the very visible participation of immigrant-born activists alongside those of French descent (Bryson 1987; Mestiri 1988; Jazouli 1992: 151–2). On both occasions, the protests were against government policies which were felt to be disadvantaging poorer sections of the population, particularly in the banlieues, in the struggle for access to high-quality education. The headscarf affair prompted no comparable mobilization among the student population of immigrant origin. The handful of girls confronting school authorities on a matter of Islamic conviction were almost completely isolated; support groups organized by classmates were few and far between and tended to be motivated more by anti-discriminatory than by pro-Islamic sentiments. In early 2006 huge nationwide student demonstrations forced Prime Minister Dominique de Villepin to scrap a provision he had included in the Equal Opportunities Law of that year which made it easier for employers to fire young workers. The intention was to cut youth unemployment by reducing the reluctance of employers to give new workers a try. The theory was that if employers knew they could easily fire young recruits, they would be more willing to hire them. This wide-ranging provision, added by de Villepin to a law originally conceived in response to the more specific issues raised by the November 2005 riots in the banlieues, eliminated employment protection for all young people in France. It was met by opposition that was equally wide in scope. If majority ethnic students were to the fore, minority ethnic protestors also joined the demonstrations, in which socio-economic interests outweighed ethnic differences.

While it is clear that socio-economic interests and anti-racism have generally outweighed the promotion of ethnocultural differences in mobilizing people of immigrant origin, Ireland (1994: 76, 85) has correctly pointed out that the younger generation is often reluctant to identify with traditional working-class organizations such as the French Communist Party (PCF). During the 1990 student demonstrations, for example, SOS-Racisme and the Young Communists pursued similar objectives but through competing organizational structures. In the 2004 regional elections, the PCF took 14 per cent of the first-round vote in the département of Seine-Saint-Denis, which contains relatively dense concentrations of young minority ethnic voters, when it selected Algerian-born Mouloud Aounit, leader of the anti-racist MRAP, to lead its list of candidates. Two years earlier the party's majority ethnic leader, Robert Hue, had taken only 6 per cent of the Seine-Saint-Denis vote in the first round of the presidential elections (*Le Monde*, 20 April 2004). This suggests that while the PCF may not be a strong attraction *per se* to minority ethnic voters, its fortunes can be boosted by adopting minority ethnic candidates.

The PCF, like the PS, has often behaved in an ambivalent way towards post-colonial minorities, partly because working-class people of French descent have been far from immune to racism. The anti-immigrant Front National (FN) enjoys a high level of support among working-class voters. In the first round of the 2002 presidential elections, for example, 24 per cent of workers and 30 per cent of the unemployed voted for Jean-Marie Le Pen, far more than for any other candidate; the PCF's candidate, Robert Hue, was supported by only 4 per cent of working-class voters and 2 per cent of the unemployed (CSA 2002a) Thus while real or perceived class interests are certainly significant in shaping the political behavior of immigrants and their descendants, class unity between them and members of the majority population is far from assured (Tripier 1990; Gallissot *et al.* 1994).

The 2005 riots

Where in this classificatory system are we to situate the disturbances of 2005? Before attempting to answer this question, it is worth asking a more basic one: can those events, generally described in media and political discourse as 'riots', be regarded as a form of political mobilization? One of the most striking features of the disturbances was their lack of political leadership. No spokespeople emerged, no list of demands was put forward nor did any meetings or negotiations take place between rioters and police or politicians. Yet these were not in any sense aimless or unstructured acts of violence. They took the form of ritualized attacks on selected targets, notably automobiles – symbols of the social mobility denied to inhabitants of the banlieues – and police forces seen as representatives of an exclusionary and repressive social order. Deliberate and sustained acts of defiance *vis-à-vis* those in power, these were in a very real sense political acts.

While unprecedented in scale, the events of 2005 were not in any significant respect new. At a lower level of intensity, there had been similar disorders in the banlieues since the late 1970s. Periodic flare-ups occurred in Lyon, for example, in 1981, 1983 and 1990, and in Strasbourg, where in the 1990s it became customary for hundreds of automobiles to be burnt every New Year's Eve. Nationally, some 28,000 automobiles were torched in France in 2005 alone – and that was before the 10,000 burnt during the disorders which began in late October (*Le Monde*, 3 Nov. 2005). When, on 17 November, the National Police Directorate declared that the situation was back to 'normal', it did so on the grounds that 'only' ninety-eight cars had been torched the previous night – the routine daily average throughout the year (*Le Monde*, 17 Nov. 2005).

These were the acts of young men, mainly teenagers of minority ethnic origin, in stigmatized urban areas. Significantly, the spark which set the banlieues ablaze in the autumn of 2005 was a police identity check on a group of minority ethnic youths in Clichy-sous-Bois, on the north-eastern outskirts of Paris. Fearful of police harassment, the youths fled and three took refuge in an electricity substation. When two of them – of Mauritanian and Tunisian origin respectively – died there by accidental electrocution, many in the banlieues were quick to blame their deaths on aggressive policing and took to the streets to demonstrate their anger by torching cars and attacking police stations and other public buildings. To the extent that those committing these acts, like the youths who had fled the police in Clichy-sous-Bois, saw themselves as the victims of racial discrimination, there was an ethnic dimension to these events. They were in a very real sense reacting to their ethnicization by members of the majority ethnic population, in whose eyes they were an alien presence in France because of their origins in non-European, mainly Islamic, countries. Yet there was no evidence that they were pursuing an ethnocultural agenda such as the promotion of Islam or some claim to recognition as a distinct ethnic group. On the contrary, the rioters shared to a very large extent the secular aspirations and values dominant in French society. Their violent acts arose from anger over their exclusion from the benefits of that society because of socio-economic disadvantage and racial and ethnic discrimination.

Lacking anything that could be characterized as an ethnocultural agenda, the 2005 riots clearly cannot be classified as a form of ethnic organization except in a secondary sense. If they bore the marks of minority ethnic unity to the extent that young people of diverse ethnic backgrounds acted in concert to taunt the police and attract media attention through the torching of cars and public buildings, they were equally if not indeed more fundamentally characterized by the position of the rioters in the class structure of France. Those who took to the streets came primarily from the least well educated ranks of minority ethnic youths in the most severely disadvantaged neighborhoods in France, where they experienced acute marginalization in the labor market. Unlike their parents and older brothers, who had memories of full employment or at the very least hopes for its return, the rioters of 2005, born for the most part in the late 1980s and early 1990s, had lived all their lives in neighborhoods where chronic unemployment and widespread racial discrimination were the norm, with no apparent improvement on the horizon. Their systemic marginalization in the labor market was such it was not unreasonable to describe them, as did the sociologist Immanuel Wallerstein, as an 'underclass'. As Wallerstein observed, theirs was 'a rebellion against poverty, joblessness, racist behavior by the French police and, above all, lack of acceptance as the [French] citizens they mostly are' (Wallerstein 2005). Thus while there was unquestionably a significant ethnic dimension to the disorders, to the extent that they were a reaction against negative ethnicization, it is important to underscore that they were rooted no less deeply in profound socio-economic inequalities.

3.7 Conclusion

Events such as the headscarf affair and the 2005 riots have brought to the fore French anxieties over the social incorporation of people of recent immigrant origin. Physically visible in ways that earlier immigrants were not, post-colonial minorities are incapable of 'melting' anonymously into the social fabric. As most immigrants from former colonies come from predominantly Islamic countries and the coming of age of their descendants has coincided with a more strident political posture by Islamic states and non-governmental terrorist groups, it has been easy to assume that France is faced within her own borders by potentially explosive tensions generated by the presence of new ethnocultural minorities. In fact, all the evidence examined in this chapter points in a very different direction. While some immigrants do adhere to cultural codes which clash in certain respects with the prevailing norms in France, there is little evidence to suggest that clashes of this kind are being reproduced by succeeding generations. In the overwhelming majority of cases, the descendants of immigrants – whether they come from Europe, Africa or Asia – identify more closely with France's dominant cultural norms than with those of their parents.

This is not to say that minority ethnocultural norms cease to exert any influence at all or that the role models of immigrant-born citizens – any more than those of the majority population – are purely French. On a per capita basis, the Portuguese population is believed to have a denser network of voluntary associations than any other minority group in France (Wihtol de Wenden 1988: 364; Hily and Poinard 1987). This, together with the relatively generous provision of state support for mother tongue teaching and the geographical proximity of Portugal, which makes it easy for families to pay regular visits to the home country, has enabled the Portuguese to maintain closer cultural ties than many other groups of recent immigrant origin. There is no incompatibility between this and what is universally judged to be the successful incorporation of the Portuguese into French society. Their unemployment rates are lower than those of the native population, they are seldom the victims of racial discrimination and they are virtually invisible in contentious parts of the political arena.

The spatial distribution of minority groups in France is such that mono-ethnic neighborhoods are extremely rare and never at all extensive. The densest micro-concentrations are probably those of South-East Asians, particularly ethnic Chinese, in areas such as the Choisy Triangle. It is often said that the Chinese function as a more self-enclosed community than any other minority group. Yet South-East Asians – large numbers of whom are ethnic Chinese – have exceptionally high rates of naturalization, acquiring full citizenship after only a few years of residence. It is seldom suggested that there is any contradiction between the relatively high level of economic and cultural self-sufficiency sustained by the Chinese and their rapid admission to full rights within the political community of France.

Suspicions of separatism or malevolent intentions towards French norms are reserved primarily for Muslim immigrants and their descendants. As these groups are very much larger than those originating in South-East Asia, it is theoretically conceivable that dense concentrations might provide the basis for a significant separatist project. Concentrations of that kind do not exist. No less importantly, there is no evidence to indicate that a political project inimical to the integrity of the French state is seriously harbored by anything other than the tiniest of minorities. Far from being a serious attempt at severing their links with the rest of society, the challenge to police thrown down by young people involved in urban disorders is first and foremost a distress signal: by attracting the attention of the media, those concerned hope to force the authorities to redress the lack of opportunities open to ethnicized groups relegated to the banlieues (Hargreaves 1996).

Only one in five of the young Maghrebis questioned by SOFRES for *Le Nouvel Observateur* (2 Dec. 1993) said they felt closer to the culture of their parents than to that of the French. Seven out of ten said the opposite. Nine out of ten young people from Muslim families questioned in the survey by Muxel (1988: 928) expressed a strong desire to be integrated into French society, as did eight out of ten from Catholic immigrant backgrounds.

The highest rates of endogamy recorded in Tribalat's MGIS study were among Turkish immigrants, who also displayed many other indicators of relatively high levels of insulation from the majority ethnic population (Tribalat 1995: 222–3). These included low levels of linguistic competence in French, high levels of literacy in Turkish, low usage of French between Turkish immigrants and their children, low levels of social contact with majority ethnic neighbors, high rates of employment with co-ethnics and low rates of acquisition of French cizitenship (Tribalat 1995: 39, 43, 47, 123, 170, 199). On many but not all of these indicators, high levels of insulation were also recorded among Tribalat's Portuguese and South-East Asian samples. While relatively closed in upon themselves socially, South-East Asians (unlike Turks) had very high rates of naturalization. The Portuguese had low rates of naturalization, high levels of retention of the Portuguese language and high rates of employment with co-ethnics yet at the same time high rates of sociability with majority ethnic neighbors. On most of these measures, Algerians, Moroccans and Africans from south of the Sahara were far less insulated than Turks and South-East Asians (Tribalat 1995: 47, 124, 216). The large-scale Family

Survey based on data collected in 1999 found similar patterns (Lefèvre and Filhon 2005).

These findings clearly invalidate much-pedaled stereotypes according to which non-Europeans and more particularly Muslims have supposedly been characterized by peculiar rates of resistance to acculturation. The high positioning of the Portuguese on many indicators of close identification with co-ethnics cuts across the notion that there is a fundamental attitudinal or behavioral divide between Europeans (often thought to be less prone to ethnic insularity) and non-Europeans (supposedly more inclined to retain distinctive cultural markers and less inclined to mix with other groups). The high levels of insularity found among immigrant groups from former French South-East Asia, where Islam is virtually non-existent, is equally out of line with the idea that Islam generates peculiarly high levels of resistance to acculturation. Muslims in France have shown that in their overwhelming majority they are respectful of the French code of *laïcité* and committed to cultural adjustments facilitating their incorporation within the fabric of French society.

If young Maghrebis have been more assertive politically than young Europeans of immigrant origin, this is not because they are less acculturated, but because, on the contrary, they share to a very large extent the values and aspirations of their French peers but are denied a fair chance of fulfilling their ambitions as a consequence of social and economic discrimination by members of the majority population. The biggest obstacles to 'integration' have come not from the cultural heritage of recent immigrants and their descendants but from the barriers placed in their way by members of the majority ethnic population. These obstacles, which reached a symbolic peak in the reform of French nationality laws, are examined in the next chapter.

4   National identity, nationality and citizenship

4.1 Immigration and national identity

In the modern world, the most potent forms of ethnic identification have generally been those associated with nationhood. So powerful and omnipresent are the signs of national belonging that majority populations seldom refer to themselves as ethnic groups at all. National identity is apt to be seen as the 'natural' condition of the majority, while ethnic belonging is regarded as an exceptional condition ascribed only to minorities. When this assumption is made, as is commonly the case among policy-makers and social scientists in France, it tends to posit an opposition between ethnicity and national identity (see, for example, Héran 2004: 11). In reality, nations are simply ethnocultural groups which acquire or aspire to the legitimacy associated with statehood, i.e. political sovereignty over a territory whose boundaries are recognized in international law. The extent to which immigrants and their descendants are incorporated into nation-states depends not only on socio-economic processes of the kind examined in Chapter 2 together with the values and aspirations of minority ethnic groups, considered in Chapter 3, but also on the attitudes and behavior of the majority population both in civil society and at the level of the state. This chapter considers how far immigrants and their descendants are accepted, both formally and informally, as part of the French national community.

If individual members of the receiving society are hostile towards people of immigrant origin, this self-evidently makes their incorporation more difficult. Barriers of this kind are all the more potent if they have the backing of the state. Some of the ways in which the state discriminates against non-nationals are considered in section 5.4. After an analysis of mass attitudes towards minority groups, the main focus of the present chapter falls on the rules governing the formal dividing line between French nationals and foreigners. As generally understood today, French nationality is virtually synonymous with French citizenship, and the two expressions are used more or less interchangeably, though in the past they have often diverged (Borella 1991). Nationality, and the citizenship embedded in it, consists of a range of rights and duties which are reserved for those who are recognized in law as members of the nation-state. In a formal sense, citizenship is associated particularly with political rights. Broader concepts of citizenship, pioneered by Marshall (1950), have now been stretched so wide that they sometimes embrace almost any form of social participation (Martiniello 1994). In the present context, citizenship is to be understood in the narrower sense of formal national membership, including the right to participate in the political processes through which the state is governed.

Nations have played and continue to play a crucial role in structuring the modern world, not least because of an unresolved tension between their cultural and political axes. If we define nations as cultural entities, their boundaries are contingent on subjective relationships binding together groups of individuals who may or may not constitute a spatially distinct whole. If we define nations as political units, their boundaries are marked by the territorial limits within which states exercise sovereignty. Defined thus, the cultural and political boundaries of nations seldom coincide exactly. The urge to make them coincide has, however, been a major force in modern history. Cultural communities have sought to fulfil their sense of nationhood by constructing and defending state boundaries against outsiders, while states have frequently attempted to control or in some cases eliminate cultural diversity within their borders.

By their very nature, immigrants cut across this homogenizing imperative, for they are born without the citizenship of the country in which they reside, and the cultural norms internalized in their country of origin differ from those prevailing in the receiving society. Depending on the circumstances, however, immigrants and their descendants may be accepted or even positively welcomed, while at other times they may be shunned or forcibly expelled.

In formal terms, there are two main ways in which non-nationals may be incorporated into a nationally defined society. One is by granting residence and other rights within the national territory, but not the political rights associated with formal citizenship. The other is by granting full citizenship to people of foreign origin. The extent to which national boundaries are open on either or both of these levels varies from one state to another and also across time. Compared with many other states, France has traditionally been relatively open in both respects, but after the early 1970s she became more exclusionary. During the 1970s, stricter controls on residence and work permits were introduced with the aim of limiting, and if possible reducing, the foreign population. In the mid-1980s, the laws governing access to French nationality became the subject of intense political debate, culminating in the passage of restrictive legislation in 1993.

During the 1980s, it became commonplace in France to claim that immigration was a threat to national identity.[1] Two-thirds of those questioned in a 1985 opinion poll said France was in danger of losing her national identity if nothing was done to limit the foreign population (BVA poll in *Paris-Match*, 29 Nov. 1985). By 1989, that view was shared by three-quarters of respondents (BVA poll in *Paris-Match*, 14 Dec. 1989). The theme of national identity was brought into the political limelight by the rise of the extreme right-wing Front National (FN), campaigning on a vigorously anti-immigrant platform. Responding to this shift in the political agenda, the traditional parties of both left and right organized major debates on the theme of French identity in the spring of 1985 (Espaces 89 1985; Club de l'Horloge 1985); a few months later the neo-Gaullist Rassemblement Pour la République (RPR) and centrist Union pour la Démocratie Française (UDF) announced joint proposals aimed at restricting the access of foreigners to French nationality.

While political and cultural factors certainly played a significant role in these changes, the most fundamental force pushing in this direction was economic. Growing acceptance of immigrants during the post-war period was largely attributable to the perceived need to meet labor shortages by importing foreign workers. It was no accident that more restrictive attitudes became dominant after the mid-1970s in a context of growing concern over unemployment, which was to reach sustained levels which were almost without precedent. As economic circumstances changed, the state attempted to improve conditions in the labor market by opening or closing access to it by non-nationals.

Even formal incorporation through citizenship is not enough to ensure that immigrants and their descendants enjoy genuine equality of opportunity. As was seen in Chapter 2, people of foreign descent, particularly those of non-European origin, frequently experience discriminatory treatment even when they are French nationals. Discrimination of this kind has been amply documented not only in relation to young French nationals born of African parents originating both north and south of the Sahara, but also in relation to first- and second-generation DOM-TOMiens, whose ancestors have in many cases been formally French for centuries (CNCDH 1992: 40–2; Galap 1993). While cultural differences sometimes help to account for discriminatory behavior, cruder exclusionary reflexes are often involved. In cultural terms, many of those who suffer discrimination differ little, if at all, from the mass of the population. Their exclusion arises, rather, from competition in the fields of employment or other forms of resource allocation, where some members of society seek to rig markets against vulnerable sections of the population, notably those with non-white skins, who are easily branded as 'outsiders'.

Just as the formal and informal construction of the national community is conditioned by changes over time, so it also shaped by the particularities of the outsiders with whom its members find themselves in contact. National identity derives its content from implicit or explicit dividing lines which are taken to separate the nation from those who stand outside it. The significance attached to particular others depends on the contingencies of geography and history and the way in which these are reworked in the light of current preoccupations. If some outsiders are seen as more alien than others, their incorporation into the national community is likely to appear particularly problematic. A substantial body of data exists to show that among the French at large, immigrants are viewed through the prism of a long-established ethnic hierarchy. The hierarchy itself changed relatively little in the course of the twentieth century, but its practical implications varied considerably as a consequence of political, economic and demographic changes affecting French society.[2]

Current perceptions of different ethnic groups are typified by the results of a 1989 public opinion poll in which respondents were asked to state which out of four groups of immigrants would be the most difficult to integrate into French society. For 50 per cent of respondents, the single most problematic group consisted of Maghrebis; 19 per cent were mainly concerned by sub-Saharan Africans, 15 per cent by Asians and 2 per cent by Europeans (BVA poll in *Paris-Match*, 14 Dec. 1989). Half a century earlier Georges Mauco, who was to become an influential figure in French immigration policy, had conducted a survey among employers asking which ethnic groups were the best foreign workers. The classification which emerged was headed by workers from neighboring European states such as Belgium and Italy; central Europeans were concentrated in the middle ranks, while the Chinese, Greeks and Arabs filled the last three places (1937 survey cited in Weil 1991: 35, 360).

Immediately after the Second World War, Mauco and others argued for the official adoption of a similar ethnic hierarchy through the application of quotas in French immigration policy. While not formally adopted in law, this hierarchy structured many important administrative practices (Weil 1991: 53–75), though for the reasons noted in sections 1.3 and 1.4, the authorities proved unable to prevent the main sources of migratory inflows shifting from Europe to Africa and Asia. The absence of sub-Saharan Africans from Mauco's company survey reflected their numerical insignificance in pre-war and early post-war France. In a large-scale public opinion survey conducted in 1951 by the Institut National d'Études Démographiques (INED), Maghrebis[3] were the only non-European group cited in a list of ten ethnic groups on which respondents were invited to comment. Asked to say how readily the different groups were capable of adapting to the French way of life, interviewees placed Belgians and Italians at the top of the list, central Europeans lower down and Maghrebis last of all except for Germans. An almost identical ranking emerged in response to a question on which groups were most liked (Girard and Stoetzel 1953: 144).

The close parallel between levels of personal liking and the evaluation of the capacity of different groups to fit into French society, which recurs in more recent surveys, raises an important question: are certain ethnic groups liked more than others because they fit in easily or do they appear to fit in more easily because they are made more welcome? This is linked in turn to the question of whether hierarchical ethnicization of this kind is a reflection of significant cultural differences or the product of political or other circumstances. The low regard for Germans recorded in the 1951 survey is undoubtedly a reflection of the unhappy political relationship between France and Germany, which had reached its nadir in the Nazi occupation of France during the Second World War. Similarly, while the low ranking of Asians and Arabs in the Mauco and INED surveys may well arise in part from a greater cultural distance separating them (compared with Europeans) from the native French population, it is probably also conditioned by the political fact of colonization. The ideology of colonial domination was built on the alleged inferiority of non-Europeans. The widespread view that colonized peoples differed from the French to a far greater degree than Europeans helped to underpin the colonial system, and was reinforced by it in turn.

Less than thirty years after the end of the Second World War, an INED survey showed that the Germans had risen markedly in French esteem, while Maghrebis and sub-Saharan Africans (who had now been added to the list of groups mentioned in the questionnaire) scored the lowest rankings (*Population* 1971). The healing powers of time are not in themselves sufficient to explain this evolution. Today, well over forty years after the final phase in the liquidation of France's overseas empire, marked by Algerian independence in 1962, people originating in former colonial territories still occupy the lowest positions in French perceptions of different ethnic groups. Since 1957, France and Germany have been political partners in the construction of what was initially known as the European Economic Community; in addition, under the terms of a Treaty of Friendship signed in 1963, the highest authorities in both countries have actively sought to overcome past enmities through bilateral programs of cooperation involving the public at large. There has been no comparable investment aimed at overcoming the divisive memories and attitudes inherited from the colonial period.

This legacy is clearly visible in the results of a survey conducted in 1984 asking whether different groups were perceived as well or badly integrated into French society (Table 4.1). The hierarchy which emerges is very similar to that seen in

Table 4.1 French perceptions of minority ethnic groups, 1984
Question: Here is a list of communities living in France. For each of them, can you tell me whether they are on the whole well or badly integrated into French society?

	A Well (%)	B Badly (%)	C No reply (%)	D A–B
Italians	81	9	10	+72
Spanish	81	9	10	+72
Poles	75	8	17	+67
Portuguese	70	18	12	+52
Pieds-noirs	66	21	13	+45
West Indians	57	20	23	+37
Jews from E. Europe	49	16	35	+33
Yugoslavians	43	20	37	+23
Asians	47	25	28	+22
Armenians	37	28	35	+9
Tunisians	37	42	21	−5
Black Africans	36	48	16	−12
Moroccans	33	48	19	−15
Turks	19	43	38	−24
Gypsies	21	64	.15	−43
Algerians	21	70	9	−49

Source: SOFRES opinion poll for MRAP 1984: 22.

pre-war and early post-war surveys, with west Europeans at the top, central and eastern Europeans in the middle and Africans at the bottom. Algerians, whose struggle for independence left deep scars in the French national psyche, are seen as by far the least well integrated group. Moroccans and Tunisians, who are culturally similar to Algerians but gained their independence at the cost of relatively little violence, score less badly. The relatively favorable evaluation of Asians probably reflects the political sympathy enjoyed by refugees who fled to France from South-East Asia after the fall of Saigon in 1975. Memories of the Indochina war of decolonization, which ended in French defeat in 1954 and which might have left an enduring legacy of enmity, appear to have been effaced subsequently by two decades of war between South and North Vietnam, at the end of which anti-communist middle-class South-East Asians were welcomed as victims of the Cold War rather than as former adversaries associated with anti-colonial nationalism.

While some variations of this kind have occurred, the broad hierarchical ordering of ethnic categories by the French public has remained fairly stable during the post-war period. There have, however, been marked changes in the perception of immigration and its effects on French society. In INED's 1951 survey, 45 per cent of respondents felt that foreign residents would always remain foreign, while 36 per cent thought them capable of gradually mixing in with the mass of the French population. When the same question was asked in the winter of 1973–4, only 35 per cent felt that immigrants would remain permanently foreign, whereas 56 per cent thought they would gradually mix in (*Population* 1974: 1061). This greater confidence in the capacity of French society to absorb immigrants reflects the rising prosperity experienced during the boom decades of the 1950s and 1960s. The economic utility of Maghrebis, who had by then become dominant in migratory inflows, clearly outweighed any misgivings associated with the cultural and political heritage of non-Europeans.

In 1951, only 50 per cent of respondents had felt that foreign residents in France performed useful services; by 1973–4, the figure had risen to 80 per cent (*Population* 1974: 1059). An almost identical proportion of interviewees (79 per cent) said foreign workers were doing jobs which the French themselves did not wish to do; only 14 per cent considered that immigrants were competing against French nationals in the labor market. At the same time, 65 per cent felt that, if a severe rise in unemployment were to take place, foreigners should be sacked before French nationals. Thus ticking away beneath the surface of this greater acceptance of immigrants was a time-bomb set to explode in the event of an economic downturn, the first signs of which began to appear not long after the 1973–4 survey.

With unemployment rising sharply in the late 1970s and 1980s, the repatriation of immigrant workers was regularly ranked in opinion polls as the best solution to the problem (SOFRES 1984: 221; 1991: 120). In the early 1990s, annual polls consistently showed that those who thought immigrant workers were a burden on the French economy were twice as numerous as those who regarded them as beneficial. In 1993, for example, the figures were 60 and 28 per cent respectively (CNCDH 1994: 457). There was now great uncertainty as to whether immigrants could be integrated into French society, and deep divisions over the desirability of this. In the late 1980s, interviewees were split almost exactly down the middle between those who wished to prioritize the repatriation of immigrants and those who wished to integrate them into French society (SOFRES poll in *Le Nouvel Observateur*, 23 Nov. 1989). By 1990, the proportion favoring repatriation stood at 46 per cent, against 42 per cent wishing to prioritize integration (SOFRES 1991: 125). In 1985, 42 per cent of respondents thought most immigrants were too different for it to be possible to integrate them into French society, while 50 per cent thought integration would eventually be possible; five years later the proportion declaring integration to be impossible had risen to 49 per cent, against 43 per cent who were of the contrary view (SOFRES 1991: 122).

As noted earlier, Maghrebis are the main source of concern among those who doubt whether immigrants can be successfully integrated into French society. Maghrebis have the double misfortune of occupying the lowest ranking in the ethnic hierarchy prevalent in France and of having emerged as by far the most visible component in the population of immigrant origin at precisely the time when the expansionary climate which had favored the recruitment of foreign workers in the early post-war decades was giving way to more difficult economic circumstances. It was therefore almost inevitable that the increased hostility towards immigrants and their descendants resulting from this economic downturn would focus on the Maghrebi population (Naïr 1988). Even before the first oil crisis of 1973, an outbreak of violence against Algerian immigrants in the summer of that year (Giudice 1992: 93–103) led the Algerian government to halt further emigration to France, almost a year before the blanket ban on non-EC entrants imposed by France in July 1974. Recorded cases of racist violence rose sharply during the 1980s. In the period between 1980 and 1993 Maghrebis, who represented less than 40 per cent of the foreign population, accounted for 78 per cent of all those injured and 92 per cent of those killed in attacks officially classified by the authorities as racist (CNCDH 1994: 23).

Islam is usually cited as the main obstacle to the integration of Maghrebis. Some 49 per cent of those questioned in a 1991 poll said Islam was so different from the prevailing norms in French society that it made the integration of Muslim immigrants impossible; only 40 per cent thought Muslims could eventually be integrated (CSA poll in *La Vie*, 28 Nov. 1991). These figures match up closely with the pattern noted above in the responses made to a less ethnically specific question about the chances of integrating immigrants; behind this seemingly general question, respondents had clearly sensed they were being invited to comment primarily on Maghrebis. Similarly, when 45 per cent of interviewees agreed in another poll that Maghrebis had a 'way of life' which could not be integrated into French society, compared with 42 per cent who disagreed (CSA poll in *Le Journal du dimanche*, 18 March 1990), they were no doubt thinking principally of Islam.

There are at least three possible explanations for this apparent decline in confidence among the French public concerning the chances of successful integration. One is that it reflects an objective shift in the cultural complexion of immigrants and their descendants, making them more difficult to incorporate when compared with earlier migratory inflows. It is certainly true that the mainly non-European cultures which have come to the fore during the last twenty years differ markedly from those associated with earlier, European migrants. Yet as we saw in Chapter 3, direct conflicts with the norms prevailing in French society are the exception rather than the rule, and it is by no means certain that they now occur more frequently than when immigrants were mainly Europeans. Moreover, there is overwhelming evidence to show that the inter-generational trend is towards the reduction of cultural differences when the descendants of recent immigrants are compared with the majority of the population. Their acculturation flies in the face of those who claim that integration is impossible.

An alternative explanation for those claims is that they are based on mistaken but sincerely held beliefs concerning the population of immigrant origin. Two-thirds of French respondents questioned in a 1991 survey said there were too many immigrants in France; an almost identical proportion said they had never had any significant personal dealings with immigrants (SOFRES 1991: 121–2). It is clear that the negative images associated with immigrants in general and with certain ethnicized groups in particular owe more to second-hand information and impressions than to direct personal experience. The mass media play a central role in this process. Research on the representation of minority ethnic groups on French television has shown that they are mainly visible as 'problems' in news and current affairs broadcasts. It is in the nature of journalism to highlight conflicts and difficulties rather than ordinary or benign occurrences. An understanding of the native French population based solely on news and current affairs programs would no doubt conclude that the French as a whole were riddled with conflicts and problems. News and current affairs are, however, only one part of total broadcasting output. Many other programs, such as game shows, sitcoms and variety shows, present a far more convivial picture of 'ordinary' people. Because recent immigrants and their descendants have been largely absent from these programs, viewers tend to gain a very lopsided and unattractive idea of how they fit into French society (Hargreaves and Perotti 1993). In the absence of a wider media presence, Muslims in particular suffer as a consequence of the high-profile coverage given to news stories such as the Islamic headscarf affair, for the deeply disturbing images generated by what in fact are exceptional events come to be perceived as the norm.

A third explanation for the widespread view that immigrants can no longer be integrated into French society is that those who argue in this fashion are influenced less by defective information than by their own exclusionary reflexes. The steady rise of non-Europeans in migratory inflows during the post-war period did not prevent the French from expressing growing acceptance of immigrants as long as there was rising economic prosperity and a favorable labor market. To claim now that cultural differences make integration impossible is a convenient way of blaming immigrants themselves for the alleged necessity of excluding them from French society at a time when this is also widely seen as a solution to the country's economic difficulties. During the economic downturns of the 1890s and 1930s, similar arguments were advanced concerning the alleged unassimilability of Italians and Poles, who are often held up today as examples of easily integrated immigrants in contrast with more recent arrivals from former colonies outside Europe (Schor 1985; Milza 1985: 5–6; Noiriel 1988: 247–94).

In a 1990 poll, the proportion of respondents (49 per cent) who held that immigrants were too different to be integrated into French society was almost identical to the level of support (46 per cent) expressed for repatriation in preference to integration (SOFRES 1991: 122, 125). Many respondents would no doubt argue that the second proposition followed from the first, but another reading might reverse the causal chain. While it is impossible to prove that calculations of self-interest outweigh unprejudiced analysis in shaping attitudes of this kind, it is certainly arguable that the principal obstacles now blocking the social incorporation of immigrants and their descendants lie not in their cultural particularities but in the unfavorable conditions prevailing in the labor market and the exclusionary attitudes found among the French themselves.

What is beyond doubt is that the ethnicized categories against which French images of national identity are constructed are seriously at odds with both the *de facto* participation of immigrants and their descendants within French society and their own sense of belonging. Seven out of ten young Maghrebis interviewed in a 1993 survey said they identified more closely with the lifestyle and culture of the French than with their parents' norms (SOFRES poll in *Le Nouvel Observateur*, 2 Dec. 1993). French perceptions were quite different: in a 1990 poll, only three out of ten saw second-generation Maghrebis as mainly French while five out of ten regarded them primarily as Arabs (CNCDH 1991: 210). Eight out of ten thought it would be difficult or impossible to integrate young Maghrebis born in France. Yet most of those concerned are in a formal sense already French, for French nationality has been automatically bestowed upon them under the terms of the French nationality code (CNF).[4] This disjunction between popular perceptions of the ethnicized boundaries defining French national identity and the juridical contours of French nationhood emerged as a major issue in French politics during the mid-1980s. The debate over the CNF became symbolic of the anxieties and exclusionary pressures traversing French society in the face of minority groups of immigrant origin. Before examining the details of that debate and the reform to which it led in 1993, it is important to understand first of all its historical and ideological foundations.

4.2 The republican tradition

The prevailing conceptions of nationality and citizenship in France are rooted in the Revolution of 1789. Breaking with the system of privileges associated with the division of society into rigidly stratified estates or orders, the revolution wrested sovereignty, i.e. legitimate political authority, from the monarch and invested it in the nation, all of whose members were proclaimed equal before the law. The republican values which are now most commonly associated with the revolutionary heritage include universalism, unitarism, secularism and assimilationism, though not all these terms were in use at the time of the revolution. Universalism has both an external and an internal face. The Rights of Man proclaimed in August 1789 were held to be valid not only for every individual in France, but also for the whole of humanity. Within the republican tradition the nation, including its political incarnation in the form of the state, is indivisible: no intermediary orders are recognized between the individual and the unitary state of which he or she is a member. The principle of *laïcité* (secularism), a term which entered currency only in the later part of the nineteenth century, includes both freedom of conscience, already proclaimed during the revolution of 1789, and the formal separation of the state from any religious order (Brubaker 1992: 35–49).

The revolutionary period was shot through with tensions and contradictions, some of which were already implicit in the Declaration of 26 August 1789, the formal title of which was the Declaration of the Rights of Man and of the Citizen. The fields embraced by the two terms joined together through the word 'and' coexisted but were not coterminous. While some rights belonged inalienably to all human beings, others – including, in particular, the right to share in the exercising of political sovereignty – were reserved solely for citizens. As all authority emanated from the nation, citizens were by definition members of the nation, but as the revolution unfolded gaps opened up in the apparent symmetry between citizenship and membership of the national community.

The Constitution of 1791 confirmed that citizenship was reserved exclusively for members of the nation, but distinguished between 'active' citizens, who had political rights, and 'passive' citizens, including all females and poorer members of society, who were not allowed to participate in the political processes governing the state though they remained subject to its jurisdiction. Admission to the French nation came automatically through a mixture of *jus soli* and *jus sanguinis* to anyone born on French soil and resident there or descended from a French father. In addition, foreigners who wished to become French citizens were eligible to do so after five years' residence, provided they satisfied other criteria indicating that they were incorporated into the life of the nation. The Constitution of 1793, which granted citizenship rights to most foreigners after a year's residence, was never applied. Not until 1794 did the revolutionaries declare slavery – the very antithesis of citizenship – to be abolished, but it was reinstated in the colonies under Napoleon (Borella 1991).

Most of the monarchical or authoritarian régimes which have exercised power in France at various times during the last 200 years, including that of Napoleon, have restricted access to French nationality by prioritizing *jus sanguinis* over *jus soli*. Republican régimes, by contrast, have adopted more liberal measures. In 1851, the Second Republic determined that third-generation residents of foreign origin would be French from birth provided they and one of their parents were born on French soil. Under the Third Republic, a law passed in 1889 lowered the threshold for the second generation by conferring French nationality automatically on children born in France when they reached the age of majority. In 1927, first-generation foreigners were given easier access to French nationality when the conditions governing naturalization were liberalized. Further inclusionary measures were introduced by the post-war Provisional Government in 1945 and under the Fifth Republic in 1973. Except for the late stages of the revolutionary period, the 1993 reform, which ended the automatic acquisition of French nationality by the children of immigrants at the age of majority, was the first under a republican régime to move in an exclusionary direction.[5]

At the heart of the arguments advanced by those who favored this reform was the conviction that the assimilationist assumptions on which a liberal nationality code was based were no longer well founded. The assimilationist tradition, like other aspects of the revolutionary heritage, is double-sided and steeped in ambiguity. From a political perspective, it appears universalist and egalitarian; in cultural terms, it is particularist and intolerant (Silverman 1992: 19–33). Historically and ideologically, as Brubaker (1992) has shown, the French and German constructions of nationality and citizenship differ profoundly in the relative weight accorded to political and cultural considerations. In France, a unitary state existed well before the cultural unification of those resident within its borders. Before and since the revolution of 1789, the state has pursued policies aimed at promoting cultural uniformity based on the norms prevailing among the political and social elite. In Germany, by contrast, the sense of a shared national culture preceded and to a considerable extent motivated the drive towards political unification. When a unified German state was established, nationality laws were designed to exclude those originating outside the German ethnocultural nation. Membership of the French polity was relatively open to outsiders, whose incorporation was assumed to be facilitated by a process of acculturation. This openness was partly motivated by demographic concerns, for throughout the nineteenth century and most of the twentieth, France was characterized by a much lower birth rate than most of her European neighbors, notably Germany. The incorporation of people of foreign origin helped to redress this demographic imbalance, which was widely perceived as a threat to France's international standing and military security.

In theory, the principle of assimilation was extended beyond the borders of metropolitan France into the overseas empire. Officially designated as the ultimate objective of the colonial project, assimilation appeared to promise equal political rights to the indigenous inhabitants of the overseas territories (Betts 1961). In practice, political equality would have destroyed the very foundations of the colonial system, and it was refused to all but a tiny elite among the indigenous populations on the grounds that the broad masses were insufficiently acculturated to justify the granting of citizenship (Guillaume 1991). Their low level of cultural assimilation was the inevitable consequence of the minimal or completely non-existent educational provision made available by France to the majority of her colonial subjects. In metropolitan France, by contrast, primary education was publicly funded, compulsory and universal from the 1880s onwards. Under the terms of French nationality laws, as codified in 1945, the state held the right to block the automatic acquisition of French nationality by second-generation foreigners if they were judged to be insufficiently assimilated on reaching the age of majority (Brubaker 1992: 224), but the national educational system, extended after the war into compulsory secondary schooling, effectively rendered this provision unnecessary. In the early 1980s, when more than 15,000 people a year were automatically acquiring French nationality at the age of 18, the number refused each year on the grounds of inadequate assimilation averaged less than one (Lebon 1987: 12–13).

Tainted by its colonial connotations, the word 'assimilation' fell into general disuse with the collapse of the overseas empire in the early post-war decades, but it retained a juridical existence in the CNF, where assimilation was formally enshrined as a prerequisite for the acquisition of citizenship by people of foreign origin. The concept (if not the term) continued to underlie the debate over immigration, where it resurfaced during the 1980s as one of the meanings attached to the word 'integration'. When advocates of a reform of the CNF justified their proposals on the grounds of an alleged breakdown in the traditional processes of integration, more often than not they meant that immigrants and their descendants were no longer being culturally assimilated. Almost invariably, this claim was illustrated by pointing to the rise of Islam in France. Other cultures originating outside Europe were seldom if ever mentioned, while European immigrants were regularly cited as examples of successful 'integration' and by implication, therefore, assimilation (Taguieff 1990; Silverman 1992: 140–7). It is certainly true that first-generation residents originating in Islamic countries generally remain deeply attached to the faith which they internalized during their formative years prior to emigrating. It is no less clear, however, that most of the children born in France to Muslim parents have a much weaker attachment to Islam and are far more committed to the values and aspirations commonly found among their French-born peers. On the evidence reviewed in Chapter 3, claims that 'integration' (in the sense of cultural assimilation) is no longer operative simply do not hold water.

Other arguments advanced by those wishing to limit access to French nationality were more political in nature. Again, Algerians were at the heart of these concerns. The low naturalization rates of first-generation Algerians in France were read, with some justification, as a sign of their unwillingness to accept formal membership of the French national community because of the political legacy of decolonization (Sayad 1987). Most second-generation Algerians in France automatically hold French nationality and have practical reasons to value the rights associated with this but, influenced no doubt by their parents, they often appeared indifferent, distrustful or positively hostile towards the French state. As they also held Algerian nationality, their loyalty to France appeared open to question. Stora argued convincingly that, at root, historically conditioned political factors of this kind were more significant than cultural differences in shaping the debate over contemporary immigration and the reform of the CNF:

> The difference, compared with earlier [i.e. European] immigrants, resides not in religious history but in the history of France and of French colonization. This is why the institutions designed to produce assimilation or integration suddenly seem to be misfiring. The children born from these more recent migratory waves, whose parents asserted the right to a nationality which was denied, rejected and forced underground [during the colonial period], are marked by this history ...

In France, the debate is clouded by an unreal vision of Islam, which is equated with politically motivated Islamic fundamentalism; behind this phantasm lurks once again the settling of old colonial scores; people want revenge for the Algerian war.

(Stora 1990: 38–9)

While it would be going too far to characterize the reform of the CNF as an act of revenge committed out of spite because of events that took place more than a quarter of a century earlier, it is certainly true that a lack of trust on all sides inherited from that period was a potent factor in focusing public disquiet over immigration on the population of Algerian origin. As the largest national group of non-European origin, as Muslims, and as former adversaries in a bitter war of decolonization, Algerians more than any other group came to symbolize in French eyes all the problems associated with immigration (Silverman 1992: 70–94). As Brubaker (1992: 139) observed, they were at the center of the most symbolic struggle of all – over the formal boundaries of French nationhood – though, as we shall see, for technical reasons the reform of the CNF enacted in 1993 left them virtually unscathed.

4.3 Nationality and citizenship

The main forces seeking to restrict access to French nationality were on the right of the political spectrum. While those efforts to a large extent set the terms of the debate from the mid-1980s onwards, minority ethnic groups and sympathizers on the left had been arguing since the late 1970s for no less radical but very different changes. In 1978, the Socialist Party (PS) promised that if elected to government it would amend the constitution so as to allow foreign residents to vote in local elections without first acquiring French nationality. This was seen as a way of allowing immigrants to participate in public affairs without directly confronting the symbolically charged issue of formal national membership. The proposal was included in Mitterrand's manifesto for the presidential elections of 1981. After Mitterrand's victory and that of the PS, allied with the Communist Party (PCF), in the parliamentary elections held immediately afterwards, Foreign Minister Claude Cheysson announced during a visit to Algiers that the government was planning to implement this proposal. His announcement was met by such a hostile reaction on the right and such a lukewarm response on the left that it was followed in less than forty-eight hours by a government climbdown. While Mitterrand remained on record as personally favoring local voting rights for foreign residents, the PS said it would not proceed with the proposal in the foreseeable future on the grounds that public opinion would not accept it and the necessary parliamentary majority was also unlikely to be forthcoming (Wihtol de Wenden 1987: 52–73; Weil 1988: 193–5).

Critics of the proposed reform said that it was not only unconstitutional but also fundamentally at odds with the republican values inherited from the revolution. Within the tradition of 1789, political sovereignty was indivisible and was vested solely in the nation. Seen in this light, nationality and citizenship were inseparable. Historically, this was at best no more than half true. It is certainly true that, as a general rule, nationality has been a prerequisite for citizenship. While foreigners granted citizenship rights during the revolutionary period also became by the same token French nationals, between 1889 and 1983 naturalized foreigners had to wait several years before being allowed the political rights enjoyed by the rest of the nation (Wihtol de Wenden 1994a: 45–6). Moreover, nationality has not automatically entailed citizenship. Political rights were denied to a full half of the French nation (i.e. the female half) until 1944, and the vast majority of people in the overseas empire, while officially classified as French subjects, were also excluded from citizenship (Borella 1991).

It is no accident that Cheysson made his announcement during a visit to Algeria, for the colonial legacy was nowhere more sensitive than in former French North Africa. The denial of Algerian nationhood throughout more than a century of colonial rule – during most of which Algerians were told that they were French nationals though not French citizens – and the bitter eight-year war that preceded independence made Algerians extremely reluctant to accept any outward sign of French domination (Sayad 1987). The PS's proposal to facilitate partial citizenship for immigrants without their being required to take French nationality would have made it easier for Algerians and other former colonial subjects to participate in French public life while avoiding formal allegiance to the French state.

Similar considerations led senior PS figures to consider revising Article 23 of the CNF, which attributed French nationality at birth to anyone born in France at least one of whose parents was also born on French territory. Despite Algerian independence in 1962, children born since then to Algerian immigrants in France were automatically given French nationality because Algeria was officially regarded as French territory at the time of their parents' birth. Since independence, Algeria has refused to recognize these claims on the grounds that to do so would be to legitimize France's former colonial domination. Under Algerian law, the children of emigrants are Algerian nationals. In practice, therefore, they are bi-nationals, although Algeria does not formally acknowledge French claims. In the early 1980s, Socialist ministers examined possible changes to Article 23 so as to enable the children of Algerian immigrants to choose whether or not to accept French nationality instead of having it automatically imposed on them. However, technical difficulties were encountered: it appeared impossible to change Article 23 without adversely affecting *rapatriés*, i.e. former colonial settlers of European descent, and the change might also pose administrative problems in relation to the mass of French nationals originating in metropolitan France. By 1984 the emergence into the political limelight of the FN, calling for radical restrictions on access to French nationality, led the left to abandon any thoughts of revising the CNF (Weil 1988: 195–6; 1991: 165–6; Brubaker 1992: 141–2).

France and Algeria did, however, sign an agreement in 1983 under which Franco-Algerian bi-nationals who performed their military service in either country would be exempted by the other (Babadji 1992). Until then, as nationals of both France and Algeria, the sons of Algerian immigrants had been subject to the draft in both countries. Military service is one of a range of rights and duties – some of them highly symbolic, others of great practical import – associated with nationality and citizenship. Others include the right of access to the national territory and protection from deportation, access to employment in the public sector, and the right to participate in the exercise of political sovereignty by voting and standing as a candidate in elections to the local and national institutions of government.

In the post-colonial period, French nationality and citizenship have formed a virtually indissoluble whole. The Franco-Algerian military service agreement was no more than a small crack in this amalgam. The Socialists' flirtation with the possibility of making political rights unconditional on nationality was all but abandoned by the mid-1980s, but the idea has continued to circulate among minority groups as well as anti-racist and human rights associations (Wihtol de Wenden 1987: 64–73; Balibar 1988). The project of what has become known as a New Citizenship (Bouamama *et al.* 1992) attracted considerable attention during the bicentenary celebrations of the French Revolution. Several campaigns and conferences were organized by intellectuals and grass-roots activists with the aim of advancing the cause of local voting rights for foreign residents. This was presented not as a break with French republicanism but as its true fulfilment, with the language and ideals of 1789 constantly to the fore, together with plentiful references to the Constitution of 1793. A petition in favor of local voting rights for immigrants organized by SOS-Racisme brought together dozens of associations in a collective called 89 For Equality. Shortly afterwards, hundreds of associations joined a similar collective called Here I Am and Here I Vote run by the League of Human Rights, whose founding fathers had been directly inspired by the ideals of 1789 when setting up the organization in the late nineteenth century at the height of the Dreyfus Affair (Oriol 1992: 104–7).

The emphasis of grass-roots activists has been on the local dimension of the New Citizenship. By focusing on the subnational level, they have sought to open to minorities from former colonial territories a political space uncompromised by the emotional and ideological baggage inherited from the struggle for national liberation. Following the Single European Act of 1986, however, there has been a growing realization that some of the most powerful arguments at their disposal are transnational in nature. The Act, which provided for a complete end to internal border controls between member states of the European Community (EC) by the end of 1992, highlighted the steady erosion of national sovereignty with the development of economic and political integration in western Europe. Two EC member states, Denmark and the Netherlands, had recently granted local voting rights to foreign residents. Similar rights had existed in Ireland since 1963, while in the United Kingdom all citizens of Commonwealth (i.e. ex-colonial) countries have always enjoyed full political rights at the national as well as the local level. In 1985, the European Parliament called for reciprocal voting rights in local elections for citizens of EC states residing in any member country; if implemented, this proposal would break the link between citizenship and nationality across practically the whole of western Europe, thereby demolishing the claims of those who argued that such a link was sacrosanct (Oriol 1992: 109–36).

The Maastricht Treaty of 1992 made a legal reality of this project by creating, in Article 8, a European citizenship enjoyed by the nationals of all member states, who were given voting rights in local and European elections no matter where they resided within the common frontiers of what now became known as the European Union (EU). The partial dilution of national sovereignty implied by this and other provisions of the treaty, particularly those dealing with economic and monetary union, required a constitutional amendment in France. This was approved by only a whisker in a referendum held in September 1992 after a vigorously fought campaign which split most of the main parties from top to bottom. Local voting rights even for Europeans were thus conceded only grudgingly. While a precedent was certainly set, the prospects for extending those rights to non-EU nationals were poor. For people of African and Asian origin, in the foreseeable future the only means of access to political rights in France lay in the acquisition of French nationality. Far from smoothing their path, however, the right placed new obstacles in their way through its reform of the CNF.

4.4 The reform of French nationality laws

The reform of French nationality laws was placed firmly on the political agenda in 1985, when the RPR and UDF included it in their joint manifesto for the 1986 parliamentary elections. In a more draconian form, such a reform had long been advocated by the FN (Le Gallou and Jalkh 1987), but little attention had been paid to this extreme right-wing party until it began to score significant electoral successes in 1983–4. Anxious to staunch the loss of their supporters to the FN, the traditional center-right parties hardened their policy platform on immigration and related issues. After gaining a narrow election victory in March 1986, they formed a government under the premiership of RPR leader Jacques Chirac, who announced that the government would introduce legislation ending the automatic acquisition of French nationality by people of foreign origin.

This would require the reform or abolition of Articles 23 and 44 of the CNF. However, when the government began drafting the necessary legislation, it found that Article 23 could not be changed without running into unwanted and unacceptable side-effects. If Article 23 were to be abolished, this would remove the simplest mechanism open to the mass of French citizens for proving their nationality. The production of two birth certificates – that of the person concerned and that of at least one parent – showing that both births had taken place on French soil sufficed to prove that the person was French, and the government was advised that it would be unwise to tinker with this. If the provisions of Article 23 were to be declared inoperative only with reference to Algeria and other former colonies, this would be tantamount to denying the historical legitimacy of French colonization; it would also raise difficulties for the *rapatriés*. For these reasons, the government reluctantly left Article 23 in place and focused instead on Article 44 (Brubaker 1992: 151–2).

As it stood, Article 44 gave French nationality automatically to people born on French soil of foreign parents when they reached the age of majority. Certain conditions applied: it was necessary to have resided in France during the five years prior to this procedure, French nationality could not be acquired by any person who had committed certain criminal offences, and the state could in principle refuse French nationality to a person judged to be of unacceptable morals or inadequately assimilated. However, these latter provisions were almost never invoked, and none of the conditions attached to Article 44 altered the central point that those acquiring French nationality in this way did so without having to request it. The centerpiece of the Chirac government's draft legislation was the revision of Article 44 in such a way as to require those covered by it to request French nationality instead of receiving it automatically.

One of the justifications advanced by the government in favor of this reform was that it would give more freedom to young people of immigrant origin: instead of having French nationality forced upon them, they would be free to choose whether or not to take it. This voluntarist argument was unconvincing for two main reasons. In the first place, second-generation foreigners were already permitted to decline French nationality in the year leading up to their eighteenth birthday if they so wished. Thus freedom of choice already existed, and the proposed reform did nothing to widen it. On the contrary – and here was the second reason for doubting the government's liberalist claims – in its revised form, Article 44 added important new conditions on the basis of which applicants could be refused access to French nationality. The range of criminal convictions disqualifying applicants was greatly extended and it would in future be necessary to swear an oath of allegiance to the French Republic before being admitted to citizenship (Brubaker 1992: 152–3).

The latter provision was openly acknowledged by the government to be aimed at weeding out people of foreign origin whose loyalty to France might be open to doubt. At a more subtle level, the very fact of forcing the children of immigrants to request French nationality instead of receiving it passively was calculated to have a similar effect. The prime targets of these measures were the children of immigrants from former colonies who, because of parental influences, might be more reluctant than those of European origin to actively request French nationality. Because the government had found itself compelled to leave Article 23 intact, there was a certain amount of shadow-boxing involved in all this. Had the government had its wish, young Franco-Algerians, whose loyalty was doubted more than that of any other group, would have fallen under the terms of the revised version of Article 44. As it turned out, they were protected from this by the retention of Article 23, which ensured that they automatically held French nationality from birth. However, throughout the debate over the CNF, perceptions of practical realities were frequently obscured from view by gestures of highly charged political symbolism.

The outcry against the proposed reform voiced by opposition parties on the left, trade unions, church leaders, anti-racist and human rights associations, grass-roots activists and others of both immigrant and native origin was so strong and came at a time when the government was already vulnerable on other fronts that a tactical retreat was soon ordered (Wayland 1993). Even before the bill was formally tabled in Parliament in November 1986, Justice Minister Albin Chalandon announced that while second-generation foreigners would still have to request French nationality, they would not, after all, be required to swear an oath of allegiance. A month later, faced with the prospect of massive demonstrations against the bill, Prime Minister Chirac said the reform would not be brought forward in the next parliamentary session. In January 1987 the prospective legislative timetable was slowed down still further by the decision to set up a special commission to conduct a comprehensive review of the CNF as a whole.

Composed essentially of experts from outside the field of party politics, the Nationality Commission was encouraged to look beyond the government's existing proposals and to make whatever recommendations it considered appropriate for the modernization of French nationality laws. Given *carte blanche*, the Commission was free to explore all the issues currently exercising public opinion as well as a range of technical issues brought to its attention by civil servants and jurists. Not surprisingly, Muslims in general and Algerians in particular occupied center-stage in the Commission's deliberations. Their resonance was greatly increased by the Commission's decision to hold public hearings which, quite uniquely by French norms, were broadcast live on French television (Hargreaves 1988). Only as an afterthought did the Commission add an extra session so that it could hear evidence from activists and academics of Asian and Portuguese origin; by then, the television cameras had been switched off. One of the Commission members, Dominique Schnapper, later acknowledged that they had been particularly concerned to

> examine head-on the problems preoccupying public opinion, including the most sensitive issues. There is particular public concern over dual nationality, military service and Islam, so we prioritized those problems and perhaps went a bit far. It was only in the final public session that we heard evidence from Asian and Portuguese contributors.
>
> (Schnapper 1988: 15)

Bearing in mind the alarmist atmosphere in which the Commission had been set up, the expert evidence which it heard was surprisingly reassuring. Dual nationality, including arrangements covering military service similar to those agreed by France and Algeria, was shown to be commonplace. France had bilateral agreements on military service with no less than fourteen states and had signed a multilateral agreement with a dozen others under the auspices of the Council of Europe; among Franco-Algerian bi-nationals (the only specific group for which the Commission requested detailed figures), no more than one in five was opting to do military service in Algeria (*Être Français aujourd'hui et demain* 1988, vol. 1: 211–21, vol. 2: 259–61).[6] Where Islam was concerned, the tone was set during the first televised hearing by a leading researcher, Bruno Étienne, who pointed out that it had taken France 300 years to successfully manage the presence of a Protestant minority and 150 years to do the same for Jews; he thought it not unreasonable to aim to accomplish something similar in relation to Muslims within a mere half century. 'French identity strikes me as being far more threatened by the globalization of culture and by Europe than by the Beurs [i.e. second-generation Maghrebis]', Étienne told the Commission (*Être Français aujourd'hui et demain* 1988, vol. 1: 131).

The Commission presented its report, including a full transcript of the hearings, in January 1988 (*Être Français aujourd'hui et demain* 1988). While agreeing that Article 44 should be revised so as to require a positive decision to opt into French nationality, its recommendations were in most other respects far more liberal than the abortive proposals which had been put forward by the government. Assent to the acquisition of French nationality would be as simple as ticking a box and adding a signature; no oath of allegiance would be required. People born in France of foreign parents would be able to benefit from these procedures between the ages of 16 and 21. While certain criminal offences would disqualify them if they applied after reaching the age of 18, between the age of 16 and 18 their right to French nationality would be absolute, subject only to the condition of their having resided in France during the five years preceding the application. The Commission not only ruled out the extra conditions which the government had wished to impose on Article 44 candidates, but also recommended abolishing the state's right to refuse French nationality on the grounds of poor morals or inadequate assimilation, powers which were regarded as unnecessary in the light of the period of socialization spent in France.

In line with the desire to establish a closer harmonization between acculturation and political incorporation, the Commission also recommended a limited revision of Article 23. This rested on a distinction between former colonies which had been officially classified as fully fledged French départements (Algeria being the most important instance) and those which had had the status of French overseas territories (which included most of French sub-Saharan Africa). No change was envisaged in relation to Algeria and other ex-départements, but it was recommended that Article 23 should no longer apply to other former colonies on the grounds that these had not been as fully subject to French cultural influences as Algeria. The effects of this recommendation were, however, partially canceled out by the Commission's proposal that there should be easier access to French nationality for applicants originating in independent states (among which were many former colonies) where French was now the official language.

By the time the report appeared, it was too late for legislation to be brought forward before the presidential elections due to be held in the early summer of 1988, but Chirac indicated that if he were elected in place of Mitterrand, he would hold a referendum to reform the CNF in line with the Commission's recommendations. In the event, Mitterrand won a second term of office, and the center-right parties lost their majority in the parliamentary elections held immediately afterwards. When they returned to office five years later under the premiership of Edouard Balladur, the first significant legislative text submitted to Parliament was the reform of the CNF. Almost simultaneously, two other pieces of legislation were introduced, providing for tougher immigration controls and more widespread identity checks by the police. Together, these became known as the

Pasqua laws by reference to Interior Minister Charles Pasqua, who was the guiding force behind them. Their combined effect would be such that anyone failing to acquire French citizenship in future would be more vulnerable to deportation.

Balladur was pushed into prioritizing the CNF reform by pressure from hard-line RPR deputies. As Justice Minister, the UDF centrist Pierre Méhaignerie assumed formal responsibility for the bill, but it had in fact been drafted by RPR deputy Pierre Mazeaud, who served as its *rapporteur* (i.e. principal spokesperson) (*Le Monde*, 15 April and 12 May 1993). Méhaignerie had opposed the reform originally proposed by the Chirac government in 1986, but said he favored the new bill because it was based solely on the recommendations of the Nationality Commission, which had been widely praised when first published in 1988. The Minister claimed that the purpose of the legislation was to foster integration, but Mazeaud offered a more revealing insight into the thinking behind it when he told the National Assembly that citizenship should be acquired only by those willing to make an act of commitment to the French nation and added: "The role of Islam stands out more and more – Islam, and particularly the fundamentalist threat, which refuses all adherence to our society' (*Le Monde*, 13 May 1993).

With the hard-liners still not satisfied by the bill, the government introduced a number of amendments which went well beyond the Nationality Commission's recommendations. The most politically symbolic of these was an amendment to Article 23. In addition to ending its application to ex-colonies such as those in sub-Saharan Africa, as suggested by the Commission, the government now proposed to impose a residence qualification on Algerians. Children born in France to Algerian parents would be French from birth only if one of their parents had lived in France for at least five years prior to the birth. Méhaignerie justified this on the grounds of the need to combat the fraudulent use of Article 23 by pregnant Algerian women allegedly traveling to France with no other purpose than to gain residence rights for them and their children by giving birth there. No figures were given to indicate the extent of this 'fraud', but it seems unlikely to amount to more than a few hundred cases a year at most (Wihtol de Wenden 1994a: 51). Once again, the symbolic weight of the gesture outweighed its practical significance.

The revised bill was adopted by Parliament in June 1993 and took effect on 1 January 1994. The speedy passage of the 1993 reform was in marked contrast to the débâcle of 1986–8. In his analysis of the Chirac government's initiative, Brubaker attributed its failure to 'the prevailing idiom of nationhood' among French political and cultural elites, and thought it unlikely that a future government of the right would succeed in enacting an exclusionary citizenship reform (Brubaker 1992: 162–4). On this view, while mass opinion was more attached to a narrow ethnocultural vision of nationhood, the majority of French intellectuals, politicians and civil servants were deeply committed to 'an open, inclusive definition of citizenship' (Brubaker 1992: 164). How, then, are we to explain the adoption of exclusionary legislation by the traditional center-right parties only a few years after their withdrawal of a similar project?

Wayland (1993) has underlined important differences in the political opportunity structure prevailing at the time of the Chirac and Balladur governments, as well as differences in resource mobilization by those opposed to the reform. In 1986, the RPR and UDF held only a wafer-thin majority in Parliament, and there were known to be dissensions within its ranks on the issue of the CNF. The government's loss of nerve following massive demonstrations in the autumn of 1986 against its educational reform proposals, combined with the very broad front successfully mobilized against its CNF reform project, led Chirac to pull back rather than risk another humiliating defeat. In 1993, by contrast, Balladur had a landslide parliamentary majority, the opposition parties were beset by internal feuds and the old alliance of anti-racist and other pressure groups was able to generate far less momentum than in 1986.

On both occasions, the right was playing to the gallery of public opinion which, as was seen in section 4.1, has been preoccupied by the issue of immigration since the early 1980s. Yet while mass opinion was strongly influenced by a feeling that 'something needs to be done' about immigration, the evidence yielded by opinion polls on the question of nationality laws did not indicate an overwhelming desire for exclusionary legislation. Certain polls indicated support for the general idea of a reform of the CNF (CSA poll in *L'Événement du jeudi*, 12 May 1988), but when more precise questions were asked, respondents did not usually favor tougher laws. In particular, when asked specifically if children born to immigrants should automatically acquire French citizenship on reaching the age of majority, those in favor of retaining this provision generally outnumbered those against by two to one (SOFRES poll in *Le Nouvel Observateur*, 13 Sept. 1990; SOFRES poll in *Le Figaro Magazine*, 21 Sept. 1991). A very similar ratio – but this time of a hostile nature – was regularly recorded in polls asking whether non-nationals resident in France should be allowed to vote in local elections (BVA poll in *Le Figaro Magazine*, 4 Nov. 1989; SOFRES poll in *Le Nouvel Observateur*, 13 Sept. 1990).

It is clear from these findings that the republican-inspired idiom of nationhood described by Brubaker is strong not only among French elites but also among the public at large. There is a wide consensus in favor of the view that citizenship is to be reserved for members of the nation, and that the nation should be open to people of foreign origin who have internalized its norms, as have most young people born and socialized in France. While open at the level of political incorporation, the assimilationist aspect of this idiom is closed to cultural difference. This is true at both the elite and mass levels. Few politicians or civil servants are prepared to endorse the concept of multiculturalism. In opinion surveys, those who say immigrants must adapt or wholly conform to French cultural norms regularly outnumber by three to one those who feel they should be allowed to retain the traditions of their country of origin (IPSOS poll in *Le Point*, 30 Oct. 1989; CSA poll in CNCDH 1994: 465).

The 1993 reform of the CNF was calculated to serve as a symbolic gesture of the government's intent to 'do something' about immigration without fundamentally infringing the values associated with France's republican tradition (cf. Weil 1994: 268–9). In particular, it was designed to appeal to the sizeable minority among the electorate which was tempted by the more exclusionary arguments of the FN. Had it not been for the rise of the FN in the mid-1980s and the threat this posed to the electoral base of the RPR and UDF, it is doubtful whether the traditional center-right parties would have implemented or even proposed the changes which were made in the CNF in 1993. The debate over French nationality laws was thus symptomatic of a party-political contest in which, since the mid-1980s, a large part of the agenda had been set by the anti-immigrant platform of the FN. The wider dynamics of party politics and their impact on public policy formation are considered in more detail in the next chapter. Before examining them, it is useful to consider the impact of the 1993 reform and subsequent changes in public attitudes on citizenship and associated matters.

4.5 Wrong targets and missed opportunities

In the early 1990s, around 24,000 young men and women were estimated to be acquiring French nationality each year under Article 44 of the CNF. After the 1993 reform, it soon became clear that it had made virtually no difference to the number of immigrant-born youths acquiring French citizenship. Far from the number falling (as anticipated by many of those who backed the law), if anything it actually rose because of the speed with which immigrant-born youngsters opted to exercise their rights under the newly defined terms of access to citizenship. Under the new law, young people of immigrant origin had several years in which to opt into French citizenship. By 1995, the number of youngsters taking French citizenship in this way was running at about 30,000 a year, suggesting not only that most were opting into citizenship but also that many were doing so at the earliest opportunity rather than at the last minute. The rate of citizenship acquisitions remained at this level until 1997, when the newly elected Socialist-led government reversed the reform and reinstated automaticity of citizenship for immigrant-born youths. The new administration also opened up the option of acquiring French citizenship by declaration prior to the age of majority. Most young people – the numbers were again running at around 30,000 per annum by the beginning of the new century – exercised that option instead of waiting to acquire citizenship by automaticity (Table 1.2).

The 1993 reform thus appeared a sterile exercise. While it completely failed to reduce the number of young people of immigrant origin acquiring French citizenship, it may nevertheless have caused significant attitudinal damage for it was interpreted by many of those targeted by it as a sign of majority ethnic suspiciousness if not indeed hostility towards them. The reform was pushed through as part of the Pasqua laws of 1993, which also imposed severe new restrictions on the settlement of family members of migrants and made it easier to deport them. These new laws resulted in numerous anomalies, including growing numbers of *sans-papiers* (undocumented migrants) who could neither be regularized nor deported, as well as fierce protests over forcible deportations (Fassin *et al.* 1998; Simeant 1998). The humanitarian crisis resulting from this reached a climax in the summer of 1996, when Pasqua's successor as Interior Minister, Jean-Louis Debré, sent the CRS riot police into churches where families of *sans-papiers* threatened with deportation had sought refuge. Live television coverage of police officers in riot gear hauling traumatized women and children out of churches was a public relations disaster for the government. While two-thirds of those questioned in a public opinion poll immediately after the police operation said they supported the Pasqua laws, which had provoked the *sans-papiers* crisis, at the same time 46 per cent said they felt sympathetic towards the *sans-papiers*, compared with 36 per cent expressing hostility (IPSOS opinion poll in *Le Monde*, 27 Aug. 1996).

When the left returned to power in 1997 under the premiership of Lionel Jospin it reversed most of the Pasqua laws, including the reform of the CNF. Considering how much energy had been expended on putting those laws into place, their repeal met with remarkably little opposition. Moreover, on their return to government in 2002, the center-right parties made no attempt to reinstate the nationality laws they had created nine years earlier. What in 1993 had been presented as an urgent necessity had in the intervening period disappeared almost without trace from the political agenda. This may well have been due in part to the patent fact that, when operationalized, the 1993 CNF reform had made virtually no difference to the number of young people becoming French. It was also due to a gradual but unmistakable change in both the terms and the substance of the public policy debate together with public opinion in general which began to make itself felt from 1997 onwards.

The humanitarian disaster created by the Pasqua laws may have been one factor helping to soften public opinion *vis-à-vis* immigrant minorities. Other changes also helped to improve the climate of public opinion. Beginning in 1997, France began to experience the first sustained fall in unemployment seen in over twenty years. Economic insecurity, which more than any other single factor had been the motor driving the politicization of immigration, began to abate. By the end of the 1990s, opinion surveys indicated that improved labor market conditions were reflected in reduced levels of economic insecurity (though other types of insecurity had grown) and greater tolerance towards immigrant minorities (IPSOS poll in *Le Monde*, 18–19 July 1999; CECOP data analyses in *Le Monde*, 15–16 Aug. 1999). There was also a marked change in public opinion on the question of political citizenship. In the early 1990s, opinion surveys consistently showed that most people in France were opposed to granting local voting rights to foreigners. The Maastricht Treaty of 1992 committed all EU member states, including France, to grant voting rights in local and European elections to citizens of EU countries. In the course of the decade opposition to local voting rights for foreigners of all nationalities declined steadily and by the beginning of the new century polls showed a clear and rising majority in favor of granting those rights to all foreigners, including non-Europeans (IPSOS 2003b; CSA poll in *La Lettre de la citoyenneté*, Sept. 2003). No less remarkably, in 2003 and again in 2005, public opinion surveys found that a substantial majority supported positive discrimination in favor of people of immigrant origin (IFOP poll in *Le Journal du Dimanche*, 16 Dec. 2003; BVA 2005).

Political discourse had also begun to undergo significant changes. The Socialist-led administration elected in 1997 reversed most of the Pasqua laws and announced that anti-discrimination policy was for the first time to be a government priority. Center-right politicians also began to re-examine their own positions. Amid the euphoria surrounding the victory of France's multi-ethnic soccer team in the 1998 World Cup, Pasqua, whose laws had created the *sans-papiers* crisis, declared that he was in favor of regularizing the selfsame *sans-papiers* (*Le Monde*, 17 July 1998). Alain Juppé too, who had been Prime Minister when the *sans-papiers* were dragged out of churches and deported, ate humble pie, regretting the clumsiness with which he had handled the affair, courting minority ethnic voters, and lending his support to the creation of an independent anti-racist authority (*Le Monde*, 1 Oct. 1999). Edouard Balladur, under whose premiership the Pasqua laws had been passed, discovered the virtues of 'difference' and defended the rights of minority ethnic groups to 'integration' without requiring their outright 'assimilation' (Balladur 1999).

Tangible changes on the ground were more elusive. Institutional initiatives to fight racism under the Jospin administration proved timid and largely ineffective, with no measurable lessening of discrimination. After peaking at 13 per cent just before Jospin took office in 1997, the national unemployment rate dropped to 10 per cent in 2000 but then hovered stubbornly at between 9 and 10 per cent, far higher than in most other west European countries. When the twenty-first century dawned, youth unemployment was running at around 40 per cent in the most disadvantaged of the banlieues (HCI 2003: 38), where a new generation of teenagers saw little, if any, reason to hope for any abatement in the chronic unemployment and discrimination which, during the 1990s, had become the norm in such areas. Evidence of hardening attitudes among younger members of minority ethnic groups was apparent in opinion surveys and, most graphically, in the 2005 riots. An opinion survey conducted in January 2004 showed for the first time a small majority of Muslims was opposed to a law banning the Islamic headscarf; amongst the sample, those in the youngest age group (18–24) showed the highest levels of opposition (CSA 2004a). The survey was conducted at the height of the renewed controversy over the headscarf following Chirac's announcement of legislation to ban the garment from state schools. Bearing in mind the very small numbers of young women wearing the headscarf (see section 3.4), it seems likely that this apparent shift of opinion – all previous surveys had shown a majority of Muslims in favor of banning the headscarf – had more to do with hostility towards what was perceived as a discriminatory law than with enthusiasm for the headscarf itself.

In the spring of 2003, support among the general population for an anti-headscarf law had been at an all-time low, almost equally balanced by opposition to such a law. It was only after Chirac stirred the matter up by establishing the Stasi Commission and then announcing legislation to ban the headscarf that this course of action regained high levels of support (CSA 2004b). Other surveys conducted amid the furore surrounding the new law indicated that local voting rights for foreigners, which had had majority support since the beginning of the new century, were now opposed by most majority ethnic respondents (CSA poll in *La Lettre de la citoyenneté*, May 2004).

While attitudes are by no means static and can sometimes swing rapidly in response to current events – a survey conducted in the immediate aftermath of the

November 2005 riots showed a significant worsening in majority ethnic attitudes towards minority ethnic groups (CSA poll in CNCDH 2006: 333–42) – during the last ten years there appears to have been an underlying softening of majority ethnic sentiments towards immigrant minorities while attitudes among minorities, especially younger age groups, appear to have been more prone to harden. Disaffection among young members of minority ethnic groups owes much to the sense of despair engendered by the perceived long-term inability or unwillingness of the Republic to improve conditions in the banlieues. With unemployment falling in the late 1990s and public opinion becoming more sympathetic towards immigrant minorities, politicians who since the mid-1980s had been nervous about appearing soft on immigration because of the electoral threat posed by the FN had an important opportunity to address the socio-economic inequalities and entrenched patterns of discrimination which were making conditions in the banlieues intolerable. The Socialist-led administration which took office in 1997 and the center-right government which replaced it in 2002 both made genuine efforts to address those problems but their initiatives have so far proved too limited and too late to turn the tide of disillusionment. The riots of 2005 showed that the fabric of national unity in France was threatened not by easy access to French citizenship, as proponents of the 1993 reform had claimed, but by government failures to provide effective remedies to long-standing problems of socio-economic inequality and racial discrimination.

5   Politics and public policy

5.1 From *laissez-faire* to state intervention

The politicization of immigration during the final quarter of the twentieth century is all the more striking when contrasted with the marginal position of this issue in political debate during most of the post-war period. The present chapter has two main aims: to delineate and account for the emergence of immigration as a key issue in French party politics, and to analyse how this has translated into substantive changes in the field of public policy. First, however, we need to understand something of how immigration was handled by political elites prior to the 1980s.

It is a remarkable fact that no legislation relating directly to immigration was passed by the French Parliament at any point in the post-war period before 1980. The fundamental lines which were to guide public policy during most of this period were laid down in an ordinance (an executive order having the force of law) issued in November 1945 by the provisional government installed the previous year under the leadership of General de Gaulle pending the organization of France's first post-war parliamentary elections, which took place with the creation of the Fourth Republic in 1946. The marginal role of Parliament in shaping immigration policy until the end of the 1970s is partly a reflection of the relatively limited powers enjoyed by the legislature compared with the executive under the constitution of the Fifth Republic, the terms of which were set by de Gaulle in 1958. Yet even under the Fourth Republic, which gave much more extensive powers to the legislature, immigration seldom attracted parliamentary attention (Verbunt 1985: 156–60).

At root, the absence of parliamentary debate reflected the relatively uncontroversial nature of immigration policy at a time of labor shortages as well as the executive's preference for dealing with potentially sensitive aspects in a technocratic fashion away from the glare of party politics (Freeman 1979: 99–130). As noted in section 1.2, an important debate took place within the provisional government immediately after the war over the relative importance of demographic and economic considerations in the recruitment of immigrants, together with the desirability of setting ethnic quotas (Weil 1991: 53–62). The 1945 ordinance empowered the state to control the overall level of recruitment according to economic and demographic needs, but did not set out any formal ethnic preferences since it was felt these might appear too reminiscent of Nazi ideology, from which Europe had only just been liberated. An ethnic hierarchy favoring Europeans over Africans and Asians nevertheless commanded wide assent, and while never formally codified in law it underlay the actions of successive governments to the extent that they pursued a proactive recruitment policy.

However, state control over the recruitment process was in practice undercut by three main forces: unexpectedly low inflows from European countries such as Italy, the exemption of Algerians from formal immigration controls and the reluctance of French employers to comply with the procedures laid down by the 1945 ordinance. Under the terms of that ordinance, employers were required to request from the state-controlled Office National d'Immigration (ONI) advance authorization for the entry of each would-be immigrant. While ONI offices established in Italy failed to secure the anticipated number of recruits, entirely separate developments in colonial policy gave Algerians complete freedom of movement in and out of France beginning in 1947, thereby removing them from immigration controls. From the mid-1950s onwards, economic expansion and labor shortages were such that ONI's procedures were increasingly flouted by employers anxious to hire foreign workers as quickly as possible. By the late 1960s, the overwhelming majority of new entrants were technically illegal immigrants before being regularized *ex-post facto* by ONI after they had found jobs in France. Government ministers acquiesced uncomplainingly in these developments. In 1966, for example, the Minister for Social Affairs, Jean-Marcel Jeanneney, stated: 'Illegal immigration has its uses, for if we adhered rigidly to the regulations and international agreements we would perhaps be short of labor' (quoted in Wihtol de Wenden 1988: 161).

A laissez-faire approach thus came to dominate official policy on migratory inflows, which were effectively left to the free play of the labor market.[1] A similar lack of intervention characterized to a large extent public policy concerning the welfare of immigrants once they had arrived in France. In principle, ONI's procedures required employers to make suitable arrangements for the housing of immigrant workers; in practice, most were left to fend for themselves. There was an acute housing shortage in post-war France. Many immigrant workers were employed in construction projects designed to remedy this shortage, but they were not among the planned beneficiaries of these programs. Instead, they faced severe discrimination in the housing market and, with low disposable incomes, were relegated to its most marginal sectors, such as inner-city slums and bidonvilles (shantytowns) thrown up illegally on vacant land. The Fonds d'Action Sociale (Social Action Fund – FAS), a public agency created in 1958, invested significant sums in hostel accommodation initially designed specifically for Algerians; its terms of reference were extended in 1964 to include all immigrants. This program made only a limited impact on the overall housing problem, however, and in other respects social assistance for immigrants was left largely to voluntary agencies.

By the late 1960s, the public authorities were increasingly troubled by two main consequences of the laissez-faire approach: their loss of control over the ethnic composition of the foreign population and the appalling social conditions in which many immigrants were living. Beginning in 1968, a series of measures was introduced aimed at reducing inflows of non-European, especially Algerian, immigrants while continuing to facilitate migration from Europe, notably Portugal. Circulars issued by Interior Minister Raymond Marcellin and Labor Minister Joseph Fontanet in 1972 made regularization contingent on more stringent employment and housing criteria, with deportation orders being served on those unable to satisfy them. At the same time, the state began to take a more interventionist role in matters relating to the welfare of immigrants, particularly housing. The twin principles of controlling primary inflows and integrating immigrants legally resident in France, which were to become the leitmotif of public policy, thus began to emerge during this period. Both trends became sharply accentuated in 1974, when the admission of non-EC labor migrants was halted altogether and for the first time a wide-ranging social policy was developed for the population of immigrant origin.

5.2 Europeanization and globalization

Changes in France associated with immigration and the settlement of immigrant minorities have been taking place within an international context which, since the end of the Cold War in 1989, has frequently been characterized in terms of globalization. While complex and contested in many respects, the concept of globalization is generally understood to include at least two key dynamics: a process whereby virtually all parts of the world are becoming increasingly interconnected and a redistribution of power whereby the sovereignty of long-established nation-states is being steadily eroded by powerful trans- and multinational forces.

Prior to 1989 it was commonplace to view the world in terms of two polarized blocs – developed capitalist nations led by the United States in one camp versus the Soviet-dominated communist bloc in the other – together with a residual group of relatively poor countries in Africa, Asia and Latin America generally referred to as the Third World. That tripartite division has been rendered obsolete by the collapse of the communist bloc, the steady erosion of barriers to international trade and the ever more rapid development of international telecommunications, making it increasingly difficult to insulate any country or region from other parts of the world. The capacity of national governments to shape the fabric of the societies over which they hold nominal sovereignty has been increasingly challenged by large-scale corporations whose operations routinely traverse national boundaries, multilateral groupings of states such as the European Union, and numerous other developments which mean that the lives of ordinary individuals are now touched in multiple ways by spaces beyond the boundaries of the state of which they hold citizenship.

For governments and ordinary citizens accustomed to the notion that collective identities and destinies are shaped primarily by nation-states, these changes have raised many concerns. Nowhere have those challenges been more keenly felt than in France, where the erosion of national sovereignty has been widely portrayed as a threat to national identity and individual well-being. Key factors contributing to this have been the longer history of France as a centralized national polity compared with many other European states, making national sovereignty appear an all the more 'natural' state of affairs, and the determination of post-war political elites to efface the humiliation of the Nazi occupation of France by restoring the nation's prestige in the international arena. The high water mark of those efforts was reached under the presidency of Charles de Gaulle, who served as first President of the Fifth Republic from 1958 to 1969. His successors have found it increasingly difficult to halt or conceal the erosion of national sovereignty.

Numerous powers which were previously the prerogative of national governments – including significant aspects of immigration and 'integration' policy – have been transferred by France and other member states to the EU in the belief that this multilateral pooling of sovereignty will afford greater benefits than any single state can hope to achieve on its own. The enormous economic repercussions resulting from the oil shocks of the 1970s, a by-product of the politics of the Middle East, demonstrated the vulnerability of France, like other developed nations, to international forces beyond its control. Since the Iranian Revolution of 1979 the resurgence of Islam in the international arena, seen most graphically in the attacks of 11 September 2001 in the United States, has been widely perceived as a further threat to the security of France, where international migration has brought the settlement of the largest Muslim population in western Europe.

French public policy on international migration and settlement has been directly affected by outside forces on three main levels internationally: bilateral, regional and global. In response to labor shortages after the Second World War, France signed bilateral agreements with many states, initially in Europe and subsequently in Africa, which in each case imposed on both parties a number of rights and obligations by which they had not previously been bound. Simultaneously, France was signing regional and global-level agreements which in due course were to impact significantly on international migration, though this was not always anticipated at the time.

For instance, when the European Convention on Human Rights (ECHR) was signed in 1950, the agreement was not generally seen as being of particular salience to international migration. Yet it became so in the 1970s when government attempts to prevent family members from joining economic migrants in France were found to be unlawful under the terms of the ECHR. The impossibility of blocking family reunification was of crucial importance in the transformation of what had originally been thought of as temporary labor migration from African countries into the permanent settlement of immigrant minorities. Another multilateral agreement, the UN's 1951 Geneva Convention on Refugees, also acquired greater importance than originally anticipated. Under the terms of the Convention, persons who have well-founded fears of persecution in their home country are entitled to asylum in signatory states, where they must be granted refugee status. Until the late 1970s asylum-seekers in France were relatively small in number, almost all came from the Soviet bloc and most were granted refugee status. During the 1980s the number of new asylum-seekers grew rapidly and where previously most had come from Europe now the majority came from Africa and Asia. Although the rejection rate also increased, mainly on suspicions that would-be economic migrants were trying to circumvent the ban on labor migration, France was bound under the terms of the Convention to accept all those meeting the criteria for refugee status. The net result was a significant rise in the total number of refugees granted residence permits and a further shift in the composition of France's foreign population in favor of non-Europeans. By the mid-1990s, 70 per cent of all foreigners taking up residence in France each year were doing so under the combined terms of the ECHR and the UN Convention on Refugees.

What is now the twenty-five-member European Union began in 1958 as the six-member European Economic Community. As the Community developed, adding member states and intensifying their cooperation, a growing number of policy areas shifted from inter-governmental status (where each national government effectively held a veto) to community competence (where majority voting could override the wishes of individual governments).[2] These changes have been fiercely opposed by various political factions in France, especially on the extreme right and hard left. In 1992, the Maastricht Treaty transferred to the EU level major powers over economic policy, preparing the way for the abolition of national currencies, and gave voting rights in local and European elections to migrants from EU states. When submitted to a referendum in France, the treaty was ratified by only a wafer-thin majority. In 1997, the Amsterdam Treaty created community competence in important new spheres including aspects of immigration control and integration policy, notably anti-discrimination. Unwilling to risk a negative referendum vote, Chirac instead arranged for ratification by Parliament, where he was assured of a majority. In 2005, he opted against the parliamentary route and chose instead to submit the European Constitution to a referendum which he lost by a wide margin.

Opinion surveys showed that the highest rates of negative voting in 2005 were among the most economically insecure parts of the population. Some 70 per cent of workers on short-term contracts voted against the European Constitution, as did a similar proportion of the unemployed and of those with no educational qualifications; two-thirds of low-income voters cast their votes negatively, compared with only a quarter of high-income voters (CSA survey in *La Tribune*, 30 May 2005; IPSOS survey in *Le Figaro*, 30 May 2005). It was among these same highly insecure parts of the electorate that the extreme right-wing Front National had been garnering its strongest levels of support since the mid-1980s, when Le Pen's party made its first electoral breakthrough. In the eyes of these voters, they were being ill served by policies which ceded sovereignty over the nation's destiny to supranational powers and allowed immigrants to settle in France. A generation earlier, many among these disadvantaged social groups would have vented their disaffection by supporting the French Communist Party and its class-based agenda. Now they were blaming the ills that afflicted them on the dilution of French sovereignty and the settlement of ethnic minorities.

5.3 The ethnicization of politics

If we define ethnic politics as political behavior conditioned to a significant degree by conscious processes of ethnic differentiation, it was not until the mid-1970s that stirrings of this kind became apparent in mainstream party-political activities, and it is only since the early 1980s that they have played a sustained role in French national politics. The absence of ethnic politics prior to the mid-1970s is attributable to three main factors: the insulation of policy-making in the field of immigration from parliamentary debate, the largely non-interventionist role of the state prior to 1968, particularly where the social welfare of immigrants was concerned, and above all the conditions of full employment and rapid economic growth which prevailed until the oil shocks of the 1970s. The ethnicization of French politics which has been witnessed since then has its roots in radical changes in all three respects.

The government habit of treating immigration as an almost private affair in which parliamentarians had no rightful role was challenged during the second half of the 1970s by a series of legal rulings, the most important of which emanated from the Conseil d'État, France's highest administrative court. Major immigration controls imposed by executive order (circulars, decrees, etc.) were declared to be unlawful, forcing the government to amend the measures and/or submit them to Parliament in the form of draft legislation open to analysis and argument from all sides of the political spectrum. The party-political divisions revealed by the parliamentary debates of 1979–80 were so deep that the legislation passed in January 1980 amounted to little more than a shadow of the draconian measures which had been initially proposed by the government with the aim of forcing the mass repatriation of non-European immigrants (Wihtol de Wenden 1988: 232–43). Every government elected since 1981 has brought forward important legislative proposals in the field of immigration, as a consequence of which parliamentary debate of this issue has become a standard feature of French politics.

The state has become more active not only in the field of immigration controls but also in measures designed to assist in the settlement of people of immigrant origin. These measures, discussed in greater detail later in this chapter, have included initiatives designed to reduce some of the chronic socio-economic disadvantages suffered by minority groups. As Crowley (1993: 629–31) has observed, improvements of this kind became increasingly visible from the mid-1970s onwards, particularly in the field of social housing. At the same time, groups of recent immigrant origin were becoming greater consumers of other welfare services as a consequence of family settlement. With unemployment rising, members of the majority population exposed to increased social insecurity have been inclined to see minority groups as competitors for scarce resources to a greater degree than when they were confined to the outer margins of housing and other markets. Competition over resource allocation at a time of growing socio-economic insecurity has been the single most important force pushing towards the ethnicization of French party politics.

Where mass opinion is concerned, resistance to immigration has always existed among certain sections of the population, but as was seen in section 4.1, this hostility declined during the post-war boom before gathering strength with the onset of a more difficult economic climate beginning in the mid-1970s. Even before the economic downturn seen in the later part of the decade, Algerians were the target of considerable racial violence during the early 1970s (Giudice 1992: 55–103). This prompted the Algerian government to suspend emigration by its citizens to France in 1973, a year before the introduction of France's blanket ban on non-EC labor migrants. However, ethnic tensions of this kind were not generally exploited by mainstream political parties during the early post-war decades. A very different pattern began to emerge after 1973. While the structural change conditioning this shift lay in the macro-economic situation, the particular forms in which it manifested itself owed much to the tactical contingencies of inter-party rivalry (Schain 1988).

At the national level, the center-right governments presided over by Valéry Giscard d'Estaing between 1974 and 1981 argued unsuccessfully but ever more stridently for the reduction of the immigrant population as a response to unemployment among the native population, which by the late 1970s had become the single most important preoccupation of the French electorate (Weil 1991: 108). The left was by no means immune to the temptations of ethnic politics. At the local level, minority ethnic groups are concentrated in poorer districts, where the French Communist Party (PCF) is traditionally strong. Schain (1985) has shown that from the mid-1970s onwards a growing number of Communist-run municipalities recast disputes over the allocation of social resources (particularly housing) around the division between natives and immigrants, rather than presenting them within the party's habitual ideological mold, based on the antithesis between capital and labor. It thus championed one part of the working class (white French nationals, who could vote) against another (visible minorities, most of whom lacked political rights). During the campaign for the 1981 presidential elections, the ethnic card was also played by the PCF's national leadership, most notoriously through its support for the Communist mayor of Vitry, in the south-eastern suburbs of Paris, when he ordered the demolition of a hostel housing African immigrant workers on Christmas Eve 1980.

Socialist Party (PS) leaders, too, have sometimes resorted to ethnicized representations of social issues. During the winter of 1982–3, the French automobile industry was hit by a wave of strikes arising from massive job losses among unskilled immigrant workers, mainly from Islamic countries. Exasperated by the difficulties he faced on the economic front, Socialist Prime Minister Pierre Mauroy claimed that the strikers were being 'stirred up by religious and political groups motivated by factors which have little to do with labor relations' (interview in *Nord-Eclair*, 27 Jan. 1983). Interior Minister Gaston Defferre and Labor Minister Jean Auroux lent support to this view, claiming that the culprits were Islamic fundamentalists (Kepel 1987: 253–4). Yet there was no evidence to support these claims, in which a classic conflict between capital and labor was grotesquely misrepresented as a struggle between ethnocultural groups.

Shortly afterwards, in the final stages of the campaign for the municipal elections held in March 1983, Defferre and his center-right opponent for the mayordom of Marseilles, Jean-Claude Gaudin, vied with each other in their claims as to who would be toughest in dealing with the city's Arab population. The election campaigns in many other localities were marked by similar rhetoric highlighting the alleged dangers of immigration.

It was against this backdrop that the extreme right-wing Front National (FN) emerged from almost total obscurity into the political limelight in a series of local elections held in 1983. The most notable of these took place in Dreux, thirty miles (fifty kilometers) to the west of Paris, where the party scored 17 per cent of the vote in September 1983 (Gaspard 1990). The FN had been founded under the leadership of Jean-Marie Le Pen in 1972. During the first ten years of its existence, it failed to score even 1 per cent of the vote in any nationwide election. Since the European elections of 1984, when it was supported by 11 per cent of voters, it has taken between 10 and 18 per cent of the national vote (Figure 5.1). The only exception to this was in the 1999 European elections, when internal dissensions within the FN led to the formation of a breakaway party under the leadership of Bruno Mégret, causing a split in the extreme-right vote. Mégret's Mouvement National (MN) subsequently faded while Le Pen bounced back in the presidential elections of 2002, when the left's share of the vote was splintered across multiple candidates. Because of these divisions on the left, Le Pen's 17 per cent score in the first round of voting was sufficient to put him ahead of Socialist Prime Minister Jospin, placing the FN leader second only to the incumbent, Jacques Chirac. In

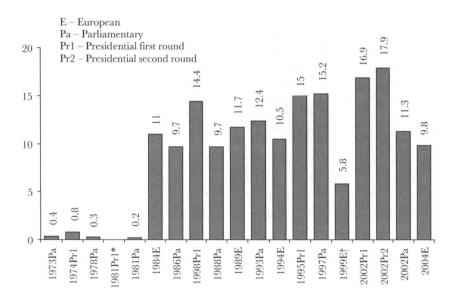

Figure 5.1 Front National's percentage share of vote in nationwide elections, 1974–2004

Notes
* No candidate; † Mouvement National splinter party scored 3.3%; FN + MN = 9.1%.

the absence of a candidate of the left in the second round run-off vote, in which Chirac was pitted head-to-head against Le Pen, most of the left's electorate joined center-right supporters in voting for Chirac, leaving Le Pen with 18 per cent of the vote. While many were shocked by Le Pen's success in ousting the left from the presidential race, it should be noted that this was due primarily to splits on the left. Le Pen's share of the first-round vote in 2002 was only slightly higher than the 15 per cent he had scored in the 1995 presidential elections and in the 2002 run-off he failed to significantly improve on his first-round vote. The FN's success in taking between 10 and 18 per cent of the vote in virtually every national election during the last twenty years has undoubtedly had a major impact on politics and public policy. At the same time, the 2002 elections showed the limits of the extreme-right vote, which though considerable has not grown significantly since the FN's breakthrough in the 1980s.

Le Pen's party has long stood on a vigorously anti-immigrant platform, with the mass repatriation of non-Europeans, the restrictive reform of French nationality laws and the exclusion of non-nationals from social security benefits foremost among its aims.[3] Its sudden electoral successes cannot be explained by a shift in FN policies or tactics. It reflects, rather, the growth of insecurity among a significant part of the electorate during a period of rising unemployment and a shift in the terms of political debate towards ethnic scapegoating for which the mainstream parties of both left and right had already paved the way (Schain 1987; Shields 1991).[4]

The heightened salience of immigration in French politics is clearly visible in a variety of indicators ranging from agenda-setting by political elites to public opinion polls and voting patterns at a mass level. Increased media coverage of immigration and minority ethnic groups (Bonnafous 1992; Gastaut 1994) has served as an important relay in this process. While the mainstream parties had already begun to talk up the issue before the FN's electoral breakthrough, the sudden, highly publicized emergence of Le Pen's party placed immigration at the center of political debate, for it forced the other parties to react to his agenda. The way in which the initiative had been seized by the FN was encapsulated in a remark made in 1985 by Socialist Premier Laurent Fabius, who stated that Le Pen was asking some of the right questions even though he was giving the wrong answers (*Le Monde*, 29 Oct. 1985). Fear of appearing 'soft' on immigration in the face of the FN contributed to a toughening of the policy platforms not only of the traditional center-right parties but also of the Socialists. The left's reintroduction of repatriation assistance and tighter restrictions on family reunification in 1984 were in part a response to the FN's initial electoral breakthrough. Similarly, the FN's parliamentary by-election victory in Dreux in December 1989 in the wake of the Islamic headscarf affair (Roy 1990) prompted Socialist Premier Michel Rocard to announce tougher controls against illegal immigrants.

Since 1977, unemployment has generally been the single most important issue named by voters when asked to explain their party preferences. While immigration has not generally featured as the overriding issue, it has often ranked close behind. *Insécurité* (literally, 'insecurity'), which in political debates denotes concerns over a range of subjects including law and order and personal safety, has been another high-ranking issue, sometimes – in the 2002 presidential elections, for example – ahead of immigration. In the minds of FN voters, who consistently attach the highest levels of importance to immigration and *insécurité*, these two issues are closely intertwined with each other as well as with unemployment (Freedman 2004). FN supporters, who have been alone in consistently identifying immigration as their prime concern also express higher levels of insecurity than those found among the supporters of any other party (Mayer 1995). While economic insecurity is only one element in a much wider network of anxieties ranging from concern over law and order and personal safety to fears about the erosion of French national identity – all of them linked in the minds of FN voters to threats associated with the banlieues and people of immigrant origin – it would be a mistake to underrate the significance of economic concerns. In an exit poll conducted during the first round of voting in the 1993 parliamentary elections, 72 per cent of FN supporters (compared with 31 per cent of voters as a whole) said immigration had been an important consideration when casting their vote. At the same time, 64 per cent of FN voters said unemployment was an important concern, a figure practically identical to the 68 per cent of all interviewees attaching importance to this issue (CSA poll in *Le Parisien*, 22 March 1993). While inclined to perceive economic problems as the symptoms rather than the causes of a wider national malaise, FN voters nevertheless see a close connection between immigration and unemployment. In their eyes, minority ethnic groups are both the cause and – if migratory flows were to be reversed – the potential solution to practically every difficulty facing the nation, including unemployment.

The FN regularly takes a larger share of the national vote than the PCF, which in the early post-war period enjoyed greater popularity than any other party. It is particularly noteworthy that Le Pen's party has become very much more popular than the PCF among the young as well as among manual workers and the unemployed (BVA poll in *Libération*, 23 March 1993; CSA poll in *Le Parisien*, 22 March 1993; SOFRES 1994: 144; CSA 2002a), groups to whom the Communists traditionally looked for strong support. Platone and Rey (1989) have shown that there is little evidence to suggest that large numbers of former Communist voters have defected to the FN. The PCF appears by and large to have retained the allegiance of voters who entered the Communist fold before the mid-1970s, but while these have advanced in years the party has failed to replenish its electoral base by recruiting among young voters from disadvantaged social backgrounds who in earlier decades might have been its natural supporters and who instead are voting for the FN. High levels of job insecurity and long-term unemployment have placed many young voters beyond the reach of organized labor, which in the past was a key recruitment ground for the PCF.

The biggest transfer of votes to the FN came not from the PCF but from former supporters of the traditional center-right parties, the Union pour la Démocratie Française (UDF) and more particularly the Rassemblement pour la République (RPR). From the mid-1980s onwards the RPR and UDF were presented with a troubling dilemma: in order to win back their lost supporters, should they argue against Le Pen's ideas, make deals with the FN or try to undercut its electoral appeal by stealing some of the party's program? RPR and UDF leaders veered between these different approaches, and in so doing further accentuated the ethnic dimension in political discourse.

In September 1983, senior party figures gave their blessing to a local pact between the FN and the traditional center-right parties which enabled them to win power in Dreux (Gaspard 1990). A commitment to reform French nationality laws, included in the joint RPR–UDF manifesto for the 1986 parliamentary elections, was clearly inspired by the FN's proposals in this area. While RPR leader Jacques Chirac officially refused to countenance a national deal with Le Pen and just secured enough seats to form a government in 1986 without the support of the extreme right, he turned a blind eye to local alliances forged at the same time which enabled his party and the UDF to gain control of several regional councils with the support of the FN. Another senior RPR figure, Michel Noir, declared that he would prefer to see the center-right parties lose the 1988 presidential elections rather than their own soul by making a pact with Le Pen (*Le Monde*, 15 May 1987). While no such pact was made nationally, there were again local deals in the south of France during the parliamentary elections held in the summer of 1988 immediately after François Mitterrand's successful bid for a second presidential term. In the early 1990s, the mainstream center-right parties appeared to turn their backs on deals of this kind (none was made in the 1992 regional elections), but the barrage of legislation relating to immigration introduced when they returned to power nationally following the parliamentary elections of 1993 (Costa-Lascoux 1994a)[5] was clearly designed to enable them to recapture the initiative in the struggle for voters attracted by the FN.

The alternation of the left and right in government during the 1980s and early 1990s did nothing to halt the seemingly inexorable rise in unemployment, which was the foremost concern of most voters throughout this period. Less than half a million in 1973, the total number of unemployed stood at one million in 1977, 1.5 million in 1980, two million in 1982, 2.7 million in 1987 and 3.3 million at the end of 1993. During most of the post-war period, the rhetoric of political debate in France was dominated by the division between right and left over how to manage relations between capital and labor. The left came to power in 1981 promising to tilt the balance against private capital after almost a quarter of a century of center-right rule. After only two years, it abandoned the attempt to break out of recession by reflationary policies and fell back on orthodox austerity measures. Unhappy with the open acceptance of capitalist economics, the Communists, who had served as junior partners in the administration formed in 1981, stood down in 1984, leaving the Socialists to govern alone.

In 1981, 43 per cent of those interviewed by SOFRES found the distinction between left and right a valid framework for understanding French politics, compared with 33 per cent who thought it out of date. Three years later, only 37 per cent felt the distinction was still valid, while 49 per cent said it was out of date. By 1991, the proportion finding it valid had fallen to 33 per cent, against 55 per cent who considered it out of date (SOFRES 1992: 59). By the late 1980s, a large majority of survey interviewees felt that in practically every policy field there were few differences between left and right. Immigration had become – and in the 1990s remained – the only policy issue where a majority considered the left and the right to be divided by major differences (1988 and 1989 polls in SOFRES 1990: 18; 1992 poll in SOFRES 1993: 223).

When respondents were asked in 1991 to rank key words indicating *ideas* most commonly associated with the left, welfare protection topped the list. By contrast, when the same respondents were asked about 'the *reality* of the left during the last ten years' (SOFRES 1992: 68; emphasis in the original), anti-racism emerged at the top of the list, ahead of the construction of Europe and social welfare, in second and third places respectively. The identification of the left's policies with the protection of a relatively small minority of the population – that of immigrant origin – more than with its classic role as the guarantor of welfare protection for all in need is a striking development. It tells us much about the ethnicization of political debate but relatively little about the substance of public policy. As we shall see in the remainder of this chapter, after a series of liberal measures enacted by the left during the early 1980s, policy differences between left and right in the field of immigration have often been more apparent than real. Summarizing the present section, however, three important points should be noted: the centrality of socio-economic insecurity in shaping mass opinion during the last two decades, the ineffectiveness of public policy in addressing that issue and the growing tendency among political elites and the public at large to focus on ethnic differences within French society rather than on the traditional cleavage between capital and labor.

5.4 Division and consensus in public policy

From the founding of the Fifth Republic in 1958 until 1981, the presidency, government and parliament were all under center-right control. Because presidential and parliamentary elections were not always in phase, during the presidencies of Socialist François Mitterrand (1981–95) and of conservative Jacques Chirac (1995–2007), the distribution of power was less uniform: at times, parliament and government were of the same political hue as the president, while at other times the president and prime minister came from opposing political parties. Broadly speaking, when the presidency and government were aligned all major policy areas were under the control of the president; when the presidency and government were in the hands of opposing political camps, immigration and integration policy were controlled by the Prime Minister and his or her government.

A consensus among political elites to keep immigration out of inter-party rivalry largely prevailed until the 1970s, when it broke down (Freeman 1979: 99–130). Since then, politicians have tended to emphasize their differences rather than their common ground where immigration and ethnic relations are concerned. A rare exception to this came in a televised debate in October 1985 between Socialist Premier Laurent Fabius and RPR leader Jacques Chirac. Fabius's insistence that he agreed to a large extent with Chirac in the field of immigration policy was heavily criticized by the left and generally judged to have cost him the debate (Weil 1991: 191, 203–4). Cross-party talks organized by Socialist Prime Minister Michel Rocard in the spring of 1990 with the aim of defusing immigration as a political issue following the FN's capitalization on the Islamic headscarf affair ended inconclusively, with the right clearly unwilling to sacrifice the tactical advantage derived from the left's poor opinion poll ratings in this field (Schain 1993: 69–70). Yet while important differences certainly exist on a number of questions, behind the bluster of political rhetoric there has been substantive agreement among the mainstream parties on some of the most fundamental policy issues, most notably firm controls against fresh inward migration and the social incorporation of those who wish to remain permanently in France.

Since the formal end of non-EC labor migration in 1974, none of the main parties has questioned the principle of this ban. The two most divisive issues have concerned the degree to which people of immigrant origin already in France should be encouraged or even forced to leave and the extent to which those permanently settled in the country should be allowed to live in culturally distinct ways. The right has generally taken a tougher line on both questions, while the left has been identified with a more sympathetic attitude towards the population of immigrant origin. Both issues generated intense controversy during the late 1970s and early 1980s. The first was effectively settled by a unanimous National Assembly vote in 1984 granting more secure residence rights to most immigrants, while the second became the object of a broad consensus during the late 1980s and early 1990s, when the concept of 'integration' became the watchword of all the main parties, except for the FN. This *de facto*, though seldom acknowledged, consensus was facilitated by the right's renunciation of mass repatriation as a policy goal together with the left's decision to pull back from a flirtation with multiculturalism in the early 1980s (Vichniac 1991; Weil 1991: 187–204).

In very broad terms, three major periods may be distinguished since the 1974 halt on labor migration. The first, under Giscard d'Estaing's center-right presidency from 1974 to 1981, was characterized by increasingly tough policies on immigration control, hostility towards the settlement of non-European immigrants and a mixture of carrots and sticks aimed at their repatriation. From 1981 to 1997, while immigration controls remained firmly in place, policies of forced repatriation were abandoned and 'integration' became the cross-party watchword, though significant aspects of center-right government policies appeared to cut across this, notably in the field of nationality and citizenship laws. Since 1997 a third phase has emerged in which the inadequacies of 'integration' policies have been increasingly recognized and serious attention has been given to the need for effective anti-discrimination policies.

Within that overarching chronology, the main shifts in government policy may be summarized as follows:

- Between 1974 and 1977, the center-right governments headed initially by Jacques Chirac and then by Raymond Barre under the presidency of

Valéry Giscard d'Estaing displayed considerable ambivalence over the long-term future of non-European minorities already resident in France.

- From 1977 to 1981, the emphasis fell firmly on measures designed to encourage or force the repatriation of non-Europeans.

- When the left came to power in 1981 with the election of François Mitterrand as President and the appointment of Pierre Mauroy as Prime Minister, it ended the official pursuit of repatriation and introduced liberal measures designed to improve the rights and living conditions of minority groups.

- By the end of 1984, however, Laurent Fabius had replaced Mauroy as Prime Minister, this liberalizing phase was largely over, assistance for voluntary repatriation had been reintroduced and family reunificaton had been made more difficult.

- On returning to government under the premiership of Jacques Chirac in 1986, the RPR and UDF attempted unsuccessfully to reform the French nationality code (CNF), but mass repatriation no longer featured as a policy goal.

- While the Socialist-led governments headed succesively by Michel Rocard, Edith Cresson and Pierre Bérégovoy between 1988 and 1993 proved more cautious than those of 1981–6 in their attitude towards minority groups, the main thrust of their policies lay in measures designed to facilitate integration.

- The center-right administration which took over in 1993 under the premiership of Edouard Balladur introduced a raft of new legislation known as the Pasqua laws which brought in tighter immigration controls, easier police identity checks and a restrictive reform of the CNF, all of which destabilized immigrant minorities, though the principle of integration was officially retained.

- The government led by Socialist Prime Minister Lionel Jospin from 1997 to 2002 reversed the CNF reform and other parts of the Pasqua laws and began to address the need for more effective action against racial and ethnic discrimination.

- When the center-right returned to government in 2002 under the premiership of Jean-Pierre Raffarin, who was succeeded in 2005 by Dominique de Villepin, additional weight was given to anti-discrimination policy while Interior Minister Nicolas Sarkozy moved to strengthen immigration controls and President Chirac pushed through legislation banning the Islamic headscarf from state schools.

Thus despite periodic changes in the political complexion of governments and important differences of emphasis associated with these, public policy since 1981 has been characterized by the twin principles of control (externally) and integration (internally). The way in which these principles have been applied is examined in more detail below.

Control

In attempting to control migratory flows, states have at their disposal a range of levers. Some of these regulate the admission to the national territory of would-be entrants, while others limit the duration for which residence is authorized and the terms under which the repatriation of foreign residents may be facilitated or required. The center-right governments which held office prior to 1981 took vigorous action on each of these fronts. They sought to end not only labor migration from non-EC countries, but also the entry of family members of migrants already in France. Although the principle of banning family reunification was declared to be unlawful by the Conseil d'État, the government continued to place administrative obstacles in the path of dependants seeking to join their breadwinner in France. From 1977 onwards, financial inducements known as *aide au retour* (repatriation assistance) were offered in a largely unsuccessful attempt to encourage immigrants to return to their countries of origin. At the same time, executive orders were drawn up by Interior Minister Christian Bonnet and the minister responsible for immigrant affairs, Lionel Stoléru, with the aim of reducing the number of immigrants holding work permits and deporting those who were unemployed. When the Conseil d'État ruled that these orders were unlawful, the government attempted to implement the same policy by draft legislation brought before Parliament in 1979. While the Bonnet law of January 1980 tightened up on entry and residence rights, Stoléru's failure to secure parliamentary backing for the wide-scale non-renewal of work permits rendered impossible the deportation of hundreds of thousands of immigrants already living in France, as had been intended. On a very much smaller but symbolically significant scale, the Ministry of the Interior nevertheless used its executive powers to deport thousands of foreigners who were deemed to be a threat to *l'ordre public* (public order),[6] mainly because of criminal convictions (Wihtol de Wenden 1988: 189–275; Weil 1991: 89–138).

On taking office in 1981, the left called a halt to administrative expulsions of this kind. Court orders would in future be required for most deportations, and certain categories of foreigners – particularly young people who had spent most or all of their lives in France – were protected altogether from expulsion. The procedures governing family reunification were eased and an amnesty was declared for illegal immigrants. While the latter move helped to create an image of the left as 'soft' on immigration, it is important to note that those eligible for regularization had to prove both that they had entered the country before 1981 and that they held a job. The 132,000 who were regularized in this way were thus a legacy from the period when the right had been in office, and their work record was a clear sign of their economic utility. Simultaneously with this amnesty, the new government brought in stiffer penalties for employers whom it hoped to dissuade from hiring illegal immigrants in future.

The most enduring liberal initiative taken by the left in the field of immigration controls was a law passed in July 1984 granting automatically renewable ten-year combined work and residence permits to the majority of foreigners legally settled in France. The law, which enjoyed all-party support in the National Assembly, put an end to much of the complexity and insecurity which had until then been associated with the renewal of permits. Its acceptance by the right was a clear signal that mass deportations linked directly to conditions in the labor market were no longer on the agenda of any electorally significant party, except for the FN. The rise of Le Pen nevertheless led the left to toughen its stance in other respects. Deportations justified on the grounds of threats to public order began to rise again in 1983, voluntary repatriation assistance renamed *aide à la réinsertion* was reintroduced in the spring of 1984, and at the end of the year family reunification was made conditional on stringent housing conditions which many immigrants were unable to meet (Wihtol de Wenden 1988: 276–305; Weil 1991: 138–86).

When the right returned to power in 1986, Interior Minister Charles Pasqua brought forward legislation which gave back to the executive control over deportations on the grounds of threats to public order and widened the categories of those liable to be expelled; access to the ten-year residence and work permit was also made subject to certain restrictions. His Socialist successor, Pierre Joxe, reversed some of these provisions in 1989 (Harris 1991), but in 1993 they were reinstated and toughened by the Pasqua laws, which also placed more severe restrictions on the settlement of the family members of migrants. These measures resulted in a humanitarian crisis (see section 4.5) which the left attempted to resolve when it returned to power in 1997 by reversing the 1993 Pasqua laws and regularizing most of their victims.

Since the mid-1980s, the member states of the European Community have moved increasingly towards a common policy concerning the entry of non-EC nationals across external frontiers.[7] This has been necessitated by the abolition of internal border controls between most member states. The Schengen Agreement, initially negotiated by France and four other member countries in 1985, took effect in most EU states in 1995, abolishing internal border controls between them. In 1990, all twelve EC member states signed the Dublin Convention harmonizing procedures for handling asylum applications. Following the closure of EC borders to labor migrants in the mid-1970s, it was widely felt that the increase in asylum applications during the 1980s arose from abuses by would-be economic migrants. The 1993 Pasqua laws included provisions limiting the rights of asylum-seekers in line with the Schengen and Dublin agreements. This necessitated a constitutional revision, which was passed by Parliament in November 1993. Although the Socialists voted against it (*Le Monde*, 20 Nov. 1993), they had in fact signed both the Schengen and Dublin agreements. They had also introduced administrative reforms in 1990 which speeded up the processing of applications, the great majority of which were rejected, leading to a sharp fall in the overall number of requests for asylum (Wihtol de Wenden 1994b). Thus here too, overt displays of discord belied an underlying consensus in favor of tight border controls.

Integration

While admission to EU states is increasingly managed at a multilateral level, policy relating to the social welfare of immigrants, especially those who are not

EU nationals, is still largely determined by each national state. Although the French state is in this sense master in its own house, many of the issues thrown up by the settlement of immigrants and their descendants are fundamentally similar in all receiving countries. Despite historical, cultural and institutional variations which have given European states contrasting starting points in the rhetoric and sometimes the substance of their policies, a *de facto* process of convergence is visible in many areas (Schnapper 1992; Lapeyronnie 1993). After phases of marginalization or exclusion, the realization that settlement is now permanent has led most states to embrace policies designed to incorporate minority ethnic groups into the receiving societies. In France, a clear consensus in favor of integration emerged during the mid-1980s, after a decade of division and uncertainty.

The laissez-faire approach which characterized immigration controls prior to the 1970s was replicated in the field of social policy by a minimal level of state intervention in favor of immigrants and their families (Tapinos 1975). Not until 1974 was a ministry created with specific responsibility in this field. Antoine Postel-Vinay was appointed Minister of State for Immigrant Workers[8] in June 1974. He immediately proposed an end to further labor recruitment, coupled with an ambitious program designed to improve the living conditions of immigrants already resident in France, particularly their housing. The suspension of labor recruitment was implemented early in July, but Postel-Vinay resigned a few weeks later when it became clear that his housing proposals would not receive the required funding. He was replaced by Paul Dijoud, who announced a wide-ranging package of measures in October 1974. Until his own replacement by Lionel Stoléru in March 1977, Dijoud pursued a policy which was characterized by deep ambiguity over the long-term future of immigrants. On the one hand, improvements in housing, which implicitly favored the settlement of immigrant families, were facilitated by a major increase in funding in 1975; on the other hand, immigrants and their descendants were encouraged to retain close contact with the cultural systems of the sending countries in the hope that repatriation would remain a practical possibility.

The most important initiative in the field of housing was the decision to earmark part of a payroll tax for the specific purpose of assisting immigrants. Since 1953, companies with more than ten employees had been required to pay 1 per cent of their total salary bills to public bodies which invested the money in new housing. In 1975, a fifth of the money raised by this tax was earmarked to assist in the housing of immigrants and a new body, the Commission Nationale pour le Logement des Immigrés (National Commission for the Housing of Immigrants – CNLI), was set up to supervise the use of these funds. Some of the money was to be spent on the construction or refurbishment of hostels for foreign workers whose families were still in the country of origin, but most of the funds were invested in social housing (HLMs) for family occupation. Although this source of funding was later reduced, the net effect was to greatly increase the number of immigrant families living in social housing. As many had previously been housed in slum properties or shantytowns, this represented a significant improvement in their living conditions

(Barou 1989). At the same time, when combined with discriminatory practices in the housing units allocated to them (see section 5.5), this policy had the effect of concentrating minority ethnic groups in the most disadvantaged and stigmatized areas of French cities, generally referred to as the banlieues.

A number of initiatives were also taken to facilitate the distinctive cultural traditions of minority ethnic groups. Agreements were signed with sending states permitting them to fund limited amounts of mother tongue teaching for the children of immigrants within French state schools. A weekly television program for immigrants entitled *Mosaïque*, launched in 1977, placed a strong emphasis on the cultural traditions of sending states, especially in the Maghreb, which supplied a considerable proportion of the broadcast material. Despite France's constitutional commitment to *laïcité*, i.e. the separation of the state from religious organizations, public bodies facilitated the installation of Islamic places of worship in hostels for foreign workers, HLM blocks housing immigrant families and factories of state-controlled companies such as Renault, which employed large numbers of Muslims (Weil 1991: 245–9).

Under Dijoud, the aim of these initiatives was to keep open repatriation as a policy option. That option became a positive preference when Stoléru replaced Dijoud in 1977. In parallel with his plans for forced repatriation, Stoléru set up an advisory commission called Culture et Immigration with instructions to consider the cultural needs of minority ethnic groups who, he said, were 'legitimately asking for the right to be different and to choose their own future' (letter from Stoléru dated 13 November 1979 in *Culture et immigration* 1980: 99). The seemingly liberal connotations of 'le droit à la différence' (the right to be different) were of course undercut by the executive orders and draft laws prepared by Stoléru with the aim of ensuring that many people of immigrant origin would be anything but free to choose their own future. If they were found to be surplus to the requirements of the French labor market and did not choose the 'right' way, Stoléru intended to ensure that they were deported. The maintenance of their cultural heritage was thus conceived as the very antithesis of integration (Sayad 1978).

For different reasons, the concept of 'le droit à la différence' commanded widespread support on the left, particularly among members of the Socialist Party. Decolonization and the near-revolution of May 1968 had led many on the left to adopt a favorable attitude towards cultural pluralism. Mitterrand explicitly endorsed the principle of 'le droit à la différence' during his campaign for the 1981 presidential elections (campaign statement in *Le Droit de vivre* 1981: 17). In abolishing repatriation assistance and halting deportations, the administration installed at the beginning of his first presidency made it clear that minority ethnic groups of recent immigrant origin were now expected to settle permanently in France.[9] New measures were introduced to improve the housing, employment and educational prospects of minority groups. They were also allowed the free right of association (previously, the prior approval of the Interior Ministry had been necessary if foreigners wished to establish their own organizations), and substantial state funding was made available to support such initiatives.

The word most favored at this time in official circles to describe the social incorporation of people of immigrant origin was 'insertion'. It featured, for example, in the title of a report on measures designed to improve the social and economic welfare of second-generation members of minority groups (Marangé and Lebon 1982). It implied that those concerned could be 'inserted' into the social fabric of France while still retaining a distinctive cultural identity. 'Insertion' was thus implicitly contrasted with assimilation, a term felt to have been tainted by its association with colonial policies which had denigrated non-European cultures. Although the word 'multiculturalism' was almost never used, this was implicitly the direction in which the policies of the left seemed to point during their early years in office.

The rise of the FN, campaigning on a platform claiming that immigration threatened not only employment and law and order but also national identity itself, led the left to pull back from its apparently multiculturalist posture. References to 'le droit à la différence' all but disappeared, and a separate junior ministry with specific responsibility for immigrants was abolished when Laurent Fabius replaced Pierre Mauroy as Prime Minister in 1984. Issues relating to the social incorporation of minority groups were subsumed within the Ministry of Social Affairs, headed by Georgina Dufoix. This reflected the Socialists' desire to play down the notion of immigrants as distinct socio-cultural groups. Since then, whether the left or the right has been in power, no ministry has carried an explicit reference in its title to the population of immigrant origin.

Massive media coverage of the Islamic headscarf affair in the autumn of 1989 led to a spurt of institutional initiatives designed to reassure the public that people of recent immigrant origin were being successfully incorporated into French society. It was at this point that 'integration' became officially consecrated as the watchword of public policy relating to minority groups, though in practice it had already been structuring the policies of both the left and the right for several years. In December 1989, only days after the FN's by-election victory in Dreux, Rocard created a new administrative post, that of Secretary-General for Integration, within the Prime Minister's office. Hubert Prévot, the senior civil servant appointed to this post, was given the task of coordinating government policy aimed at sections of the population who were in danger of being socially excluded. To generate relevant policy proposals, Rocard set up a think-tank called the Haut Conseil à l'Intégration (High Council for Integration – HCI), which subsequently produced a series of reports and recommendations. In theory, Prévot and the HCI were concerned with integrating into mainstream society all those threatened by marginalization, including members of the native population. In practice, they focused almost exclusively on the population of immigrant origin.

The extreme sensitivity associated with any suggestion of ethnic separatism was apparent in the terminological coloration of Rocard's initiatives. Although fears over the cultural 'threat' associated with Islam had triggered these moves, there was no explicit reference to immigration in their formal designation. Instead, the whole thrust of the preferred term, 'integration', was to suggest that any differences separating minorities from the majority population were being reduced or eliminated by enlightened public policy. For the same reason, Rocard refused to set up a separate ministry responsible for minority groups.

His successor, Edith Cresson, did appoint a Minister of State for Integration, Togolese-born Kofi Yamgnane. The appointment of Yamgnane, who as a Catholic championed the cultural norms dominant in France and displayed a frosty attitude towards Islam, was clearly calculated to demonstrate that people of immigrant origin could be integrated into the very heart of the French state without this threatening the cultural integrity of the nation (Quemener 1991; *Le Monde*, 10 Oct. 1991).

The rapidity with which the Balladur government tightened entry and residence rights for foreigners and reformed the French nationality code (CNF) in 1993 signaled its determination to take a tough stance on immigration (Costa-Lascoux 1994a). Had the CNF reform made it impossible for large numbers of people of immigrant origin to acquire French citizenship, this might have served as an indirect method of facilitating mass deportations. In practice, relatively few would be barred from citizenship, and there was no substantive deviation from the core objective of integration inherited from the Socialist-led administrations of 1988–93.

Integration remains in many ways an ambiguous concept. For many on the right, it is little more than a euphemism for assimilation, while some on the left see it as a more palatable term for something akin to insertion. No less importantly, however, as Weil and Crowley (1994: 113–16) have pointed out, the consensus surrounding this word removed other ambiguities attaching to earlier terms which helped the FN to establish its political legitimacy during the early 1980s. The concepts of insertion and of 'le droit à la différence' were adaptable to the most extreme and opposed of policy positions, ranging from unbridled multiculturalism to mass deportations. The extreme right was only too glad to acknowledge cultural differences – and to infer from them the right of one ethnocultural group to exclude another. For all its ambiguities, 'integration' presupposed the irreversibility of the settlement of minority groups. By the same token, its widespread adoption during the late 1980s and early 1990s came to differentiate at a symbolic level all of the older established political parties more clearly from the FN than had previously been the case.

5.5 Discrimination, anti-discrimination and positive discrimination

Discrimination

The FN's policy platform is encapsulated in what the party calls 'la préférence nationale' (priority to French nationals). If implemented, this policy would legitimize systematic discrimination against foreigners in practically every area of social life from employment and housing to education and welfare. There are in principle enormous legal obstacles to a policy of this kind. All EU nationals, for example, enjoy legal protection from this type of discrimination, and the FN has said it will respect these obligations, while the nationals of many other states enjoy certain rights under bilateral treaties negotiated with France which cannot be unilaterally abrogated. The seemingly universal principle of non-discrimination is enshrined in a 1972 French law prohibiting discrimination on the grounds of ethnic origins, nationality, race or religion (Costa-Lascoux 1994b).

Yet in practice, very few prosecutions have been successfully brought under this law, while the French state has, like many other receiving states, discriminated both officially and unofficially against foreign residents on a massive scale (Lochak 1992). The formal rights of foreigners have been limited not only with regard to political citizenship, discussed in Chapter 4, but also in many other spheres, particularly employment. In unofficial ways, public authorities have often discriminated against minority ethnic groups, notably in the allocation of housing.

The system of work permits which operated until 1984 enabled the state officially to limit the geographical areas and types of jobs in which most foreigners were allowed to work. They were thus prevented from competing on a wholly equal footing within the national labor market. The relatively small number of foreigners working as tradespeople before 1984 was one of the consequences of this system (Ma Mung 1992: 40). Foreigners remained excluded from most public-sector jobs, which tend to be among the most secure in the whole economy. Almost all states exclude foreigners from areas where national security could be said to be involved (the army, the police, the senior civil service, etc.), but France draws exceptionally wide boundaries around public-sector employment, so that non-nationals are generally unable to work in state-owned sectors such as public transport, the postal service, education and health care, except for temporary and usually low-grade posts (Costa-Lascoux 1989: 53–70). Taking the private and public sectors together, in the year 2000 about 30 per cent of all wage-earning jobs in France were reserved for French nationals (GED 2000: 6). Although these are now being opened up to citizens of EU states, they remain closed to non-Europeans.

In mainly unofficial ways, the authorities responsible for publicly funded housing have discriminated against people of immigrant origin in many cities. In theory, the system of earmarking funds supervised by the CNLI, formally instituted in 1975, came close to a form of positive discrimination, since the money was to be used specifically for the housing of immigrants. Weil (1991: 249–56) has shown that in practice, these funds were frequently misused. Substantial sums were awarded to HLM authorities in exchange for agreements to house set numbers of immigrant families. Often, the money was spent on constructing or refurbishing homes which were then offered to members of the native population. The homes given to immigrants were concentrated in decaying parts of the public housing stock. In some cases, no extra immigrants were housed at all, since the authorities claimed that they were meeting their obligations if they undertook to replace an existing immigrant family with another one. Partly because of these abuses, the proportion of payroll tax funds earmarked for the housing of immigrants was gradually reduced before being virtually abolished in 1987 (Weil 1991: 274–5).

Despite the fact that ethnic quotas are in principle prohibited by the 1972 law against racial discrimination, they have in practice been applied by public housing authorities in many French cities. Those targeted have been 'visible' minorities, i.e. groups perceived as non-Europeans, including in many cases DOM-TOMiens, despite the fact that they are French citizens. Because the authorities are not obliged to make public their reasons for accepting or refusing individual housing applications, it is only rarely that documentary proof of discrimination can be brought before the courts (Blanc 1990: 86). Compelling evidence that a general policy of ethnic quotas has been applied on a wide scale has nevertheless been adduced by researchers such as Schain (1985: 176–82), Weil (1991: 254–6) and Villanova and Bekkar (1994: 47–89).

This has often involved a consensus between national and local arms of government, even when these have been controlled by parties of different political persuasions. Many of the poorer municipalities containing substantial areas of social housing are controlled by the left, particularly the PCF. During the second half of the 1970s, many left-controlled municipalities sought to limit the number of housing units allocated to visible minorities, notably Maghrebis, Africans and DOM-TOMiens. They were often assisted in this by the local representatives of the central state, which at that time was under the control of the center-right parties. Since 1981, when the left introduced a policy of decentralization, mayors have often used their increased powers to refuse construction permits for new social housing liable to bring into their locality additional minority ethnic families; at the same time, rigid quotas have been applied to existing housing stocks (Weil 1991: 270–6).

This approach has often been justified on the grounds of the so-called *seuil de tolérance* (threshold of tolerance), a level of immigrant concentrations beyond which the process of social incorporation is held to be threatened (Grillo 1985: 125–7). It is claimed that if this threshold – often put at between 10 and 15 per cent of the population – is crossed in a given locality, the capacity of the native population to absorb minority ethnic groups would be stretched beyond breaking point. There is no reliable evidence to indicate that such a threshold exists. While fears of ethnocultural 'ghettos' may have inspired some of those who pursued this policy, anxieties over a possible electoral backlash among native voters were probably a primary concern. One of the ironies of the pattern which developed is that because housing authorities tended to allocate their least desirable properties to immigrant families, relatively dense micro-concentrations of minority ethnic groups often arose despite the imposition of lower overall limits across given localities (Weil 1991: 254–6).

Anti-discrimination

Since 1997, major changes have taken place in the discourse and policies of both the left and center-right in the field of ethnic relations. While incremental rather than sudden, these changes have now become so substantive that policy development concerning France's immigrant minorities can be seen to have entered a significant new phase. Dominant between 1981 and 1997, the discourse of 'integration' has been increasingly supplanted by a new lexicon in which the buzz words are diversity, anti-discrimination and equal opportunities. Changes in political discourse do not always translate into changes in public policy. Many important policies inherited from the earlier period remain in place but they are being increasingly complemented and in some cases supplanted by a new agenda in which anti-discrimination is pivotal.

Until 1997, few politicians felt there was a need for stronger measures against racial and ethnic discrimination. Some virtually denied the existence of discrimination. Most took the view that, as racial discrimination was banned by the 1958 Constitution and the law of 1972, the problem had been dealt with (Bleich 2003). But in the course of the 1990s a growing body of evidence emerged of widespread discrimination against people of non-European origin (IGAS 1992; de Rudder *et al.* 1994; Bataille 1997). No less importantly, it became increasingly clear that anger and resentment among the victims of discrimination was fueling a growing threat to public order, which generated enormous media coverage and public concern over what was commonly called *l'insécurité*, a by-word for threats to personal safety and law and order.

This threat took three main forms. First, there was a steady stream of clashes between police and disaffected youngsters in the banlieues. The most violent of these clashes were sparked by police shootings of unarmed youths. Those shot were sometimes at the wheel of stolen vehicles; on other occasions they were being held in police custody. Car theft and joyriding afforded temporary access to the kinds of social goods denied to the victims of discrimination by their exclusion from the job market. Street battles with the police gave them the chance to vent their anger on the representatives of a state which was perceived to have failed to deliver on its promises of equality. There were sporadic incidents of this kind in the early 1980s, but they became much more widespread during the 1990s, attracting heavy media coverage and generating considerable public concern (Hargreaves 1996). A high impact cinematic representation of this spiral of violence was Mathieu Kassovitz's 1995 movie *La Haine* (Hate), inspired by events surrounding the death of a 16-year-old Zairean youth, Makomé Bowole, who was shot at point blank range in 1993 while being questioned in police custody.

A second type of violence took the form of terrorist bombings. In 1995, for the first time small numbers of second-generation Maghrebis aligned themselves with Islamic militants from Algeria and conducted under their direction organized attacks on civilian targets in France. If these attacks were at one level a spillover from the civil war raging in Algeria between Islamic guerrillas and a military-dominated régime which they accused France of backing, the bombing campaign was also rooted in the sense of rejection experienced by many young Maghrebis in their dealings with the rest of French society (see section 3.4). During a meeting arranged with minority ethnic residents in Lyon following the 1995 bombings, President Chirac was told by the writer and sociologist Azouz Begag that discrimination against minority ethnic youths was rife. Many nightclubs, for example, systematically refused entry to them. Chirac declared himself to be shocked by this revelation and eventually raised it at a cabinet meeting (*Le Monde*, 14 Oct. 1995 and 8 Nov. 1996). Although Alain Juppé's center-right government took only limited steps to redress the situation – no one in authority seems to have even suggested that club owners should be prosecuted for breaking the law – these developments may well have contributed to a request made by Juppé to the Haut Conseil à l'Intégration (HCI) for a report on racial discrimination and proposals for combating it. By the time the report was delivered (HCI 1998), Juppé's administration had been replaced by a Socialist-led government under the premiership of Lionel Jospin, in which it fell to Martine Aubry to address these questions.

By now, a third and in many ways more insidious form of violence was manifesting itself widely. There were growing reports of relatively small but increasingly numerous acts of violence by disadvantaged youths in schools, on buses and in other public places. Quantitative data confirming this upward trend were disclosed in a report commissioned by the Interior Ministry (Body-Gendrot and Le Guennec 1998). These appeared to be the actions of young people who had given up on the system because they were convinced the system had given up on them. By the late 1990s, many minority ethnic teenagers had spent all their lives in stigmatized neighborhoods where unemployment was taken as the norm and discriminatory treatment appeared to block any prospect of social advancement. In these circumstances, growing numbers were now engaging in acts of petty (and sometimes more serious) violence that seemed designed to spite people who were seen as representatives or beneficiaries of a social system that excluded them. Where earlier forms of violence had been largely confined to fairly localized confrontations between disaffected youths and the police, now schoolteachers, bus drivers and ordinary members of the public were exposed to often lower level but very unpleasant incidents on a much wider scale. Having been left to fester, the situation in the banlieues appeared to be in danger of spinning out of control.

Public concerns about *insécurité* had traditionally been played upon more by the right than the left. It was therefore a mark of the seriousness of the situation that in 1997 Socialist Prime Minister Lionel Jospin declared the fight against *insécurité* to be second only to the reduction of unemployment in the priorities of his government. The Interior, Education, Employment and Urban Affairs ministries announced numerous initiatives to strengthen law enforcement and personal security in the banlieues, but it was clear that these alone would not suffice. Action was also required over the seething resentment against discrimination that was helping to fuel much of this anti-social behavior. In the autumn of 1998, Martine Aubry, Minister for Employment and Solidarity, duly announced that she was making the fight against racial discrimination a priority area of 'integration' policy (Aubry 1998). Until then, 'integration' policy had focused on two main concerns: social disadvantage and cultural differences. It had been assumed that if these issues were satisfactorily addressed, disadvantaged minorities would be able to participate fully and harmoniously in French society. To this end, public authorities had been charged with the twin tasks of alleviating unemployment and poor housing and ensuring that immigrant minorities adapted to majority ethnic cultural norms. Although the existence of racism was acknowledged, it was not recognized in the policy-making community as a serious obstacle to integration requiring public action on a scale comparable with that undertaken in the social and cultural fields. While cosmetic improvements were made in some aspects of housing, attempts to curb unemployment failed dismally, sending the jobless rate among minority ethnic groups spiraling in the banlieues. The notion that they had failed to integrate themselves culturally exasperated second- and third-generation members of minority ethnic groups, who shared overwhelmingly in the values, aspirations and cultural codes of the majority ethnic population. They knew full well that their social exclusion arose not from some imaginary cultural deficit but from the discriminatory treatment to which persons of color were commonly subjected. Recognizing this, Aubry called into question the usefulness of 'integration' as a concept in public debate: 'We truly ought to think about finding another concept: today, the issue is not so much that of integration – the people we are talking about have long since been "integrated" culturally – but that of the struggle against discrimination and for equal rights' (Aubry 1999). Although Aubry's speech attracted little attention at the time and the new path which it mapped out was to prove long and tortuous, it marked a significant step in the process of terminological evolution which was eventually to dislodge 'integration' from its central position in public debate.

Aubry was one of three senior ministers who, during the premiership of Jospin (1997–2002), pursued this new agenda in a variety of ways. The others were Interior Minister Jean-Pierre Chevènement and Justice Minister Elisabeth Guigou. They disagreed over the most appropriate means for tackling discrimination, lacked coordination and by the time they left office appeared to have made little impact on the problem they had been endeavoring to address.

Of the three, Aubry was under the greatest pressure to act for it was on her desk that the HCI report requested by Juppé landed in the autumn of 1998. The seriousness of the situation described in the report was underlined by the HCI's proposal to effectively wind itself up and then reconstitute itself as an independent authority dedicated to the fight against racial discrimination. Equally astonishing was the HCI's suggestion that Britain's Commission for Racial Equality (CRE) – a state-funded agency with extensive powers for investigating alleged discrimination, assisting victims and promoting good 'race' relations – might serve as an institutional model for this new incarnation. Until then, the HCI had been one of numerous public bodies in France which had habitually demonized British 'race relations' institutions as the antithesis of the French 'republican' model of integration. In her statement, Aubry announced a number of initiatives aimed at consciousness-raising and improved arrangements for mediation, but she was cautious about the proposal for an independent anti-racist authority and such a body never saw the light of day under the Jospin administration.

Before the HCI report was published, Guigou had already indicated her support for an independent anti-racism authority (*Le Monde*, 9 Oct. 1998). She had also preceded Aubry in attempting to make more effective use of existing institutions, issuing a circular in July 1998 urging state prosecutors to pursue incidences of discrimination with greater vigor. In January 1999, apparently without consulting Aubry, Interior Minister Jean-Pierre Chevènement launched a further initiative, instructing prefects (representatives of the central state at département level) to set up coordinating agencies to be known as Commissions d'Accès à la Citoyenneté (CODACs) to monitor and combat cases of racial discrimination (*Le Monde*, 28 Jan. 1999). These measures, too, were to prove largely ineffectual. As the police, widely distrusted by minorities (Body-Gendrot and Wihtol de Wenden 2003), were among the public services running the CODACs, the system offered no guarantee of impartiality to the victims of discrimination. This may have been one of the factors inhibiting minorities in coming forward with complaints. At the end of its first year of operation, the nationwide network of CODACs reported that it had been notified of a total of 353 alleged cases of racial discrimination across the whole of France. Fewer than fifty of these had been notified to the public prosecutor, who had secured a total of just seven convictions. These figures showed no perceptible increase on the tiny number of convictions for racial discrimination seen each year prior to the creation of the CODACs.[10]

There were moreover huge gaps in the statutory powers relating to discrimination which no one in government appeared willing to address. Although Guigou declared her support for an independent anti-discrimination authority, she also asserted that no changes in the law were necessary (*Le Monde*, 9 Oct. 1998). The implication of this was that, while an independent authority might in principle offer improved support to victims of racism, its sphere of competence would be confined within the parameters of the 1972 law against racial discrimination. This covers only cases of direct discrimination, where individuals behave in an explicitly racist fashion, and it has been notoriously difficult to obtain proof of this. It offers no protection against racists who camouflage their motives or against indirect discrimination, i.e. institutional practices which have the effect of disadvantaging certain ethnic groups without this necessarily being intended.

In May 2000 a free nationwide telephone number was opened to enable victims of discrimination to lodge complaints and seek assistance from the authorities. By September some 861,453 calls had been made, of which less than 1 per cent were followed up by the CODACs. The data provided stunning evidence of the scale of the problem and the inadequacy of the government's response. A report into the functioning of the free phone number carried out for Aubry's ministry concluded that it was corrosive in its effects, engendering among callers 'profound disillusionment' and 'a very negative image of the services offered by the state' (Gorgeon *et al.* 2001: 15).

Five years after an EU Directive requiring every member state to set up an independent anti-racism authority, Chirac inaugurated the Haute Autorité de Lutte contre les Discriminations et pour l'Égalité (HALDE) in June 2005. It had hardly begun to operate, still less demonstrate any tangible effects, when, in the autumn of 2005, the banlieues erupted in the worst disturbances seen in France for decades. The Equal Opportunities Law adopted in March 2006 in response to those disorders gave additional powers to the HALDE but it was still very far from clear that the organization had the means to make real headway against racial discrimination. In the absence of tangible results such as a rise in successful prosecutions against perpetrators of discrimination, there were few grounds for expecting any abatement in the despair and disillusionment which had fueled the 2005 riots. Without a system of ethnic monitoring, indirect discrimination still remained largely beyond the reach of legal redress. The chair of the HALDE, Louis Schweitzer, President Chirac and Prime Minister Dominique de Villepin were all implacably opposed to any system of ethnic monitoring, which was being called for by growing numbers of expert reports and anti-racist campaigners who argued that without such a system it was impossible to document institutional biases against minority groups and measure progress in combating discrimination. The risk was that, in the absence of such evidence, victims of discrimination would remain disillusioned and prone to vent their frustration in fresh outbursts of violence.

Ethnic monitoring

In attempting to redress the inequalities resulting from past and present discrimination, some states have implemented policies designed to favor disadvantaged groups. In the United States, affirmative action programs have sometimes involved the appointment or promotion of people from disadvantaged groups who are less well qualified than candidates or employees from other ethnic backgrounds. That kind of affirmative action would be unlawful in Britain, where successive Race Relations Acts have prohibited any form of discrimination, including so-called positive discrimination in favor of disadvantaged groups. However, the Commission for Racial Equality (CRE), which was established under the terms of the 1976 Race Relations Act, encourages companies and other organizations to engage in ethnic monitoring as a check against racial discrimination as part of a policy approach known as positive action. This involves comparing the ethnic composition of personnel within the organization with that of qualified applicants or the population as a whole, and if necessary instituting measures (such as additional training programs) designed to achieve a fairer balance. In France, such approaches were until recently almost universally condemned as Anglo-Saxon devices leading to quotas, ghettos and *communautarisme*, i.e. ethnic separatism.

   In considering these matters it is important to distinguish three separate issues which are often confused in France: ethnic monitoring, ethnic targets and positive discrimination. Ethnic monitoring is a system of measurement which does not in itself imply favorable or unfavorable treatment for any of the groups measured, though it provides data which may be used to argue for such treatment. Ethnic targets are proportions of workforces, student enrolments or other measurable entities which companies, universities or other organizations are encouraged or in some cases required to meet, usually for reasons of social equity. Such targets do not necessarily imply positive discrimination, i.e. the awarding of jobs, housing, educational opportunities or other social goods to members of certain groups even if they are less well qualified than others. In the US, affirmative action has sometimes involved positive discrimination through quotas for minority groups. In the pursuit of ethnic targets in the UK, it has never been permissible to award jobs, university places or any other social goods to members of ethnic minorities who are less well qualified than applicants from other ethnic groups.

At least three main reasons are commonly advanced in France for the rejection of any measure or policy based on ethnic criteria. One is a deep attachment to the republican tradition of refusing to recognize differences based on separate origins. While originally grounded in opposition to the hereditary transmission of socio-economic privileges, which the revolutionaries of 1789 set out to abolish, the principle of egalitarianism is widely understood to require that in their dealings with the state, individuals should be treated without regard for their religious, national or ethnic origins (Noiriel 1992a: 70–1). A second factor is the widespread fear of strengthening ethnocultural differences by giving state recognition and/or state funds to minority groups, thereby undermining national cohesion. Finally, there are painful memories associated with the Vichy régime, which during the Second World War used state-compiled registers listing Jews and other minorities to collaborate actively in Nazi Germany's extermination policies. Since the resurgence of the extreme right in the early 1980s, it has seemed to many liberally minded French nationals that the ethnic categorization of the population would create a body of information which in the wrong hands might be used against (rather than in favor of) disadvantaged groups.

Despite these endless protestations about the alleged incompatibility of ethnic categorization with republican principles, the historical fact of the matter is that the French Republic brazenly used such categories over a long period overseas and it has also used them in more discreet ways at home. Overseas, the colonial empire was founded on such distinctions, which served as the basis for institutionalized discrimination against non-Europeans (Bancel *et al.* 2003). In Algeria, for example, a juridical distinction was drawn between French citizens or Europeans on the one hand (although not exactly coterminous, the two terms overlapped closely), and on the other, French subjects constituting the mass of the population who were generally referred to in official documents as *indigènes musulmans* (Muslim natives). In the twilight years of the colonial era, when a succession of new statutes moved towards formal equality of citizenship for the whole of the population, natives were still distinguished from settlers through official terms such as *Français musulmans d'Algérie* (French Muslims of Algeria), *citoyens de statut local* (local status citizens) and *Français de souche nord-africaine* (FSNA – French people of North African origin) (Henry 1987–8).

In census data for metropolitan France, immigrants from Algeria and other colonial possessions were customarily treated as if they were foreigners though they were juridically French nationals prior to independence. Even in the 1954 census, when migrants originating in the overseas empire (at that time known as the Union française) were included among the global figure for French nationals, Algerian Muslims were at another level tabulated separately, and the data relating to them were incorporated in analyses devoted to foreigners (Silberman 1992:

121). With Algerian independence in 1962, Algerians of non-European origin were deemed by the French authorities automatically to lose French nationality unless they specifically opted to retain it. In this way, most economic migrants ceased to be French and appeared in subsequent census data as foreigners (although many of their children were to have dual nationality). Yet the *harkis* who opted to retain French nationality after fleeing to France, whose sovereignty they had unsuccessfully fought to uphold in Algeria, were still classified by the census authorities separately from other French nationals. The continued use in the 1968 census of the category *Français musulmans* reflected the perception that these were not normal members of the national community. Although this disappeared as a separate category in the 1975 census, it lived on in other official documents, being gradually reformulated into *Français musulmans rapatriés* and, subsequently, *Rapatriés d'origine nord-africaine* (RONA) (Wihtol de Wenden 1993).

Official census data are based on the statements made by individual members of the public to the census enumerators. The authorities permit themselves to reclassify answers where these appear to be incomplete or erroneous. In the past, many residents of Alsace and Lorraine who declared themselves to be German were routinely reclassified as French. By contrast, although the authorities have produced estimates of the number of Franco-Algerian dual nationals who have been incorrectly declared as foreign, those concerned have not been formally reclassified as French (Silberman 1992: 119).[11] French officialdom clearly regards certain categories of French citizens as less authentic members of the nation than others.

More generally, as noted above, in the allocation of social housing ethnically based policies have been widely (and illegally) practised with the aim of dispersing minority groups, thereby reducing the risk of ethnic ghettos. Ironically, however, in applying housing quotas (an allegedly Anglo-Saxon invention) and concentrating immigrant families in poor-quality properties, public authorities have at times come close to creating something akin to the very ghettos which they profess to abhor.

During the 1990s social scientists such as Michèle Tribalat (1991, 1993) and Patrick Simon (1993) began calling for the census authorities and other organizations to use ethnic criteria in data collection. It was not until the end of the decade that a number of public officials came out in support of this. In a report submitted to Martine Aubry in March 1999 Jean-Michel Belorgey, a member of the Conseil d'État, not only backed the HCI's call for an independent anti-discrimination authority; he also recommended a form of monitoring explicitly modeled on that used by the UK's Commission for Racial Equality (Belorgey 1999). Although the word 'ethnic' was not used by Belorgey, it was clearly implied by his recommendation.

A few weeks earlier, in an effort to reduce distrust of the police, Interior Minister Chevènement had announced that he wanted police forces to recruit more officers from minority ethnic groups. As formulated by Chevènement, the objective was to ensure 'that the nation's police force is a reflection of its population' (Chevènement 1999). This was similar in spirit to the situation in Britain, where police forces were expected to reflect the ethnic composition of the population. Without using the word 'ethnic', Chevènement was in effect laying down a target for ethnic equity.

Yet in the absence of clearly quantified targets or any system of ethnic monitoring of the type employed in the UK and the US, in France there was no way of measuring progress, identifying good practice or pinpointing failure.

Chevènement called for particular efforts to be made in recruiting minority ethnic youths[12] into newly created auxiliary units set up to help keep the peace in the banlieues. These used cheap labor – mainly unemployed youths – to take the pressure off fully qualified (and fully paid) police officers. When the Paris Police Prefecture sought to demonstrate the progress being made by disclosing that minority ethnic groups accounted for 35 per cent of certain auxiliary units,[13] eyebrows were raised. As public bodies were forbidden from recording ethnically based data, how could such figures be compiled? This disclosure fueled long-standing suspicions that ethnic categories were often used unofficially by police forces, often to the disadvantage of minorities. Nationally, the Interior Ministry blurred these issues by announcing that 19 per cent of youths hired as *adjoints de sécurité* (auxiliaries) came from neighborhoods designated as Zones Urbaines Sensibles, an official term for the most acutely disadvantaged banlieues (*Le Monde*, 21 Sept. 1999). Data of this kind complied more faithfully with the traditional ban on ethnic categories, but by the same token they were of doubtful utility as a measure of progress in the incorporation of minority ethnic groups.

A few months later government officials and the regulatory body for radio and television, the Conseil Supérieur de l'Audiovisuel (CSA), began announcing what has since become a long series of measures to redress the underrepresentation of people of color in the French media. In May 2000 Catherine Tasca, Minister of Culture and Communications, announced that publicly owned television channels would in future be required to 'pay due attention to the richness and diversity of the origins and cultures which make up contemporary society' (*Le Monde*, 20 May 2000) and the CSA inserted an almost identically worded requirement in the contract of the privately owned Canal +. Shortly afterwards, the CSA sparked off a fierce controversy by publishing a summary of the findings of a study it had financed entitled 'Présence et représentation des minorités visibles à la télévision française' (The Presence and Representation of Visible Minorities on French Television) (CSA 2000). To the guardians of republican orthodoxy, public funding for a study bearing such a title was deeply shocking for in their eyes the word 'minority' was as unacceptable as 'ethnic'. Criticism of the ethnically based methodology of the study was so fierce that the CSA canceled publication of the full text. Yet in the course of the next few years, it became increasingly commonplace for journalists, researchers and to a lesser extent government officials to speak of 'visible minorities' and although 'ethnic' and 'origins' are still largely eschewed, in government circles 'diversity' is now a highly fashionable albeit coded way of talking about the multi-ethnic nature of French society.

Moreover, instead of being dismissed out of hand, as used to be the case, the question of ethnic monitoring has become the subject of a vigorous debate among government officials and ministers (Cour des Comptes 2004: 146–9; Cusset 2006). The debate has been fueled by recommendations in favor of ethnic monitoring in a growing number of government-commissioned and parliamentary reports

(Belorgey 1999; Bébéar 2004; Fauroux 2005; Zimmermann 2005). By early 2005 Prime Minister Pierre Raffarin was quoted as encouraging employers to engage in ethnic monitoring while the Commission Nationale de l'Informatique et des Libertés (CNIL), the government agency responsible for data protection including restrictions on the collection of ethnically based data, was authorizing experimental systems of ethnic monitoring in a number of French companies (*Le Figaro*, 4 Feb. 2005). Under an agreement signed under the aegis of the Employment Ministry in June 2005, France Télévisions, responsible for France's publicly owned television channels, committed itself to 'an independent audit of the real or supposed representation of the diversity of which French society is composed [in the workforce of] France Télévisions as indicated by surnames, provided the CNIL grants prior approval for this' (Ministère de l'Emploi, de la Cohésion Sociale et du Logement 2005). Although the word 'ethnic' was avoided, that intention was clearly that ethnically marked surnames would be used as a lightly camouflaged method of what in all but name was ethnic monitoring. But in a report published a few weeks later, the CNIL threw a major spanner into the works by ruling that employers should not collect ethnically based data except by the legally sanctioned criteria already in general use, principally nationality (CNIL 2005: 64). France Télévisions was told that it could not use surnames. Other ethnic markers were also ruled out.

Although Dominique de Villepin, who succeeded Raffarin as Prime Minister in June 2005, was opposed to ethnic monitoring, he appointed as Minister for Equal Opportunities Azouz Begag, who was better disposed towards the idea. Begag commissioned a survey designed to determine the acceptability of such a practice to the general public. The results, published in July 2006, showed that only a minority of those interviewed were hostile to ethnic monitoring (Simon and Clément 2006). In March 2006, de Villepin had pushed through Parliament an Equal Opportunities Law which, among other things, required the CSA to ensure that radio and television stations reflect the 'diversity' of French society and report annually on their efforts. Yet in the absence of a legally sanctioned method of measuring ethnic diversity (of which nationality was a patently inadequate indicator), it was unclear how the CSA could comply with this statutory obligation other than in a quite fuzzy fashion. No less importantly, the interdiction on ethnic monitoring made it impossible to collect evidence of institutional bias or discrimination in housing, employment and numerous other spheres.

The makers of French public policy had thus painted themselves into an uncomfortable corner. On the one hand, there was now almost universal support for the slogan of 'diversity'. On the other hand, many senior statesmen and public officials still could not bring themselves to embrace the statistical apparatus which would be necessary to measure compliance with that slogan. As the CNIL observed (2005: 64), it appeared that the circle could be squared only by new legislation lifting the ban on ethnically based data. As neither Prime Minister de Villepin nor President Chirac favored such a change, it was unlikely to come before the 2007 elections but, depending on the outcome of those elections, it could certainly not be ruled out afterwards.

Positive discrimination

Ethnic monitoring is one of three major taboos which, until a few years ago, were almost completely off-limits in French public debate. The others are multiculturalism (Wieviorka 1997; Hargreaves 1997b) – still a delicate area but rendered slightly less sensitive by the new, albeit ambiguous, vogue for 'diversity' – and positive discrimination, now widely debated in government and academic circles (Calvès 2004; Sabeg and Sabeg 2004). The cat was set among the pigeons when, in an interview in 2003, Interior Minister Sarkozy said it was time to acknowledge the failures of French integration policy and redress these through a policy of positive discrimination (*Le Monde*, 22 Nov. 2003). As Sarkozy illustrated his thinking by citing the need for more Muslims to accede to senior professional and public positions, he was widely understood to be calling for positive discrimination based on religious or ethnic criteria. There can be little doubt that he had intended to create a stir, not least because, as he acknowledged in the same interview, he had ambitions for the presidential elections of 2007, in pursuit of which part of his strategy was to demonstrate the distance between himself and the incumbent, Jacques Chirac. The President duly obliged by declaring that ethnically based positive discrimination was unacceptable (*Le Monde*, 7 Dec. 2003).

It subsequently became clear that the impression created by Sarkozy's remarks had more to do with grabbing media headlines than with a genuine commitment to ethnically based measures. In 2005, in a long speech devoted to 'la discrimination positive à la française' (French-style positive discrimination) delivered just a day before the banlieues began to burn, Sarkozy made it unequivocally clear that his conception of positive discrimination was territorially not ethnically based (Sarkozy 2005). Such an approach was a long-established part of French public policy aimed at reducing inequalities. For at least a quarter of a century it had been used to address issues related to immigration by targeting disadvantaged localities in which minority ethnic groups were concentrated. Because the modus operandi was not restricted to particular ethnic groups, all residents in the targeted localities benefited, irrespective of their origins. It was certainly intended that populations of immigrant origin would be prominent beneficiaries of such policies. This point was often made by government officials and ministers, but seldom in the provocative terms chosen by Sarkozy, who was clearly aiming to create a stir when, in his 2003 interview, he illustrated the need for positive discrimination by making specific reference to Muslims and announcing that he would shortly be appointing a 'Muslim prefect [representative of the central state at departmental level]'. But in his 2005 speech, Sarkozy repeatedly denied favoring special measures for Muslims or other minorities, insisting that, as he had indeed briefly said in his 2003 interview, he wanted such groups to benefit from measures targeting all the inhabitants of disadvantaged localities. Contrary to appearances, there was at root nothing new in principle in Sarkozy's stance.

There was nevertheless something incrementally new in Sarkozy's imple-mentation of that principle, for he was one of several public actors widening the field of its application. Until recent years, measures targeting disadvantaged areas had been mainly concerned to improve conditions directly within those localities. Since the late 1970s there has been a long series of publicly funded programs aimed at improving housing and job opportunities in the most disadvantaged of the banlieues, and additional support for schools was also made available from 1981 onwards. It was not until the year 2000 that special measures began to be made to help young people from the banlieues enter top-ranking institutions of higher education in which the nation's future elites are trained. The apparent egalitarianism of France's university system, open at minimal cost to any student with the *baccalauréat* (high school diploma) has in practice long been overshadowed by the extremely unegalitarian *grandes écoles*. Access to these elite institutions of higher education, whose graduates are guaranteed top public- and private-sector jobs, is by competitive examinations in which the overwhelming majority of those admitted come from high-income families. Young people from low-income families lack the means to attend special preparatory classes for the competitive exams and are often ignorant about how the system works. In the year 2000 France's top political science institute, the Institut d'Études Politiques de Paris, known more commonly as Sciences-Po, announced that it was opening an additional mode of entry reserved for high school students from ZEPs (Zones d'Education Prioritaires) situated in severely disadvantaged neighborhoods in the banlieues (Sabbagh 2004). Although the scheme was not explicitly targeted at minority ethnic groups, these groups in practice represented at least two-thirds of the students admitted in this way (*Le Monde*, 21 June 2006). Other *grandes écoles* soon followed Sciences-Po's lead by instituting similar measures. When, in his 2005 speech, Sarkozy proposed that special preparatory classes be created to help young people in disadvantaged areas sit the civil service entry exams, he was following in the same trajectory.

These measures are similar in spirit to programs adopted in recent years in US states such as Texas and Florida, where ethnically based affirmative action has been abolished and replaced in the educational field by procedures enabling the best high school students in all localities, including the most disadvantaged, to enter the public university system. More generally, much of what has been happening in France has paralleled in many respects similar measures in Britain (Lapeyronnie 1993), where they are commonly referred to as 'positive action' policies. As in Britain, some of the measures taken in France have in fact been based directly on ethnic criteria, though that expression is never used. For many years, the most important institution funding programs of this kind was the Fonds d'Action Sociale (Social Action Fund), which was required by law to target people of immigrant origin, with the central aim of integrating them into French society.[14] The training programs included among the FAS's spending programs were similar to those which the CRE encourages in Britain with the aim of improving the qualifications of disadvantaged groups. Because France refuses to institute ethnic monitoring, the effectiveness of these programs has been difficult to gauge, but the underlying principle is similar in all but name to the British concept of positive action. Bearing in mind that in the 1990s the FAS had a budget ten times larger than that of the CRE (Lapeyronnie 1993: 198), and that the whole of it was designated for the exclusive benefit of immigrants and their descendants, the *de facto* commitment of the French state to positive action has been not inconsiderable.[15]

The Zones d'Éducation Prioritaires (Educational Priority Zones – ZEPs) introduced by the left in 1981 parallel similar initiatives taken in Britain under Section 11 of the 1966 Local Government Act. In both cases, additional state funding has been made available to schools with high concentrations of immigrant-born pupils. French schools most likely to benefit are those which have 30 per cent or more foreign pupils. However, ZEP funding is not reserved for minority ethnic groups. An ethnic element is included in the criteria by which schools are designated for ZEP status because concentrations of minority groups are statistically one of the surest indicators of social deprivation. Although the ZEPs are often seen as a camouflaged 'immigrant' program, they are not in any sense designed to promote ethnic diversity. On the contrary, their prime aim is to better prepare young people from disadvantaged backgrounds, whatever their ethnic origins, to function effectively in French society. Extra teachers and other facilities are provided with the central aim of improving the delivery of mainstream teaching programs, thereby countering high drop-out rates and poor examination results (Costa-Lascoux 1989: 91–5; Lorcerie 1994c).

A similar principle has informed a long succession of government initiatives designed to remedy poor housing and the wider problems of urban decay afflicting many French cities. These are similar to the Urban Programme launched in Britain in 1968 during a phase of so-called 'color-blind' policy-making, the effect of which was to assist minority ethnic groups within the framework of wider programs tackling the problems of socio-economically disadvantaged areas. Since 1977, when a government committee called Habitat et Vie Sociale (Housing and Social Life – HVS) was created, the institutional framework of French initiatives in this field has undergone various transformations and gained an ever more prominent position in the machinery of government.

Rocard's decision to set up a Ministry for Urban Affairs in December 1990 was prompted by the disorders which had taken place a few months earlier in Vaulx-en-Velin, a suburb of Lyon typifying the problems of the French banlieues: high unemployment, poor-quality housing and neighborhood infrastructure, and difficult relations between the police and local inhabitants, particularly those of minority ethnic origin. A key plank of the policy pursued by the Ministry and its institutional predecessors was a system of contracts under which central and local government agreed to provide additional funding for areas suffering high levels of social disadvantage (Champion *et al.* 1993). Although these jointly aided districts contain relatively dense concentrations of minority ethnic groups, who have often been to the fore in disturbances such as those in Vaulx-en-Velin, the difficulties they face are grounded primarily in socio-economic circumstances rather than ethnic particularities. By the same token, the aid granted to these areas is designed to improve the living conditions of all those in need, regardless of their ethnic origins.

In 1991 Michel Delebarre, who had been appointed head of the new Urban Ministry, piloted through Parliament what the media called an 'anti-ghetto' law.

This was designed to force local authorities to accept in the future a more even distribution of social housing (HLMs), thereby reducing concentrations of the kind seen in Vaulx-en-Velin and Mantes-la-Jolie, where further disturbances had taken place immediately before the new legislation was adopted. Despite the ethnic connotations of the nickname given to this law by the media, the central aim was to address socio-economic disparities rather than ethnic differences *per se*. The law was watered down by the center-right government which took office in 1993 but under the Socialist-led administration of Jospin the drive towards a more even distribution of low-income HLM housing was reactivated and in December 2000 new teeth were added to the law, forcing local authorities to pay fines if they did not meet a nationwide minimum target of 20 per cent of social housing in all localities. In 2006, *députés* from wealthy localities containing little social housing attempted once again to overturn these requirements but this time the center-right government refused to back them and the law remained in force. The scale of the problem the law was attempting to address was symbolized by the fact that more than 50 per cent of the social housing in the Île-de-France region, centered on Paris, was still located in less than 9 per cent of the localities making up the region (*Libération*, 13 July 2006). It was in the HLMs in those overrepresented localities that minority ethnic groups were most heavily concentrated. By the same token, to the extent that the law is enforced, it will disperse not only poverty but also minority ethnic concentrations.

5.6 Pluralism, exclusion or cooption?

Majority ethnic fears of spatial concentrations of minority ethnic groups have been closely intertwined with anxieties about cultural differences associated with immigration which have helped to make the notion of multiculturalism, caricatured as synonymous with ethnic separatism, a no-go area in French political discourse (Hargreaves 1997b). Broadly speaking, three alternative policy approaches may be distinguished in the treatment of cultural minorities. A pluralist approach allows or positively fosters the coexistence of diverse cultural systems, with no real attempt at reducing differences. An exclusionary approach seeks to eliminate differences either by forcing minorities to assimilate totally into the dominant culture or by expelling them from the national territory. A policy of cooption tolerates differences but seeks to ensure that minorities limit their distinctive patterns of behavior in ways that are compatible with the dominant cultural norms. While pluralist or exclusionary tendencies have sometimes been apparent, the dominant approach in French public policy, particularly since the mid-1980s, has been that of cooption.[16]

The right has consistently shown itself to be more tempted than the left by exclusionary reflexes. Ironically, it has also been responsible for some of the most pluralist initiatives taken by the state. During the presidency of Giscard d'Estaing, minorities of recent immigrant origin were encouraged to retain their distinctive cultural traditions. While pluralist in its effects, this approach was to a large extent motivated by exclusionary considerations, which dominated public policy from

1977 onwards, when mass repatriation of non-European immigrants, particularly Maghrebis, became a prime objective. If immigrants and their descendants were to be lured or forced into repatriation, it appeared desirable that they should feel at home with the cultural norms prevailing in the sending states. It was in this spirit that the right encouraged the teaching of Langues et Cultures d'Origine (Homeland Languages and Cultures – LCO) in state schools during the second half of the 1970s.[17]

However, the effects of this policy should not be exaggerated. While hoping that minority groups would retain sufficient competence in homeland cultures to make repatriation feasible, Giscard and those who served under him were firmly committed to the domination of French cultural norms as long as immigrants and their descendants remained in France. The LCO program was in every respect half-hearted when compared with the overall educational experience of immigrant-born children within state schools. France did not invest a penny in LCO provision. The recruitment and funding of teachers were the responsibility of sending states, which generally lacked the resources to provide tuition for more than a small proportion of their expatriates' children (see section 3.2). On average, no more than one in five children received tuition of this kind (Costa-Lascoux 1989: 92; Boyzon-Fradet 1992: 158). For those who received such tuition the time available for LCO classes was in any case limited to three hours a week, a quite marginal proportion bearing in mind that the rest of the week was devoted to the standard French curriculum.

The LCO program turned into a political boomerang during the 1980s, when it was frequently attacked by the right for weakening cultural cohesion in France.[18] During the headscarf affair of 1989, media reports suggested that some of the teachers recruited by sending states were using their classes to spread Islamic fundamentalism, in violation of the secular principles governing the state education system. There was little documentary evidence to support these claims (Lorcerie 1994b), but they were indicative of the widespread anxieties generated by what was now perceived to be the permanent settlement of cultural minorities of immigrant origin.

The left had appeared more genuinely committed to pluralism when it came to power in 1981. By granting freedom of association to foreigners, it made it easier for minority groups to mobilize around projects which diverged from the cultural norms dominant in France. Additional funds were made available to support minority associations, principally through the FAS, and for the first time people of immigrant origin were included in its decision-making machinery. Similarly, the Conseil National des Populations Immigrées (National Council of Immigrant Populations – CNPI), created in 1984, gave representatives of minority ethnic groups a consultative role in the formation of government policy.

Between 1980 and 1986, the FAS's budget doubled, and the number of organizations receiving financial assistance from it increased fourfold (Weil 1991: 176). By 1991, it was funding more than 4,000 associations serving minority ethnic groups, compared to only a few hundred in 1981. Again, however, it is important to keep a sense of perspective in assessing the significance of these changes. Noting that the FAS had an annual budget of around 1,200 million francs, McKesson (1994: 28) claimed that much of it was spent assisting ethnically based associations which promoted communitarianism, thereby undermining the official project of integration. In fact, over two-fifths of the total budget was allocated to housing, more than a quarter was spent on training designed to improve the employment prospects of immigrants and their descendants, and scarcely a tenth was devoted to culturally based associations, of which no more than a small proportion (if any) might arguably be described as communitarian (Costa-Lascoux 1989: 96–7).

In its allocation of funding to minority-based associations, the fundamental aim of the FAS has been to coopt people of immigrant origin who, while retaining certain differences, basically respect the cultural and legal norms prevailing in France. That principle has guided the FAS consistently despite the alternation of the left and the right in government since the mid-1980s. It has governed the distribution of FAS subsidies to organizations active in radio, television and other media productions, discussed in Chapter 3, and to pressure groups such as the Maghrebi-dominated France-Plus and the multi-ethnic SOS-Racisme (*Passages* 1989), which have explicitly committed themselves to the project of integration, understood as a process of constructive participation within French society by people of diverse origins. Similarly, Ni putes ni soumises (Neither sluts nor slaves), the pressure group set up in 2003 by minority ethnic women to campaign against abusive behavior by young men in the banlieues, received substantial support from the FAS and from other powerful figures, including the center-right president of the National Assembly, Jean-Louis Debré, in whose eyes this was a way of countering arguments that the Republic was to blame for the ills afflicting the banlieues.

It should not be forgotten, moreover, that simultaneously with its pluralist initiatives, the left instituted in 1981 the ZEP program, which aims at improving mainstream educational provision in French schools containing dense concentrations of minority ethnic groups. In the mid-1990s the ZEPs were funded by the Ministry of Education alone to the tune of 1,360 million francs; in addition, other ministries and government agencies were estimated to contribute four times as much, making a total budget of around 7,000 million francs (Lorcerie 1994c: 35–6). Granted that the children of immigrants represented around 30 per cent of those benefiting from this program, (equivalent to about 2,000 million francs on a pro rata basis), and that this was an extra layer reinforcing the much larger budget allocated to the basic education program, state investment in the acculturation of immigrant-born children clearly dwarfed the sums spent by the FAS on cultural activities of all kinds.

Islam has been by far the most important concern of French officials and politicians worried about cultural differences. That concern has sometimes been fed by grossly distorted perceptions and misrepresentations, most notably during the Islamic headscarf affairs. In the eyes of the anti-headscarf camp, anxiety over claims that girls wearing the garment were being manipulated by Islamic extremists completely overrode any consideration of what the headscarf might mean to those actually wearing it. The 2004 law banning the headscarf from

French state schools bore testimony to the strength of that camp. Yet the same center-right government that outlawed the headscarf had been simultaneously pursuing the objective, first set by the left in 1990, of coopting Islamic organizations into partnership with the Republic. Those efforts were crowned with success in 2003 when, with the blessing of the government, the Conseil Français du Culte Musulman (CFCM) held its first elections for a nationwide assembly representing all the major Islamic federations in France. A key milestone paving the way for those elections was an agreement signed in the year 2000 at the instigation of the Socialist-led government of the day whereby all the Islamic federations that were to participate in the CFCM committed themselves to support the principles of *laïcité*, as codified in the law of 1905.

An important element in this strategy of cooption concerns the training and recruitment of imams (Islamic prayer-leaders), who at a grass-roots level serve as the spiritual leaders and principal figureheads of local Muslim communities. Until the 1990s, there were virtually no formal training facilities for imams in France. As a consequence of this, practically all the imams active in France were trained and recruited abroad, where it was impossible for the French authorities to exert any significant influence. Shortly before losing government office in 1993, the Socialists signaled their wish to reduce this reliance on foreign-trained spiritual leaders by refusing visas to dozens of Algerian and Egyptian imams, extra numbers of whom were normally allowed into France during the month of Ramadan (*Le Monde*, 28 Feb. 1993). They also attempted to exert tight control over the recruitment of staff and students in the first training institute for imams in France, which was set up in 1991 by the Union des Organisations Islamiques de France (UOIF), which had a reputation for radicalism. Two other such institutes were founded in 1993, one at the initiative of the Moroccan-dominated Fédération Nationale des Musulmans de France (FNMF) and the other under the auspices of the Grande Mosquée de Paris, closely aligned with the Algerian government (*Migrations société* 1994). Because the last of these was regarded by the Balladur government as the most moderate, it received the support of center-right Interior Minister Charles Pasqua and of his colleague in the RPR, Jacques Chirac, who as Mayor of Paris had already provided a subsidy for the renovation of the Grande Mosquée de Paris (*Le Monde*, 30 July 1994).

In September 1994, Pasqua turned out in person to inaugurate a new mosque in Lyon whose leaders, like those of the Grande Mosquée de Paris, were regarded as politically moderate. This, it should be recalled, was the same minister who had given his name to a raft of hard-line laws tightening immigration controls and access to French citizenship, and who, in response to the civil war raging in Algeria, had instigated several roundups of alleged Islamic fundamentalists in France, some twenty of whom were deported by Pasqua only a month before he opened the Lyon mosque (*Le Monde*, 2 Sept. 1994). His speech in Lyon included a revealing statement of government policy:

> We need to treat Islam in France as a French question instead of continuing to see it as a foreign question or as an extension into France of foreign problems

... It is no longer enough to talk of Islam in France. There has to be a French Islam. The French Republic is ready for this.

(Le Monde, 1 Oct. 1994)

In sketching this vision of a 'French Islam' independent of foreign forces, Pasqua was effectively inviting Muslims to participate in the conjuring trick through which France has traditionally sought to minimize or efface public recognition of the diverse ethnic origins from which the population is descended (cf. sections 1.2, 1.3). Those whom the minister had expelled a few weeks earlier could have no place in this scheme of things, since they were alleged to be aiding terrorist networks set up in Algeria after the government there banned the fundamentalist Front Islamique du Salut (FIS). By supporting institutions such as the Grande Mosquée de Paris, whose leadership was appointed by the fiercely anti-fundamentalist Algerian government, Pasqua hoped to foster among the broad mass of Muslims in France a moderate form of Islam compatible with the republican tradition of *laïcité*.[19]

Although this is considerably less than the full-blown policy of multiculturalism once apparently favored by some on the left, it also falls a long way short of the intolerant mono-culturalism for which right-wing nationalists have traditionally argued. In pursuing a strategy of cooption, which in the early years of the twenty-first century chimed with the new buzz word of 'diversity', governments of both left and right have effectively accepted that cultural differences associated with recent migratory inflows are to be accommodated in France provided they are not felt to threaten the basic principles of republicanism and *laïcité*. The evidence examined in section 3.4 suggests that those principles are indeed being internalized by Muslims. Hugely publicized confrontations between small numbers of Muslims and public agencies such as those seen during the Islamic headscarf affairs of 1989, 1994 and 2003–4 have masked this underlying trend. Similarly, behind the divisive rhetoric generated by the tactical exigencies of party-political rivalry, French policy-makers reflecting most shades of the political spectrum appear now to be committed to the social incorporation of minorities who continue to display cultural particularities derived from their pre-migratory past.

Conclusion

In November 2005, Blandine Kriegel, president of the Haut Conseil à l'Intégration (HCI), published an article commenting on the riots which had recently torn through the French banlieues. Kriegel was indignant over suggestions that the disturbances showed the French 'republican' model of integration to have failed. She warned that those who made such claims were out to subvert republican principles by replacing them with Anglo-Saxon *communautarisme* (ethnic separatism). The riots had erupted, she said, not because there was anything wrong with the republican model, but because there had not been enough time to apply it (Kriegel 2005). Kriegel's diagnosis was both complacent and insensitive. While it was true that recent initiatives such as the Haute Autorité de Lutte contre les Discriminations et pour l'Égalité (HALDE), inaugurated in June 2005 to support victims of discrimination, had not had time to bear fruit, Kriegel made no reference to the fact that an entire decade or more had been lost because the dominance enjoyed by the discourse of republican theory had in practice led to the neglect of discrimination and other chronic problems in the banlieues. A powerful case can be made for the view that, properly applied, republican principles offer an admirable basis for the social incorporation of immigrants and their descendants. But it is disingenuous to suggest that there has been insufficient time to apply those principles. On the contrary, the gravity of the problems facing France in 2005 arose in no small measure from the failure of successive governments throughout the 1990s to seriously address endemic abuses of republican values, above all in the form of racial and ethnic discrimination.

Senior politicians such as President Chirac, Prime Minister de Villepin and Interior Minister Sarkozy were more lucid than Kriegel. They all acknowledged that the events of 2005 necessitated a more critical review of the republican model. In the years immediately preceding the 2005 riots, significant changes had been taking place in both political discourse and public policy. While still audible in certain quarters, the tired clichés which habitually accompanied the discourse of 'integration' had been increasingly displaced by a new emphasis on equal opportunities. The overall goal – the successful incorporation of immigrants and their descendants into French society – was not significantly different but the new policy approach recognized the seriousness of problems which had previously been ignored, most notably discrimination, and included new tools designed to address them. But tangible results remained elusive. Almost a decade after Martine Aubry first announced that anti-discrimination policy was to become a major government priority, successful prosecutions against perpetrators of discrimination remained extremely small in number and, even if progress were being made in reducing discrimination (which was far from certain), in the absence of ethnic monitoring it was difficult if not impossible to demonstrate this. The riots of 2005 showed that the political neglect in which the banlieues had languished during the 1990s had generated despair and distrust which were now so deep that it would be far more difficult to dispel them than if action had been taken earlier.

The picture is not entirely bleak. Since the mid-1990s there have been significant changes not only in public policy but also in public opinion (discussed in section 4.5) and French popular culture. Rap, imported from the ghettos of the US and saturated in cultural hybridity forged in the French banlieues, has become the most popular musical form among young people of all ethnic backgrounds in France. In 1998 the Académie Française, habitually a jealous guardian of cultural conservatism, awarded its 'grande médaille de la chanson française' (Gold medal for French song-writing) to a leading figure on the French rap scene, MC Solaar. Since captaining France's victorious multi-ethnic soccer team in the 1998 World Cup, Zinédine Zidane, from an Algerian immigrant family, has been repeatedly named the most popular personality in France. Even Zidane's sending off in the 2006 World Cup final, which France lost to Italy, was quickly forgiven by the French public, for whom Zidane remained a national hero (CSA 2006). In 2002 another young man from the banlieues, humorist Jamel Debbouze, a second-generation Moroccan, had become the best paid cinema actor in France, overtaking long-time box office favorite Gérard Dépardieu.

There is still a stark and disturbing contrast between the growing visibility of minority ethnic entertainers, soccer players and other athletes and the near-invisibility of minority figures in national politics (Bekkouche 2005). While the DOM-TOM have long been represented in the French parliament by *députés* (members) of color, in 2006 there was still not a single *député* of Maghrebi, sub-Saharan African or Caribbean descent elected within metropolitan France in the 577-member National Assembly.[1] In 1999, the French constitution was amended to permit positive discrimination – diplomatically termed *parité* (parity) – in favor of female political candidates to elected office. No comparable measure has been taken nor is any on the horizon in favor of minority ethnic groups, though a handful of ministerial appointments have been made from their ranks. Unlike in the United Kingdom, where government ministers must first be members of either the upper or lower chamber in parliament, in France ministers are barred from simultaneously holding parliamentary seats and a significant number have never run for elected office. Not uncommonly, therefore, ministers owe their positions purely to powers of patronage. There has been no shortage of *députés* and senior government ministers of European immigrant descent and originating among the pied-noir (white settler) population in North Africa. Recent examples include center-right politicians such as Prime Minister Dominique de Villepin (born in Morocco just before independence from France) and Interior Minister

Nicolas Sarkozy (the son of a Hungarian immigrant) as well as Socialists such as Catherine Tasca and Raymond Forni, both born of Italian immigrants, who served respectively as Minister of Culture and President of the National Assembly. Not until 2002 were a couple of junior ministerial appointments given to ethnic North Africans and it was only in 2005 that Azouz Begag became the first French citizen of North African immigrant origin appointed to a ministerial position of full cabinet status.

While the pace of change in some fields is slow, since the suspension of labor recruitment from non-EC countries in 1974, French perceptions of immigration and its social consequences have nevertheless changed radically. A process which was once seen as narrowly economic has now become highly politicized, and its cultural dimensions have raised searching questions about French national identity. Anxieties over the degree to which people of immigrant origin can or should be incorporated into French society crystallized during the 1980s and 1990s in the debate over 'integration' (Wieviorka 1990). Among politicians and the public at large, there was a widely held view that integration had become more difficult because recent immigrants and their descendants were both more different in their cultural traditions and more resistant to cultural change than were earlier minority groups. It is true that the cultural roots of today's minorities, which are predominantly of African and Asian origin, are often more distant from the norms prevailing in France than are the traditions in which most European immigrants were raised. Yet if recent immigrants and their descendants appear less well incorporated than earlier minority groups, the evidence examined in the course of this study suggests that this is due far more to socio-economic and political changes which have taken place within the receiving society than to differences in the cultural complexion of the minority population.

Marked contrasts in the pattern of ethnic relations frequently emerge when periods of economic expansion and labor shortages are compared with times of high unemployment and job insecurity (Milza 1985; Noiriel 1988: 247–93). After being welcomed during the labor shortages of the 1920s, the Europeans who dominated migratory inflows at that time became subject to xenophobic charges of 'unassimilability' and in some cases deportation during the economic depression of the 1930s. Although migratory inflows from Africa, Asia and the Caribbean outstripped those from Europe soon after the Second World War, it was not until the labor market turned sour in the second half of the 1970s that these new minorities became the subject of intense public debate.

The almost relentless rise in unemployment and job insecurity witnessed in France since the 1970s has made the process of social incorporation correspondingly difficult for growing numbers of people. Prior to this period, first-generation members of minority ethnic groups experienced a relatively high degree of functional incorporation within the booming post-war labor market. Their children and grandchildren have been reaching adulthood in very different circumstances. Across the country as a whole, unemployment is particularly high among young people, and some (but not all) minority ethnic groups have been particularly badly hit. As was shown in Chapter 2, the high unemployment levels suffered by certain visible minorities cannot be accounted for solely by reference to below-average levels of certified skills and still less in terms of cultural differences among those concerned. If young people of South-East Asian origin fare less badly than other minority groups, this may be due in part to better educational qualifications, but they appear also to be less vulnerable to discrimination by employers than young Maghrebis and others of African descent, whose unemployment rates far exceed the national average. Although the descendants of Portuguese immigrants are often as badly qualified as second-generation Maghrebis, their unemployment rate is well below the national average.

While the poor qualifications gained by many young people of immigrant origin are sometimes blamed on a school system which tends to perpetuate social inequalities from one generation to the next, the state educational system has nevertheless proved extremely effective as an institution of acculturation. The evidence reviewed in Chapter 3 demonstrates clearly that most of the descendants of immigrants identify more closely with the cultural codes dominant in France than with those prevailing in sending countries, and it is clear that the educational system (together with the mass media) has played a central role in this. The disorders which have broken out periodically in certain banlieues containing high concentrations of minority ethnic youths are not in any sense a mark of inadequate acculturation or ethnic separatism. On the contrary, it is precisely because they share to a large extent the values and aspirations common to the majority of young people in France, but are denied equal opportunities for the fulfilment of their ambitions, that immigrant-born youths have sometimes vented their frustration in violent attacks on property and the representatives of the state, most notably the police (Lapeyronnie 1987; Body-Gendrot 1993; Mucchielli 2005; Clémentine *et al.* 2006).

Schain (1994) has pointed out that through institutions such as the Fonds d'Action Sociale (FAS), the French state has come to deal directly with associations organized along ethnic lines to a far greater degree than was previously the case. It is important to note, however, that the official recognition of ethnically based associations and the decline of other organizations of a more 'universal' nature as instruments in the social incorporation of immigrants and their descendants are rooted primarily in changes in the receiving society. French trade unions, for example, which are universal in character in the sense that they are open to all workers, irrespective of ethnic origins, have traditionally played a significant role in inducting immigrants into organizational structures alongside native members of the labor force. During the 1980s, economic restructuring saw the number of trade union members as a proportion of the total labor force fall from about one in five to one in ten; among 18–24 year olds it is estimated to have plummeted from about one in ten to one in 100 (SOFRES 1992: 39). High levels of youth unemployment, which are particularly severe among minority groups, mean that many people of immigrant origin now have little, if any, direct contact with organized labor. This has inevitably weakened the role of trade unions in the social incorporation of minority groups.

As immigrants have generally been concentrated in manual occupations, they have in the past tended to affiliate with French organizations based in the working classes, particularly the French Communist Party (PCF) and its trade union ally, the Confédération Générale du Travail (CGT), which has traditionally served as recruiting ground for the party. The PCF has always depended more than any other party on the support of blue-collar workers, particularly in manufacturing and other sectors with relatively high rates of unionization. The party has therefore been greatly weakened by the rapid contraction of these sectors in recent years. Until the late 1970s, the PCF was by far the most powerful party of the left. Since then, it has been eclipsed by the Socialist Party (PS), which has been strongly influenced by a more pluralist vision of French society than was generally encountered in French politics until the near-revolutionary upheaval of 1968.

Ireland (1994) has shown that where, at a local level, the PCF retained organizational strength, it continued to play a significant role in structuring the incorporation of first- and second-generation members of minority groups. Thus throughout the 1980s in the Paris suburb of La Courneuve, where the Communists retained control of the municipal council while losing power in many other localities, 'ethnic-based organizing remained tributary to the working-class movement' (Ireland 1994: 123). The fact that this became increasingly untypical of the national pattern of minority incorporation arises not from the influx of Maghrebi and other post-colonial migrants (who are strongly represented in La Courneuve as in other parts of the country), but from the wave of economic restructuring which has cut through much of French industry, severely weakening the PCF in many of the urban areas where its strength was traditionally concentrated.

In the northern textile town of Roubaix, the PCF has always been weaker than the Socialists and Catholic centrists, who governed the city in coalition throughout the post-war period until 1977. The PS then took overall control with minority PCF support. Compared with the Communist municipality of La Courneuve, the Socialist-led administration in Roubaix adopted a much more pluralist approach towards people of immigrant origin. Typical of this was the creation in 1978 of a Commission Extra-Municipale aux Étrangers (Associate Municipal Commission for Foreigners – CEM), a consultative body made up of representatives of the town's immigrant population. Similar consultative bodies were established for other types of minority groups such as the old and the disabled (Ireland 1994: 123–4). These initiatives were undertaken in the spirit of 'participation', a rallying cry from 1968 which inspired the PS to favor the greater democratization of French society.

The same spirit was at work when the Socialists came to power nationally, again with minority PCF support, in 1981. Decentralization was an early priority, with substantial powers being shifted from the national government in Paris to regional and local councils. The regionalization of the Fonds d'Action Sociale and the introduction of people of immigrant origin into its decision-making bodies in 1983 were part of the same process, as was the creation in 1984 of the Conseil National des Populations Immigrées. While this increased willingness to formally recognize people of immigrant origin within consultative or decision-making public institutions was welcomed by many of those concerned, it is important to note that it came about primarily as a consequence of changes among French political elites, rather than in response to new demands from minority groups.

Members of older established European minorities in France such as the Italians and Spanish have taken advantage of the liberal rights of association granted to foreigners in 1981 no less than have more recent arrivals of African or Asian origin (Campani *et al.* 1987; *La Tribune Fonda* 1991; Diantelli 1992). On a per capita basis, the Portuguese probably developed a denser network of voluntary associations than any other minority ethnic group (Hily and Poinard 1987). The more vigorous presence of ethnically based organizations is in this respect unconnected with the increased weight of non-Europeans among the population of recent immigrant origin.

Central and local arms of the state have recently encouraged Muslims to become more involved in the organization of community life than was previously the case. In Mantes-la-Jolie, for example, judicial and police authorities supported by the Socialist mayor, Paul Picard, and his center-right rival, Pierre Bédier, arranged for local Muslims to hold widely based elections to the governing council of the town's mosque in December 1994 with the aim of ousting a small fundamentalist faction which had taken control of this institution (*Le Monde*, 20 Dec. 1994).[2] National initiatives undertaken by the Interior Ministry since 1990 under governments of both left and right have had a similar objective: to encourage the establishment of representative institutions reflecting the aspirations of the broad mass of Muslims in France, thereby marginalizing the minority of fundamentalists among them.

An important element implicit in this strategy is the conviction that most Muslims understand and accept the norms governing religious practices within the French tradition of *laïcité*. Interior Minister Charles Pasqua said as much only a day after deporting an Algerian imam accused of inciting violence in November 1994. During a parliamentary debate Raoul Béteille, who, like Pasqua, was a member of the center-right Rassemblement pour la République (RPR), called on the minister to confront what he called the single most important question facing France at the end of the twentieth century: was the country not in danger of losing its identity because of the settlement of Muslim immigrants? Pasqua replied that while he would be uncompromising in the repression of anti-French religious propaganda, the situation was far less worrying than many people thought, since the overwhelming majority of Muslims in France were as opposed to intolerance as the rest of the population (*Le Monde*, 8 and 9 Nov. 1994).

After a period of acute discord in the late 1970s and early 1980s, most of France's political elite came to recognize that recent migratory inflows were irreversible. The question was no longer whether but how immigrants and their descendants should best be incorporated into French society. The discourse of 'integration' contained many ambiguities, and widespread acts of discrimination placed many obstacles in the way of minority groups. Even a radical improvement in the economic climate may not entirely remove those obstacles, but behind the sound and fury generated by party-political rivalry, the position of minority ethnic groups now appears somewhat less insecure than when the 'end' of immigration was decreed in the mid-1970s.

Many years that could have been used to build greater social cohesion have nevertheless been wasted, especially during the 1990s. If politicians had spent their time applying republican principles instead of building what many regarded as discriminatory barriers, such as the nationality law reform of 1993 and the anti-headscarf law of 2004, the banlieues might not have lapsed into despair. While the left took the lead in putting anti-discrimination policy on the agenda in 1997, its initiatives proved too timid. It was only after the EU issued a Race Directive in 2000 requiring all member states to set to up within the next three years an independent anti-discrimination authority that, five years later, Chirac inaugurated the HALDE, with powers and resources still significantly smaller than those of Britain's Commission for Racial Equality.

At every step in the incremental changes seen since 1997, the anti-discrimination initiatives taken by governments of both the left and the center-right have been half-baked and some would say half-hearted. Yet significant changes have unquestionably taken place in both the discourse and substance of French public policy. In place of the tired discourse of 'integration', the new political correctness is expressed in terms of diversity and equal opportunities, code words for protecting the interests of ethnic minorities and promoting anti-discrimination policies. Britain and the United States, previously demonized for their allegedly communitarian policies, are now commonly cited by French politicians and officials as examples of good practice. Each year the French Prime Minister of the day selects a major national concern as 'la grande cause nationale de l'année' (the year's national cause). The year 2006 was declared by de Villepin to be the Year of Equal Opportunities. It would be unfair to regard this as simply hot air. The fight against discrimination, which until ten years ago was widely regarded as a non-problem, has been the object of a growing number of policy initiatives under the premiership of de Villepin and his immediate predecessors. An independent authority similar in spirit to Britain's CRE, albeit with more limited means at its disposal, has been established and there are now serious debates among the policy-making community in France about questions such as ethnic monitoring and 'positive discrimination' (affirmative action), which until very recently were regarded as completely taboo. While positive discrimination on ethnic grounds still looks very unlikely in France, it would not be surprising if a form of ethnic monitoring were to be introduced in the coming years. If so, when combined with determined action against discrimination it will enable those in authority to demonstrate their seriousness and effectiveness in ensuring that republican principles are respected. Without such action, the social cohesion of the Republic remains seriously weakened.

Chronology

Year	French executive	French public policy	Other developments
1968	31 May: Center-right government reshuffle under PM Georges Pompidou; Raymond Marcellin appointed Interior Minister 11 July: Maurice Couve de Murville appointed PM of center-right government	1 and 29 July: Reassertion of control over migratory inflows by restricting 'regularization' procedures and imposing quotas on Algerians	May–June: France paralysed by student demonstrations and workers' strikes 23 and 30 June: Center-right parties win landslide majority in parliamentary elections
1969	15 June: Georges Pompidou elected President following resignation of Charles de Gaulle 22 June: Jacques Chaban-Delmas appointed PM of center-right government; Joseph Fontanet appointed Labor Minister		29 Feb.: Report to Conseil Économique et Social by Corentin Calvez recommends tighter immigration controls, ethnic selection and improved social provisions
1970			
1971			March–May: Nine die in anti-Algerian attacks

Year	French executive	French public policy	Other developments
1972		Jan.–Feb.: Marcellin-Fontanet circulars further tighten immigration controls	
	5 July: Pierre Messmer appointed PM of center-right government	1 July: Parliament passes law prohibiting racial discrimination and incitement to racial violence	
1973	5 April: Georges Gorse appointed Labor Minister		4 and 11 March: Center-right victory in parliamentary elections
			19 Sept.: Algerian government halts emigration following further racist killings in France
			Oct.: Middle East war, followed by oil crisis and fears of economic downturn in West
1974	1 March: Jacques Chirac appointed Interior Minister		
	19 May: Valéry Giscard d'Estaing elected President		
	27 May: Jacques Chirac appointed PM of center-right government; Michel Poniatowski appointed Interior Minister		
	8 June: André Postel-Vinay appointed Minister of State for Immigrant Workers	5 July: Suspension of labor migration by non-EC nationals	
	22 July: Paul Dijoud replaces Postel-Vinay as Minister of State for Immigrant Workers	9 Oct.: Government adopts 25-point package for tighter immigration controls and improved social provisions	

Year	French executive	French public policy	Other developments
1975			April: Communist victory over US-backed régime in South Vietnam prompts exodus of asylum-seekers from South-East Asia
1976	25 July: Raymond Barre appointed PM of center-right government		
1977	29 March: Christian Bonnet appointed Interior Minister; Lionel Stoléru appointed Minister of State for Manual and Immigrant Workers	26 April: Creation of *aide au retour* (repatriation assistance)	
1978		Stoléru conducts inconclusive negotiations aimed at mass repatriation of non-EC immigrants	
1979		Dec.: Insufficient parliamentary support to carry legislation proposed by Stoléru to facilitate large-scale forcible repatriations	
1980		10 Jan.: Bonnet Law tightens entry and residence regulations	24 Dec.: Communist Mayor of Vitry orders demolition of hostel for African workers

Year	French executive	French public policy	Other developments
1981	10 May: François Mitterrand elected President	29 May: Most expulsions halted	April: Hunger strike in Lyon against administrative expulsions
	21 May: Pierre Mauroy appointed PM of Socialist-Communist government; Gaston Deferre appointed Interior Minister		
	23 June: François Autain appointed Minister of State for Immigrants	Aug.–Nov.: Family reunifications made easier; amnesty announced to permit 'regularization' of illegal immigrants; foreigners granted free right of association; aide au retour abolished	14 and 21 June: Left wins large majority in parliamentary elections July–Aug.: Disorders in Lyon suburbs
1982		June: End of amnesty for illegal immigrants, with a total of 132,000 regularized	
1983	22 March: Georgina Dufois appointed Minister of State for Family, Population and Immigrant Workers		6 and 13 March: Right makes gains in municipal elections after campaign marked by heavy emphasis on immigration Summer: Young Maghrebis targetted in upsurge of racist killings 4 Sept.: Front National scores 17 per cent of first-round vote in municipal by-election in Dreux Oct.–Dec.: March Against Racism from Marseilles to Paris

Year	French executive	French public policy	Other developments
1984		27 April: Reintroduction of repatriation assistance, now called *aide à la réinsertion*	
		29 May: Creation of Conseil National des Populations Immigrées (CNPI), consultative body on immigration and minority ethnic groups	17 June: FN takes 11 per cent of national vote in European Parliament elections
	19 July: Laurent Fabius appointed PM of Socialist government	17 July: ten-year combined work and residence permit for most immigrants approved by Parliament	
	23 July: Pierre Joxe appointed Interior Minister; Georgina Dufoix appointed Minister for National Solidarity and Social Affairs	4 Dec.: New restrictions on family reunifications	
1985			15 June: SOS-Racisme's first rock concert in Paris attracts crowd of 300,000
			7 Dec.: Start of ten-month bombing campaign in Paris by Middle East-linked terrorists
1986			16 March: Center-right parties win narrow overall majority in parliamentary elections
	20 March: Jacques Chirac appointed PM of center-right government; Charles Pasqua appointed Interior Minister; Philippe Seguin appointed Minister for Social Affairs	9 Sept.: Pasqua Law toughens entry and residence regulations for foreigners	Dec.: Student demonstrations against proposed university reforms
		12 Nov.: Government agrees draft legislation for reform of French nationality laws (CNF)	

Year	French executive	French public policy	Other developments
1987		17 Jan.: Government delays CNF reform	
		14 March: Government announces special commission to examine CNF	
1988	8 May: François Mitterrand re-elected President		
	10 May: Michel Rocard appointed PM of Socialist-led government		
	12 May: Pierre Joxe appointed Interior Minister; Claude Evin appointed Minister for Solidarity		5 and 12 June: Socialists win relative majority in parliamentary elections
1989		2 Aug.: Joxe Law softens Pasqua Law	Autumn: Islamic headscarf affair in Creil
		19 Dec.: Creation of Haut Conseil à l'Intégration	3 Dec.: FN candidate wins parliamentary by-election in Dreux
1990	19 Dec.: Michel Delebarre appointed Minister of State for Urban Affairs		Oct.: Disorders in Vaulx-en-Velin
1991			Jan.–March: Gulf War
	15 May: Edith Cresson appointed PM of Socialist-led government		March: Disorders in Sartrouville
	16 May 1991: Philippe Marchand appointed Interior Minister; Jean-Louis Bianco appointed Minister for Social Affairs and Integration		May: Disorders in Mantes-la-Jolie
	25 May: Kofi Yamgnane appointed Minister of State for Social Affairs and Integration	13 July: Parliament passes 'anti-ghetto' law, requiring more even distribution of social housing	

Year	French executive	French public policy	Other developments
1992	2 April: Pierre Bérégovoy appointed PM of Socialist-led government; Paul Quilès appointed Interior Minister; René Teulade appointed Minister for Social Affairs and Integration; Bernard Tapie appointed Minister for Urban Affairs		12 Jan.: Suspension of elections in Algeria, triggering terrorist violence by Islamic groups within Algeria and security operations against alleged supporters in France

20 September: Referendum approves Maastricht Treaty |
| 1993 | 29 March: Edouard Balladur appointed PM of center-right government; Charles Pasqua appointed Interior Minister; Simone Veil appointed Minister for Social Affairs, Health and Urban Affairs | July–Aug.: Pasqua laws reform access to French nationality, facilitate easier identity checks by police and limit entry and residence rights of foreigners

19 Nov.: Parliament approves constitutional revision tightening asylum laws | 21 and 28 March: RPR and UDF win sweeping majority in parliamentary elections |
| 1994 | | | Autumn: Education Ministry circular sparks new school confrontations over Islamic headscarf |
| 1995 | 7 May: Jacques Chirac elected President

17 May: Alain Juppé appointed PM of center-right government

18 May: Jean-Louis Debré appointed Interior Minister; Eric Raoult appointed Minister for Integration and Counter-Exclusionary Measures | 23 Aug.: Debré announces regular charter flights to increase deportations of illegal immigrants | 11–18 June: FN candidates elected mayors of Toulon, Orange and Marignane

July–Oct.: Ten killed and 130 injured in wave of terrorist attacks by Islamic militants in major French cities |

Year	French executive	French public policy	Other developments
1996			18 March–24 Aug.: Sit-ins and hunger-stikes by Africans (many of them victims of Pasqua laws) seeking regularization of illegal residence status
			3 Dec.: fresh bombing campaign by Islamic terrorists
1997		26 March: Debré reform of Pasqua laws passed by Parliament	9 Feb.: FN mayor elected in fourth southern town, Vitrolles
	2 June: Lionel Jospin appointed PM of Socialist-led government		25 May and 1 June: Left wins majority in parliamentary elections
	4 June: Martine Aubry appointed Employment and Solidarity Minister; Jean-Pierre Chevènement appointed Interior Minister	June 1997–Oct. 1998: Regularisation of 77,000 'sans-papiers' (undocumented migrants)	
		Dec.: Parliament passes Guigou and Chevènement laws, partially reversing Pasqua and Debré laws	
1998			March: Regional elections provoke splits within UDF and RPR over local pacts with FN permitting election of center-right Assembly Presidents in four regions: Rhône-Alpes, Bourgogne, Picardie, Languedoc-Roussillon
			12 July: Multi-ethnic soccer team wins World Cup for France
			21 Oct: Aubry declares anti-discrimination to be a government policy

Year	French executive	French public policy	Other developments
1999		18 Jan.: Constitutional amendment by parliament permits ratification of Amsterdam Treaty	13 June: Decline in vote of FN, hit by internal schisms, in European elections
2000		13 Dec.: New law strengthens promotion of more even distribution of social housing	
2001		29 Jan.: New law recognizes Armenian massacres of 1915 as 'genocide' 21 May: New law declares slavery in French colonial empire to have been a 'crime against humanity'	
2002	5 May: Jacques Chirac re-elected President 6 May: Jean-Pierre Raffarin appointed PM of center-right government; Nicolas Sarkozy appointed Interior Minister; Jean-Louis Borloo appointed Minister for Urban Affairs		21 April–5 May: Le Pen finishes second to Chirac in presidential elections 9–16 June: Center-right wins majority in parliamentary elections
2003		26 Nov.: New law limits deportation of legally resident foreigners convicted of crimes	April: Conseil Français du Culte Musulman holds its first elections
2004	30 March: Dominique de Villepin appointed Interior Minister; Jean-Louis Borloo appointed Minister for Employment and Social Cohesion	15 March: New law bans wearing of 'conspicuous' religious signs in state schools	

Year	French executive	French public policy	Other developments
2005		23 Feb.: New law requires high school teachers to teach the 'positive' role of French colonization, notably in North Africa	
	31 May: Dominique de Villepin appointed PM of center-right government	3 March: Establishment of Haute Autorité de Lutte contre les Discriminations et pour l'Égalité (HALDE)	29 May: European Constitution rejected in national referendum
	2 June: Nicolas Sarkozy appointed Interior Minister; Jean-Louis Borloo appointed Minister for Employment, Social Cohesion and Housing; Azouz Begag appointed Minister for Equal Opportunities		Nov.: Government declares state of emergency amid widespread urban disorders following deaths of two minority ethnic youths fleeing police in Clichy-sous-Bois
2006		25 Jan.: Chirac ends legal requirement to teach 'positive' role of colonization	Feb.–April: Nationwide student and worker protests force government to retract easy-hire easy-fire youth employment clause in equal opportunities law
		31 March: New equal opportunities law in response to November 2005 riots	
		6 April: New law aimed at curbing forced marriages raises marriage age for women from 15 to 18	
		June: National Assembly approves tightening of family reunification restrictions and easier labor permits for professionally skilled workers	

Internet sites

Official sources

French President
www.elysee.fr
Includes links to presidential speeches and statements.

French Prime Minister
www.premier-ministre.gouv.fr
Includes links to all government ministries.

Direction de la Population et des Migrations
www.social.gouv.fr/htm/dossiers/dpm/accueil.htm
Includes links to many official reports.

Commission Nationale Consultative des Droits de l'Homme
www.commission-droits-homme.fr
Includes links to annual report on racism and anti-racism in France.

Institut National de la Statistique et des Études Économiques (INSEE)
www.insee.fr
Website of the French census agency.

Institut National d'Études Démographiques (INED)
www.ined.fr
Website of the national demographic institute.

Haut Conseil à l'Intégration (HCI)
www.hci.gouv.fr
Website of policy advice think-tank.

Haute Autorité de Lutte contre les Discriminations et pour l'Égalité (HALDE)
www.halde.fr
Website of independent anti-racist authority.

Resource centers

Centre d'Information et d'Études sur les Migrations Internationales (CIEMI)
www.ciemi.org
Includes complete table of contents for the journal *Migrations société*.

Cité Nationale de l'Histoire de l'Immigration
www.histoire-immigration.fr
Includes full-text online version of the journal *Hommes et migrations*.

Ville-École-Intégration
www.sceren.fr/vei
Includes online searchable bibliographic database.

Public opinion

The following organizations offer free online access to many of their opinion surveys:

BVA
www.bva.fr

CSA
www.csa.fr

IPSOS
www.ipsos.fr

SOFRES
www.tns-sofres.com

Voluntary associations and pressure groups

CIMADE (Service oecuménique d'entraide)
www.cimade.org
Nationwide support network for immigrants and asylum-seekers.

Groupe d'information et de soutien des immigrés (GISTI)
www.gisti.org
Provides legal assistance to migrants and asylum-seekers.

PAJOL
pajol.eu.org
Active in support of 'sans-papiers' (undocumented migrants).

Other websites

Suffrage universel
www.suffrage-universel.be
Link to 'France' provides access to a wealth of information on minority ethnic candidates in French elections up to 2004.

Wikipedia
en.wikipedia.org
Link to 'Elections in France' provides detailed results of parliamentary and presidential elections since 1958.

Glossary

aide au retour   repatriation assistance

arrondissement   urban district, roughly equivalent to a ward in the UK or a precinct in the US

banlieues   literally, suburbs; as commonly used since the 1980s, denotes socially disadvantaged urban areas containing dense concentrations of minority ethnic residents

communautarisme   ethnic factionalism or separatism

Conseil d'État   France's highest administrative court

département   administrative unit similar to a county in the UK or the US

député   member of the National Assembly

Français par acquisition   persons born without French nationality who have since acquired it

Habitation à Loyer Modéré (HLM)   publicly subsidized low rental social housing unit

harkis   Algerian Muslim auxiliaries used by the French army against nationalist insurgents during the Algerian war of independence (1954–62)

jus sanguinis   citizenship rights based on biological descent

jus soli   citizenship rights based on place of birth or territorial residence

laïcité   the separation of the state from religious organizations

ostensible   ostensible or conspicuous

ostentatoire   ostentatious

pieds-noirs   colloquial term for European settlers in French North Africa

rapatriés   literally, repatriated citizens; official term for European settlers who migrated to France at the time of decolonization

regroupement familial   family reunification

verlan   backslang, formed by inverting the order of syllables

Zones d'Éducation Prioritaire (ZEP)   literally, 'education priority zones'; disadvantaged localities targeted for supplementary educational funding

Zones Urbaines Sensibles (ZUS)   official category designating the most chronically disadvantaged of the banlieues

Zone à Urbaniser en Priorité (ZUP)   urban development area typically containing dense concentrations of social housing

Notes

Introduction

1 While there are many valuable essays in the volume edited by Horowitz and Noiriel (1992), they are divided in their focal points between France and the US. Contributions to the volume edited by Ogden and White (1989) are scattered across a much longer historical period than that dealt with here.

2 See Freeman (1979), Grillo (1985), Schain (1985, 1987), Brubaker (1992), Hollifield (1992), Silverman (1992), Favell (1998), Lloyd (1998), Feldblum (1999), Fetzer (2000), Bleich (2003), Freedman (2004), Lebovics (2004) and Chapman and Frader (2004). A growing body of work has also been published in English on the extreme-right Front National party: see Marcus (1995), Simmons (1996), Davies (1999), DeClair (1999), Fysh and Wolfrys (2003) and Rydgren (2004). For a detailed study of majority ethnic attitudes on the Islamic headscarf affair see Bowen (2006b).

3 North Africans are the most studied minority in English: see MacMaster (1997), Silverstein (2004) and Derderian (2004). Muslims are the subject of a valuable study by Laurence and Vaisse (2006). On minority ethnic political mobilization, see Miller (1981), Safran (1986, 1992) and Ireland (1994). On minority ethnic women, see Freedman and Tarr (2000) and Keaton (2006).

4 All translations from French into English are my own.

5 In a more recent publication, Safran (1992) recognizes that, compared with Latinos in the US, Maghrebis in France have been far less able to resist the erosion of their cultural heritage.

1 Overview

1 For a fuller discussion of the limitations of French census data for the study of immigrants and their descendants, see Silberman (1992).

2 Estimates based on partial censuses conducted in 2004–5 put the total number of immigrants at 4.9 million (INSEE 2006). The last complete census in France was conducted in 1999.

3 An authoritative account of this transition is presented by Cross (1983).

4 For a convenient encyclopedic-style guide to immigration in twentieth-century France, see Amar and Milza (1990). For a guide to archival sources, see Génériques (1999). The essays edited by Ogden and White (1989) span the nineteenth and twentieth centuries. Gervereau et al. (1998) offers a richly illustrated history of the twentieth century. Surveys of the period since 1945 include Georges (1986), Mestiri (1990), Ogden (1991) and Fitzpatrick (1993). On the period since 1974, see Gaspard and Servan-Schreiber (1985), Fuchs (1987), Voisard and Ducastelle (1990), Taguieff (1991) and Bernard (2002).

5 In 1987 the name of this organization was changed to the Office des Migrations Internationales (OMI).
6 Census officials estimate that in addition to the 510,000 foreigners born in France recorded in 1999, as many as 410,000 foreign minors born in France were incorrectly declared by their parents to be French in anticipation of their acquisition of French citizenship on or before the age of majority (INSEE 2005: 34).
7 For surveys of the literature, see Yinger (1985) and Bulmer and Solomos (1999).
8 For a defense of this approach, see Banton (1991); for a critique, see Miles (1993).
9 On the history of French perceptions of Islam and the marginal role of this religion within French society prior to the post-war period, see Sellam (1987).
10 Cf. Rath (1993) on the related concept of 'minorization'.

2 Socio-economic structures

1 The notion of the ghetto as a place for outsiders has been present in Europe since the term was introduced in the sixteenth century, when it denoted a neighborhood in which Jews were forced to live.
2 For an analysis of French perceptions of this kind, see Crowley (1992).
3 Cultural differences are, however, only part of the picture. Until the mid-1980s, Algerian and other African women legally resident in France were not uncommonly refused work permits, whereas Portuguese women enjoyed unrestricted access to the labor market (Costa-Lascoux 1989: 7).
4 For a literature review of this field, see Aldrich and Waldinger (1990).

3 Minority ethnic identification and mobilization

1 For an incisive critique of the supposed opposition between ethnicity and modernization, see Safran (1987).
2 Through the codification and enforcement of laws governing kinship structures, the state does, of course, play a major role in shaping the broad parameters within which family relationships develop. Todd (1994) has argued that differences in family structures are an important factor in conditioning the pace of acculturation among minority groups and the willingness of receiving societies to accommodate cultural differences.
3 In 2001, the name of the FAS was changed to FASILD (Fonds d'Action et de soutien pour l'intégration et la lutte contre les discriminations – Action Support Fund for Integration and Anti-Discrimination), reflecting the new priority given to anti-discrimination measures. In 2006, the FASILD was programd for absorption into a new umbrella agency for equal opportunities.
4 A useful overview of French educational policy in relation to the children of immigrants is provided by Boyzon-Fradet (1992).
5 As Roy (1994: 64) has pointed out, this formally involves the state in recognizing *religious* – but not *ethnic* – minorities. Although this distinction is in some respects a fine one (most – but not all – Muslims in France are of immigrant origin), it is important from the perspective of French republicanism. Recognition of religious organizations is considered acceptable because their members choose freely to associate with each other; by contrast, state recognition of ethnic groups would be a denial of personal freedom, since the origins of individuals are, as a matter of biological fact, beyond their control. The objective of the French state is to separate Muslims as far as possible from their foreign origins, treating them as individuals exercising their freedom of conscience – albeit through organized forms of religious belief – within the overarching framework of France's republican tradition.
6 *Ostensible* may be translated into English as 'ostensible' or 'conspicuous'. Because of the importance of this particular term and the closely related word *ostentatoire* (ostentatious) in the debate leading up to the 2004 law, both have been retained in French.

7 Chirac and others used the term 'Islamic veil' as a generic expression embracing the headscarf and analagous Islamic garments.

8 On the illogicalities associated with the distinctions between 'ostensible' and 'ostentatoire' and other verbal acrobatics performed by proponents of the new law, see Gemie (2004). For more wide-ranging accounts of the 2003–4 resurgence of the headscarf affair and its historical context, see Gunn (2004), Gresh (2004), Gunn and Chélini-Pont (2005) and Bowen (2006b).

9 As noted above, Chirac was one of many participants in the headscarf debate who used the words 'veil' and 'headscarf' more or less interchangeably.

10 These ratios have been calculated by assuming that a total of approximately 125,000 girls from Muslim families were attending French state secondary schools in 1994 (data derived from Conseil Économique et Social 1994: 57). The figure of 350,000 quoted by Rocard in 1989 included Muslim girls of primary as well as secondary school age. Although at least one girl had been expelled from a primary school for wearing a headscarf (*Le Monde*, 26 Nov. 1994), it was normally only girls of secondary school age who might potentially be involved. If the ratios were calculated on the basis of the total given by Rocard, the proportion of Muslim girls wearing headscarves would be one in twenty-three on the higher estimate advanced by the Interior Ministry or one in 175 on the higher estimate given by the Education Ministry.

11 On the problematic nature of the concept of the 'home country' or 'homeland', see Safran (1990) and Morley (2000).

12 Citing a news magazine account of the 1990 French Defense Ministry report, Safran (1991: 229) says it 'revealed that only 25 per cent of Beurs ... fulfilled their military obligations in France (the remainder either serving in Algeria or getting exemption)'. This highly selective account of the report – echoed in Fitzpatrick's assertion that three-quarters of Franco-Algerian conscripts have 'found ways of avoiding it [i.e., military service] or opted to do it in the Algerian army' (1993: 113) – passes over the fact that no more than three in ten have been opting for Algeria, and as almost two-thirds of these have been declared unfit for service only about one in ten has actually served in the Algerian armed forces (Faivre 1990: 33). Under Algerian law, the age of majority is 21. The French Defense Ministry believes that some Algerian fathers have used their parental rights to enlist their sons in the Algerian armed forces prior to their reaching the age of majority; once this has been done, the young men concerned have been prevented from serving in France (Biville 1990: 10). A clear majority of Franco-Algerian bi-nationals have nevertheless been opting for France, where about half have been declared unfit for service (Faivre 1990: 33); hence the seemingly low participation rate quoted by Safran. Contrary to the gloss put on these figures by Fitzpatrick, rejection by the French authorities cannot in all fairness be described as a way of 'avoiding' military service.

4 National identity, nationality and citizenship

1 On the wider context within which anxieties over French national identity have developed, see Safran (1991: 223–4) and Freedman (2004).

2 In a perceptive essay, Silberman (1992: 118–21) has shown that, despite the official silence on ethnic origins maintained by the census authorities, traces of this ethnic hierarchy are clearly visible just below the surface of seemingly technical aspects of French census data.

3 Maghrebis were referred to at this time as North Africans. In Mauco's pre-war survey, they appeared as Arabs.

4 Until 1993, the Code de la Nationalité Française (CNF) was formally separate from the main body of civil laws, which are collectively known as the Code civil. Besides revising the laws governing French nationality, the 1993 reform incorporated them within the Code civil. In this sense, the CNF no longer exists as a separate entity.

5 On the historical evolution of French nationality laws, see Masson (1985), Laacher (1987), Decouflé (1992) and Weil (2004). Prior to 1993, the acquisition of French nationality by second-generation foreigners was automatic in the sense that it was conferred upon them without their having to request it. Although certain conditions applied, an act of volition was not formally among them. To prove their citizenship, those concerned had to demonstrate that they were born in France and had lived there during the five years preceding the age of majority; in formal terms, the submission of the necessary documents did not constitute a request for citizenship, but served to prove that it was already held.

6 The calculation of data on military service is made complex by a number of factors, one which is the fact that, depending on their personal circumstances, draftees were permitted to enlist at any point between the age of 18 and 29. A Defense Ministry report compiled in 1990, based on a longer run of data than that submitted to the Nationality Commission in 1987, indicated that up to three in ten Franco-Algerian bi-nationals were opting to serve in Algeria (Biville 1990; Faivre 1990: 33). The military draft was abolished in France with effect from 1997.

5 Politics and public policy

1 As Ogden (1991: 300) has observed, an important exception to this lay in the DOM-TOM, where the French government actively recruited migrant workers from the early 1960s onwards.

2 On EU immigration policy, see Bigo and Guild (2005). On European citizenship, see Dell'Olio (2005) and Hansen and Weil (2001). On EU anti-discrimination policy, see Geddes and Giraudon (2004).

3 For an analysis of the FN's policy platform, see Taguieff (1989). On the party's organizational structures and electoral strategies, see Fysh and Wolfreys (1992). On its origins and development within the wider historical context of the extreme right in France, see Hainsworth (1992).

4 Valuable analyses of the evidence available on sources of support for the FN include Mitra (1988), Husbands (1991), Perrineau (1991) and Mayer and Perrineau (1993).

5 These new measures – covering entry and residence rights, police identity checks and access to French nationality – were generally dubbed the Pasqua laws (cf. Costa-Lascoux 1994a). Although Interior Minister Charles Pasqua was directly responsible for most of this legislation, the nationality reform did not technically fall within his ministerial brief, but was the formal responsibility of Justice Minister Pierre Méhaignerie.

6 On the French concept of 'public order', see HCI (1992b: 17–25).

7 On the growing role of the EC (now the EU) in French public policy, see section 5.2.

8 The French designation was 'Secrétaire d'État aux Travailleurs Immigrés'. This is sometimes misleadingly translated as Secretary of State for Immigrant Workers. In Britain, the term Secretary of State applies only to very senior ministers, and in the US it denotes the minister responsible for foreign affairs, whereas a *Secrétaire d'État* is a junior French minister responsible for a particular sector of activities, usually within a larger government department. Postel-Vinay, for example, was a subordinate of the Minister of Labor, Michel Durafour. Verbunt (1985: 137) captures the technical sense of *Secrétaire d'État* by translating it as Vice-Minister. The nearest formal equivalent in Britain is Minister of State.

9 A similar signal was sent by placing the new Minister of State for Immigrants, François Autain, within the Ministry of National Solidarity (a new name for the Ministry of Social Affairs), rather than within the Ministry of Labor.

10 The total number of convictions for racial and ethnic discrimination had averaged around half a dozen per annum throughout the 1990s. These figures covered discriminatory treatment in employment, housing and goods and services of all kinds

(CNCDH 1999: 313–16). In 2004, the number of convictions totaled about a dozen, including a single case in the field of employment (CNCDH 2006: 59–60).

11 The numbers involved are by no means insignificant. According to the 1982 census returns, there were 805,116 Algerians in France. It is estimated that 240,000 of these also had French nationality and ought therefore not to have been classified as foreigners. The 1990 census put the number of Algerians at 614,207, of whom 110,000 are thought to have been French. See Lebon (1992: 20).

12 In line with the seemingly non-ethnic lexis favored in government circles, he spoke of these minorities as 'jeunes issus de l'immigration' (young people of immigrant origin) (Chevènement 1999).

13 Explicitly ethnic categories were again avoided but were nevertheless unambiguously present in the statement that '35 per cent [among the units concerned] are of immigrant origin' (*Le Monde*, 21 Sept. 1999).

14 The Fonds d'Action Sociale was created in 1958 with the initial purpose of assisting Algerian immigrant workers. Its brief was later widened to include all immigrant workers and their families and its title was expanded to reflect this change, becoming the Fonds d'Action Sociale pour les Travailleurs Immigrés et leurs Familles (Social Action Fund for Immigrant Workers and their Families). In 2001, a further change of name turned it into the FASILD (Fonds d'action et de soutien pour l'intégration et la lutte contre les discriminations – Action Support Fund for Integration and Anti-Discrimination), reflecting the new priority given to anti-discrimination policy. The 2006 Equal Opportunities Law programd the FASILD's absorption and transformation into a new umbrella agency for equal opportunities.

15 On the history and operational structures of the FAS, see Caron (1990: 11–12), Khellil (1991: 122–9), Lapeyronnie (1993: 177–85).

16 For a literature review dealing with cultural policy in the field of immigration, see ADRI (1994).

17 The first experimental program of this kind, aimed at the children of Portuguese immigrants, began in 1973. The scheme was widened to include children of other nationalities from 1975 onwards. While initially conceived in response to the wishes of sending states anxious to ensure that the cultural heritage of their expatriates was maintained, the LCO program soon came to be regarded by the French authorities as a valuable tool in preparing the ground for repatriation (Boyzon-Fradet 1992: 155–7).

18 The drastic reform or even abolition of the LCO program was called for in official reports such as those of the Haut Conseil à l'Intégration (HCI 1992b: 51–3) and the Conseil Économique et Social (1994: 124).

19 Although the current *Recteur* (head) of the Grande Mosquée de Paris, Dalil Boubakeur, was appointed by the Algerian government in 1992, it is important to note that he is a French national and the son of an earlier *Recteur*, Si Hamza Boubakeur, who sided with the French during the Algerian war of independence (*Libération*, 13 April 1992). Complex from the outset, the juridical status of the Grande Mosquée de Paris, inaugurated in 1926, became the subject of labyrinthine disputes after decolonization: see Kepel (1987: 61–94, 313–52) and *Independent* (12 Feb. 1992).

Conclusion

1 In France's second parliamentary chamber, the 321-seat Senate, where members are elected by city and rural councillors, not by direct elections, there are now two members of North African descent.

2 These hopes were vindicated by the results of the elections, held in January 1995 (*Le Monde*, 24 Jan. 1995).

Bibliography

Abelkrim-Chikh, R. (1991) 'Les Femmes exogames: entre la loi de Dieu et les droits de l'homme', in B. Étienne (ed.), *L'Islam en France: islam, état et société*, Paris: CNRS, pp. 235–54.

Abou Sada, A. (1990) 'L'Avenir des travailleurs immigrés dans le contexte de la restructuration des entreprises', in A. Abou Sada *et al.* (eds), *L'Immigation au tournant*, Paris: CIEMI/L'Harmattan, pp. 157–68.

ADRI (Agence de Développement des Relations Interculturelles) (1990) *Dossier de presse sur l'affaire du foulard*, 4 vols, Paris: ADRI.

—— (1994) *Action culturelle et intégration: un bilan des connaissances*, Paris: ADRI.

Aissou, A. (1987) *Les Beurs, l'école et la France*, Paris: CIEMI/L'Harmattan.

Aldrich, H.E., and Waldinger, R. (1990) 'Ethnicity and Entrepreneurship', *Annual Review of Sociology*, 16: 111–35.

Aldrich, R. (2005) *Vestiges of the Colonial Empire in France: Monuments, Museums and Colonial Memories*, Basingstoke: Palgrave Macmillan.

Amadieu, J.-F. (2004) 'Enquête "Testing" sur CV', Paris: Observatoire des discriminations. Online: http://cergors.univ-paris1.fr/docsatelecharger/pr%E9se ntation%20du%20testing%20mai%202004.pdf (accessed 31 July 2006).

—— (2005) 'Discriminations à l'embauche: de l'envoi du CV à l'entretien', Paris: Observatoire des discriminations. Online: http://cergors.univ-paris1.fr/ docsatelecharger/Discriminationsenvoientretien.pdf (accessed 31 July 2006).

Amar, A. and Milza, A. (1990) *L'Immigration en France au xxe siècle*, Paris: Armand Colin.

Amara, F. and Zappi, S. (2003) *Ni putes ni soumises*, Paris: La Découverte.

Anstett, S. (1992) 'Suspension de l'immigration et besoins de l'économie française', *Revue française des affaires sociales*, 46 (Dec.): 105–26.

Assemblée Nationale (2004) 'Commission des Affaires culturelles, familiales et sociales: compte rendu no. 25'. Online: http://www.assemblee-nationale.fr/12/cr-cafc/03–04/c0304025.asp (accessed 31 July 2006).

Aubry, M. (1998) 'La Politique d'intégration. 21 octobre 1998. Communication en conseil des ministres de Mme Martine Aubry, ministre de l'emploi et de la solidarité'. Online: http://www.santé.gouv.fr/htm/actu/34_981021_1.htm (accessed 19 July 1999).

——(1999) 'Table Ronde sur les Discriminations Raciales dans le monde du travail', 11 May. Online: http://www.vie-publique.fr/documents-vp/aubry11051999. shtml (accessed 30 Aug. 2006).

Auvolat, M. and Benattig, R. (1988) 'Les Artisans étrangers en France', *Revue européenne des migrations internationales*, 4(3): 37–55.

Babadji, R. (1992) 'Le Mixte franco-algérien: remarques à partir des conventions sur le service national et les enfants de couples mixtes séparés', in K. Basfao and J.-R. Henry (eds), *Le Maghreb, l'Europe et la France*, Paris: CNRS, pp. 323–42.

Bachmann, C. and Basier, L. (1984) 'Le Verlan: argot d'école ou langue des Keums?', *Mots*, 8 (March): 169–87.

Balibar, É. (1988) 'Propositions sur la citoyenneté', in C. Wihtol de Wenden (ed.), *La Citoyenneté et les changements de structures sociale et nationale de la population française*, Paris: Edilig/Fondation Diderot, pp. 221–34.

—— and Wallerstein, I. (1988) *Race, nation, classe: les identités ambiguës*, Paris: La Découverte.

Balladur, E. (1999) *L'Avenir de la différence*, Paris: Plon.

Bancel, N., Blanchard, P. and Vergès, F. (2003) *La République coloniale: essai sur une utopie*, Paris: Albin Michel.

Banton, M (1983) *Racial and Ethnic Competition*, Cambridge: Cambridge University Press.

—— (1991) 'The Race Relations Problematic', *British Journal of Sociology*, 42(1): 115–30.

Barbara, A. (1986) 'Discriminants et jeunes "beurs"', in G. Abou-Sada and H. Milet (eds), *Générations issues de l'immigration: 'mémoires et devenirs'*, Paris: Arcantère, pp. 123–38.

—— (1993) *Les Couples mixtes*, Paris: Bayard.

Barbulesco, L. (1985) 'Les Radios arabes de la bande FM', *Esprit*, 102 (June): 176–85.

Barou, J. (1989) 'L'Insertion des immigrés passe par leurs conditions de logement', *Hommes et migrations*, 1118 (Jan.): 29–37.

—— (1992a) *L'Immigration en France des ressortissants des pays d'Afrique noire*, Paris: Secrétariat Général à l'Intégration.

—— (1992b) 'Des Chiffres en général et de ceux de l'INSEE en particulier', *Migrants-formation*, 91 (Dec.): 5–10.

Barreau, J.-C. (1992) *De l'immigration en général et de la nation française en particulier*, Paris: Le Pré aux Clercs.

Bastenier, A. and Dassetto, F. (1993) *Immigration et espace public: la controverse de l'intégration*, Paris: CIEMI/L'Harmattan.

Bataille, P. (1997) *Le Racisme au travail*, Paris: La Découverte.

Battegay, A. (1992) 'L'Actualité de l'immigration dans les villes françaises: la question des territoires ethniques', *Revue européenne des migrations internationales*, 8(2): 83–100.

Bazin, C. and Vermes, G. (1990) 'L'Enseignement du portugais et de l'arabe dans le secteur associatif: premiers résultats d'une recherche-action', *Migrants-formation*, 83 (Dec.): 76–97.

Beaud, S. and Noiriel, G. (1991) 'Penser l'"intégration" des immigrés', in P.-A. Taguieff (ed.), *Face au racisme*, vol. 2, *Analyses, hypothèses, perspectives*, Paris: La Découverte, pp. 261–82.

Beaugé, G.L. (1990) 'Immigration et nouvelles formes de salariat dans la crise du BTP', in G. Abou Sada, B. Courault and Z. Zeroulou (eds), *L'Immigration au tournant*, Paris: CIEMI/L'Harmattan, pp. 181–93.

Bébéar, C. (2004) *Des enterprises aux couleurs de la France. Minorités visibles: relever le défi de l'accès à l'emploi dans l'entreprise*, Rapport au Premier Ministre. Paris: La Documentation Française.

Begag, A. (1986) *Le Gone du Chaâba*, Paris: Seuil; trans. by Naïma Wolf and Alec G. Hargreaves as *Shantytown Kid*, Lincoln, NE: University of Nebraska Press, 2007.

—— (1989) *North African Immigrants in France: The Socio-Spatial Representation of 'Here' and 'There'*, Loughborough: European Research Centre.

—— (1991) 'Voyage dans les quartiers chauds', *Les Temps modernes*, 47(545–6, Dec.): 134–64.

Begag, A. and Delorme, C. (1994) *Quartiers sensibles*, Paris: Seuil.

Bekkouche, A. (ed.) (2005) *La Sous-représentation des Français d'origine étrangère: crise du système représentatif ou discrimination politique?*, Paris: L'Harmattan.

Belaïd, L., *et al.* (1996) 'Islamistes: les réseaux de l'ombre', *L'Evénement du jeudi* (11 April): 14–17.

Bellil, S. and Stoquart, J. (2002) *Dans l'enfer des tournantes*, Paris: Denoël.

Belorgey, J.-M. (1999) *Rapport sur la lutte contre les discriminations*, Paris: Ministère de l'emploi et de la solidarité. Online: http://www.social.gouv.fr/htm/pointsur/discrimination/index_bel.htm (accessed 31 July 2006).

Berger, S. and Piore, M.J. (1980) *Dualism and Discontinuity in Industrial Societies*, Cambridge: Cambridge University Press.

Beriss, D. (1990) 'Scarves, Schools and Segregation: The *Foulard* Affair', *French Politics and Society*, 8(1): 1–13.

Bernard, P. (2002) *L'Immigration: le défi mondial*, Paris: Gallimard.

—— (2004) 'Communautarisme et cloisonnement des mémoires', *Le Monde* (23 June).

Berrier, R.J. (1985) 'The French Textile Industry: A Segmented Labour Market', in R. Rogers (ed.), *Guests Come to Stay: The Effects of European Labor Migration on Sending and Receiving Countries*, Boulder, CO: Westview Press, pp. 51–68.

Betts, R.F. (1961) *Assimilation and Association in French Colonial Theory and Practice*, New York: Columbia University Press.

Bigo, D. and Guild, E. (eds) (2005) *Controlling Frontiers: Free Movement into and within Europe*, Aldershot: Ashgate.

Biville, Y. (1990) 'Les Jeunes d'origine maghrébine et le service national', *Hommes et migrations*, 1138 (Dec.): 7–18.

Blanc, M. (1990) 'Les Politiques d'attribution de logements sociaux aux minorités ethniques en France, Grande-Bretagne et Allemagne fédérale', *Migration*, 7: 69–91.

—— (1992) 'From Substandard Housing to Devalorized Social Housing: Ethnic Minorities in France, Germany and the UK', *European Journal of Intercultural Studies*, 3(1): 7–25.

Bleich, E. (2003) *Race Politics in Britain and France: Ideas and Policymaking since the 1960s*, Cambridge: Cambridge University Press.

Body-Gendrot, S. (1993) *Ville et violence: l'irruption de nouveaux acteurs*, Paris: Presses Universitaires de France.

Body-Gendrot, S. and Le Guennec, N. (1998) *Mission sur les violences urbaines*, Paris: La Documentation Française.

Body-Gendrot, S. and Wihtol de Wenden, C. (2003) *Police et discriminations raciales: le tabou français*, Paris: Éditions de l'Atelier/Éditions Ouvrières.

Bonnafous, S. (1992) 'Le Terme "intégration" dans *Le Monde*: sens et non-sens', *Hommes et migrations*, 1154 (May): 24–6.

Borella, F. (1991) 'Nationalité et citoyenneté', in D. Colas, C. Emeri and J. Zylberberg (eds), *Citoyenneté et nationalité: perspectives en France et au Québec*, Paris: Presses Universitaires de France, pp. 209–29.

Borrel, C. and Simon, P. (2005) 'Les Origines des Français', in C. Lefèvre and A. Filhon (eds), *Histoires de familles, histoires familiales*, Paris: INED, pp. 425–41.

Bouamama, S. (1989) 'Elections municipales et immigraton: essai de bilan', *Migrations société*, 1(3): 22–45.

—— (1994) *Dix ans de marche des Beurs: chronique d'un mouvement avorté*, Paris: Desclée de Brouwer.

—— Cordeiro, A. and Roux, M. (1992) *La Citoyenneté dans tous ses états: de l'immigration à la nouvelle citoyenneté*, Paris: CIEMI/L'Harmattan.

Boulot, S. and Boyzon-Fradet, D. (1987) 'Un siècle de réglementation à l'école', in G. Vermes and J. Boutet (eds), *France, pays multilingue*, vol. 1, *Les Langues en France, un enjeu historique et social*, Paris: L'Harmattan, pp. 163–204.

—— (1988) *Les Immigrés et l'école: une course d'obstacles*, Paris: CIEMI/L'Harmattan.

Boumaza, N., Rudder, V. de and Maria, M.F. de (1989) *Banlieues, immigration, gestion urbaine*, Grenoble: Institut de Géographie Alpine.

Bourdin, M.-J. (1992) '"Tu ne couperas point"', in E. Rude-Antoine (ed.), *L'Immigration face aux lois de la République*, Paris: Karthala, pp. 165–75.

Bourgeba-Dichy, M. (1990) 'Des militants maghrébins de la deuxième génération en France', *Revue du Tiers Monde*, 31(123): 623–36.

Bowen, J.D. (2006a) 'France's Revolt: Can the Republic Live up to its Ideals?', in *Boston Review* (Jan.–Feb.). Online: http://bostonreview.net/BR31.1/bowen.html (accessed 20 Aug. 2006).

—— (2006b) *Why the French Don't Like Headscarves: Islam, the State and Public Space*, Princeton, NJ: Princeton University Press.

Boyer, A. (1998) *L'Islam en France*, Paris: Presses Universitaires de France.

Boyzon-Fradet, D. (1992) 'The French Education System: Springboard or Obstacle to Integration?', in D.L. Horowitz and G. Noiriel (eds), *Immigrants in Two Democracies: French and American Experiences*, New York and London: New York University Press, pp. 148–66.

Brenner, E. (ed.) (2002) *Les Territoires perdus de la République: Antisémitisme, racisme et sexisme en milieu scolaire*, Paris: Mille et une nuits.

Brouard, S. and Tiberj, J. (2005) *Rapport au politique des Français issus de l'immigration*, Paris: CEVIPOF.

Brubaker, R. (1992) *Citizenship and Nationhood in France and Germany*, Cambridge, MA: Harvard University Press.

Brunel, E. (1992) 'Les Chinois à Marne-la-Vallée', *Revue européenne des migrations internationales*, 8(3): 195–209.

Bryson, S.S. (1987) 'France through the Looking Glass: The November–December 1986 French Student Movement', *French Review*, 61(2): 247–60.

Bulmer, M. and Solomos, J. (eds) (1999) *Ethnic and Racial Studies Today*, London: Routledge.

BVA (2005) 'L'Opinion en question: Les Français et la question de l'intégration des étrangers', 31 Jan. Online: http://www.bva.fr/new/index.asp (accessed 31 July 2005).

Cachin, O. (1996) *L'Offensive rap*, Paris: Gallimard.

Cahier de l'Observatoire de l'intégration (1994) 'L'Apport de la migration espagnole: bibliographie analytique', no. 11 (May).

Calvès, G. (2004) *La Discrimination positive*, Paris: Presses Universitaires de France.

Campani, G., Catani, M. and Palidda, S. (1987) 'Italian Immigrant Associations in France', in J. Rex, D. Joly and C. Wilpert (eds), *Immigrant Associations in Europe*, Aldershot: Gower, pp. 166–200.

Cannon, S. (1997) '*Paname City Rapping*: B-Boys in the *Banlieues* and Beyond', in A.G. Hargreaves and M. McKinney (eds), *Post-Colonial Cultures in France*, London and New York: Routledge, 150–66.

Caron, M. (1990) 'Immigration, intégration et solidarité', *Regards sur l'actualité*, 116 (Dec.): 3–45.

Castellan, M., Marpsat, M. and Goldberger, M.F. (1992) 'Les Quartiers prioritaires de la politique de la ville', *INSEE Première*, 234 (Dec.): 1–4.

Castles, S. and Kosack, G. (1973) *Immigrant Workers and Class Structures in Western Europe*, London: Oxford University Press, for the Institute of Race Relations.

Catani, M. and Palidda, S. (1989) 'Devenir Français: pourquoi certains jeunes étrangers y renoncent?', *Revue européenne des migrations internationales*, 5(2): 89–106.

Centre des Cultures Méditerranéennes (1989) *Les Immigrés et la participation à la vie locale*, Paris: Adels/Syros.

Céreq (2004) 'Les Jeunes issus de l'immigration: de l'enseignement supérieur au marché du travail', *Bref*, 205 (Feb.): 1–4.

Cesari, J. (1989) 'Les Stratégies identitaires des musulmans à Marseille', *Migrations société*, 1(5–6): 59–71.

—— (1992) 'L'Émergence d'une élite intermédiaire parmi les Franco-Maghrébins', in K. Basfao and J.-R. Henry (eds), *Le Maghreb, l'Europe et la France*, Paris: CNRS, pp. 401–13.

—— (1993) 'Les Leaders associatifs issus de l'immigration maghrébine: intermédiaires ou clientèle?', *Horizons maghrébins*, 20–1: 80–94.

—— (1998) *Musulmans et républicains: les jeunes, l'Islam et la France*, Brussels: Complexe.

Chaabaoui, M. (1989) 'La Consommation médiatique des Maghrébins', *Migrations société*, 1(4): 23–40.

Chaïb, Y. (1994) 'Le Lieu d'enterrement comme repère migratoire', *Migrations société*, 6(33–4): 29–40.

Chaker, S. (1988) 'Le Berbère: une langue occultée en exil', in G. Vermes (ed.), *Vingt-cinq communautés linguistiques en France*, vol. 2, *Les Langues immigrées*, Paris: L'Harmattan, pp. 145–64.

Champion, J.-B., Goldberger, M.-F. and Marpsat, M. (1993) 'Les Quartiers "en convention"', *Regards sur l'actualité*, 196 (Dec.): 19–28.

Chapman, H. and Frader, L.L. (eds) (2004) *Race in France: Interdisciplinary Perspectives on the Politics of Difference*, New York and Oxford: Berghahn.

Chauviré, Y. (1993) 'Répartition spatiale des principales nationalités étrangères en France', *Espace, populations, sociétés*, 3: 533–40.

Chevènement, J.-P. (1999) 'Discours de Monsieur Jean-Pierre Chevènement, Ministre de l'Intérieur, à la réunion des préfets', 15 Feb. Online: http:www.interieur.gouv.fr/organisation/ministere/discours/9915_02.html (accessed 20 March 1999).

Chirac, J. (2003) 'Discours prononcé par M. Jacques Chirac, Président de la République, relatif au respect du principe de la laïcité dans la République', 17 Dec. Online: http://www.elysee.fr/elysee/elysec.fr/francais/interventions/discours_ et_declarations/2003/decembre/discours_prononce_par_m_jacques_chirac_ president_de_la_republique_relatif_au_respect_du_principe_de_laicite_dans_la_ republique-palais_de_l_elysee.2829.html (accessed 31 July 2006).

—— (2005) 'Déclaration aux Français de M. Jacques Chirac, Président de la République', 14 Nov. Online: http://www.elysee.fr/elysee/elysee.fr/francais/ interventions/interviews_articles_de_presse_et_interventions_televisees./2005/ novembre/declaration_aux_francais.32000.html (accessed 31 July 2006).

Citron, S. (1987) *Le Mythe national: l'histoire de France en question*, Paris: Éditions ouvrières/ Études et documentation internationales.

Clémentine, A., *et al.* (eds) (2006) *Banlieue, lendemains de révolte*, Paris: La Dispute/ Regards.

Club de l'Horloge (1985) *L'Identité de la France*, Paris: Albin Michel.

CNCDH (Commission Nationale Consultative des Droits de l'Homme) (1991) *1990: La Lutte contre le racisme et la xénophobie*, Paris: La Documentation Française.

—— (1992) *1991: La Lutte contre le racisme et la xénophobie*, Paris: La Documentation Française.

—— (1993) *1992: La Lutte contre le racisme et la xénophobie*, Paris: La Documentation Française.

—— (1994) *1993: La Lutte contre le racisme et la xénophobie*, Paris: La Documentation Française.

—— (1999) *1998: La Lutte contre le racisme et la xénophobie*, Paris: La Documentation Française.

—— (2004) *2003: La Lutte contre le racisme et la xénophobie*, Paris: La Documentation Française.

—— (2006) *2005: La Lutte contre le racisme et la xénophobie*, Paris: La Documentation Française.

CNIL (Commission Nationale de l'Informatique et des Libertés) (2005) *26e Rapport d'Activité*, Paris: La Documentation Française. Online: http://lesrapports. ladocumentationfrancaise.fr/BRP/064000317/0000.pdf (accessed 31 July 2006).

Comité de Réflexion sur l'Application du Principe de Laïcité dans la République (2004) *Rapport au Président de la République*, Paris: La Documentation Française.

Conseil Économique et Social (1994) *La Scolarisation des enfants d'immigrés*, Paris: Conseil Économique et Social.

Conseil Supérieur de l'Audiovisuel (2000) 'Présence et représentation des minorités visibles à la télévision française', *La Lettre du CSA*, 129: 12–14.

Coroller, C. (2004) '"Ostensible", le mot mot qui s'est imposé', *Libération* (28 Jan.).

Costa-Lascoux, J. (1983) 'L'Immigration algérienne et la nationalité des enfants d'Algériens', in L. Talha *et al.*, *Maghrébins en France: émigrés ou immigrés?*, Paris: CNRS, pp. 299–320.

—— (1989) *De l'immigré au citoyen*, Paris: La Documentation Française.

—— (1994a) 'Les Lois "Pasqua": une nouvelle politique de l'immigration', *Regards sur l'actualité*, 199 (March): 19–43.

—— (1994b) 'French Legislation Against Racism and Discrimination', *New Community*, 20(3): 371–9.

Courault, B.A. (1990) 'Les Étrangers "catégorie" du marché dual ou "vecteur" de la flexibilité du travail', in G. Abou Sada *et al.* (eds), *L'Immigration au tournant*, Paris: CIEMI/L'Harmattan, pp. 109–22.

Cour des Comptes (2004) *L'Accueil des immigrants et l'intégration des populations issues de l'immigration.* Online: http://www.ccomptes.fr/Cour-des-Comptes/publications/rapports/immigration/immigration.pdf (accessed 31 July 2006).

Courtois, S. (1989) *Le Sang de l'étranger: les immigrés de la MOI dans la résistance*, Paris: Fayard.

Cross, G.S. (1983) *Immigrant Workers in Industrial France: The Making of a New Laboring Class*, Philadelphia: Temple University Press.

Cross, M. (1995) '"Race", Class Formation and Political Interests: A Comparison of Amsterdam and London', in A.G. Hargreaves and J. Leaman (eds), *Racism, Ethnicity and Politics in Contemporary Europe*, Aldershot: Edward Elgar, pp. 47–78.

Crowley, J. (1992) 'Minorités ethniques et ghettos aux Etats-Unis: modèle ou anti-modèle pour la France?', *Esprit*, 182 (June): 78–94.

—— (1993) 'Paradoxes in the Politicisation of Race: A Comparison of the UK and France', *New Community*, 19(4): 627–43.

CSA (2002a) 'L'Élection présidentielle: explication du vote et perspectives politiques', 21 April. Online: http://www.csa-tmo.fr/dataset/data2002/opi20020421b.htm (accessed 31 July 2006).

—— (2002b) 'Le Vote des Français d'origine étrangère au premier tour de l'élection présidentielle', 29 April. Online: http://www.csa-tmo.fr/dataset/data2002/opi20020421e.htm (accessed 31 July 2006).

—— (2004a) 'Les Musulmans et la laïcité', 26 Jan. Online: http://www.csa-tmo.fr/dataset/data2004/opi20040121b.htm#2 (accessed 31 July 2006).

—— (2004b) 'Les Français et la rentrée scolaire', 20 Sept. Online: http://www.csa-tmo.fr/dataset/data2004/opi20040915b.htm (accessed 31 July 2006).

—— (2006) 'Les Français, le parcours de l'équipe de France et Zinédine Zidane', 11 July. Online: http://www.csa-tmo.fr/dataset/data2006/opi20060710a.htm (accessed 31 July 2006).

Culture et immigration (1980) Rapport de la commission mixte 'Culture et immigration' installée le 21 novembre 1979 par le Président de la République, Paris: ICEI.

Cunha, M. do C. (1988) *Portugais de France: essai sur une dynamique de double appartenance*, Paris: L'Harmattan.

Cusset, P.-Y. (2006) 'Les Statistiques ethniques en France: où en sommes-nous?', *La Note de veille*, 22 (31 July): 1–4.

Dabène, L. and Billiez, J. (1987) 'Le Parler des jeunes issus de l'immigration', in G. Vermes and J. Boutet (eds), *France, pays multilingue*, vol. 2, *Pratiques des langues en France*, Paris: L'Harmattan, pp. 62–77.

Davies, P. (1999) *The National Front in France: Ideology, Discourse and Power*, London: Routledge.

Debré, J.-L. (1996) 'Depuis 1994, la frontière entre militants islamistes et délinquants est devenue incertaine et perméable', *Le Monde* (4 April).

DeClair, E.G. (1999) *Politics on the Fringe: The People, Policies and Organization of the French National Front*, Durham, NC: Duke University Press.

Decouflé, A.-C. (1992) 'Historic Elements of the Politics of Nationality in France', in D.L. Horowitz and G. Noiriel (eds), *Immigrants in Two Democracies: French and American Experiences*, New York and London: New York University Press, pp. 357–67.

Decouflé, A.-C. and Tétaud, M. (1993) *La Politique de la nationalité en 1992: données chifrées et commentaires*, Paris: Ministère des Affaires Sociales, Direction de la Population et des Migrations.

Déjeux, J. (1989) *Image de l'étrangère: unions mixtes franco-maghrébins*, Paris: Boîte à documents.

Dell'Olio, F. (2005) *The Europeanization of Citizenship: Between the Ideology of Nationality, Immigration and European Identity*, Aldershot: Ashgate.

Derderian, R. (2004) *North Africans in Contemporary France: Becoming Visible*, New York: Palgrave Macmillan.

Désir, H. (1985) *Touche pas à mon pote*, Paris: Grasset.

Desplanques, G. (1985) 'Nuptialité et fécondité des étrangères', *Économie et statistique*, 179 (July–Aug.): 29–46.

Desplanques, G. and Tabard, N. (1991) 'La Localisation de la population étrangère', *Économie et statistique*, 242 (April); 51–62.

Diantelli, E. (1992) 'L'État espagnol et les associations d'émigrés en France: une relation structurante', *Migrations société*, 4(19): 35–43.

Dignan, D. (1981) 'Europe's Melting-Pot: A Century of Large-Scale Immigration into France', *Ethnic and Racial Studies*, 4(2): 137–52.

Dreyfus, M. and Milza, P. (1987) *Un siècle d'immigration italienne en France (1850–1950): état des travaux*, Paris: CEDEI/CHEVS.

Le Droit de vivre (1981) Campaign statements by presidential candidates, May, pp. 15–17.

Dubet, F. (1987) *La Galère: jeunes en survie*, Paris: Fayard.

—— (1989) 'Immigrations: qu'en savons-nous?' Special issue of *Notes et études documentaries*, 4887.

Dubet, F. and Lapeyronnie, D. (1992) *Les Quartiers d'exil*, Paris: Seuil.

Duhamel, O. and Jaffré, J. (1987) 'L'Opinion publique et le chômage: réflexions sur trois courbes', *Les Temps modernes*, 42(496–7, Nov.–Dec.): 305–18.

Durmelat, S. (1998) 'Petite histoire du mot *beur*', *French Cultural Studies*, 9(2) : 191–207.

Echardour, A. and Maurin, E. (1993) 'La Main-d'œuvre étrangère', in *Données sociales*, Paris: INSEE, pp. 504–11.

Économie et statistique (1991) 'Les Étrangers en France', no. 42 (April).

Espaces 89 (1985) *L'Identité française*, Paris: Tierce.

Ethnic and Racial Studies (1991) 'Migration and Migrants in France', 14(3).

Étienne, B. (1987) *L'Islamisme radical*, Paris: Hachette.

—— (1989) *La France et l'islam*, Paris: Hachette.

—— (ed.) (1991) *L'Islam en France: islam, état et société*, Paris: CNRS.

Être Français aujourd'hui et demain (1988) Rapport de la Commission de la nationalité présente par M. Marceau Long, président, au Premier Ministre, 2 vols, Paris: Union Générale d'Éditions.

Faivre, M. (1990) 'Le Service militaire des binationaux', *Hommes et migrations*, 1138 (Dec.): 32–7.

Fassin, D., Morice, A. and Quiminal, C. (eds) (1998) *Les Lois de l'hospitalité: les politiques de l'immigration à l'épreuve des sans-papiers*, Paris: La Découverte.

Fauroux, R. (2005) *La Lutte contre les discriminations ethniques dans le domaine de l'emploi*, Paris: Ministre de la cohésion sociale.

Favell, A. (1998) *Philosophies of Integration: Immigration and the Idea of Citizenship in France and Britain*, Basingstoke: Macmillan.

Feldblum, M. (1993) 'Paradoxes of Ethnic Politics: The Case of Franco-Maghrebis in France', *Ethnic and Racial Studies*, 16(3): 52–74.

—— (1999) *Reconstructing Citizenship: The Politics of Nationality Reform and Immigration in Contemporary France*, Albany, NY: State University of New York Press.

Fetzer, J. (2000) *Public Attitudes toward Immigration in the United States, France and Germany*, Cambridge: Cambridge University Press.

Filhon, A. and Varro, G. (2005) 'Les Couples mixtes, une catégorie hétérogène', in C. Lefèvre and A. Filhon (eds), *Histoires de familles, histories familiales*, Paris: INED, pp. 483–501.

Finkielkraut, A. (2005) Interview in *Haaretz* (17 Nov.). Online: http://www.haartez.com (accessed 27 Nov. 2005).

Fitzpatrick, B. (1993) 'Immigrants', in J.E. Flower (ed.), *France Today*, London: Hodder & Stoughton, pp. 99–125.

Freedman, J. (2004) *Immigration and Insecurity in France*, Aldershot: Ashgate.

Freedman, J. and Tarr, C. (eds) (2000) *Women, Immigration and Identities in France*, Oxford: Berg.

Freeman, G.P. (1979) *Immigrant Labor and Racial Conflict in Industrial Societies: The French and British Experiences*, Princeton: Princeton University Press.

—— (1992) 'The Consequences of Immigration Policies for Immigrant Status: A British and French Comparison', in A.M. Messina *et al.* (eds), *Ethnic and Racial Minorities in Advanced Industrial Democracies*, New York: Greenwood Press, pp. 17–32.

Fuchs, G. (1987) *Ils resteront: le défi de l'immigration*, Paris: Syros.

Fysh, P. and Wolfreys, J. (1992) 'Le Pen, the National Front and the Extreme Right in France', *Parliamentary Affairs*, 45(3): 309–26.

—— (2003) *The Politics of Racism in France*, Basingstoke: Palgrave Macmillan.

Gabizon, C. (2002) 'La Gauche a perdu le monopole des Beurs', *Le Figaro* (28 May).

Galap, J. (1993) 'Phénotypes et discriminations des Noirs en France: questions de méthode', *Migrants-formation*, 94 (Sept.): 39–54.

Gallissot, R., Boumaza, N. and Clément, G. (1994) *Ces migrants qui font le prolétariat*, Paris: Méridiens Klincksieck.

Garson, J.-P. and Mouhoud, E.M. (1989) 'Sous-traitance et désalarisation formelle de la main-d'œuvre dans le BTP', *La Note de l'IRES*, 19: 36–47.

—— and Tapinos, G. (eds) (1981) *L'Argent des immigrés: revenus, épargne et transferts de huit nationalités immigrées en France*, Paris: Presses Universitaires de France.

Gaspard, F. (1990) *Une petite ville en France*, Paris: Gallimard.

Gaspard, F. and Khosrokhavar, F. (1995) *Le Foulard et la République*, Paris: La Découverte.

Gaspard, F. and Servan-Schreiber, C. (1985) *La Fin des immigrés*, rev. edn, Paris: Seuil.

Gastaut, Y. (1994) 'Les Mutations du thème de l'immigration dans le journal *Le Monde* (1958–1992)', *Migrations société*, 6(31): 40–51.

—— (2000) *L'Immigration et l'opinion en France sous la Ve République*, Paris: Seuil.

GED (Groupe d'Études sur les Discriminations) (2000) *Une forme méconnue de discrimination: les emplois fermés aux étrangers*, Paris: GED.

Geddes, A. and Giraudon, V. (2004) 'Britain, France, and EU Anti-Discrimination Policy: The Emergence of an EU Policy Paradigm', *West European Politics*, 27(2): 334–53.

Geertz, C. (ed.) (1963) *Old Societies and New States: The Quest for Modernity in Asia and Africa*, New York: Free Press.

Geisser, V. (1992) 'Les Élites politiques issues de l'immigration maghrébine: l'impossible médiation', *Migrations société*, 4(22–3): 129–38.

Gemie, S. (2004) 'Stasi's Republic: The School and the "Veil", December 2003–March 2004', *Modern and Contemporary France*, 12(3): 387–97.

Génériques (1999) *Les Étrangers en France: Guides des sources d'archives publiques et privées, xixe–xxe siècles*, 3 vols, Paris: Génériques/Direction des Archives de France.

Georges, P. (1986) *L'Immigration en France: faits et problèmes*, Paris: Armand Colin.

Gervereau, L., Milza, P. and Temime, E. (eds) (1998) *Toute la France: Histoire de l'immigration en France au xxe siècle*, Paris: Somogy, Éditions d'Art.

Gillette, A. and Sayad, A. (1984) *L'Immigration algérienne en France*, 2nd edn, Paris: Entente.

Gilroy, P. (1993) *The Black Atlantic: Modernity and Double Consciousness*, London: Verso.

Ginesy-Galano, M. (1984) *Les Immigrés hors la cité: le système d'encadrement dans les foyers (1973–1982)*, Paris: L'Harmattan/CIEM.

Girard, A. and Stoetzel, J. (1953) *Français et immigrés*, vol. 1, *L'Attitude française: L'Adaptation des Italiens et des Polonais*, Paris: Presses Universitaires de France/Institut National d'Études Démographiques.

Girard, B. (2006) *Banlieues, insurrection ou ras-le-bol?*, Paris: Les points sur les i.

Giudice, F. (1992) *Arabicides: une chronique française 1970–1991*, Paris: La Découverte.

Gokalp, A. (1992) 'L'Immigration turque: repères communautaires et transition générationnelle', *Migrations société*, 4(20): 41–6.

Gonzales-Quijano, Y. (1988) 'Les "Nouvelles" Générations issues de l'immigration maghrébine et la question de l'islam', in R. Leveau and G. Kepel (eds), *Les Musulmans dans la société française*, Paris: Presses de la Fondation Nationale des Sciences Politiques, pp. 65–76.

Gordon, M.M. (1964) *Assimilation in American Life: The Role of Race, Religion and National Origins*, New York: Oxford University Press.

Gorgeon, C., Amaouche, M.-D., Audebrand, É. and Barilero, B. (2001) 'La Mise en œuvre locale du 114', *Migrations études*, 99 (May–June): 1–16.

Green, N. (1991) 'L'Immigration en France et aux États-Unis: historiographie comparée', *Vingtième siècle*, 29 (Jan.–Feb.): 67–82.

Gresh, A. (2004) *L'Islam, la République et le monde*, Paris: Fayard.

Grillo, R.D. (1985) *Ideologies and Institutions in Urban France*, Cambridge: Cambridge University Press.

Guillaume, S. (1991) 'Citoyenneté et colonisation', in D. Colas, C. Emeri and J. Zylberberg (eds), *Citoyenneté et nationalité: perspectives en France et au Québec*, Paris: Presses Universitaires de France, pp. 123–36.

Guillon, M. and Taboada-Leonetti, I. (1986) *Le Triangle de Choisy: un quartier chinois à Paris*, Paris: CIEMI/L'Harmattan.

Gunn, J. (2004) 'Religious Freedom and *Laïcité*: A Comparison of the United States and France', *Brigham Young University Law Review*, 2004(2): 419–501.

Gunn, J. and Chélini-Pont, B. (2005) *Dieu en France et aux États-Unis: Quand les mythes font la loi*, Paris: Berg International.

Hainsworth, P. (1992) 'The Extreme Right in Post-War France: The Emergence and Success of the Front National', in P. Hainsworth (ed.), *The Extreme Right in Europe and the USA*, London: Pinter, pp. 29–60.

Hall, S. (1992) 'The Question of Cultural Identity', in S. Hall, D. Held and T. McGrew (eds), *Modernity and its Futures*, Cambridge: Polity Press, in association with the Open University, pp. 273–325.

Hames, C. (1989) 'La Construction de l'islam en France', *Archives en sciences sociales des religions*, 68: 79–82.

Hamoumou, M. (1993) *Et ils sont devenus harkis*, Paris: Fayard.

Hansen, R. and Weil, P. (eds) (2001) *Towards a European Nationality: Citizenship, Immigration and Nationality Law in the EU*, Basingstoke: Palgrave.

Hargreaves, A.G. (1988) 'The French Nationality Code Hearings', *Modern and Contemporary France*, 34 (July): 1–11.

—— (1990) 'Algerians in France: The End of the Line?', *Contemporary French Civilization*, 14(2): 292–306.

—— (1991) 'The Political Mobilization of the North African Immigrant Community in France', *Ethnic and Racial Studies*, 14(3): 350–67.

—— (1992a) 'L'Europe, les pays anglo-saxons et le Tiers-Monde chez les jeunes issus de l'immigration maghrébine en France', in K. Basfao and J.R. Henry (eds), *Le Maghreb, l'Europe et la France*, Paris: CNRS, pp. 379–89.

—— (1992b) 'Ethnic Minorities and the Mass Media in France', in R. Chapman and Nicholas Hewitt (eds), *Popular Culture and Mass Communication in Twentieth Century France*, Lewiston, NY: Edwin Mellen Press, pp. 165–80.

—— (1993a) 'Figuring out their Place: Post-Colonial Writers of Algerian Origin in France', *Forum for Modern Language Studies*, 29(4): 335–45.

—— (1993b) 'Télévision et intégration: la politique audiovisuelle du FAS', *Migrations société*, 5(30): 7–22.

—— (1995a) *Immigration, 'Race' and Ethnicity in Contemporary France*, London and New York: Routledge.

—— (1995b) 'Perceptions of Place among Writers of Algerian Immigrant Origin in France', in R. King, J. Connell and P. White (eds), *Writing across Worlds: Literature and Migration*, London and New York: Routledge, pp. 89–100.

—— (1996) 'A Deviant Construction: The French Media and the *Banlieues*', *New Community*, 22(4): 607–18.

—— (1997a) *Immigration and Identity in Beur Fiction: Voices from the North African Immigrant Community in France*, 2nd, expanded edn, Oxford and New York: Berg.

—— (1997b) 'Multiculturalism', in C. Flood and L. Bell (eds), *Political Ideologies in Contemporary France*, London and Washington, DC: Pinter, pp. 180–99.

—— (2000) 'Half-Measures: Anti-Discrimination Policy in France', *French Politics, Culture and Society*, 18(3): 83–101.

Hargreaves, A.G. and Mahdjoub, D. (1997) 'Satellite Television Viewing among Ethnic Minorities in France', *European Journal of Communication*, 12(4): 459–77.

Hargreaves, A.G. and Perotti, A. (1993) 'The Representation on French Television of Immigrants and Ethnic Minorities of Third World Origin', *New Community*, 19(2): 251–61.

Hargreaves, A.G. and Stenhouse, T.S. (1991) 'Islamic Beliefs among Youths of North African Origin in France', *Modern and Contemporary France*, 45 (April): 27–35.

Hargreaves, A.G. and Stenhouse, T.S. (1992) 'The Gulf War and the Maghrebian Community in France', *Maghreb Review*, 17(1–2): 42–54.

Harris, N. (1991) 'La "Loi Joxe" et son substrat politique et symbolique', *Contemporary French Civilization*, 15(1): 18–34.

HCI (Haut Conseil à l'Intégration) (1991) *Pour un modèle français de l'intégration*, Paris: La Documentation Française.

—— (1992a) *La Connaissance de l'immigration et de l'intégration novembre 1991*, Paris: La Documentation Française.

—— (1992b) *Conditions juridiques et culturelles de l'intégration*, Paris: La Documentation Française.

—— (1993a) *La Connaissance de l'immigration et de l'intégration, décembre 1992*, Paris: La Documentation Française.

—— (1993b) *Les Étrangers et l'emploi: décembre 1992*, Paris: La Documentation Française.

—— (1993c) *L'Emploi illégal des étrangers*, Paris: La Documentation Française.

—— (1998) *Lutte contre les discriminations: faire respecter le principe d'égalité*, Paris: La Documentation Française.

—— (2003) *Le Contrat et l'intégration*, Paris: La Documentation Française.

—— (2004) *Observatoire statistique de l'immigration et de l'intégration: Groupe permanent chargé des statistiques. Rapport 2002–2003*, Paris: Haut Conseil à l'Intégration.

Hechter, M., Friedman, D. and Appelbaum, M. (1982) 'A Theory of Ethnic Collective Action', *International Migration Review*, 16(2): 412–34.

Heisler, M.O. and Schmitter Heisler, B. (1986) 'Transnational Migration and the Modern Democratic State: Familiar Problems in New Form or a New Problem?', *Annals of the American Academy of Political and Social Science*, 485 (May): 12–22.

Henry, J.-R. (1987–8) 'La Norme et l'imaginaire: construction de l'altérité juridique en droit colonial algérien', *Procès*, 18: 13–27.

Héran, F. (1993) 'L'Unification linguistique de la France', *Population et sociétés*, 285 (Dec.): 1–4.

—— (2004) 'Une approche quantitative de l'intégration linguistique en France', *Hommes et migrations*, 1252 (Nov.–Dec.): 10–24.

Héran, F., Filhon, A. and Deprez, C. (2005) 'La Dynamique des langues en France au fil du XXᵉ siècle', in C. Lefèvre and A. Filhon (eds), *Histoires de familles, histoires familiales*, Paris: INED, pp. 505–12.

Hessel, S. (ed.) (1988) *Immigrations: le devoir d'insertion*, 2 vols, Paris: La Documentation Française.

Hily, M.-A. and Poinard, M. (1987) 'Portuguese Associations in France', in J. Rex, D. Joly and C. Wilpert (eds), *Immigrant Associations in Europe*, Aldershot: Gower, pp. 126–65.

Hollifield, J.F. (1992) *Immigrants, Markets and States: The Political Economy of Postwar Europe*, Cambridge, MA: Harvard University Press.

Hommes et migrations (1991a) 'Elles… femmes en mouvement(s)', no. 1141 (March).

Hommes et migrations (1991b) 'Aux soldats méconnus: étrangers, immigrés, colonisés au service de la France (1914–1918 et 1939–1945)', no. 1148 (Nov.).

Hommes et migrations (1993) 'Le Bouddhisme en France', no. 1171 (Dec.).

Hommes et migrations (2002) 'Migrants.com', no. 1240 (Nov.).

Horowitz, D.L. and Noiriel, G. (eds) (1992) *Immigrants in Two Democracies: French and American Experiences*, New York and London: New York University Press.

Humblot, C. (1989) 'Les Émissions spécifiques: de "Mosaïque" à "Rencontre"', *Migrations société*, 1(4): 7–14.

Husbands, C.T. (1991) 'The Support for the *Front National*: Analyses and Findings', *Ethnic and Racial Studies*, 14(3): 382–416.

IGAS (Inspection Générale des Affaires Sociales) (1992) *Enquête sur l'insertion des jeunes immigrés dans l'entreprise*, 2 vols, Paris: IGAS.

INSEE (Institut National de la Statistique de des Études Économiques) (1986) *Les Étrangers en France:* Contours et caractères, Paris: INSEE.

—— (1992a) *Recensement de la population de 1990: nationalités, résultats du sondage au quart*, Paris: INSEE.

—— (1992b) *INSEE Première:* 'La Fécondité des étrangères en France se rapproche de celle des Françaises', no. 231 (Nov.).

—— (1994) *Les Étrangers en France:* Contours et caractères, Paris: INSEE.

—— (2002a) *Recensement général de la population de 1999*, Tableaux thématiques 'Population immigrée, population étrangère', CD-ROM, Paris: INSEE.

—— (2002b) *INSEE Île-de-France à la page:* 'L'Île-de-France, region privilégiée des migrants des DOM-TOM', no. 207 (Jan.).

—— (2005) *Les Immigrés en France:* Contours et caractères, Paris: INSEE.

—— (2006) *INSEE Première:* 'Enquêtes annuelles de recensement 2004 et 2005. Près de 5 millions d'immigrés à la mi-2004', no. 1098 (Aug.).

IPSOS (2003a) 'L'Opinion des Français musulmans', 7 April. Online: www.ipsos.fr/CanalIpsos/poll/7756.asp (accessed 31 July 2006).

—— (2003b) 'Islam, intégration, immigration: l'opinion des Français', 15 May. Online: http://www.ipsos.fr/CanalIpsos/poll/7771.asp (accessed 31 July 2006).

Ireland, P. (1994) *The Policy Challenge of Ethnic Diversity: Immigrant Politics in France and Switzerland*, Cambridge, MA: Harvard University Press.

Jazouli, A. (1986) *L'Action collective des jeunes maghrébins de France*, Paris: CIEMI/L'Harmattan.

—— (1992) *Les Années banlieues*, Paris: Seuil.

Jones, T. (1993) *Britain's Ethnic Minorities*, London: Policy Studies Institute.

Kastoryano, R. (1986) *Être Turc en France: réflexions sur familles et communauté*, Paris: CIEMI/L'Harmattan.

Keaton, T.D. (2006) *Muslim Girls and the Other France: Race, Identity, Politics and Social Exclusion*, Bloomington: Indiana University Press.

Kelkal, K. (1995) 'Moi, Khaled Kelkal', *Le Monde* (7 Oct.).

Kepel, G. (1987) *Les Banlieues de l'islam: naissance d'une religion en France*, Paris: Seuil.

—— (2004) 'L'Islamisme gagnera-t-il la bataille de l'Europe?', *Le Monde* (2 Nov.).

Kessas, F. (1990) *Beur's Story*, Paris: L'Harmattan.

Khellil, M. (1991) *L'Intégration des Maghrébins en France*, Paris: Presses Universitaires de France.

Kokoreff, M. (1991) 'Tags et zoulous: une nouvelle violence urbaine', *Esprit*, 169 (Feb.): 23–36.

Kriegel, B. (2005) 'Crises des banlieues: la défaite de la République', *Le Figaro* (23 Nov.).

Laacher, S. (ed.) (1987) *Questions de nationalité: histoire et enjeux d'un code*, Paris: CIEMI/ L'Harmattan.

Lallaoui, M. (1993) *Du bidonville aux HLM*, Paris: Syros.

Lapeyronnie, D. (1987) 'Assimilation, mobilisation et action collective chez les jeunes de la seconde génération de l'immigration maghrébine', *Revue française de sociologie*, 28(2) (April–June) : 287–318.

—— (1993) *L'Individu et les minorités: La France et la Grande-Bretagne face à leurs immigrés*, Paris: Presses Universitaires de France.

Laurence, J. and Vaisse, J. (2006) *Integrating Islam: Political and Religious Challenges in Contemporary France*, Washington, DC: Brookings Institution.

Lebon, A. (1987) 'Attribution, acquisition et perte de la nationalité française: un bilan (1973–1986)', *Revue européenne des migrations internationales*, 3(1–2): 7–34.

—— (1992) 'Des chiffres et des hommes', *Revue française des affaires sociales*, 46, hors série (Dec.): 15–27.

—— (1993) *Immigration et présence étrangère en France: le bilan d'une année 1992–1993*, Paris: Ministère des Affaires Sociales, Direction de la Population.

Lebovics, H. (2004) *Bringing the Empire Back Home: France in the Global Age*, Durham, NC: Duke University Press.

Le Bras, H. (1998) *Le Démon des origines: démographie et extrême droite*, Paris: L'Aube.

Lee, S.M. (1993) 'Racial Classifications in the US Census, 1890–1990', *Ethnic and Racial Studies*, 16(1): 75–94.

Lefèvre, C, and Filhon, A. (eds) (2005) *Histoires de familles, histoires familiales*, Paris: INED.

Lefort, F. and Néry, M. (1985) *Émigré dans mon pays*, Paris: CIEM/L'Harmattan.

Le Gallou, J.-Y. and Jalkh, J.F. (1987) *Être Français, cela se mérite*, Paris: Albatros.

Lehembre, B. (1984) 'L'Immigration sur la bande FM', *Im'média magazine*, 1 (Autumn): 30–3.

Le Huu Khoa (1985) *Les Vietnamiens en France: insertion et identité*, Paris: CIEM/ L'Harmattan.

—— (1987) *Les Jeunes Vietnamiens de la deuxième génération: la semi-rupture au quotidien*, Paris: CIEMI/L'Harmattan.

Lemoine, M. (1992) 'Les Difficultés d'intégration profesionnelle des jeunes étrangers ou d'origine étrangère', *Revue française des affaires sociales*, 46 (Dec.): 173–80.

Le Pen, J.-M. (1984) *Les Français d'abord*, Paris: Éditions Carrère-Michel Lafon.

Le Pors, A. (1977) *Immigration et développement économique et social*, Paris: La Documentation Française.

Lequin, Y. (ed.) (1988) *La Mosaïque France: Histoire des étrangers et de l'immigration en France*, Paris: Larousse.

Leveau, R. (1988) 'The Islamic Presence in France', in T. Gerholm and Y.G. Lithman (eds), *The New Islamic Presence in Western Europe*, London: Mansell, pp. 107–22.

Leveau, R. and Wihtol de Wenden, C. (1991) *Modes d'insertion des populations de culture islamique dans le système politique français*, Paris: Mission Interministérielle Recherche Expérimentation.

Liebkind, K. (ed.) (1989) *New Identities in Europe: Immigrant Ancestry and the Ethnic Identity of Youth*, Aldershot: Gower.

Lloyd, C. (1991) 'Concepts, Models and Anti-Racist Strategies in Britain and France', *New Community*, 18(1): 63–73.

—— (1998) *Discourses of Antiracism in France*, Aldershot: Ashgate.

Lochak, D. (1992) 'Discrimination Against Foreigners under French Law', in D.L. Horowitz and G. Noiriel (eds), *Immigrants in Two Democracies: French and American Experiences*, New York and London: New York University Press, pp. 391–410.

Long, M. and Weil, P. (2004) 'La Laïcité en voie d'adaptation', *Libération* (26 Jan.).

Lorcerie, F. (1994a) 'Les Sciences sociales au service de l'identité nationale: le débat sur l'intégration en France au début des années 1990', in D.-C. Martin (ed.), *Cartes d'identité: comment dit-on 'nous' en politique?*, Paris: FNSP, pp. 245–81.

—— (1994b) 'L'Islam dans les cours de "langue et culture d'origine": le procès', *Revue européenne des migrations internationales*, 10(2): 5–43.

—— (1994c) 'Les ZEP 1990–1993 pour mémoire', *Migrants-formation*, 97 (June): 30–48.

McKesson, J. A. (1994) 'Concepts and Realities in a Multiethnic France', *French Politics and Society*, 12(1): 16–38.

MacMaster, N. (1997) *Colonial Migrants and Racism: Algerians in France, 1900–62*, Basingstoke: Macmillan.

Malik, S. (1990) *Histoire secrète de SOS-Racisme*, Paris: Albin Michel.

Ma Mung, E. (1992) 'L'Expansion du commerce ethnique: Asiatiques et Maghrébins dans la région parisienne', *Revue européenne des migrations internationales*, 8(1): 39–59.

—— and Guillon, M. (1986) 'Les Commerçants étrangers dans l'agglomération parisienne', *Revue européenne des migrations internationales*, 2(3): 106–34.

Marangé, J. and Lebon, A. (1982) *L'Insertion des jeunes d'origine étrangère dans la société française*, Paris: La Documentation Française.

Marcus, J. (1995) *The National Front and French Politics: The Resistible Rise of Jean-Marie Le Pen*, Basingstoke: Macmillan.

Marie, C.-V. (1988) 'L'Immigration clandestine et l'emploi des travailleurs étrangers en situation irrégulière', in S. Hessel (ed.), *Immigrations: le devoir d'insertion: Analyses et annexes*, Paris: La Documentation Française, pp. 331–74.

—— (1992) 'Les Étrangers non-salariés en France, symbole de la mutation économique des années 80', *Revue européenne des migrations internationales*, 8(1): 27–38.

—— (1993) 'Les Antillais en France: histoire et réalités d'une migration ambiguë', *Migrants-formation*, 94 (Sept.): 5–14.

Marshall, T.H. (1950) *Citizenship and Social Class and Other Essays*, Cambridge: Cambridge University Press.

Martiniello, M. (1994) 'La Citoyenneté à l'aube du 21ième siècle: questions et enjeux majeurs', rapport de recherche préparé à la demande et pour la Fondation Roi Baudoin, Brussels.

Mason, D. (1990) 'A Rose by Any Other Name …? Categorisation, Identity and Social Science', *New Community*, 17(1): 123–33.

—— (1991) 'The Concept of Ethnic Minority: Conceptual Dilemmas and Policy Implications', *Innovation*, 4(2): 191–209.

Masson, J. (1985) 'Français par le sang, Français par la loi, Français par le sang', *Revue européenne des migrations internationales*, 1(2): 9–19.

Maurin, E. (1991) 'Les Étrangers: une main-d'œuvre à part?', *Économie et statistique*, 242 (April): 39–50.

Mayer, N. (1987) 'De Passy à Barbès: deux visages du vote Le Pen à Paris', *Revue française de science politique*, 37(6): 891–906.

—— (1995) 'Ethnocentrism and the Front National Vote in the 1988 French Presidential Elections', in A.G. Hargreaves and J. Leaman (eds), *Racism, Ethnicity and Politics in Contemporary Europe*, Aldershot: Edward Elgar, pp. 96–111.

—— and Perrineau, P. (1993) 'La Puissance et le rejet ou le lepénisme dans l'opinion', in SOFRES, *L'État de l'opinion 1993*, Paris: Seuil, pp. 63–78.

M'Barga, J.-P. (1992) 'Excision, fonctions et conséquences de sa répression en milieu migrant en France', in E. Rude-Antoine (ed.), *L'Immigration face aux lois de la République*, Paris: Karthala, pp. 165–75.

Mela, V. (1988) 'Parler verlan: règles et usages', *Langage et société*, 45 (Sept.): 47–70.

Merckling, O. (1987) 'Nouvelles politiques d'emploi et substitution de la main-d'œuvre immigrée dans les entreprises françaises', *Revue européenne des migrations internationales*, 3(1–2): 73–95.

Mestiri, E. (1988) 'Le Souffle d'une jeunesse: jeunes d'origine étrangère dans le mouvement étudiant de l'automne de 1986', *Tribune immigrée*, 24–5 (Jan.–March): 118–19.

—— (1990) *L'Immigration*, Paris: La Découverte.

Meurs, D., Pailhé, A. and Simon, P. (2005) 'Mobilité intergénérationnelle et persistance des inégalités: l'accès à l'emploi des immigrés et de leurs descendants en France', in *INED Documents de travail*, 130:1–35.

Migrants-formation (1990) 'Religions et intégration', no. 82 (Sept.).

Migrations société (1992) 'Immigrés de Turquie', 4(20).

Migrations société (1994) 'Intermédiaires culturels: le champ religieux', 6(33–4).

Miles, R. (1989) *Racism*, London: Routledge.

—— (1993) *Racism After 'Race Relations'*, London: Routledge.

Miles, R. and Phizacklea, A. (1977) 'Class, Race, Ethnicity and Political Action', *Political Studies*, 25(4): 491–507.

Miller, M.J. (1981) *Foreign Workers in Western Europe: An Emerging Political Force*, New York: Praeger.

Milza, P. (1985) 'Un siècle d'immigration étrangère en France', *Vingtième siècle*, 7 (July–Sept.): 3–18.

Ministère de l'Éducation Nationale (1989) 'L'Enseignement des langues et cultures d'origine dans le premier degré en 1988–1989', *Note d'information*, Paris: Ministère de l'Éducation Nationale, 89–53.

Ministère de l'Emploi, de la Cohésion Sociale et du Logement (2005) 'Lutte contre les discriminations: accords avec les partenaires publics et privés pour lutter contre les discriminations et pour favoriser l'insertion professionelle des personnes issues de l'immigration', 24 June. Online: http://www.social.gouv.fr/IMG/html/sommaccords-2.html#frtele240605a (accessed 31 July 2006).

Mitra, S. (1988) 'The National Front in France: A Single-Issue Movement?', *West European Politics*, 11(2): 47–64.

Moreau-Desportes, A. (1990) 'Les Émissions des radios locales privées', *Hommes et migrations*, 1136: 46–8.

Moreira, P. (1987) *Rock métis en France*, Paris: Souffles.

Morley, D. (2000) *Home Territories: Media, Mobility and Identity*, London: Routledge.

Morokvasic, M. (1990) 'Le Comportement économique des immigrés dans le secteur de la confection', in G. Abou Sada, B. Courault and Z. Zeroulou (eds), *L'Immigration au tournant*, Paris: CIEMI/L'Harmattan, pp. 237–48.

Morokvasic, M., Phizacklea, A. and Rudolph, H. (1986) 'Small Firms and Minority Groups: Contradictory Trends in the French, German and British Clothing Industries', *International Sociology*, 1(4): 397–419.

Moulier Boutang, Y. (2005) *La Révolte des banlieues ou les habits nus de la République*, Paris: Éditions Amsterdam.

Mouvement des Indigènes de la République (2006) 'La Part des anges: la crise de l'automne 2005 dans les quartiers pauvres en France et la démonologie des banlieues', 14 March. Online: http://www.indigenes-republique.org/article.php3?id_article=12 (accessed 31 July 2006).

MRAP (Mouvement contre le Racisme et pour l'Amitié entre les Peuples) (1984) *Vivre ensemble avec nos différences*, Paris: Éditions Différences.

Mucchielli, L. (2005) *Le Scandale des 'tournantes': derives médiatiques, contre-enquête sociologique*, Paris: La Découverte.

—— (ed.) (2006) *Quand les banlieues brûlent … Retour sur les émeutes de novembre 2005*, Paris: La Découverte.

Muller, M. (1987) *Couscous pommes frites: le couple franco-maghrébin, d'hier à aujourd'hui*, Paris: Ramsay.

Munoz-Perez, F., and Tribalat, M. (1984) 'Mariages d'étrangers et mariages mixtes en France: évolution depuis la Première Guerre', *Population*, 3 (May–June): 427–62.

Muxel, A. (1988) 'Les Attitudes socio-politiques des jeunes issus de l'immigration maghrébine en région parisienne', *Revue française de science politique*, 38(6): 925–40.

Naïr, S. (1988) 'L'Immigration maghrébine: quelle intégration? Quelles citoyenneté?', in C. Wihtol de Wenden (ed.), *La Citoyenneté et les changements de structures sociale et nationale de la population française*, Paris: Edilig/Fondation Diderot, pp. 257–79.

Nielsen, J.S. (1992) *Muslims in Western Europe*, Edinburgh: Edinburgh University Press.

Nini, S. (1993) *Ils disent que je suis une Beurette*, Paris: Fixot.

Noiriel, G. (1988) *Le Creuset français: histoire de l'immigration, XIXᵉ–XXᵉ siècles*, Paris: Seuil.

—— (1991) *La Tyrannie du national: le droit d'asile en Europe (1793–1993)*, Paris: Calmann-Lévy.

—— (1992a) 'Difficulties in French Historical Research on Immigration', in D.L. Horowitz and G. Noiriel (eds), *Immigrants in Two Democracies: French and American Experiences*, New York and London: New York University Press, pp. 66–79.

—— (1992b) 'Français et étrangers', in P. Nora (ed.), *Les Lieux de mémoire*, iii, *Les France*, vol. 1, *Conflits et partages*, Paris: Gallimard, pp. 275–319.

Nous sommes les Indigènes de la République (19 January 2005). Online: http://toutesegaux.free.fr/article.php3?id_article=90 (accessed 31 July 2006).

OFPRA (Office Français de Protection des Réfugiés et Apatrides) (1994) *Bilan de treize années de fonctionnement de l'OFPRA (1981–1993)*, Fontenay-sous-Bois: OFPRA.

—— (2006) *Rapport d'activité 2005*, Fontenay-sous-Bois: OFPRA.

Ogden, P.E. (1991) 'Immigration to France since 1945: Myth and Reality', *Ethnic and Racial Studies*, 14(3): 294–318.

Ogden, P.E. and White, P.E. (eds) (1989) *Migrants in Modern France: Population Mobility in the Later 19th and 20th Centuries*, London: Unwin Hyman.

Olzak, S. (1983) 'Contemporary Ethnic Mobilization', *Annual Review of Sociology*, 9: 355–74.

Oriol, P. (1992) *Les Immigrés devant les urnes*, Paris: CIEMI/L'Harmattan.

Panoramiques (1991) 'Islam, France et laïcité: une nouvelle donne?', no. 1 (June–Aug.).

Passages (1989) 'Immigration business: l'état, la politique, les immigrés et l'argent', (Sept.): 21–30.

Pellegrini, C. (1992) *Le FIS en France, mythe ou réalité*, Paris: Édition°1.

Perotti, A. and Thépaut, F. (1990) 'L'Affaire du foulard islamique: d'un fait divers à un fait de société', *Migrations société*, 2(7): 61–82.

Perotti, A. and Toulat P. (1990) 'Immigration et médias: le "foulard" surmédiatisé?', *Migrations société*, 2(12): 9–45.

Perrineau, P. (1991) 'Le Front National: du désert à l'enracinement', in P.-A. Taguieff (ed.), *Face au racisme*, vol. 2, *Analyses, hypothèses, perspectives*, Paris: La Découverte, pp. 83–104.

Petek, G. (2004) 'Les Elco, entre reconnaissance et marginalisation', *Hommes et migrations*, 1252: 45–55.

Pew Research Center (2006) 'Muslims in Europe: Economic Worries Top Concerns About Religious and Cultural Identity. 13–Nation Pew Global Attitudes Survey'. Online. Available HTTP: http://pewglobal.org/reports/display.php?ReportID=254 (accessed 31 July 2006).

Piet, E. (1992) 'Excision et prévention', in E. Rude-Antoine (ed.), *L'Immigration face aux lois de la République*, Paris: Karthala, pp. 189–203.

Piore, M. (1979) *Birds of Passage: Migrant Labor and Industrial Societies*, Cambridge: Cambridge University Press.

Platone, F., and Rey, H. (1989) 'Le FN en terre communiste', in N. Mayer and P. Perrineau (eds), *Le Front National à découvert*, Paris: FNSP, pp. 268–83.

Poinsot, M. (1993) 'Competition for Political Legitimacy at Local and National Levels among Young North Africans in France', *New Community*, 20(1): 79–92.

Poiret, C. (1992) 'Le Phénomène polygamique en France', *Migrants-formation*, 91 (Dec.): 24–42.

Poiret, C. and Guégan, C. (1992) *L'Habitat des familles polygames en région Île-de-France*, étude réalisée pour le compte du FAS, du Plan Architecture Construction et du GIAPP, Paris: Vivre la Ville.

Ponty, J. (1988) *Polonais méconnus: histoire des travailleurs immigrés en France dans l'entre-deux-guerres*, Paris: Publications de la Sorbonne.

Population (1971) 'Attitudes des Français à l'égard de l'immigration étrangère: enquête d'opinion publique', no. 5: 827–75.

Population (1974) 'Attitudes des Français à l'égard de l'immigration étrangère: nouvelle enquête d'opinion', no. 6: 1015–69.

Portes, A. (1981) 'Modes of Structural Incorporation and Present Theories of Immigration', in M.M. Kritz, C.B. Keely and S.M. Tomasi (eds), *Global Trends in Migration*, New York: Center for Migration Studies, pp. 179–298.

Presse et mémoire (1990) *France des étrangers, France des libertés*, Paris: Mémoire Génériques Éditions/Éditions Ouvrières.

Quemener, H. (1991) *Kofi, histoire d'une intégration*, Paris: Payot.

Questions clefs (1982) 'Jeunes immigrés hors le murs', no. 2 (March).

Rachedi, N. (1994) 'Elites of Maghrebian Extraction in France', in B. Lewis and D. Schnapper (eds), *Muslims in Europe*, London and New York: Pinter, pp. 67–78.

Raffarin, J.-P. (2004) 'Discours du Premier Ministre: cité nationale de l'histoire de l'immigration – 8 juillet 2004', *Hommes et migrations*, 1251 (Sept.–Oct.): 91–7.

Rath, J. (1993) 'The Ideological Representation of Migrant Workers in Europe: A Matter of Racialisation?', in J. Wrench and J. Solomos (eds), *Racism and Migration in Western Europe*, Oxford: Berg, pp. 215–32.

Raulin, A. (1990) 'La Consommation médiatique: une passion des minorités urbaines?', *Mediaspouvoirs*, 17 (Jan.–March): 19–28.

Rawlings, L. (2004) 'The *Sans-Papiers* Movement since the French Presidential Elections of 2002', *Modern and Contemporary France*, 12(1): 97–101.

Revue de linguistique et de didactique des langues (1990) 'Les Langues et cultures des poplations migrantes: un défi à l'école française', no. 2.

Rex, J. (1986a) *Race and Ethnicity*, Milton Keynes: Open University Press.

—— (1986b) 'Preface', in J. Rex and D. Mason (eds), *Theories of Race and Ethnic Relations*, Cambridge: Cambridge University Press.

—— (1988) *The Ghetto and the Underclass: Essays on Race and Social Policy*, Aldershot: Avebury.

Rex, J. and Tomlinson, S. (1979) *Colonial Immigrants in a British City*, London: Routledge and Kegan Paul.

Rimani, S. (1988) *Les Tunisiens de France: une forte concentration parisienne*, Paris: CIEMI/ L'Harmattan.

Rodrigues, N., Chapelle, J., Najgeborn, O. and Vieira, J. (1985) *La Ruée vers l'égalité*, Paris: Mélanges.

Rogers, R. (1986) 'The Transnational Nexus of Migration', *Annals of the American Academy of Political and Social Science*, 485 (May): 34–50.

Roy, O. (1990) 'Dreux: de l'immigration au ghetto ethnique', *Esprit*, 159 (Feb.): 5–10.

—— (1991) 'Ethnicité, bandes et communautarisme', *Esprit*, 169 (Feb.): 37–47.

—— (1993) 'Les Immigrés dans la ville: peut-on parler de tensions "ethniques"?', *Esprit*, 191 (May): 41–53.

—— (1994) 'Islam in France: Religion, Ethnic Community or Ethnic Ghetto?', in B. Lewis and D. Schnapper (eds), *Muslims in Europe*, London and New York: Pinter, pp. 54–66.

—— (2004) *Globalized Islam: The Search for a New Ummah*, New York: Columbia University Press.

Roux, M. (1991) *Les Harkis: les oubliés de l'histoire*, Paris: La Découverte.

Rudder, V. de (1990) 'Notes à propos de l'évolution des recherches françaises sur "l'étranger dans la ville"', in I. Simon-Barouh and P.-J. Simon (eds), *Les Étrangers dans la ville: le regard des sciences sociales*, Paris: L'Harmattan, pp. 60–80.

—— (1992) 'Immigrant Housing and Integration in French Cities', in D.L. Horowitz and G. Noiriel (eds), *Immigrants in Two Democracies: French and American Experiences*, New York and London: New York University Press, pp. 247–67.

Rudder, V. de and Goodwin, P. (1993) 'Théories et débats sur le racisme en Grande-Bretagne', *L'Homme et la société*, 110 (Oct.–Dec.): 5–19.

Rudder, V. de and Guillon, M. (1987) *Du marché d'Aligre à l'îlot Chalon*, Paris: L'Harmattan.

Rudder, V. de, Tripier, M. and Vourc'h, M. (1994) *La Prévention du racisme dans l'entreprise en France*, Paris: URMIS.

Rude-Antoine, E. (1991) 'La Polygamie et le droit français', *Regards sur l'actualité*, 176 (Dec.): 38–49.

Rufin, J.-C. (2004) *Chantier sur la lutte contre le racisme et l'antisémitisme*, Paris: Ministère de l'intérieur.

Rydgren, J. (2004) *The Populist Challenge: Political Protest and Ethno-Nationalist Mobilization in France*, New York: Berghahn.

Sabbagh, D. (2004) 'Affirmative Action at Sciences-Po', in H. Chapman and L.A. Frader (eds), *Race in France: Interdisciplinary Perspectives on the Politics of Difference*, New York: Berghahn, pp. 246–58.

Sabeg, Y. and Sabeg, Y. (2004) *Discrimination positive: pourquoi la France ne peut y échapper*, Paris: Calmann-Lévy.

Safran, W. (1985) 'The Mitterrand Regime and its Policies of Ethnocultural Accommodation', *Comparative Politics*, 18(1): 41–63.

— — (1986) 'Islamicization in Western Europe: Political Consequences and Historical Parallels', *Annals of the American Academy of Political and Social Science*, 485 (May): 98–112.

—— (1987) 'Ethnic Mobilization, Modernization, and Ideology: Jacobinism, Marxism, Organicism and Functionalism', *Journal of Ethnic Studies*, 15(1): 1–32.

—— (1990) 'Ethnic Diasporas in Industrial Societies: A Comparative Study of the Political Implications of the "Homeland" Myth', in I. Simon-Barouh and P.-J. Simon (eds), *Les Étrangers dans la ville: le regard des sciences sociales*, Paris: L'Harmattan, pp. 163–77.

—— (1991) 'State, Nation, National identity and Citizenship: France as a Test Case', *International Political Science Review*, 12(3): 219–38.

—— (1992) 'Sociopolitical Context and Ethnic Consciousness in France and the United States: Maghrebis and Latinos', in A.M. Messina, L.R. Fraga, L.A. Rhodebeck and F.D. Wright (eds), *Ethnic and Racial Minorities in Advanced Industrial Democracies*, New York: Greenwood, pp. 67–87.

Salgues, B. (1988) 'Les Flux financiers des travailleurs immigrés' in S. Hessel (ed.), *Immigrations: le devoir d'insertion. Analyses et annexes*, Paris: La Documentation Française, pp. 393–5.

Sarkozy, N. (2005) 'Un défi républicain: la discrimination positive à la française', 26 Oct. Online: http://www.interieur.gouv.fr/misill/sections/a_l_interieur/le_ministre/interventions/26–10–2005–discrimination/view (accessed 31 July 2006).

Sayad, A. (1975) 'El Ghorba: le mécanisme de reproduction de l'émigration', *Actes de la recherche en sciences sociales*, 2 (March): 50–66.

—— (1978) *Les Usages sociaux de la culture des immigrés*, Paris: CIEMI.

—— (1979) 'Qu'est-ce qu'un immigré?', *Peuples méditerranéens*, 7 (April–June): 3–23.

—— (1987) 'Les Immigrés algériens et la nationalité française', in S. Laacher (ed.), *Questions de nationalité: histoire et enjeux d'un code*, Paris: L'Harmattan, pp. 125–203.

Schain, M. (1985) 'Immigrants and Politics in France', in J.S. Ambler (ed.), *The French Socialist Experiment*, Philadelphia, PA: Institute for the Study of Human Issues, pp. 166–90.

—— (1987) 'The National Front in France and the Construction of Political Legitimacy', *West European Politics*, 10(2): 229–52.

—— (1988) 'Immigration and Changes in the French Party System', *European Journal of Political Research*, 16(6): 597–621.

——(1993) 'Policy-Making and Defining Ethnic Minorities: The Case of Immigration in France', *New Community*, 20(1): 59–77.

—— (1994) 'Policy and Policy-Making in France and the United States: Models of Incorporation and the Dynamics of Change', paper presented to the conference of the Association for the Study of Modern and Contemporary France, Portsmouth, England, 16–18 Sept.

Schmitter Heisler, B. (1986) 'Immigrant Settlement and the Structure of Emergent Immigrant Communities in Western Europe', *Annals of the American Academy of Political and Social Science*, 485 (May): 76–86.

Schnapper, D. (1988) 'La Commission de la Nationalité, une instance singulière', *Revue européenne des migrations internationales*, 4(1–2): 9–28.

——(1990) *La France de l'intégration: sociologie de la nation en 1990*, Paris: Gallimard.

—— (1992) *L'Europe des immigrés: essai sur les politiques d'immigration*, Paris: François Bourin.

Schor, R. (1985) *L'Opinion française et les étrangers en France, 1919–1939*, Paris: Publications de la Sorbonne.

Sellam, S. (1987) *L'Islam et les musulmans en France*, Paris: Tougui.

Shields, J.S. (1991) 'The Politics of Disaffection: France in the 1980s', in J. Gaffney and E. Kolinsky (eds), *Political Culture in France and Germany*, London and New York: Routledge, pp. 69–90.

Siblot, P. (1992) 'Ah! Qu'en termes voilés ces choses-là sont mises', *Mots*, 30 (March): 5–17.

Silberman, R. (1992) 'French Immigration Statistics', in D.L. Horowitz and G. Noiriel (eds), *Immigrants in Two Democracies: French and American Experiences*, New York and London: New York University Press, pp. 112–23.

Silverman, M. (1992) *Deconstructing the Nation: Immigration, Racism and Citizenship in Modern France*, London and New York: Routledge.

Silverstein, P.A. (2004) *Algeria in France: Transpolitics, Race and Nation*, Bloomington: Indiana University Press.

Simeant, J. (1998) *La Cause des sans-papiers*, Paris: Presses de Sciences-Po.

Simmons, H. G. (1996) *The French National Front: The Extremist Challenge to Democracy*, Boulder, CO: Westview Press.

Simon, P. (1992) 'Belleville, un quartier d'intégration', *Migrations société*, 4(19): 45–68.

——(1993) 'Nommer pour agir', *Le Monde* (28 April).

Simon, P. and Clément, M. (2006) 'Comment décrire la diversité des origines en France? Une enquête exploratoire sur les perceptions des salariés et des étudiants', *Population et sociétés*, 425 (July–Aug.): 1–4.

Sindonino, P. (1993) 'Les Africains de Vincennes', *Migrations société*, 5(25): 58–67.

Smaïn (1990) *Sur la vie de ma mère*, Paris: Flammarion.

SOFRES (1984) *Opinion publique: Enquêtes et commentaires: 1984*, Paris: Gallimard.

——(1990) *L'État de l'opinion 1990*, Paris: Seuil.

——(1991) *L'État de l'opinion 1991*, Paris: Seuil.

——(1992) *L'État de l'opinion 1992*, Paris: Seuil.

——(1993) *L'État de l'opinion 1993*, Paris: Seuil.

——(1994) *L'État de l'opinion 1994*, Paris: Seuil.

Souida, A. (1990) 'Roubaix, les "RONA" dans la cité', *Hommes et migrations*, 1135 (Sept.): 59–64.

Stora, B. (1990) '1789–1989: Nationalité et citoyenneté (histoire d'un couple, histoire d'une crise)', in *1789–1989: Actes du colloque organisé à la Maison de la Culture d'Amiens les 27, 28 et 29 octobre dans le cadre de la commémoration du bicentenaire de la révolution française*, Amiens: Association de Soutien à l'Expression des Communautés d'Amiens, pp. 20–41.

—— (1991) *La Gangrène et l'oubli*, Paris: La Découverte.

Streiff-Fenart, J. (1989) *Les Couples franco-maghrébins en France*, Paris: L'Harmattan.

—— (1993) 'The Making of Family Identities among Franco-Algerian Couples', in A.G. Hargreaves and M.J. Heffernan (eds), *French and Algerian Identities from Colonial Times to the Present: A Century of Interaction*, Lewiston, NY, and Lampeter: Edwin Mellen, pp. 225–37.

Taboada-Leonetti, I. (1982) 'Identité nationale et liens avec le pays d'origine', in H. Malewska-Peyre *et al.* (eds), *Crise d'identité et déviance chez les jeunes immigrés*, Paris: La Documentation Française, pp. 205–47.

—— (1987) *Les Immigrés dans les beaux quartiers: la communauté espagnole dans le 16e siècle*, Paris: CIEMI/L'Harmattan.

—— (1989) 'Cohabitation pluri-ethnique dans la ville: stratégies d'insertion locale et phénomènes identitaires', *Revue européenne des migrations internationales*, 5(2): 51–70.

Taguieff, P.-A. (1989) 'The Doctrine of the National Front in France (1972–1989): A "Revolutionary" Programme?', *New Political Science*, 16–17 (Fall–Winter): 29–70.

—— (1990) 'The New Cultural Racism in France', *Telos*, 83: 109–22.

—— (ed.) (1991) *Face au racisme*, 2 vols, Paris: La Découverte.

Talha, L. (1989) *Le Salariat immigré dans la crise*, Paris: CNRS.

Tapinos, G. (1975) *L'Immigration étrangère en France, 1946–1973*, Paris: Presses Universitaires de France.

—— (1992) 'Immigration féminine et statut des femmes étrangères en France', *Revue française des affaires sociales*, 46 (Dec.): 29–60.

Tévanian, P. (2005) *Le Voile médiatique. Un faux débat: 'l'affaire du foulard islamique'*, Paris: Raisons d'agir.

Todd, E. (1994) *Les Destin des immigrés: assimilation et ségrégation dans les démocraties occidentales*, Paris: Seuil.

Toubon, J.-C. and Kessamah, K. (1990) *Centralité immigrée: le quartier de la Goutte d'or. Dynamique d'un espace pluriethnique: succession, compétition, cohabitation*, Paris: CIEMI/L'Harmattan.

Tribalat, M. (ed.) (1991) *Cent ans d'immigration: étrangers d'hier, Français d'aujourd'hui*, Paris: Presses Universitaires de France/INED.

—— (1993) 'Les immigrés au recensement de 1990 et les populations liées à leur installation en France', *Population*, 6: 1911–46.

—— (1995) *Faire France: une enquête sur les immigrés et leurs enfants*, Paris: La Découverte.

—— (1996) *De l'immigration à l'assimilation: enquête sur les populations d'origine étrangère en France*, Paris: La Découverte.

—— (2004a) 'Le Nombre de musulmans en France: qu'en sait-on?', in Y.C. Zarka (ed.), *L'Islam en France*, Paris: Presses Universitaires de France, pp. 21–31.

—— (2004b) 'Une estimation des populations d'origine étrangère en France', *Population*, 59(1): 51–82.

La Tribune Fonda (1991) 'Associations et immigration: 10 ans de liberté associative pour les étrangers en France', nos. 82–3 (Nov.).

Tripier, M. (1990) *L'Immigration dans la classe ouvrière en France*, Paris: CIEMI/ L'Harmattan.

UNESCO (1986) *Mass Media and the Minorities*, Bangkok: UNESCO Regional Office for Education in Asia and the Pacific.

Van Eeckhout, L. (2006) 'Immigration familiale: les faits', *Le Monde* (5 Jan.).

Varro, G. and Lesbet, D. (1986) 'Le Prénom révélateur', in G. Abou-Aada and H. Milet (eds), *Générations issues de l'immigration: 'mémoires et devenirs'*, Paris: Arcantère, pp. 139–53.

Verbunt, G. (1985) 'France', in T. Hammar (ed.), *European Immigration Policy: A Comparative Analysis*, Cambridge: Cambridge University Press, pp. 127–64.

Verhaeren, R.-E. (1990) 'Avenir de l'immigration face aux mutations du marché du travail', in G. Abou Sada, B. Courault and Z. Zeroulou (eds), *L'Immigration au tournant*, Paris: CIEMI/L'Harmattan, pp. 123–36.

Vichniac, J.E. (1991) 'French Socialists and the *droit à la différence*: A Changing Dynamic', *French Politics and Society*, 9(1): 40–56.

Villanova, R., and Bekkar, R. (1994) *Immigration et espaces habités*, Paris: CIEMI/ L'Harmattan.

Voisard, J. and Ducastelle, C. (1990) *La Question immigrée*, rev. edn, Paris: Seuil.

Vuddamalay, V., White, P. and Sporton, D. (1991) 'The Evolution of the Goutte d'or as an Ethnic Minority District of Paris', *New Community*, 17(2): 245–58.

Wacquant, L.J.D. (1992) 'Banlieues françaises et ghetto noir américain: de l'amalgame à la comparaison', *French Politics and Society*, 10(4): 81–103.

Wallerstein, I. (2005) 'The Inequalities that Blazed in France will Soon Scorch the World', *Guardian* (3 Dec.).

Wayland, S. (1993) 'Mobilising to Defend Nationality Law in France', *New Community*, 20(1): 93–110.

Weil, P. (1988) 'La Politique française d'immigration (entre 1974 et 1986) et la citoyenneté', in C. Wihtol de Wenden (ed.), *La Citoyenneté et les changements de structures sociale et nationale de la population française*, Paris: Edilig/Fondation Diderot, pp. 189– 200.

—— (1991) *La France et ses étrangers: l'aventure d'une politique de l'immigration, 1938–1991*, Paris: Calmann-Lévy.

—— (1994) 'La Politique française de l'immigraton depuis 1945', in B. Falga, C. Wihtol de Wenden and C. Leggewie (eds), *Au miroir de l'autre: de l'immigration à l'intégration en France et en Allemagne*, Paris: Éditions du Cerf, pp. 251–69.

—— (2004) *Qu'est-ce qu'un Français? Histoire de la nationalité française depuis la Révolution*, rev. edn, Paris: Seuil.

—— (2005) *La République et sa diversité: Immigration, intégration, discriminations*, Paris: Seuil.

Weil, P. and Crowley, J. (1994) 'Integration in Theory and Practice: A Comparison of France and Britain', *West European Politics*, 17(2): 110–26.

White, P.E. (1989) 'Immigrants, Immigrant Areas and Immigrant Communities in Postwar Paris', in P.E. Ogden and P.E. White (eds), *Migrants in Modern France:*

Population Mobility in the Later 19th and 20th Centuries, London: Unwin Hyman, pp. 195–211.

Wieviorka, M. (1990) 'La Crise du modèle français d'intégration', *Regards sur l'actualité*, 161 (May): 3–15.

—— (ed.) (1997) *Une société fragmentée? Le multiculturalisme en débat*, Paris: La Découverte.

—— (2005) *La Tentation anti-sémite: Haine des Juifs dans la France d'aujourd'hui*, Paris: Robert Laffont.

Wihtol de Wenden, C. (1987) *Citoyenneté, nationalité et immigration*, Paris: Arcantère.

—— (1988) *Les Immigrés et la politique*, Paris: Presses de la Fondation Nationale des Sciences Politiques.

—— (1993) 'The *Harkis*: A Community in the Making?', in A.G. Hargreaves and M.J. Heffernan (eds), *French and Algerian Identities from Colonial Times to the Present: A Century of Interaction*, Lampeter and Lewiston, NY: Edwin Mellen, pp. 189–201.

—— (1994a) 'Le Cas français', in B. Falga, C. Wihtol de Wenden and C. Leggewie (eds), *Au miroir de l'autre: de l'immigration à l'intégration en France et en Allemagne*, Paris: Éditions du Cerf, pp. 41–59.

—— (1994b) 'The French Response to the Asylum Seeker Influx, 1980–93', *Annals of the American Academy of Political and Social Science*, 534 (July): 81–90.

Wilson, W.J. (1987) *The Truly Disadvantaged*, Chicago, IL: Chicago University Press.

—— (ed.) (1989) 'The Ghetto Underclass: Social Science Perspectives', special issue, *Annals of the American Academy of Political and Social Science*, 501.

Yinger, J.M. (1985) 'Ethnicity', *Annual Review of Sociology*, 11: 151–80.

Yok-Soon, N.G. (ed.) (1991) *Guide de la communauté chinoise en France, 1991–1992*, Paris: Éditions les Cent Fleurs.

Zaleska, M. (1982) 'Identité culturelle des adolescents issus des familles de travailleurs immigrés', in H. Malewska-Peyre *et al.*, *Crise d'identité et déviance chez les jeunes immigrés*, Paris: La Documentation Française, pp. 177–204.

Zamora, F. and Lebon, A. (1985) 'Combien d'étrangers ont quitté la France entre 1975 et 1982?', *Revue européenne des migrations internationales*, 1(1): 67–80.

Zappi, S. (2004) 'Le Mouvement antiraciste rate son rendez-vous unitaire', *Le Monde* (7 Nov.).

Zimmermann, M.-J. (2005) *Rapport d'activité au nom de la Délégation aux droits des femmes et à l'égalité des chances entre les hommes et les femmes*, Paris: Assemblée Nationale.

Index

Routledge History

Asylum Seekers and Refugees in the Contemporary World

David Whittaker

Examining a number of case studies, including Palestinian, Afghan and Iraqi refugees, David J. Whittaker's book provides a balanced introduction to this very controversial subject.

Fuelled by extensive coverage in the media, the issue of asylum seekers and refugees is one of the most talked about subjects in contemporary politics. Whittaker cuts through the emotive language to give an objective introduction to the subject.

Asylum Seekers and Refugees in the Contemporary World discusses the international as well as national implications of the issue, and the book looks in detail at the issue as it has affected Britain and Europe in particular, as well as including material on the UN and its response to the refugee 'problem'.

Asylum Seekers and Refugees in the Contemporary World is essential reading for all students of the history of the modern world and is ideal for newcomers to the subject.

ISBN10 0-415-36090-0 (Hbk)
ISBN10 0-415-36091-9 (Pbk)
ISBN13 978-0-415-36090-6(Hbk)
ISBN13 978-0-415-36091-3 (Pbk)

Routledge History

The Course of French History

Pierre Goubert

This stimulating one-volume history traces the social and economic evolution of France as a nation from the founding of the monarchy in 987, to the present day.

Against a background of structural change, Goubert etches a vivid account of key events and personalities. His perspective is a popular one, and his main interest is in how political events and famous people affect the nation as a whole. The book incorporates the findings and perspectives of recent monographic studies with clarity and precision, but it is Goubert's own judgements, direct, forceful and iconoclastic, which make this an invaluable text.

ISBN10 0-415-06671-9 (Pbk)
ISBN13 978-0-415-06671-6 (Pbk)

Routledge History

Decolonization

2nd Edition

Raymond F. Betts

The mid-twentieth century saw the end of colonial empires, a global phenomenon that brought about profound changes and created enormous problems. Decolonization played a major part in shaping the contemporary world order and the domestic development of newly emerging states in the 'Third World'.

In the second edition of this concise introduction to the phenomenon, Raymond F. Betts brings the discussion up to date and looks at contemporary concerns such as the growth of Islamic Fundamentalism, 9/11, globalization and the AIDS pandemic.

ISBN10 0-415-31820-3 (Hbk)
ISBN10 0-415-31821-1 (Pbk)
ISBN13 978-0-415-31820-4 (Hbk)
ISBN13 978-0-415-31821-1 (Pbk)

Available at all good bookshops
For ordering and further information please visit:
www.routledge.com

Routledge History

Aspects of Contemporary France

Sheila Perry

France is defined by claims of uniqueness made by or about the French. *Aspects of Contemporary France* illuminates the contemporary economic, cultural, political and social climate of France. Using a multidisciplinary approach, this book explains the historical background to controversial issues. It also traces France's road to nationhood through religion, language and territory.

Each chapter is by a specialist in the field and is based on the most up to date information and research. Beginning with the present day, the book traces the historical background to events and provides a context for evaluation. The wide-ranging and varied themes covered include:

* Political parties
* Regions in the market place
* Television and film
* Women
* Secularism and Islam
* Linguistic policies
* French consumers

The book also offers a helpful chronology at the end of each chapter, a detailed bibliography and a recommended reading list.

Aspects of Contemporary France presents an analytical as well as informative approach to French Studies. It provides a readily accessible but in-depth understanding for students of France or French civilization at undergraduate and postgraduate levels.

ISBN10 0-415-13179-0 (Hbk)
ISBN10 0-415-13180-4 (Pbk)
ISBN13 978-0-415-13179-7 (Hbk)
ISBN13 978-0-415-13180-3 (Pbk)